THE STAIN

Also by Harry Lee Kraus, Jr.

Stainless Steal Hearts

Fated Genes

Lethal Mercy

THE STAIN

Harry Lee Kraus, Jr., M.D.

CROSSWAY BOOKS • WHEATON, ILLINOIS
A DIVISION OF GOOD NEWS PUBLISHERS

This is a work of imagination. None of the characters found within these pages reflect the character or intentions of any real person. Any similarity is coincidental.

Cover design: Cindy Kiple

First printing, 1997

Printed in the United States of America

Library of Congress Cataloging-in-Publication Data
Kraus, Harry Lee, 1960–
    The stain / Harry Lee Kraus, Jr.
      p.   cm.
    ISBN 0-89107-972-6
    I. Title.
PS3561.R2875S7 1997
813'.54—dc21   97-16775

07	06	05	04	03	02	01	00	99	98	97
15	14	13	12	11	10	9	8	7	6	5	4	3	2	1

For the twins,
my sisters, Donna and Debbie,
and for the men they married,
Tim Parrish and Jeff Snyder

PROLOGUE

"A DESPERATE ACT BY A DESPERATE MAN."
—THE DEER FALLS DAILY

"AN INTENTIONAL CRIMINAL COVER-UP,
A DESPICABLE SHADOWING OF A PLOT THAT CAN ONLY
BE CALLED THE MOST HEINOUS ATTACK ON CHRIST
SINCE JUDAS ISCARIOT."
—THE DAILY RECORD

"A FORTUNATE BLUNDER WITHOUT WHICH
WE NEVER WOULD HAVE SEEN THE DEEPER LURKING EVIL."
—THE COAST CHRONICLE

WELL, the word is out on the street, and if we're to believe the confession of our own town physician, Seth Berringer, his problems started in earnest when he decided to take matters into his own hands and protect his job, something most of us would do, even if it means bending the appearance of the truth a little. If, on the other hand, you believe certain local staff reporters, Berringer's guilt lies more with the suspicion that the whole event was conjured up by a criminal mind capable of not only covering up a murder, but committing it in the first place.

Since there are two opposing views in the community, and the media can't seem to help, I'll add my opinion here. After all, I'm the editor, and I can print what I want. Besides, it is apparent that this act, regardless of how you've judged it, isn't bound for the courts. It is likely that Dr. Berringer will only be tried in the court of public opinion, and so on that score, I'll give my two cents.

We should at least listen to the doctor himself. What did he have to gain by bringing the facts to light? If he is guilty of more than he's confessing, why bring the whole thing up in the first place? Certainly, he knew people were bound to suspect that he was only protecting a deeper wrong.

I, for one, would like to side with Berringer. He's naive, if anything. Certainly we should explore the facts that have led to the events as we know them. If our doctor is telling the truth, a portion of the blame needs to rest with the mega-health-care-provider Coast Care, for creating the impersonal environment that made the doctor fear for his job.

And what of the nearly unbelievable story of human DNA cloning and the assessment of Christ's divinity? What would motivate Berringer to twist such a tall tale in the first place? Most of us find this all a bit unbelievable and wonder if this won't be a larger stain on Berringer's image. If he's not a murderer, then he certainly has an imagination bent on the implausible.

How will history judge our local family physician? A hero who uncovered a diabolical plot? A murderer who confessed to a lesser sin just to hide his own guilt? An imbecile who sought national attention by his outlandish imagination? A compassionate physician who cradled the people of his own community as if they were his own family?

A hero? A murderer? An imbecile? A compassionate physician?

I want more information.

And when it comes, I want to weigh my judgment in the light of Berringer's history in this town. Don't we at least owe him that? Wasn't he the only one to stay when other physicians had given up on Deer Falls? How many of us have bothered him in the middle of the night with calls about our sick children? Who else provided care for the uninsured in our town when the silo plant closed? Who organized the fund-drive to help pay for little Holly's bone marrow transplant?

Let's look at history, folks. Sure, all of this seems a bit outrageous right now. But he hasn't been found guilty in any court of law, so let's refrain from assuming he's guilty before all the facts are in.

Well, that's how I see it.

Tim Snyder
Editor
Deer Falls Gazette

CHAPTER
1

SETH Berringer looked at his watch. His Saturday E.R. shift would be over in five minutes. Things at Chesapeake General Hospital's emergency department had settled to a dull roar, and Dr. Berringer looked forward to getting home. Ever since being bought out by Coast Care, his practice and his office had been streamlined—the hard way. One of the changes was the physician coverage of the emergency room. He was now expected to cover two twelve-hour shifts a month in addition to maintaining his family practice at Deer Falls Family Medicine Clinic. His replacement, Dr. James Grim, was late. Again.

Just then the radio broke the silence. It was a Deer Falls rescue unit. "We're en route with a six-year-old male, the victim of a bicycle versus car accident. The patient is unresponsive, with rapid, shallow respirations. We should be in your facility in two minutes."

Trauma was what most surgeons loved and what Berringer hated the most. Just the mention of the word brought him vague discomfort. He looked at his watch and knitted his brow in anxiety. *Where's Jimmy?*

He glanced at his scrubs. At least he hadn't changed into his street clothes yet. He looked at his nursing staff and gave the assignments for the expected patient arrival. "Mary, start the IV and send off a trauma blood panel. Del, call respiratory therapy and have them set up a ventilator. It sounds like we'll need it." He looked at the unit secretary. "Laurie, phone the surgeon on call. Tell him I'm going to need him right away. Then call an X-ray tech and have him come on down." He turned away and then back, adding quietly, "Could you also call Dr. Grim? Remind him it's time to be at work." He smiled thinly.

In another minute the trauma team was assembled in the first bay.

Moments later rescue unit 1 arrived with the focus of all their attention, a small boy in the center of a rapidly rolling stretcher. A rescue worker was depressing the patient's chest with rhythmic compressions.

Seth's anxiety rose a hundred percent. "When did he code?"

Sandy, an experienced paramedic, saw the fear in the young family doctor's eyes. "Right after we called. He just quit breathing. We couldn't find a pulse. We would have called again, but we were right on top of you by then."

"Let's move him! One, two, three!" The team moved the boy on a backboard to the E.R. stretcher.

At the head of the stretcher, a respiratory therapist took over the responsibility of bagging the patient, slowly and rhythmically forcing oxygen into the patient's lungs through a small tube inserted into the windpipe.

Seth laid his stethoscope on the small chest. "Your tube is in, but he's not moving much air on the right." He wrinkled his brow again. "Where's the surgeon?"

"In O.R.," a nurse responded. "Laurie just got off the phone with the folks up there."

"Great! A six-year-old is going to die without a chest tube, and the surgeon is tied up!" He looked at the monitor. "What's his pressure?"

Mary, a veteran nurse, looked up from the blood pressure gauge. "Fifty systolic with CPR."

Berringer cursed. "Set up for a chest tube. I can't wait for a surgeon!" He began to pace in the crowded cubicle. "How much IV fluid has he received?"

"Only 500 so far. I'm squeezing the bag as much as I can," Mary responded.

Seth quickly wiped some Betadine prep on the skin of the patient's right chest. He put on a pair of sterile gloves and picked up the scalpel from the open sterile tray. His hands trembled as he made the incision, a jagged cut that was longer and deeper than he'd intended. *Great, Berringer*, he chided himself silently. *You'll need to sew this up if he survives!*

He took a clamp and bluntly dissected his way into the chest cavity. Fortunately, the child was thin, so the distance to the pleural cavity was closer to the surface than in an adult.

Whoosh! The trapped air in the right chest forced itself through the incision with an audible rush. Seth awkwardly pushed a plastic tube through the small wound and connected it to a collection chamber. Immediately, the chamber turned crimson as it filled with the patient's blood.

Berringer and the nursing staff looked at the collecting tubing and gasped. "His whole blood volume must have been in the chest," Mary observed.

Seth blanched as he wondered if his tube could have entered the heart by mistake. *No. Mary is right. I performed the procedure correctly. The poor lad had already lost his blood into his chest!* He looked up at the team. "What are his pupils like?"

Del focused a small light beam into the patient's eyes. "Fixed and dilated."

"We've lost this one, doc."

Seth shook his head. He couldn't afford to lose another patient during an E.R. shift. Coast Care just didn't understand.

Mary sensed his turmoil. "He was dead before he arrived, Seth," she responded, touching his arm. "There was nothing you could do."

Seth stripped off his rubber gloves and looked up into the sheepish grin of his finally-arriving replacement.

"Sorry. I overslept."

The harried Dr. Berringer silently threw his gloves into the trash container and braced himself for a difficult discussion with the patient's family.

◆ ◆ ◆

As far as the institute was concerned, her code name was Surrogate Two. Her real name was Lisa Dale, but at this moment she would have preferred the anonymity of just being somebody—*anybody*—in a crowd. She splashed water in her face and stared at the eyes looking back at her in the bathroom mirror, eyes that couldn't belie the terror she felt or disguise the lack of sleep she so desperately needed. She tried to remember the forty-eight hours since she'd fled to save her own life and the life of her baby.

She looked at herself a second time and sighed. *Twenty-two, looking more like forty-two,* she thought. Her blonde hair hung tangled and thick, unwashed, contaminated by the smoke of too many cheap restaurants to remember. Her beauty, however, could not be hidden by her present physically disheveled state.

Fear remained the only real threat to her attractiveness. Cold, sweat-producing anxiety, an ulcer-producing gnawing, tightened her pleasant face in a steel gaze of dread.

She needed sleep, but every time she'd tried to yield to the needed rejuvenation, a thousand thoughts of her would-be captors had pushed the slumber away again. She feared being caught and dreaded what would happen to her baby. If she had known, she would never have consented . . .

Lisa exited the bathroom in the lobby of Deer Falls' only motel, the Deer Falls Inn. It sounded nicer than it was and had a local reputation for rooms to rent for a night or part of a night or even an hour, depending on the customer's desire. She planned to spend at least a night or two here, to determine whether her own apartment was under surveillance. Certainly being in Deer Falls, even without family, would be safer than anywhere else. At least she prayed so.

Lisa approached the desk and glanced at the woman behind it, a rotund female with an obvious infatuation with blue eye shadow. The older woman shoved a form under Lisa's nose.

"Fill out the top part," she snapped. She eyed Lisa with disdain. "You need the room all day?"

Lisa looked up. "One or two nights. Can I let you know?"

Lou Ellen Boatwright squinted suspiciously behind large, gold-rimmed glasses that failed to make the woman's face look smaller. "Suit yourself. You don't see anyone else standin' in line, do ya?"

Lisa looked around the lobby. She had been here for twenty minutes, counting her time in the restroom.

Under "Name," she carefully printed "Anne Dustin." Anne was her middle name, Dustin her mom's maiden name. She had to be careful. She hoped she'd be safe in the motel. Although Deer Falls was a small town, she'd never been in the center of town life and had never even been in the Inn before. She certainly hadn't spoken to the eye-shadow lady, at least not that she could remember.

Lisa paid in cash, the same way she'd handled all her transactions since leaving the institute, thus leaving a nearly invisible trail—a trail she hoped would be next to impossible to trace. In Denver she had purchased three tickets—one for Chicago, one for New York, and one for New Orleans. She waited at the New Orleans gate until her flight to Chicago was on final boarding call, then rushed onto the plane. Once in Chicago, she followed a similar plan, getting on a plane bound for Charlotte at the last possible moment. The plan was expensive, but at least she had been paid well for her part in the research.

She touched her lower abdomen instinctively. Softly she muttered, "I should have been paid even more, considering what they did to me."

Lou Ellen took the money without question. She never argued with cash customers. "Room's on the first floor. Go outside, then around to the right. Number 12. Extra blankets are in the dresser."

"Thanks." Lisa picked up her backpack and clutched her coat around her to prepare for the cold. Arriving outside, her pace quickened, her thoughts focused on a shower and a bed.

Once inside, she frowned at the lack of a dead bolt. "Oh well," she muttered, "what can you expect in Deer Falls?"

She lowered the venetian blind and closed the curtain before peeling the layers of clothing from her body. As she stepped into the bathroom, a disturbing dread resurfaced—the fear of discovery. She shook her head.

In a few moments steam began to fill the small bathroom, and Lisa slowly surrendered to the urge to cry. Large tears quickly mixed with a constant stream of water and soap.

She paused to take inventory. She was alone, but at least she knew this area well and had a few friends here who could perhaps help her sort out her problems. She sobbed through a prayer. "What am I going to do with a baby? I'm not married . . . I'm a virgin, for heaven's sake! . . . O God, what did they do to me?"

Outside, someone tried to open door number 12. "We should've grabbed her before she went inside. Let's get a key from the lobby," the taller of two men whispered.

"Right, like this lady's just going to give us a key!" a younger-looking man with Asian features responded.

"It will be easy. Ben told me about this place. We just need to talk to Ms. Boatwright. She always sets him up for a real good time."

◆ ◆ ◆

Seth Berringer, M.D. pushed aside the tattered copy of *Time* magazine and sighed. The bar was crowded. Although the environment encouraged socializing, the doctor sat alone. He had come here to escape, and to think. He certainly hadn't come to drink, although after his shift in the E.R., the thought had crossed his mind.

"Another Coke, doc?"

Seth looked up. "No thanks, Lanny. I think I've had enough."

Lanny looked at the wrinkled magazine. "What do you think, doc? Do you suppose this really is Jesus?" He lifted the cover of the periodical, emblazoned with a scientist's rendition of the physical image of Christ. Under the picture, the words "The Real Jesus?" stood out in stark red against a black background.

Seth shook his head. "I don't know. Really haven't had time to— "

"Best thing to happen to the holy church in 2,000 years, if you ask me," Lanny interrupted. "Finally some real proof we can sink our teeth into."

Seth huffed, "Apparently you're not alone." He looked at the subtitle beneath the image: "A Skeptical Scientific Community Examines the DNA Evidence of Jesus."

"What do you think, doc?" the bar owner asked for a second time.

"I really haven't had— "

"Made me think twice," Lanny interrupted again. "I might even have to get back over to St. Vincent's. It's been a while since I . . ."

His voice trailed as he walked back to the kitchen, never missing a beat in his ongoing commentary.

Deer Falls' only family doctor shook his head. The shroud . . . the image of Jesus. He really had been too busy to think about much outside his own life lately.

He was only thirty-two. He had returned to Deer Falls to join a thriving family medicine group three years earlier. Since then, his two partners had left, unable or unwilling to compete with a growing managed care market. Berringer had decided to stay—to practice on his own in the town of his youth and to remain independent as long as he possibly could. As it turned out, it was only a year before he was forced to sell out to the largest managed care network in the east, Coast Care. First they had signed up all the folks at the Deer Falls Silo company, then all the employees at the fish market, and a few more at Peninsula Lumber. Pretty soon everyone who used to be his patient was considered a "covered life" by Coast Care. He was welcome to sell his practice to the managed care giant or go hungry. After missing a second mortgage payment on his white farmhouse, he sold.

That was before his fees were cut and his hours were dictated by the giant. Even before they sent him a nurse practitioner, they warned him of his expendability. After fending off one frivolous malpractice suit, Coast Care sent him to a required conference on avoiding malpractice claims. Not how to practice good medicine, mind you, but how to avoid getting sued while practicing the least expensive managed medicine around. At the conclusion of the conference, he'd been given his warning: Do it our way, and don't get sued, or you'll be looking for another job.

Another job? Berringer had been devastated. He'd sacrificed half his life with the goal of returning to Deer Falls to serve the people he loved the most. Besides, where would he go? Physician oversupply had nearly dictated that he choose another field already.

And so Dr. Seth Berringer had stayed—and had slumped into a depression that paralyzed him from practicing the way he knew he should. Now he ordered tests because Coast Care required them, not because he thought they were necessary. Now he referred his patients to the surgeons in the next town, not because they were the best, but because they were also owned by Coast Care. One big happy family.

In the last month he had endured two reviews by the health care giant. Now, after another death in the E.R., he knew he would face them again. In the past reviews they had complimented his compliance. Evidently they felt he was an efficient provider and cared only about his generating an abundance of high-level evaluation and management codes—the ones that led to a higher rate of pay-out by the insurance carriers. During both reviews, however, they frowned at the number of deaths that had occurred during his emergency room shifts. Each time he had to carefully defend his actions. Each time they seemed quietly annoyed but satisfied with his explanations. After each review, he left feeling contaminated by the oily feeling of the bottom line.

It wasn't as if he didn't like the practice of medicine. He loved the people, the thrill of making a difficult diagnosis, the initiation of a successful treatment. It was the business of medicine that soured his outlook. But if participating with Coast Care was the only job available in town, he would have to play their little games to stay close to the folks he loved. He had occasionally considered leaving, but then he realized that Coast Care had rapidly consumed 80 percent of the eastern U.S. market. If he left Deer Falls, they would certainly lock him out of a job elsewhere. So he decided to stay and play.

Now, however, his anxiety over losing the trauma patient in the E.R. crowded his other worries about malpractice suits and the competitive physician market aside. If Coast Care didn't dump him because of another frivolous lawsuit, they would at least make him a scapegoat for the E.R. death-rate!

Look at yourself, Berringer. These people are having fun with their friends, and all you have to show for your years is a degree and a managed care headache! He glanced at three men approximately his age at a nearby table, each with a young female on his arm. *What about that, doctor? Been too busy to even establish a proper relationship in your life?* He stared into his empty Coke glass. *And what about your debts? Your education wasn't cheap. And you just nod your head when Coast Care lowers your fees? It's time for inventory, Seth. You're thirty-two, you've got a decent job and make a decent wage, you're in good health, and you still have a rugged look that most women adore. But so what? You're on the verge of losing everything you've spent years obtaining. Mess up again and you'll be driving the local ambulance. And after that fiasco in the E.R. tonight, you might as well start preparing to take a driving test!*

Seth looked up as Sheriff Wayne Boatwright settled into his chair at the corner table. The only thing bigger than his waistline was his ego—and his appetite for Lanny's award-winning shrimp fritters. Just what award they had won was an item Seth hadn't questioned, and he had jokingly stated that Lanny was responsible for more gallbladder attacks than anyone else in Chesapeake County.

The sheriff enjoyed sitting at his big table but quickly spread out a few papers to make it appear that important work was at hand. He placed a routine order for a large side of fritters and sipped on the Coke that he pulled straight from an icy bottle. Boatwright liked large things—a large table with a large order of fritters and the large campaign billboard that cast a shadow on Lanny's unpaved parking lot: "Reelect Wayne Boatwright Sheriff of Chesapeake County." His smiling face on the billboard had quickly yellowed in the bright sun. Seth swore it must be the fritters.

A few minutes later, Wayne Boatwright talked boisterously with a circle of friends and swallowed a fritter. A quiet belch announced his delight.

Lanny walked over with a platter of soft drinks. He nodded at the customers and repeated their names in greeting, then looked at the sheriff. "Phone's for you."

The sheriff was about to ask for the portable one, but Lanny's expression dictated otherwise. Boatwright rose. "I'll take it in the kitchen."

Lanny walked back with him, wiping his hands on a large, well-used cotton apron. "It's Lou Ellen. Sounds like trouble."

The sheriff frowned. Whenever his sister called Lanny's place to find him, it was trouble. "What's up, Lou?" he demanded.

"I got a problem up here, Wayne. Some customers must be gettin' out of hand."

The sheriff wrinkled his forehead. His sister's inn was a sore spot in his reelection bid. As long as things stayed quiet, people seemed content to look the other way while more than a few men fed their lustful addictions. A few of them were prominent men in Deer Falls whom Wayne Boatwright couldn't afford to alienate. A blowup in the routine at the Inn could scandalize his already oily campaign. "What do you mean?"

"I let a few men in to see one of the girls. She must be new. I didn't recognize her."

"A new girl?"

"That's not unusual, Wayne. They always come and go." Lou Ellen smacked her gum into the phone and opened a small makeup mirror to check her eye shadow.

"You said a few men?"

"Hey, I don't make the rules—"

"Lou Ellen!" The sheriff raised his voice, then turned his back away from the entrance to Lanny's front room.

"I heard her scream, and I thought she might be in trouble. I just thought I'd let you know, that's all."

The sheriff huffed and checked his watch. "What's the room number?"

"Twelve."

Not bothering to say good-bye, he sighed, hung up the receiver, and shook his head.

He strode across the room and dismissed himself from the party. He was tempted to call Rick, his deputy, but had second thoughts, wanting to keep any potential trouble at the Inn to himself—at least for the next few weeks.

He walked to his car, chewing a shrimp fritter as he went. *Maybe Lou Ellen made an apple pie.*

◆ ◆ ◆

"I have to go to the bathroom!" Lisa cried. "Please!"

"Hold still!"

Lisa stiffened again as she stared into the barrel of the revolver, held by the older of the two men.

The Asian pulled out the speculum. "It's hard to see. I can't see any evidence of cervical dilatation. We have inadequate lights, and she isn't cooperating! This is going to take forever!" he complained. "Tell me again why we can't just take her back to the institute."

"Stop whining. It has to look like a back-alley job."

A knock at the door interrupted the operation.

The man with the revolver looked at Lisa. "Into the bathroom," he hissed. "Now!" Lisa scrambled from the bed, grabbing her clothes, and stumbled toward the bathroom. "Not a word from you!"

The younger man moved slowly to the window. He pulled back the curtain an inch, then looked back at his partner and mouthed, *It's a cop!*

The other man put his revolver under his coat, and the Asian opened the door.

"Evenin', gentlemen. Everything OK?"

"Just fine. Just fine," the Asian responded.

"Just investigatin' a noise complaint. Any trouble here?"

A second man nearly filled the doorway, but the sheriff cast a glance over the shorter man's shoulder. Were those rubber gloves?

In the bathroom, Lisa contemplated screaming. But she knew that would just make her enemies angry enough to kill her more quickly. Besides, the new arrivals might be reinforcements. She rose from the commode where she had collapsed a moment before. She gasped at the amount of blood she saw there. She had to hurry. When she heard a man's voice ask the two men to step outside, she grabbed her jeans.

Surveying the little room with a frightened glance, she spotted a small window above the commode. If she stood on the toilet seat, she could reach the window.

Lisa put on her jeans and blouse, omitting her underwear, hopelessly torn from her encounter with her captors. Feeling dizzy when she stood on the commode, she paused momentarily before forcing the window open with a grunt. The cold air reminded her to take her coat, hanging on the inside of the bathroom door. She grabbed it and flung it through the window ahead of her.

Outside, Sheriff Wayne Boatwright took a dark delight in keeping the two men under his thumb for a few minutes. He wouldn't arrest them. He thought he knew what they were up to all right. He just wanted to make them sweat, to see how they would respond to his trivial questions. After all, he was The Law in this town. Everyone, even outside strangers, had to pay him the respect he was due.

After a while Wayne invited the two men to Lanny's to enjoy the local cuisine. "It's just down the hill on the right. You can't miss it." He smiled a practiced, toothy grin, a flashy political one, the one he reserved for billboards and official photos.

The two men shifted uncomfortably on the cold sidewalk. "Thanks. Maybe we'll settle for room service," the older man offered, clearing his throat.

The sheriff laughed. "The only room service you'll get here is what you bring in yourself." He tossed his head toward the road. "Burger Mac is up on the left, if you shy away from seafood." He kicked a small stone in the parking lot. "Lanny's is the best, though. Not much to look at, mind you, but the shrimp fritters can't be beat."

"Well, sure, uh . . . thanks," the Asian said.

"Course, if you stay for breakfast, Clara's is the place to go. Near the silo factory. Best cinnamon rolls east of River Town." He patted his generous waist and winked at the two men. "I oughta know."

"Yes, I guess so. Listen, we have some business to attend to. We've really not had any trouble, so—"

"Yes, sir," the sheriff interrupted again, "I'll be up talkin' to Lou Ellen for a few minutes if you need anything." The uniformed man stepped forward to open the door for the men, hoping for one last glimpse into their room.

The two men quickly filled the doorway and slipped inside, shutting the door with a sharp thud.

Wayne Boatwright grimaced, then smiled again as his sister approached carrying a cup of steaming coffee and a hearty slice of apple pie.

Inside, the older man rattled the locked bathroom door. "Open up . . . right now!"

Silence. He looked around and shook his head in frustration. "What kind of motel is this anyway? Whoever heard of bathroom doors with locks in a motel room?"

The man rubbed the back of his neck and cast a furtive glance at his partner, a man he had always called "Doc." Doc looked worried. The first man repeated his command in a raspy, hushed tone. "Open the door!"

Doc, clearly irritated, suggested, "Use the room key, Einstein. Maybe she's passed out."

"I could blow the lock away," his partner suggested excitedly, fingering his revolver again.

"Good idea, with the sheriff right outside," Doc replied smugly. He picked up the room key and tossed it to his accomplice, who hastily opened the door.

Glancing around the room, he saw the blood in the commode and the underwear on the floor. He pulled back the shower curtain, then focused on the open window. He cursed.

"Hey, quiet down! You want the fat man with the badge back in here?"

The taller, older man with graying hair stumbled into the room. With his face pale and his breathing fast and short, he stuttered, "S-she's gone, Doc! She's gone!"

CHAPTER
2

LISA Dale needed help, and she needed it fast. She rounded the corner of the motel just in time to see her two captors talking with a large uniformed man. She thought about screaming but instinctively pulled back into the shadows again. She doubted that anyone who could laugh with the two goons would be reliable help.

She ran behind the Inn and crossed the street. She needed someone, anyone, but the small town seemed deserted. As she staggered up the street, she pushed her hands deep into her coat pockets, fighting for warmth. Her hand instinctively squeezed a postcard she had scribbled to a friend. Until this moment she had been ambivalent about sending it. Now it seemed like her only chance to deliver the truth. "No one will believe me," she mumbled. "I'm not even sure I believe me."

She fought to concentrate as the dizziness returned full-force. She put her hand to her neck and counted. Her heart rate was easily over 150. She needed a hospital!

She stumbled forward. Now, in addition to the dizziness, her lower abdomen burned—first with a barely noticeable throb, then growing to a constant, knife-like agony.

She looked toward an approaching sound. A truck-load of teens yelled, "Hey, baby!" as they passed.

She looked up to see the headlights speed by. She weakly waved for help, but that only prompted a second guttural yell.

She passed an old white house with no lights on. She had to find a doctor! She strained to focus, distracted temporarily by the sticky warmth in her pants. "I'm bleeding to death! I'm going to lose my baby!" The silent house mocked her. She sullenly turned her attention back to the street. As she passed the house's mailbox, she slid the small postcard into it. She squinted to read a sign pointing to the right: "H." A hospital! She thought back to her opening semester at college when she'd first visited Deer Falls and came down with severe stomach flu. She remembered being treated at Chesapeake General Hospital. Terrified by the increasing pain, she decided to cut across the field to get help more quickly. She stumbled back across the road, her head spinning.

In the darkness, with time running out, she limped slowly through the tall grass on the vacant lot.

◆ ◆ ◆

With his head full of self-criticism and worries over malpractice and job security, Seth Berringer made the first of two very bad decisions that autumn night—he asked Lanny for a drink.

Lanny eyed him curiously, but Seth's expression said, *Don't ask.* So Lanny said nothing and fulfilled the request.

Seth hadn't taken a drink since watching his father die of cirrhosis during his second year at Duke University Medical School. "It's familial, son," his father's doctor had warned. "It's best not to tempt fate."

He had heeded the warning and swore off the party scene, ironically so popular among his medical student compadres. As he got into residency and practice, he found that his openness about his family's struggles with the bottle endeared him to several of his hard-to-reach patients.

Now, however, he wanted only to ease the constant internal accusations that screamed about his ineptitude in life. He sipped at the yellow fluid, which burned his throat but did little to push aside the fresh memory of his E.R. experience. What had his patient's father yelled? "He was alive when the rescue squad took him away! What have you done? You killed my son!"

As he stared at the scotch in the bottom of an iced glass, his soul fought with itself. He thought of his father, yellow with jaundice, spewing forth his embittered life-story. "You've become your dad," he moaned quietly to himself. "Just look at you."

Just then, Jamie Edwards walked in. He stumbled in, to be exact. Seth hung his head and hoped he wouldn't be seen. He had often counseled the young man about the evils of drink; he had also spent more than a few sessions dealing with Jamie's obsessive compulsive personality disorder. Jamie improved with counsel and medication but worsened with every drinking binge.

You hypocrite! Great example you are! Seth turned toward the wall as Jamie tottered to a back table.

Relieved, Seth took another sip of his drink and repositioned himself in the shadow of the cash register.

He tried to relax and let the alcohol quiet his accusing conscience. "I'll have another," he responded when he caught Lanny's eye.

"Doc, you don't usually—"

"Skip the preaching, Lanny. I've done some things today I'd rather forget."

Lanny frowned. "Haven't we all?" he muttered as he served a second round.

Seth sipped the golden liquid but refused to be comforted. He stole a look at his patient and was relieved to see he was facing the other way. He thought about Jamie's obsessions about the girls around him, his fears that he would harm his friends, that he would rape them or worse. He seemed to focus on a woman he'd met a while back at the library, an assistant by the name of Lisa. His fantasies were dark, to be sure, but Jamie never showed any other violent tendencies. Dr. Berringer had talked long and hard with him and felt sure Jamie was not capable of actually performing the viciousness he feared so much. Seth had told him his fears were irrational, and Jamie seemed relieved to know he could share so openly with a professional. Seth saw no need to break a medical confidence and warn the women of Jamie's fantasies.

He cast a glance over his shoulder and saw Jamie hoisting an icy brew. The fact that both Jamie and he were drinking to escape troubled him. He continued to sip quietly for a moment, feeling his head tingle from the alcohol. *Another example of what's bad about Coast Care,* he mused. *I should have had that guy in the hands of a good psychiatrist long ago. As it is, I'm rewarded for saving my patient from a high-priced specialist, while Coast Care racks up more incentives for me to care for every problem myself.*

Seth continued to drink, his remorse growing the longer he sat. He stared at the glass. The scotch was supposed to make him feel better. Instead, his gut churned. *I have to get out of here before I get sick!*

◆ ◆ ◆

"What's he doing out there anyway?"

Doc pulled back the blind and looked out the window. "He's eating. Just sitting in the patrol car with that motel dame and eating!" he grumped. "Why don't you slip out the back like the girl did?"

"Like I can fit through that little window!"

Doc rolled his eyes and glanced back out the front window. He cursed. "Great! The woman is crying." He threw back the blinds. "Now the fat man's gonna stay forever!" He walked to the bathroom. "Maybe I can fit through that hole," he added, looking up at the window. He pulled himself up but quickly saw that the opening was too narrow. Climbing back down, he placed his hand on the window ledge but quickly withdrew it. "Blood!" He washed his hands. "We'd better start cleaning this place up or we'll have to do it after we get the girl."

"I say we kill her outright this time."

The Asian shook his head. "We can't lose our heads over this. We've tracked her across the country. We need to be patient!"

The older man picked up a spray bottle and a rag. "I've got a bad feeling about this one, Doc, a real bad feeling."

"Shut up, Bill." The muscular, mustached Asian grabbed the clothing on the bathroom floor. "Here, I'll help you clean up."

◆ ◆ ◆

Exiting the smoky atmosphere of Lanny's Grill did little to clear Seth's cloudy thinking. He looked around the parking lot three times before remembering he had left his car at Chesapeake General. He had wanted to walk, and to think. Now he just wanted to get home to his own bathroom and his own bed. *Maybe I can make better time if I cut across the field.* He looked at the tall weeds and, against his better sober judgment, started across the uncut grass.

He stumbled after only traveling a few yards. "I'm not ready to drive anyway," he scoffed at himself. "The walk will do me good."

He tripped again after striding only a few feet, twisting his ankle painfully in an unseen hole. *Great! Maybe I'll go back to the E.R. and get Jimmy to wrap my ankle.*

He slowed his pace and squinted at the ditch ahead. He hadn't realized how little light there was with the moon behind the clouds. He limped his way forward a few more steps before a light rain began to fall. "This is all I need!"

After another minute, with only fifty feet more to go, Seth stumbled again, this time plunging facedown into the thick grass. An unseen object, hidden in the tall weeds, had caused him to fall. He uttered a curse and sat up, his ankle screaming with pain. As he pushed himself to a sitting position, his hand contacted the article that had made him hit the ground. It was soft, a jacket. Instinctively, Seth pulled his hand away. He fumbled in his coat pocket for his pen-light, a tool he always kept at hand for patient exams. Why hadn't he thought of using it before?

He pointed the light at his feet. There in the tall grass lay a body!

He scrambled to his knees to inspect the body more carefully. It was a girl, badly beaten, with blood on her buttocks and legs. For a moment he forgot all else and became a physician assessing a trauma patient. She had no pulse. Her skin was cool to the touch, her mouth gapped slightly, and her eyes were open, with dilated pupils. She was dead, but for how long? Seth guessed an hour. The blood between her legs was still damp, and by the look of her, she'd been raped and probably dumped here by her attacker.

Seth searched her for identification and retrieved a tattered, brown wallet from her coat pocket. He lifted her driver's license from a leather slot. The name leaped from the small card and sent an immediate chill down his back: "Lisa Dale." The girl Jamie Edwards had fantasized about! He stared at the body, trying to decide what to do. He shook his head in desperation. *I misjudged him. I should have warned her. I had a professional duty to alert her, and I followed my gut instinct instead! And now . . .*

He thought back to the psychiatric case studies he'd looked at during the malpractice conference he'd been required to attend. They had talked about this very thing—placing oneself at risk for malpractice by failing to break the confidence of someone who confesses homicidal fixation!

He collapsed back into the tall grass and tried to slow his breathing. It was all outlined in the office records—all the damning evidence anyone could ever want, clearly documenting Jamie's homicidal obsessions and Seth's negligence! Had the young man seen Seth when he walked into Lanny's? He had avoided his physician/counselor, hadn't he? In retrospect, Jamie was probably glad the doctor had his back turned.

Seth knew he had to get to those medical records. That would have been easy before he sold out to Coast Care, but the corporation had centralized the records of all the practices it owned. They daily gave Seth only the charts of the people he was scheduled to see that day. Coast Care had taken over billing, record-keeping, and transcription—all part of one efficient operation. So, getting a chart in a hurry could be a challenge. With the management office closed for the weekend, Jamie's chart was out of reach until Seth could request it on Monday morning.

Nothing could bring the girl back to life, but he had to do something to keep her death from ruining his career. Coast Care had warned him: No more lawsuits!

Seth began to tremble, more from fear than from the cold. With his head spinning from his preoccupation with losing his career and his disgust over losing the young trauma victim, with his judgment shadowed by his first alcohol intake in eight years, he began to form a dark plan: What if the authorities didn't know she died from an assault? What if . . . ?

He dry-swallowed at the thought of tampering with the death scene. He tried to focus in spite of his pain and in spite of the steady rain. What if they attributed her death to other causes? Seth's thoughts raced. Then no one would suspect Jamie, and no one would question him and thus discover his violent fantasies, and no one would know that he had told Seth Berringer about the event ahead of time.

The idea was a preposterous one but one that, in his desperate, confused state of mind, had begun to look like the most favorable of several dreaded options.

At least if they didn't realize it was a sexual assault, he would have some time to destroy his office records, and no one would be able to prove that Jamie had confessed his intentions to the physician.

He lay still for a moment, trying to understand the implications of the action he was contemplating. His thoughts were muddied by pain, despair, and alcohol. He wanted to protect himself, and yet . . . He couldn't let a murderer get off without penalty, could he? He thought about his patient and his mental illness. He likely felt very guilty for this, just as he had for the obsessions themselves. If Seth confronted him, he'd likely confess. And if he didn't, the doctor could threaten to turn him in. In the meantime, he'd have a little time to alter the office records. He just needed a few days. If he could alter the public perception of the crime long enough to cover his trail . . .

He lay still a few minutes longer, trying to focus, hoping his mind would clear. He knew he was not visible from the road, but when it became light again . . . He could hear an occasional vehicle but couldn't see anything because of the tall grass. He estimated he was a good 300 to 400 yards from the hospital parking lot.

He stood and stepped away a few feet. The body was essentially invisible at five yards. He looked around and tried to memorize a few landmarks. If he walked straight out to the road, he could leave something by the road as a marker. He looked back at the girl, then stooped to remove one of her shoes.

He walked to Chesapeake Avenue, a four-laner, counting his paces as he went. It was only twenty-two generous steps to a small ditch at the road's edge. He carefully placed the shoe on the soft shoulder. Then he limped toward the hospital parking lot, looking more like an arthritic patient than the young man that he was.

He planned to return in an hour. That would make it very unlikely that any other cars would be around. If he was caught with a dead body, how would he ever explain that?

As he stumbled on toward the parking lot, his thinking took a dangerous twist. With his judgment flawed by alcohol, exhaustion, and fear, he reviewed his desperately contrived plan. He had to do something—his career was at stake. But would he really be able to . . . ? He shook his head and tried to muster some courage. Failing to see the danger in his clouded thinking, he squelched his reasonable doubts about his scheme. *Maybe if I have another drink, I'll be able to do what's needed. I'll buy a few beers at the convenient mart on my way home. I'm not sure I can do this without a little extra nerve.*

◆ ◆ ◆

"I thought that guy would never stop eating," the older man complained.

"Forget about him, and keep your eyes open."

The silver BMW crept slowly along Chesapeake Avenue.

"How do you know she's around here?"

Doc was clearly irritated. "She can't have gone far." He rubbed the back of his neck. "I can't believe she got away right in the middle of the procedure."

"I don't want to think about what Mr. Davis will do if we come back without a tissue sample."

"What can he do?"

"Not pay us."

"Just shut up and watch for the girl."

A sign caught Bill's attention. "Hey, a hospital. I bet she went there."

The Asian lifted his eyebrows. "Now you're thinking. From the amount of blood we cleaned up in that bathroom, I'd say she might be looking for help."

"Where's the file?"

"Backseat. I'll let you handle this. No one would believe I'm related to the girl."

The older man pulled a picture out of a manila file. "Pull into the emergency parking." He pointed to his left.

William Guessford wore khaki pants and a shirt with a button-down collar. He was physically strong and wiry, with thick, unruly, gray hair. He put the picture in his wallet. He looked all the world like a typical American yuppie.

"Go find out if she's here." He sighed. "I'll wait in the car."

The older man shoved his wallet into his rear pocket and walked to the emergency entrance.

◆ ◆ ◆

Kerri Barber was managing the triage desk as a favor to a friend. This was supposed to be her weekend off, but she had traded with Jody McMullen, who wanted to attend a wedding. Kerri loved the emergency department. "Hours of boredom, moments of terror," she would report with a smile. She found the patient interactions invigorating and enjoyed the family contacts. Working with people in crisis gave her many opportunities to offer a prayer or a supportive touch.

Kerri had turned twenty-two the day she started her new job in the E.R. five years before. She began fresh out of nursing school, never once questioning the area of nursing she wanted to be in.

Tonight, as she often did during the slow hours of the morning, she prayed. This time it was for a family who had lost a six-year-old in a bicycle accident earlier during her shift. She prayed too for Dr. Seth Berringer, the young family physician who had worked so hard to save the young boy.

He looked so hurt, Father, she prayed silently, *and he's seemed so out of sorts lately. Comfort him, Lord.* She felt strangely ill at ease thinking about Seth. *If he's in trouble, God, or if he needs you, direct his pathway to you.*

She looked up just in time to see an anxious-appearing man approaching her desk.

"May I help you?" Kerri smiled.

"I hope so." The man fumbled with his wallet. "My niece didn't arrive home when we expected. I thought I'd check." He pulled out a color photograph.

Kerri's eyes brightened when she saw the portrait. "That's Lisa!"

The man stuttered, "Y-you h-have her here?"

Kerri shook her head. "No, we don't. I've been on duty all evening." She smiled again. "No one gets in here without me knowing it."

"Do you know her then?" The man seemed overly concerned.

"I met her at the Y. We used to play volleyball together." She shook her head again. "Come to think of it, I haven't seen her for a few months." She studied Lisa's "uncle," then added, "I didn't know she had any relatives around here."

The man stepped back, quickly replacing the photo, and retreated toward the exit. "I just moved here." He turned to go.

As she watched him leave, she played with her short, brown hair. She was sure Lisa had said she didn't have any family. She shrugged. *I wonder if Lisa was hiding something.*

◆ ◆ ◆

Bill shook his head and climbed back into the car. "No luck."

"Don't say that. It would have been a real challenge getting her away from the hospital."

"True."

Doc started the car and eased toward Chesapeake Avenue. The street was deserted, or so he thought at first inspection. Then he looked down to the right and squinted. "What the—"

Bill looked at a maroon van parked along the road a few hundred yards away, where the street lamps provided dim illumination. "Let's have the binoculars. What's that guy doing?"

Doc handed him the field glasses. "It looks like that guy is carrying something."

Bill squinted through the binoculars. "Or someone." He raised his voice. "He's got a body!"

"Bet you ten, he has our girl." He squirmed nervously. "What's he doing?"

"Beats me. He's putting the girl in the back of the van."

Doc cursed. "That's all we need."

"He must be in a hurry. Let's follow him."

The van pulled out with a squeal of the tires. After two blocks it veered right onto a side street, and the headlamps went off.

"Don't lose him!"

By the time the BMW arrived at the side street, the van had vanished.

◆ ◆ ◆

Inside the van, Seth's heart was pumping wildly. "Someone's coming, Berringer!" he yelled at himself. He accelerated, pushing his speed to nearly 80, then slammed his brakes, turned right, and shut off his headlights. Behind him, his cargo thudded against the van's interior.

"Slow down," he chided himself. "All you need is to have an accident and be found with a murder victim in your van!"

He made an immediate left, then another right, and climbed a small hill bordered by a long metal fence that hid Abe's Junkyard. Once he had crested the hill, he turned left again, heading past Deer Falls Elementary School toward the town limit. He passed a small sign welcoming visitors to Deer Falls, "The Friendly City."

Seth looked in the mirror. No headlights. He tried to slow his breathing. He hoped he had lost the other vehicle.

By now his head was pounding. He pulled in behind Jake's Exxon and turned off the engine. The station was deserted.

Fatigue, pain, alcohol, and fear about his future in medicine robbed Seth of rational thinking. *What am I doing? Disturbing a murder scene has to be some sort of a crime.* He brushed an empty beer bottle off the seat beside him and quickly dispelled the rational thought. He touched his forehead, then looked anxiously at his gloved hands. There was blood on his hands! He shook his head. *I only need a few days. I'll convince Jamie to come clean— after I'm sure no one can link him to me.* He wasn't hurting anything—just delaying the truth for a few days, that's all.

He waited for twenty minutes, to be sure he hadn't been followed. In that time he didn't even hear another vehicle.

He pulled open the van's back door and hoisted the corpse over his shoulder. The body was getting stiff. He hoped he hadn't waited too long.

He limped to the front of the station and dropped the dead woman onto the road, face up. He then positioned her so her legs were sprawled open to expose her bloody pelvis.

He moved quickly back to his car, his ankle screaming with every step. *Everything is ready now. I just have to make it look like she was run down by a car . . .*

◆ ◆ ◆

Back on Chesapeake Avenue, the silver BMW prowled slowly, looking for any clue as to what the mysterious man in the van might have been up to.

"Look over there." Doc pointed excitedly.

"It looks like a shoe."

Doc pulled over. There, clearly visible in the headlight's beam, was a shoe—a bloody shoe.

Bill jumped out and picked it up, holding it gingerly at arm's length. "It's hers," he reported, leaning into the open car window. "We were right. Our girl's in the van."

Doc shook his head without speaking and let out a sigh.

"We have to get that body."

Doc nodded his head. "Get in. This is going to get messy."

◆　◆　◆

Seth accelerated down the deserted street, his face twisted into a wild snarl, bracing himself for the impact.

His aim brought the right front wheel over the center of Lisa Dale's lower pelvis.

A sickening crunch followed as the van lurched up and over the body before skidding to a stop across the yellow center line.

It was time to get out of there and end the nightmare.

He drove for half a mile before turning on his lights. Ten minutes later he was sitting alone in his driveway.

He had to do one more thing, just to be sure everyone knew how she'd died.

He picked up his cellular phone, knowing they wouldn't be able to trace the call.

With trembling fingers he slowly pressed 911.

The operator picked up after one ring. "This is 911. What is the nature of your emergency?"

Speaking with a high tenor rasp to disguise his voice, Seth yelled with urgency, "A girl's been hit . . . Uh, I hit a girl! Right outside Jake's Exxon! I've got to help her!"

He depressed the power button on his cellular phone, ending the call.

He limped inside, threw his bloody gloves into the kitchen trash can, undressed, and stepped into the shower.

CHAPTER
3

KERRI Barber walked out of the hospital a few minutes after 7 A.M. She didn't have time to waste if she wanted to go home and change in time to make the early service at church. She needed sleep, but if the neighbor's dog would cooperate, she planned to sleep through the afternoon before going in for her next 11 to 7 shift.

She glanced at herself in the rearview mirror before backing her Taurus out of her parking spot. At twenty-seven, she looked nineteen and kept her hair cut short in a style just off her collar, so it wouldn't interfere with her work. If she had a physical flaw, she thought her figure was a bit too under-developed; but her slender frame would have been unbalanced otherwise, and her long legs more than made up for any deficiencies elsewhere. Her skin was fair in spite of her dark hair, and her face was quickly punctuated by her dimpled smile.

Pulling out, she flipped on the radio to catch the local news.

"A young woman has died from a hit-and-run accident on Route 602. A mysterious 911 call just after midnight alerted the rescue unit and the police to the incident. The victim, a female in her early twenties, was pro-nounced dead at the scene. Her name has not been released, pending noti-fication of her next of kin. The driver involved in the accident is unknown. The victim apparently died of massive internal and external injuries, but confirmation by the chief medical examiner is planned. In sports news, the Deer Falls High School Blazers posted another impressive win over . . ."

Kerri switched off the radio and moaned. She felt unsettled, disturbed. She hoped the deceased wasn't anyone she knew.

She began a silent prayer and, unknown to her, prayed for Seth Berringer for the second time in twenty-four hours. *Dear Father, comfort and guide the driver involved in the accident. Give him the courage to do what's right . . .*

◆ ◆ ◆

A sleepless Seth Berringer also heard the report and snapped off the radio with a groan. The throb in his temples was excruciating. He sat up slowly and massaged his head as memories of the night before came into focus.

It's a medical examiner case, of course! They'll probably do an autopsy! Why didn't I think of that? I wonder if the medical examiner will be able to tell how she really died?

He began to pace. At least the examiner wouldn't do the autopsy today—it was Sunday. Seth wiped the sweat from his forehead. If the medical examiner only did a cursory exam, maybe he'd miss the subtleties that would indicate Lisa had died from something besides the hit-and-run.

He looked at his hands and slumped back onto his bed. The enormity of what he had done had begun to loom as a large and ugly reality. He felt contaminated, guilty, incredulous at his desperate actions. What should he do now? Confess?

He sighed.

He had talked to the sheriff a time or two, even helped him get his blood pressure under better control. Maybe he'd understand. He thought a moment longer about the large man with a plastic smile looming above Lanny's parking lot. Understand? Naah!

Seth showered and dressed. He still hadn't decided what to do, if anything, when he realized that he'd better check the carpeting in the back of the van.

As he stepped off his front porch, a spot of purple caught his eye. Something was hanging from the bottom of his van!

He quickly dropped to his knees and looked under the vehicle. A piece of fabric was caught on the undercarriage. He recognized it immediately. The girl's coat!

He looked across the street, relieved that he appeared to be the first one up in his quiet neighborhood. He had no neighbors on his left because he lived on the corner, and he couldn't see the neighbors on the other side because of their high privacy fence.

He walked to the garage and opened the front door. He moved a grill, a bike, two lawn chairs, a card table, and an old phonograph to the side, then pulled his van inside and shut the door again.

As he inspected the vehicle, he was again horrified. The rug in the back was stained, there was blood on the gearshift handle and the steering wheel, and there were two fabric fragments wedged on the bottom.

He spent the next two hours removing the evidence. For the carpet, he tried cold water, then bleach, then a stain remover; he finally ripped up the whole wet mess. The stain was too dark and his memory too fresh to let it stay in the van any longer.

◆ ◆ ◆

Sheriff Wayne Boatwright showed the photo, enlarged from the victim's driver's license, to his sister.

Lou Ellen covered her gaping mouth with her hand. "Oh my! That's the girl from room 12!"

"I had a bad feeling about this." He shook his head. "Have you seen the two guys who were with her?"

"Not since last night." She nodded at the counter. "Her room key is on the counter there. It was turned in sometime last night. Gilda has already cleaned the room."

Lou Ellen looked as if she might cry. Wayne had seen this before, and he wanted to calm her down before her mascara started running.

"There, there, Lou." He put his meaty arm around her shoulder. "There was nothing you could do."

She sniffed and swallowed noisily. "Do you think those guys had anything to do with this?" She wiped her eyes, leaving a blue streak on her cheek. "She was run over, right?"

"Yeah, Lou Ellen, that's right." He lowered his voice. "Listen, if anyone comes by asking questions, leave out the part about the two men, would you? If there turns out to be some foul play here, the last thing I need is a scandal involving the Inn during my reelection campaign."

"Have you told her family?"

"She's an orphan, Lou. No family. Her father's been dead for five years, and he was an only child. Her mom, also an only child, died when the girl was five."

"My, oh, my," Lou Ellen sobbed. "So young, and so alone."

"We released her name to the media an hour ago. Lisa Dale."

"That's not her name." Lou Ellen straightened. "Or maybe I'm wrong." She scurried behind the counter, picked up a receipt, and shook it in the air. "See? It says right here, Anne Dustin."

"She probably made the name up," the sheriff responded, looking at the small paper. "Hmmm. Dustin, huh? I believe the computer printout said her mother was Gayle Dustin. I'd say she assumed another name for the registration form."

"Most girls who work here do."

"I don't want to know about it, Lou." He winked. "Not in an election year." He winked again and exited to his police cruiser.

◆　◆　◆

By the time the news of Lisa's death went public, Bill and Doc were a hundred miles to the south.

Doc was on the phone. The deep voice on the other end conveyed little emotion.

"Just find out who he is and what he knows. If he set it up to look like a hit-and-run, he must know something. If it's money he wants, perhaps we can help him, or at least make him think we can. Nobody successfully extorts money from me. No one, you hear?"

"Why is he protecting us?"

"Who knows? Find out, then get back here." There was an uncomfortable silence. "Any way they can link you to the girl?"

"I doubt it. Only if that fat sheriff realizes the victim is the same girl who was at the motel."

"Can they prove you did anything?"

"Of course not."

"How far along did you get anyway?"

"I used a dry spruce spike to dilate the cervix. It's an old back-alley trick. No one will link that to modern research."

"You fool! You probably lacerated her uterus or something." He cursed. "I never gave you permission to do that—"

"I was only protecting us in case something went wrong. No one will suspect she was a part of a modern experiment."

The man on the other end coughed and cursed again. "She probably ran out and bled to death." He thought for a moment. "You used a wood spike? A good pathologist will find it, you know."

"I've been thinking about that."

"Maybe you should get a hand on the autopsy report, before it gets to the media."

"Okay, but even if it does get out, people will just figure someone was covering up a bad abortion."

"Just cover your tracks and make sure the public still believes it was a hit-and-run. It's cleaner that way. We can't have anyone stumbling across this baby and running any special studies, can we?"

"Right."

"First see if you can find out who's covering for us. Find out what he knows—and silence him."

"Sure."

"And, Doc, get that tissue—this project's a bust without it."

Doc grunted. "Sure."

Click.

◆　◆　◆

By midday Seth figured he'd better see if there was a way out of the tangle he'd gotten into, preferably with his job intact. If worse came to worse and Coast Care terminated him, he hoped he could at least live with his conscience.

It would be best if he could deliver the whole story, including the perpetrator of the original crime. That would make his rash actions seem a bit more believable. The doctor and the patient he covered for coming forward together—it just might work.

First he would have to talk to Jamie Edwards and persuade him to confess. That idea, strangely enough, didn't scare him. Jamie had never exhibited violent tendencies toward his physician, even when admitting his preoccupation and fears about committing sexual crimes.

Seth thought he should confront Jamie face to face. He knew he worked on Sundays as a taxi driver for the only such company serving Deer Falls, the Blue Cab Company. The best way to talk to him was to call for a taxicab.

After making a call to the dispatcher and asking specifically for Jamie, Seth waited for ten long minutes, sitting on his broad covered porch in an old-fashioned glide-rocker.

Finally Jamie drove up and tapped the horn. "Where can I take you, doc?" He looked at the maroon van. "What's wrong with the old truck?"

Seth walked over to the passenger door without replying. When he got in, he looked at Jamie, a muscular man of about twenty-eight, and got right to the point. "I'm not going anywhere in particular."

Jamie looked at him curiously.

"Start the meter and let's go for a drive. I wanted to talk to you, that's all."

"We can talk here." He shut off the engine.

"You heard about Lisa Dale?"

Jamie nodded. "Just before I came on this shift." He hesitated. "It made me ill. I almost called in sick, but I've lost so much time lately, due to Mom's health."

"Get straight with me, Jamie. How did she die?" His voice was steady and firm.

"What are you gettin' at, doc?" Jamie pulled his head up. "The radio said she was hit by a car or something."

"That's what they're saying, but she was raped and murdered, and you know it!"

"No!" He glared at the doctor. "What are you tryin' to say?"

Berringer softened a notch and sighed. "OK, Jamie, where were you last night before I saw you at Lanny's?"

Jamie's eyes narrowed. "Is that what this is about? You saw me drinkin'?"

"Yes, I saw you. What I want to know is, what did you do before you went to Lanny's?"

"I was at the hospital visiting my mother, not that it's any of your business. I worked all day haulin' topsoil for Len Moyer, then went to the hospital to see my mother. After three hours with her, I headed for Lanny's." He took a breath. "I really didn't drink much, honest. I only had a few." He stopped again. "You don't know what it's like seein' your mom waste away like I've been doing. I had to calm the stress somehow. I—I just had a few drinks."

"Your mother is at Chesapeake General?"

"Room 302. Dr. Deputy says she had a stroke."

"I'm sorry, Jamie. I didn't know." Seth sighed and tried to comprehend this new possibility. So far it didn't compute.

He looked at Jamie. He either wasn't getting through or he'd made a terrible error. "Jamie, this isn't about drinking. I saw you last night, yes, but this isn't about that." He captured Jamie's eyes. "This is about Lisa, remember? Did you see her last night?"

"No." He pulled away from Seth's captive gaze. "Do you mind tellin' me what this is all about?"

Seth could see his patient was telling the truth. He slumped forward, burying his head in his hands. He suddenly felt nauseated. "I can't believe this," he muttered. "Man, I can't believe this. What have I—"

"Are you OK, doc?" Jamie looked genuinely concerned.

Berringer shrugged. "I'd better let you go, Jamie. Forget this conversation ever happened." He looked at the younger man. "I'm sorry for confusing you. Let's just say I messed up."

"Aw, doc, you're OK." Jamie didn't know what to say. His doctor looked as if he might cry.

That's the way Berringer felt, too, after realizing that he might have covered up for some madman on the loose.

"I have to go," the doctor responded, his voice barely above a whisper. "You'd better leave."

The doctor exited the cab and watched it pull away. He turned to the house and cursed, wishing he could erase the last twenty-four hours of his life. He'd give anything for that—anything.

How could he have been so stupid? He slumped onto his glide-rocker again. His evaluation of Jamie hadn't been so off the wall after all. His despair over losing the little boy, plus his job concerns, had made him second-guess himself. And now he was painted into a dangerous corner. He knew he'd have to straighten this all out with the law or catch the real murderer.

Seth shook his head and smiled. Amazingly, his sense of humor was still intact. *Naah! That's another bad idea.*

◆ ◆ ◆

Kerri Barber was listening to the radio and eating a large bowl of cereal for lunch. Cold cereal was easy and, if the truth be known, one of Kerri's favorite meals. Today it was oat bran flakes topped with low-fat granola and Trix. She was listening to the news when she heard the name of the hit-and-run victim—Lisa Dale.

The news hit her hard. She sighed with grief. Lisa's uncle's fears must have been correct. Kerri paused, caught short with a pointed fear. Was that guy really her uncle? Was it mere coincidence that a man came looking for Lisa on the same night she turned up dead?

The nurse shook her head and scolded herself for her paranoia. *Right, Kerri, like this guy just went out to find her so he could run her down!*

She returned to her cereal, crunching it as loudly as she pleased. Perhaps she should report her suspicions to the police. She continued crunching and poured a little more Trix into the remaining milk. *Why is the cereal always finished before the milk?* She didn't want the police to think she was stupid or watching too much TV. Maybe Lisa really did have an uncle.

Kerri thumbed through the phone directory. There were no Dales listed besides Lisa. She rested her finger on the listing for "L. Dale." What had Lisa said her mother's name was? Dusty or Dustbroom or . . . Dustin, that was it. She flipped to the d's, but there were no listings for Dustin.

Well, the alleged uncle did say they'd recently moved here. Maybe his name wasn't in the book yet. Kerri called Information to see if any Dales or Dustins were listed but received two negative responses. Did this mean anything, or was she being overly suspicious?

She looked at her watch. She needed some sleep if she wanted to function at the E.R. tonight.

She heaved a sigh and looked at the phone. If she didn't make this call, she'd wonder why she didn't. The worst that could happen would be that she'd embarrass herself. *Pride goes before a fall, girl.*

Kerri looked inside the cover of the phone-book for the number, then carefully dialed the county police department.

"Sheriff Boatwright." The gruff voice startled Kerri.

"Uh . . . Sheriff, I didn't know you'd answer the phone. I . . . uh . . . I'm Kerri Barber. I work as a nurse in the emergency room at Chesapeake General Hospital. I hope I'm not interrupting anything."

He chuckled. "Staff's a little thin around here on weekends, so occasionally I handle the phone myself." He took a bite from a powdered donut and wiped his mouth with the back of his hand. "How can I help you?" His voice was muffled.

"I wanted to report a suspicion, that's all. It's about Lisa Dale, the girl who was hit by a car last night."

The sheriff sat up straight. She had his attention now. "Did you see something, ma'am?"

"Not really. But a man came into the E.R. about midnight looking for Lisa. He claimed to be her uncle and said she was overdue at home. He said he was worried and wondered if we had seen her. The strange thing is, I am, or was, a friend of Lisa's. She told me she didn't have any family. And then she ends up dead on the same night this guy is looking for her."

"People don't always want you to know everything, now do they?" The sheriff grabbed a pencil and laid aside the half-eaten donut. "Can you describe the man?"

Kerri pulled up a mental image. "Tall, about forty-five or fifty, gray hair, one of those preppie shirts with buttons on the collar, khaki pants. That's all, I think."

The sheriff slapped his knee. *The guy at the Inn!* "Tell me something, Ms. Barber, was there anyone else with him? A younger Asian man with a mustache perhaps?"

Kerri thought for a moment. "No. I would have remembered that." She added, "I wasn't sure I should call." She shrugged. "I mean, for all I know, he was telling the truth, and I'm just wasting your time."

"Don't worry about it, ma'am. I'd rather you'd call." He paused for a moment, hoping to keep a lid on any possible scandal that could be traced back to his sister's place. "Say, before you go spreading any of this around, you'd better check with me first, OK?" Suddenly nervous, he began to stutter. "I m-mean, we really d-don't know anything for a fact, so before we go c-conjuring up any wrongdoing here, we'd better be hush-hush about things, or we m-might get an innocent person hurt. Besides, for all we know, she did have some family who were concerned about her being out at night. I doubt that Ms. Dale shared everything about her life with you."

Kerri nodded, even though the sheriff couldn't see her. "Sure." It sounded reasonable enough.

Sheriff Boatwright hung up the phone. Police records also showed that Lisa Dale didn't have any family. Was it coincidence that she ended up dead after his sister heard her scream? Was it coincidence that the fellow from the motel was out looking for her late at night? Was she that good? He chuckled to himself, until a serious thought choked his laugh short. This was beginning to smell pretty ripe, and it was going to get more and more difficult for him to come out untouched, particularly if people could point to the Inn or his sister as a source of questionable behavior.

On the other end, Kerri questioned the sheriff's reluctance to let her mention any of this to anyone else. She was starting to have suspicious thoughts about everyone, it seemed, and that bothered her. But her need for sleep overcame her. She slept peacefully until her alarm sounded at 10 P.M.

CHAPTER
4

THE room's interior appeared futuristic to anyone not initiated in the state-of-the-art world of genetic engineering. High, fluorescent-lit ceilings, a negative-flow, double-filtered ventilation system, and a huge array of glassware held in place on a complicated network of steel supports made up the basic design. Two large DNA sequencing areas dominated the central portion of the lab. Those at work there followed sterile techniques that bordered on the absurd.

Ursula Baumgarten spoke softly from behind her mask. She waved a computer printout two inches thick in the air. "It's no use. The latest information is too fragmented. We only have half the data from chromosomes 3 and 6, and number 16 is so moth-eaten, it's unrecognizable."

"That's all we have?" The sober voice came from a coworker, Dr. Harold Teets.

"I'm afraid so."

"Unless we get some tissue back from our surrogate, I'd say this project is closed."

"Any word from Mr. Davis?"

"Only that they found our girl."

Ursula's dark eyes flashed. "Excellent."

Harold looked down. "She showed up in her college town, but . . . she's dead, Ursula."

"Dead?" She dropped the stack of paper on the high-priced countertop. "That is not what I want to hear!"

"Mr. Davis said she was hit by a car or something—a freak accident—hit-and-run."

Ursula touched the back of the elastic cover containing her long, blonde hair. She let an expletive fly. "We're in trouble, Harold."

"They can't possibly link her to us."

"They can if someone begins testing that baby."

"They have no reason to do that. Don't worry—Mr. Davis has some men on it. He sent them out to do a tissue harvest. Maybe they'll just have to do it on the corpse."

Ursula cursed again. "Why were they going to do the harvest out there anyway? They should've known that was too risky. It should only have been done here in the lab."

"Mr. Davis wanted it done there, that's why. He was afraid she'd abort without the hormonal support we were providing for her here, so he sent the men after her. But it took too long to find her. He couldn't just write her off because he was afraid she'd flush the tissue and we'd be in a real fix."

"The same fix we're in now, I'd say." The woman scowled behind her mask.

The two stood quietly for a moment. Ursula sprayed the counter with a disinfectant. After she set the container down, she spoke again, her voice revealing a hint of anxiety. "What if we spliced in some healthy DNA? You know, sort of fill in the gaps?"

Dr. Teets shook his head. "That would defeat our purpose. Any problems we see in the offspring could be traced to our augmentation. Besides, Davis would never approve."

"As if he has any idea what I'm doing down here anyway." *Or you for that matter, Harold. If I act on my idea, who'll know?*

Teets eyed her suspiciously but said nothing.

Ursula returned his gaze, confident she hadn't revealed her thoughts, then turned and walked to the exit. She punched a numbered sequence on a keypad. "So, what is Mr. Davis proposing?"

"Simple. Find the body—get the clone."

She nodded resolutely. "It's the only way."

◆　◆　◆

At Chesapeake General Hospital, the E.R. was divided into acute and non-acute sides, sharing a common central nursing area. The acute side dealt with illnesses of a sudden nature, such as myocardial infarctions (heart attacks) and trauma. The non-acute side included illnesses that had been going on for more than a few days, such as routine colds and backaches. Kerri had been assigned to non-acute, and her Sunday night was full of pediatric complaints and mothers who suddenly wanted their children's runny noses checked before school the next day. She always had to watch her attitude while working non-acute. *This is an emergency?*

It wasn't until 3 in the morning that things slowed down enough to allow her to trade jobs with the triage nurse. Kerri turned her thoughts again to the strange man who had come there during her last shift on triage. She thought about her own family, her uncles and aunts who seemed to thrive on large holiday gatherings and the fellowship a large family provided. She suddenly realized the fallacy of her earlier thinking. She had uncles who had married into the family with half a dozen different names. If Lisa had an uncle, he wasn't necessarily named Dustin or Dale.

Feeling a bit foolish, she sat quietly for a moment and counted the number of admissions for her shift. Six so far. Right on par for a Sunday night. Just then Mary Blewett, a fellow nurse, walked up.

Mary sighed. "Things have finally slowed down. The only two we have in back are Mr. Jones, who's trying to pass another kidney stone, and Mr. Jenkins, who's sleepin' off a drunk."

Kerri smiled. She liked Mary. She shot straight, even if it was from the hip. "Some things never change."

"At least it's better than last night, working with the old 'trauma magnet.'"

"Dr. Berringer?"

Mary sat on the triage desk. "Yes. Didn't you ever notice the misery he attracts?"

Kerri thought for a moment. "Come to think of it—"

"Come on, girl!" Mary interrupted. "Every time he's here we end up with some old guy dyin' of heart failure or some refractive dysrhythmia or some horrendous trauma victim." She smiled thinly. "If he wasn't so cute, I'd think about trading away my Berringer shifts."

"Mary!" Kerri raised her eyebrows. "He's an excellent doctor, and he genuinely cares about people."

"Don't play that game with me! I know you've noticed him." Mary put her hand behind her head in an exaggerated glamour pose. "Who hasn't?"

Kerri dropped her eyes. Mary was right. Kerri *had* noticed the young physician. She had, if the truth be known, secretly observed him for over a year, watching his gentle manner with his patients, admiring the work he did, and enjoying his infectious love of medicine. She seemed naturally attracted to his handsome appearance and his self-effacing humor. Her attraction to him, in fact, had become a frequent stimulus for her prayers. *Lord, why can't I find a man like Seth Berringer?*

Kerri looked up and held her tongue. She had noticed Seth, to be sure, but she wasn't about to tell her talkative cohort about it.

Mary added a playful jab. "Oh, well, I'm sure you wouldn't notice a guy unless he goes to that church of yours."

The young nurse took it in stride. Mary was right again. She answered honestly, "That would help." She looked up and added, "To be truthful, I've been concerned about Dr. Berringer. He seemed pretty depressed after losing that little boy last night."

"He didn't lose him. That boy was dead when he got here. He came in dead and stayed dead, you know? And there wasn't a thing a fine, young physician like Berringer could do about it. I told him so last night."

Kerri didn't reply, and Mary went on, "Berringer's a fine doctor. I've seen a few hundred in my twenty years, and he's one of the brightest. He just needs a little more confidence. Why, he's a jewel under pressure, a real gem."

Kerri nodded.

Mary continued, "I think he takes this all a bit too seriously. If he keeps this up, he'll burn out. If anyone can judge 'em, I oughta be able to. After all," she added with a chuckle, "I married two of 'em."

Kerri raised her eyebrows. "Fred's a doctor?"

"Not Fred, honey. Fred sells insurance." She winked. "I finally got smart." She folded her hands across her chest resolutely. "I was talkin' about William and Gilbert."

"Oh." Kerri didn't want to touch that one.

"If you ask me, Berringer just needs to toughen up. He hasn't quite bounced back since that malpractice claim."

"Malpractice?"

"It was nothing, believe me. Some old guy on home oxygen supplement started feeling so much better after Berringer started it that he sued the doctor for not prescribing it sooner." Mary shook her head. "Frivolous, if you ask me. The lawyers finally saw the light and dropped the case, but not before making Berringer sweat for a year."

Kerri nodded again. She wanted to change the subject. This one felt too much like gossip.

Mary did it for her. "You know, with Berringer's luck I'm surprised the squad didn't bring us that hit-and-run victim too. Then he would have had another dead patient on his hands."

The younger nurse sat quietly for a moment. "I knew her."

"The girl?"

"Lisa Dale. I played volleyball with her."

"I didn't know. I'm sorry." Mary sat uncomfortably for a moment before adding, "I guess the funeral will be later in the week after the medical examiner has his crack at the case."

Kerri looked unusually sober. "I don't think she had many friends. Who will make the funeral arrangements?"

"Relatives," Mary answered. "Or if there aren't any, the sheriff's department. Some limited state funds are available for people without money or family, enough to pay for a cheap funeral or memorial service."

"I'd like to go."

"You should. If you need somebody to cover for you, let me know."

"Mary," the triage intercom squawked. It was Laurie, the E.R. ward secretary. "It sounds like Mr. Jenkins is waking up."

Mary stood. "Duty calls."

Kerri watched her go but couldn't stop thinking about Lisa. If she had any family, especially a concerned uncle, they would surely show up at the funeral. The nurse nodded resolutely. Now she could figure out whether her gut feelings about this mysterious uncle had any bearing in reality or whether she should take an antacid.

◆ ◆ ◆

The next morning Sheriff Wayne Boatwright outlined a twofold strategy. It was an unwritten plan, but a plan nonetheless. First, he would continue his efforts to control any information about the hit-and-run that might hint at foul play at the Inn. Second, he would keep his eyes open for the two men he'd spoken with outside room 12. If they were somehow involved in wrongdoing, at least if he were the one uncovering it, he would have a chance to save face in any media coverage.

He'd need to spend a little more time at the Inn, in case they returned. He had practically no information about the two men. He didn't even know their names. All he had were his suspicions. He knew just about everyone in Deer Falls—anyone he deemed important anyway. These men were definitely outsiders.

It would be best, he decided, if the whole unfortunate business went away quietly—an orphan pedestrian killed while out for a midnight stroll—nothing more, nothing less. He didn't really want to find the driver. It was an accident, and no one could have saved the girl anyway. Who could blame a guy for not wanting to come forward in such circumstances?

His thoughts were interrupted by Clara Thompson, the owner of the county's best breakfast spot. "More coffee, sheriff?"

"Warm it up, Clara," he said as he pushed his mug to the end of the table. "Thanks."

"You've been pretty quiet over here. Heavy business this morning?"

"The usual." He picked up his fork and stabbed a thick stack of cinnamon toast dripping with maple syrup.

Clara stood with her hand on her ample right hip. "Any idea who hit that girl the other night?"

"I'm working on it," he said in a muffled tone.

Clara handed him a napkin. "I'll bet she was drunk. You know college students these days. You should see 'em come in here on Saturday mornings." She rolled her eyes as she talked. "They look like the Devil himself. Eyes all bloodshot, moving slow like the world is on their shoulders." She shook her mountain of hair, which was jet-black but white at the roots. "It takes two or three mugs of my morning swill to get them to say anything," she added, waving the pot in her left hand to emphasize her speech.

The sheriff nodded.

Clara went on, not really needing a response from the hungry sheriff. "I guess we'll find out about any alcohol from the tests they'll do on the body. That stuff always comes out after the autopsy."

Boatwright looked up. He hadn't even thought about the autopsy! Maybe the chief medical examiner would overlook the need for one if everything appeared straightforward. At minimum, the sheriff would have to make sure the examiner didn't come up with too many questions. It would be to Boatwright's advantage if the examiner took things at face value and ruled that Lisa Dale died from the accident.

The sheriff pushed back an empty plate, which Clara quickly retrieved. "You sure do a great job with the french toast, Clara."

"Don't thank me. Millie's workin' the grill this morning." She smiled.

"Besides, it's good to see someone eat. These kids just come in and order coffee and bagels. They're nickelin' and dimin' me to death."

He put five dollars on the table and stood up. "I've got to run, Clara. Thanks again." He opened the front door, causing a small attached wind-chime to clatter, his thoughts already on his next assigned task—a visit with the chief medical examiner.

◆ ◆ ◆

Throughout the morning Dr. Seth Berringer had difficulty keeping his mind on his work. The weight of guilt he felt for diverting the law's attention away from a rape/murder was growing by the hour. His former plan—to remove any incriminating evidence from Jamie Edwards's chart—had fallen by the wayside, an unnecessary cover-up for an obviously innocent man.

Momentarily during the afternoon Berringer's thoughts were diverted to important patient considerations, and he was able to move more quickly through his ever-expanding medical care load.

After work he formulated yet another plan for getting himself out of the corner he'd painted himself into. He couldn't quite bring himself to con-fess, although the thought had crossed his mind that he could talk to Sheriff Boatwright. But whom had he wronged? Certainly not the sheriff, although he'd probably sent him on a goose chase, looking for a hit-and-run driver when he should be looking for a rapist. The thought stopped Seth for a moment as he reconsidered the facts. He'd never really checked the body that closely. He'd just assumed, knowing Lisa's identity, that Jamie had raped her, like he'd fantasized. But maybe, just maybe, there was another explanation. If the medical examiner did a thorough job, he might even be able to tell what actually happened.

That thought appealed to Seth even more. Since he'd steered every-one wrong so far, maybe he should contact the medical examiner to be sure he wasn't fooled by the tire tracks and the way the victim was found. If Seth could get the examiner to say she was dead before the accident and that she'd died for some other reason, there would be no need for Berringer to confess to altering the evidence. No harm would have been done, and Seth could return to normal life such as it was.

◆ ◆ ◆

Eric Donovan, M.D. had been a chief medical examiner for fifteen years. In that time he had seen suicide and murder in Chesapeake County rise sixteenfold. He was a forensic pathologist by trade, a medical doctor who dealt with the analysis of human specimens, including bodily fluids such as blood evidence collected in criminal investigations, and of course the analysis of the victims themselves and the evaluation of the death scenes. As a chief medical examiner, he was an employee of the state and oversaw a network of fifteen county medical examiners, appointed by local county medical societies.

He was about to embark on another traumatic hit-and-run death investigation, an automatic medical examiner's case. Unlike gunshot wound cases, which always required an autopsy, the chief medical examiner had the authority to recommend or perform an autopsy on as many or as few hit-and-runs as he or she felt were necessary.

The county medical examiner's report, which had been forwarded to him by the county sheriff's office, was on his desk, and it was in order and relatively straightforward, as far as he could see. The only catch, and the one hang-up in his mind, was the description of the death scene. There was no mention of skid marks on the road to the east of the body, the direction the vehicle would have been traveling from. That, in and of itself, was a small warning flag and could only mean that the driver had little or no chance to brake before impact. Along a dark road, that wasn't uncommon.

Dr. Donovan took his job seriously, knowing that complete information brought finality to the case, adequate information to the courts if needed, and closure to grieving family members. Tonight would be no different. Although the initial crime scene had been evaluated by the county medical examiner, Donovan would reexamine the scene tonight at approximately the same time as the 911 call came in on the night of the death, 12 midnight.

He combed his graying mustache with his fingers, a habit his wife disliked, and slowly opened the door to his new sport utility wagon, a Ford Explorer. He had used a number of four-wheel-drive vehicles in the past and put them to hard use, often traveling off-road or on the beach to investigate a traumatic accident or drowning death.

He had memorized the police report and left it on his desk. The report indicated that the vehicle was traveling out of town, toward the west. The location where the body was found was marked with paint. Beyond the paint were skid marks and the suggestion of a bloodstain.

Donovan, nearly sixty, was the outward picture of health, beyond a mild condition of glaucoma that he managed with daily eyedrops. He had brought a strong halogen lamp for the investigation but was struck by the fact that it wasn't needed. A single street lamp provided ample lighting to examine the scene.

He returned to the car and retrieved a purple winter coat from a plastic bag. He had removed it from the body before leaving his office. He laid the coat beside the road. The material was shimmery, like a modern athletic garment, and reflected the light easily.

The pathologist began to back up. Twenty yards, thirty, . . . even up to fifty yards he could easily see the jacket. He squinted into the semidarkness before making a photograph for the fatality's case file.

He repeated the process after moving the coat three times—in the road, beside the road, further off the road. Each time the jacket could be identified.

He looked at the road and confirmed the absence of skid marks before the body was struck. Did that imply that the driver intentionally struck the victim? Or perhaps that he fell asleep at the wheel or simply wasn't paying attention? Few deductions could be made from this alone.

Donovan wouldn't draw any conclusions that night, but his mind was made up. The yellow warning light that the police report had raised had turned to red in the coroner's mind. He definitely needed to stop and take a closer look.

CHAPTER
5

THE next morning, an urgency of business for Wayne Boatwright almost but not quite dictated missing breakfast at Clara's. He was drinking coffee from a large mug, thinking seriously about heading straight down to see the chief medical examiner when he saw a customer coming from Clara's carrying a large sweet roll. The sheriff took one look at his coffee and decided that thirty minutes wouldn't matter that much. Besides, for Sheriff Boatwright there wasn't anything in the world quite like a fresh sticky-bun.

The problem was, thirty minutes turned into forty-five and then into an hour as one sweet roll turned to two, plus a side of grits, two more cups of coffee, and a sausage biscuit for the road.

By that time, Seth Berringer was already on the phone with Dr. Eric Donovan.

◆ ◆ ◆

"Dr. Donovan? Dr. Seth Berringer here. I believe we've met before, when you lectured on forensic medicine over at Chesapeake General."

"Oh, yes. The October laboratory medicine conference." The examiner cradled the phone against his ear with his shoulder. "What can I do for you, Seth?"

"I'm calling for information about the hit-and-run-case." He started to pace. "You see, she was a patient of mine. Whenever one of my patients has an autopsy, I like to hear the results, to make sure he or she didn't have anything I missed." Since he had once treated Lisa Dale for a minor illness, he was technically speaking the truth, though he was holding back the main reason he was calling.

"Any reason to believe she had any serious pathology?" Donovan pulled out a pen to make notes. "Did she have any symptoms you were investigating?"

"N-no, not really," Seth stuttered. "I just wanted to know how the autopsy went."

"Well, to tell you the truth, I've done a cursory gross exam without putting a knife to her, and she looks pretty beaten up. I think we can say with a high degree of confidence that she likely died from the trauma. I'm not sure an autopsy is needed to prove that." He decided it was best not to share his misgivings about the way the accident happened with the family doctor, at least not yet.

Seth squirmed uncomfortably. "I think you should do the autopsy. No one's going to protest. I don't recall hearing of any family. In fact, I think the radio reported that her parents were deceased."

"Just the same, it's the state's money, and I'm not sure an autopsy is cost-effective." He decided to push Seth a bit, to see if he had any other reason for calling.

"I really think you should do it," Seth insisted. "Look, she was my patient, and I feel . . . I mean, we don't have clear evidence that she died from this hit-and-run accident, do we? Other than a 911 call from someone who has yet to come forward." He paused. "The whole thing smells fishy to me. I'd say you have a trauma death, but from an unsure cause. Call it a hunch or a gut feeling, but I think you have an obligation to look into it further."

"Is that why you called, Seth, to convince me to look for foul play?" The older pathologist spoke to him as he would to his own son.

"Yes," Seth responded honestly.

"I'll give it full consideration. I think you've made a valid point."

Seth mouthed a silent Yes! and closed his fist. "Thank you and . . . say, could you let me know if my hunch is correct?"

"I'll do better than that. Anyone who was involved in a patient's care before death is always welcome at the autopsy. You say you were her doctor?"

"Well, to be perfectly honest, I saw her only once, for the flu, but we do have, or did have, an active file on her."

"Hmmm," the pathologist pondered, "I'd say you'd still be welcome. I will likely do the autopsy this afternoon."

"Thanks, Dr. Donovan. Thanks a lot."

"It's Eric, Seth. Only the nurses call me Dr. Donovan."

"OK," Seth stopped short of saying "Eric."

"Don't worry. I'll consider what you said."

"Thanks again."

"You can call my secretary later for the time of the autopsy."

"Good-bye."

◆ ◆ ◆

Sheriff Boatwright flashed a politician's grin for Tammy Lynn Gaskins, Dr. Donovan's secretary and transcriptionist. "Howdy, Tammy Lynn. Is Eric in?"

Tammy stiffened. She didn't like anyone calling her boss "Eric," even if it was his name. He was "Dr. Donovan" to her and to anyone else in this office as far as she was concerned. And to this beach ball, she was "Ms. Gaskins." She stuck out her hand. "Ms. Gaskins," she corrected.

Boatwright backpedaled. "I'm sorry, Ms. Gaskins. I read your name plate."

"Dr. Donovan is working. Can I leave a message?"

"I need to talk to him about a case he's likely to consider today. It's somewhat of an emergency."

She wasn't going to bend. She picked up Dr. Donovan's daily planner. "I see he has an opening around 2 today."

"Look, Ms. Gaskins, this is police business. Now unless you want to obstruct justice, I suggest you get Dr. Donovan out here or take me to him right away!"

Easy, hotshot! I just wanted to see you get winded, that's all. She smiled thinly, silently enjoying her ability to frustrate the officer. "Come this way." She opened the door to the lab. "I hope you enjoy formaldehyde."

Eric Donovan looked up as the two came through the door. He immediately threw a sheet over Lisa Dale's exposed body, being prepared for autopsy. The doctor recognized the sheriff from the campaign posters around town.

"Sheriff Boatwright? What brings you here?" Dr. Donovan did not hold out his gloved hand, for which the sheriff was grateful.

"Hello, doctor. I was hopin' to talk with you about my hit-and-run case."

"I was about to start on the autopsy."

"Autopsy?" He chuckled confidently. "A smart man like you don't need a knife to figure out how this one died. I saw her myself. The car really smashed her." He shook his head. "Ooooh!" He wrinkled his mouth distastefully.

Dr. Donovan glanced toward the covered body. "I guess I was wanting to confirm things, that's all."

The sheriff moved closer, a move that made Donovan uncomfortable. "What's to confirm?" He hooked his thumbs in his belt. "You'd be wastin' your valuable time, doc."

"Why did you come down here, sheriff?" Donovan retreated a step.

"I'm interested in every phase of investigation when a tragedy happens in my jurisdiction." He puffed out his chest, which still appeared small above his massive waist.

The sheriff seemed harmless enough. Donovan sure wouldn't mind saving money and time by not doing the autopsy. He had a mountain of other work to do. But he couldn't forget his findings at the scene either.

He decided to bounce his ideas off the lawman. "I found it a bit odd that there was no evidence of the vehicle braking before impact." He pointed at the clothing laid out on the exam table. "It's not like that jacket is hard to see."

The sheriff nodded. "The way I see it, the driver wasn't payin' too much attention—maybe listenin' to the radio, or maybe it was a man payin' too much attention to his girl. Obviously, the man who made the 911 call had something to hide or he would've stuck around. Maybe he was with someone else's wife or somethin'." He paused and grunted. "You never know about these things. Maybe he felt so stupid for not watching the road that he wanted to avoid the embarrassment." He shuffled his feet. "Most likely the man was a respectable citizen or he wouldn't have called at all."

Donovan nodded. "Makes sense to me." Maybe this guy was smarter than he looked.

"Believe me, I've been around a long time. Pretty soon you can figure things out real quick."

Donovan wouldn't mind just doing the report on the gross exam and being done with it. What more did he need to know? He looked at the large man in front of him. Besides, that way he'd stay in the sheriff's good graces. From what the examiner knew about this county, he'd have to work with him for a long time.

"Well, you certainly have loads of experience."

The sheriff smiled, a genuine one that appeared boyish and awkward, not the flashy, practiced one he reserved for campaign photographs.

The pathologist continued, "I guess I'll do my report after inspecting the body a bit more and avoid the expense of an autopsy—unless something else comes up, of course."

Wayne Boatwright nodded. He was confident that Donovan would find enough evidence that Lisa Dale had died from the accident to avoid looking further into the situation. He breathed a sigh of relief and smiled again. As long as he didn't find evidence of the girl's occupation, no one would tie her, or her death, to the sheriff's sister's place, and that way Boatwright could avoid any potential damage to his campaign.

The lawman pivoted and looked back out toward Tammy Lynn and the front office. "I need to run. I'll expect your report later in the week, so I can get this whole case wrapped up."

"Should be no problem. I have to be done today."

The sheriff nodded, let himself out, and nodded politely to Tammy Lynn. "Good day, sheriff," she said coldly.

He glanced at the young woman one more time. Working around all these stiffs must have soured her disposition.

◆ ◆ ◆

Kerri's alarm brought forced wakefulness at 11 A.M. She had only been asleep for three hours, but she needed to make a transition to the evening shift, and she knew if she slept all day, she wouldn't be able to sleep when she got off that night.

She groaned and pulled up the shade, immediately squinting from the bright sunlight. It looked like a nice enough day. She hoped it wasn't too cold for a jog.

She pulled on a pair of sweats and poured herself a small glass of orange juice, then stepped outside to get the mail, frowning to see a relatively full stack. She winced, anticipating her monthly bills. As she walked back up her front steps, she flipped through the day's catch—an electric bill, a coupon pack, a new Mac Zone catalog, a bank statement, and a newsletter from Focus on the Family. She smiled at the last one. She wondered what Dr. Dobson was stirring up now.

As she dropped the mail onto the kitchen counter, a postcard, previously hidden behind the catalog, landed face-up, revealing a snowy picture of the Rocky Mountains. Kerri picked up the wrinkled card and began to read.

Dear Kerri,

I am so afraid. I signed up for a research project as a paid volunteer subject. Now I think I'm pregnant, and I don't know how. I've kept our commitment—honestly, I have. The researchers will be upset that I've run. They want the baby. I know you will pray. I'll call you when I get to Deer Falls. I'm in deep trouble. I didn't know who else to tell.

Kerri's heart quickened as she strained to read the signature. It seemed to be smudged. Was that blood? She held the card up to the light. She gasped as she clearly understood the sender's name: "Lisa."

Kerri read and reread the letter, trying to understand the choppy, confused message. Then she did what Lisa knew she would.

She prayed.

◆ ◆ ◆

Eric Donovan repeated his gross evaluation and description of the body. As he worked, several things bothered him. First, why would a family physician, who'd only seen the patient one time, urge him to do an autopsy because he suspected something fishy? And why was he suspicious in the first place? And second, why did he get his first personal visit by the sheriff during his involvement in this same case? Coincidence?

His other concerns about the accidental nature of the event also troubled him. Maybe the sheriff was right, and someone was distracted and not paying attention. Or was this an intentional run-down?

Now, as Donovan put together his findings, the exam grew even more interesting. First, her injuries were almost completely confined to the lower abdomen and pelvis. When pedestrians are struck, there is usually massive orthopedic or bony trauma as well as widespread injury due to impacting the car and the subsequent collision with the pavement.

But this girl had none of that! She had a smashed pelvis, to be sure, but no lower extremity trauma whatsoever. She didn't even have torso or facial abrasions from impacting the pavement. And she had no major head injury. It was as if . . . as if she was already lying down when she was struck! Could she have passed out, possibly from a heavy night of partying?

He pushed an intercom button. "Tammy, are the lab results back from Ms. Dale's tox screen?"

"I put them in your box," the feminine voice responded. "I'll be right in."

He followed her with his eyes from the moment she entered the room. She glanced at him, just to make sure he was watching. She allowed him to see a thin smile, which she quickly replaced with perfect professionalism.

She thumbed through the doctor's In box on top of a small corner desk and held out the lab work.

He stripped off his gloves and accepted the papers, studying her youthful appearance for a second before looking at the papers in his hand.

Hmmm. No ethanol in her blood at all. He flipped through a few more papers. *And no evidence of recreational drug ingestion.*

Certainly she could have died from internal bleeding from her pelvic injuries, but without chest or head trauma that usually takes quite a bit of time. If the 911 caller called right away, why was she already dead at the scene when the rescue squad arrived? Did the impact tear a major artery or something?

"Thanks, Tammy."

She left without speaking, her inviting smile all the communication the pathologist needed.

He sighed and looked back toward the body on the table.

Things weren't adding up to Donovan's liking. He had wanted to take the sheriff's suggestion and, in spite of the family doctor's hunch, avoid the autopsy, but now he wasn't so sure.

He went back over the findings, replaced his gloves, and scanned the victim's body further. Her pelvis was badly fractured, unstable for sure, and the skin was abraded. But there was no bruising on the skin of the lower abdomen. He turned her over into a prone position to inspect her buttocks again. There was no bruising there either. Just the routine color changes associated with blood pooling in the dependent areas after death.

The only way she could've had such a massive crush injury without subcutaneous hemorrhage or cutaneous ecchymosis was if the heart wasn't pumping at the time of the injury. This woman was dead before she was run over! What was going on around here?

The coroner relished the challenge. He stripped off his protective gown and gloves and walked through the doors into the outer office. "Tammy, call Dr. Berringer and tell him I'll be doing the autopsy on the Dale girl at two o'clock." He looked up to see his secretary talking to a young, muscular man with Asian features. He had jet-black hair and a mustache. "Oh, I'm sorry. I didn't mean to interrupt."

Tammy brightened at the pathologist's appearance. She stood and extended a manicured finger toward the young visitor. "Dr. Donovan, this is Dr. Yamatsu. He's a professor at Gratton University. He's here to talk to you about the hit-and-run case." She looked at the newcomer. "Dr. Yamatsu, this is our chief medical examiner, Dr. Donovan."

The man smiled and extended his hand.

The pathologist sighed. "Let me guess. You're here to talk me out of doing an autopsy on the girl, right?"

"On the contrary, doctor, we have a great interest in helping you do the right thing."

◆ ◆ ◆

Sheriff Boatwright finished his late lunch at Lanny's shortly before two o'clock. When he stood again, the plates were completely empty. Two orders of shrimp fritters, a side of steak fries, an order of hush puppies, and two tall Cokes had all been consumed without a break, except when the sheriff loosened his belt.

After lunch he checked in on Lou Ellen. Her disposition concerned him. She seemed so taken back at losing a customer.

He found her smoking in the small room behind the front desk. "Hi, Lou."

She huffed and pointed to a faded chair. "Had lunch?"

"Just came from Lanny's. Thanks." He sat for a moment, wondering what to say.

Lou Ellen looked like a mascara nightmare. Wayne thought for a moment she may have been trying to hide some bruises, then shook his head in rejection of the notion. She put on the shadow a little too thick, that's all.

He made an attempt at small talk. "Ever eat Lanny's fritters?"

"Oyster or shrimp?"

He shrugged. "Either."

"Nope. I can't eat that grease. It's hard on my complexion. My skin is very sensitive, you know. Grease gives me zits worse than a teenager on prom week."

The sheriff chuckled and shifted in his seat. "They might be greasy, but they're worth it if all you get is a few pimples."

They sat silently for a minute longer.

"You doin' all right, Lou?"

"Peachy," she scowled. "You?"

"Cut the crap, Lou Ellen. I know you were upset about that girl the other night." He considered his words. "Look, there was nothing you could've done. It's not like you chased her out or something. I talked to the pathologist this morning. He sounded pretty sure she died from the accident. He should release the official report later today."

Lou Ellen pulled out a small makeup mirror and reapplied a fresh layer of brilliant red to her ample lips. Wayne looked on with horror and fascination.

She looked over at him. "You need something to do?" She nodded her head to the side. "Freda's upstairs. I know she'd see you."

"Freda?" His eyebrows lifted. He checked his watch, then stood up to go.

"Room 21."

He looked at his sister. "Someday I'm going to bust this place, Lou."

She only smiled. "Leave your money behind the counter, sheriff." She paused. "Thanks for comin' to see me, Wayne. Mom wouldn't approve if you deserted *me* too."

The lawman rolled his eyes. "Don't start with that again, Lou. We've been over this a thousand times. She hasn't recognized me in months."

"She knows, Wayne. I can tell. She knows plenty."

He muttered under his breath, "You're livin' in a fantasy." Then louder, "Bye, Lou Ellen. Tell Mother I said hello."

CHAPTER

6

SEEING the autopsy and knowing that Dr. Donovan would report that the patient was likely dead before being run over did little to relieve the growing stain of remorse and confusion Seth Berringer felt about Lisa Dale. The more he saw, the more he realized that he'd covered up a heinous crime; and by the time he saw the damage his van had done to her pelvic organs, he felt nauseated. It was little comfort knowing she was dead at the time her body experienced the trauma.

Each organ had been examined and removed with care and swiftness by the experienced pathologist. Each organ was weighed and described on a tape that would be transcribed by Tammy Lynn. The upper abdomen was relatively normal except for some incidental gallstones. The pelvis—now that was a different story.

The bony pelvis had been crushed, sending a bone spike through the patient's urinary bladder and her rectum, changes that involved no additional bleeding because they were produced after death. The most interesting finding was the large amount of free blood within the abdominal cavity, which seemed to be related to a perforation of the uterus and a laceration of the right uterine artery from a thin wooden spike that had evidently been driven through the cervix from below.

"I've seen this before," Donovan reported in a solemn tone. "Back in the days of illegal, back-alley abortions." He rhythmically lifted the uterus in his hand, weighing it in his mind. "I'd guess she was at least two months along. For some odd reason she was apparently attempting to abort by this monstrous technique."

Sweat beaded on Seth's forehead, but he curled his lip and kept quiet.

Thinking the physician didn't quite understand the procedure, Donovan explained, "They slip a dry spike of wood into the cervix, preferably a type that will swell when it contacts water. As the wood expands, the cervix is forced open, and an abortion is inevitable." He shook his head. "But by the looks of things, the procedure didn't go well this time." He pointed at the laceration in the uterine wall and the artery that had been severed. "Must have driven it right through the uterus. I'd say, as far as I can tell at this point, that she died as a direct complication of an abortion gone awry. Then someone dumped her on the road and made the 911 call to cover his tracks."

Seth's eyes went wide. He stuttered, "It wasn't a rape? It was an abortion?"

Dr. Donovan carefully opened the uterus, beginning at the thickest part, the fundus, and glided his knife down to the entrance of the wooden spike. The opening revealed a small baby, which the spike had missed. Donovan estimated it to be three and a half months old.

"Lucky little fella," the pathologist responded sarcastically.

"It's a boy?" Seth replied timidly.

"Kind of hard to be sure, but yes, I'd guess it's a little boy."

"What will you do with it? Shouldn't you test it or something, maybe help figure out who the father is?"

"It's not easy to determine paternity. You have to have a potential father to see if there's a match."

Seth nodded.

"I doubt the state would want to pay for expensive testing, but I think I'll send a sample to a friend at the N.I.H. for genetic testing. I know a doc up there who thrives on this sort of thing. He'll do an extensive DNA analysis just for the thrill of discovery." He sighed. "It may be unnecessary though, as paternity is likely never to be questioned in a case like this."

"The N.I.H.? The National Institutes of Health?" Seth was clearly impressed.

"Sure. Have you heard of Kevin Schwab?"

"The shroud scientist?" Seth was incredulous. "Who hasn't?"

"The one and only. I helped train the boy, long before he became famous for finding a bloodstain on the shroud of Turin."

"All I really know about that is what I've read in *Newsweek* and other print media. It seems like he's launched a whole new revival of interest in the physical reality of Jesus."

"He was able to extract and analyze the genetic code of Jesus." Donovan shook his head. "Nothing short of amazing." He shook his head in disbelief. "Evidently he used modern scanning electron microscopy and then applied new extraction and restoration technology to map the DNA he obtained from white blood cells found within the bloodstain." He chuckled. "A lot has changed because of a two-millimeter stain."

Donovan looked back at the little fetus cradled in his hand. "We're getting off the subject here, aren't we?" He paused. "But the fact is, old Schwab owes me a favor. I practically had to pry him out of the pathology lab back when he was a resident. He should be glad to do this. He'll be able to tell me a lot more than the sex."

The pathologist looked over at Seth, who had taken a seat at a nearby counter. "Do you feel OK?"

He paled. "Just a little hot, that's all."

Donovan smiled. "An autopsy can be a little unnerving. Don't sweat it. Would you like to lie down?"

Seth forced a smile. "I—I'll be OK." He looked toward the front office. "Maybe I just need a little air."

Just then the intercom made an electronic chirp, followed by Tammy's voice. "Dr. Donovan? The mortician is calling again. He says he needs the body soon if he's going to be ready for the funeral."

Eric rolled his eyes, then walked over and punched the intercom button with his elbow. "Tell him I'll have the body over late tonight. He'll still have tomorrow to get ready."

"Thanks, Dr. Donovan."

Seth looked at his watch nervously. "Well, I think I've seen enough. I need to head back to my office to finish up some paperwork."

"It looks like it will be a late one for me, too," Dr. Donovan responded. "I still have to autopsy a six-year-old who died in a bike accident Saturday night."

Seth's eyes widened. He looked up at the pathologist, who was pointing to another small body bag in the corner. "From Chesapeake General?"

"Yes, I think so."

Seth mumbled a curse. "That's another one of mine." He stood to leave. "I don't think I'd better stick around for that one. I feel bad enough already."

The pathologist nodded. Was this merely a case of first-autopsy jitters or something more? Why was Berringer so upset about all this? He studied the young physician for a moment. Did he have something to hide?

◆ ◆ ◆

The knock on the motel room door startled Bill, who had anticipated at least one uninterrupted hour of sleep.

"Come on, Bill."

"Doc?" Bill cracked the door, then lurched back as it flew open and impacted his forehead. "Ooowww!"

Doc stormed past. "You should have unlocked it sooner."

"You should have taken your key." He looked in the mirror. No blood. "Why are you back? Did they already do the autopsy?"

"No. They're doing it now," his younger partner quipped. "And we're not invited."

"He didn't buy the research story?"

"Oh, he bought it all right, but evidently everybody has been sticking their nose into this case, and by the time I came along, he was fed up with requests. He said he had to go by the book on this one and couldn't authorize any tissue samples for our research, even after I showed him the signed consent form we had from the girl. He said it wasn't valid since she's dead and is now officially a ward of the state. Any deviation from protocol would take a court order." He cursed. "What a jerk." He paused, then added, "I guess we'll still have a chance at the funeral home."

"What about the autopsy report?"

The younger man flexed his arm. "I think it will be all right. I met the transcriptionist. She seems to enjoy a sensitive man who appreciates rare beauty."

Bill rolled his eyes, ignoring the comment. He continued to nurse his forehead, then stood back to comb his gray hair. He raised his eyebrows. "Did you find out who else was looking into the case?"

"The coroner was tight-lipped. Why do you ask?"

"Just a hunch." He shrugged. "Whoever pulled this hit-and-run stunt is likely to be nervous, even nervous enough to ask about the autopsy, see?"

Doc let out a groan of reluctant understanding. "The question remains, why would he try to cover up a crime he didn't commit?"

"Mr. Davis is probably right. If the guy is covering for us, he probably knows something, and he probably wants something. Why else would he pull a trick like this?"

"No one else would be that stupid." Doc laughed.

◆ ◆ ◆

Every Tuesday at four o'clock sharp, Lou Ellen Boatwright entered the Deer Falls Convalescent Home to visit her mother. Lou Ellen followed a set pattern ritualistically. She always brought a serving of applesauce. She always brought the family photo album. She always came on Tuesdays, and always at four o'clock. And to the dismay and delight of the staff, she always brought her makeup case.

Lou Ellen balanced the applesauce bowl in her left hand and her makeup case in the right and pinched the photo album against her side with her right arm, pausing only to put the case down so she could open the front door. The odor of urine and pine-scented cleaner greeted her. The smell was stronger in the winter months when the windows were kept closed.

She turned right and took the elevator to the second floor. The ambulatory residents called her by name. The janitor smiled and said hello.

"Hi, Mr. Smith."

He smiled. He could set his watch by her. He'd be home in a half hour.

Janet Sears Boatwright sat quietly in a padded vinyl chair on wheels with a tray in front of her. A white sheet crossed her lower abdomen and was tied in a large bow behind the chair. It kept her securely upright, a position that could be maintained for only a few minutes without it. The room was sparsely decorated with one potted plant and two pictures on the windowsill. The style suggested a mixture of "Early Sterile" and "Convalescent Neglect."

"Hi, Momma." Lou Ellen dumped the album and the makeup case on the hospital bed, but not before checking it for dampness first. She shed her massive coat and hung it carefully over the back of the only regular chair in the room. "I've brought your applesauce."

It was homemade. The skill passed from mother to daughter provided a comfortable part of the routine that both Lou Ellen and her mother enjoyed. She uncovered the bowl and placed it on the tray in front of her mother. She then opened the makeup case and took out a large plastic bib, which she gently placed over her mother's head. "There. Now we're ready," she announced.

She spooned the smooth sauce into her mother's mouth, scraping the spilled portions off her chin and bib, pausing occasionally to remind her to "Open" or "Swallow." "That a girl," she'd encourage every few moments.

Janet's eyes brightened for a second. A moment of recognition perhaps?

Lou Ellen noticed the dampness in her mother's eyes. "You like it, don't you, Momma?"

She answered for her mother, just as she had for the past eighteen months. "Yes, it's good. It's always been your favorite, hasn't it, Momma?"

She finished feeding her mother the applesauce, then placed the makeup case in the center of the tray. For the next thirty minutes Lou Ellen worked—first the hair, then an application of foundation, followed by blush, eye shadow, and lipstick. The fact that no one but the staff would see it would never deter Lou Ellen. She could only do so much for her mother, but this was one thing she could do.

And as she worked, she talked. It was a weekly commentary on the town. Who ate where. Any unique visitors at the Inn. The best gossip and the juiciest morsels gathered from her work at the Inn and Wayne's work at the sheriff's department.

For Lou Ellen, this was a purging time. She'd been more open to her mother since Janet's last stroke than in the previous fifty years. She recounted her teenage escapades, told more delightfully about Wayne's, and shared her feelings of inferiority, her secrets, her desire for something better. It was the listening ear she'd never had, the psychotherapy she couldn't afford.

Janet never reacted but just sat transfixed, her facial expression unchanging, with the only indication of recognition on any level being an occasional tear that brought with it a trail of bright blue mascara.

Today Lou Ellen told about Lisa Dale. Before she did, she shut the door. It wouldn't do for anyone to overhear her weekly purging today. Wayne would sooner shoot her than let her speak her mind in a public arena.

"She had that look, Momma. You know, like she was afraid. Well, most of 'em are in the beginning. I've watched most of 'em change over the weeks. Maybe she knew . . . Maybe those men did something to her. I feel awful about it. I can't believe she's dead." She dabbed the corner of her own eyes and then her mother's. "But what could I do? I called Wayne soon as I heard her scream." She blew her nose with short, rhythmic, sonorous blasts.

"I just know that room is cursed now. I tried to go in there, but I couldn't stay. There's something bad goin' on—I'm sure of it. I just don't know what I should do. Maybe I should sell out. Bob Trevors is still buggin' me for the place. Wants to fix it up like a country bed and breakfast or some such nonsense. The Inn has been the same for twenty years." She paused. "But maybe I *should* get rid of it. Especially if it's cursed or somethin'."

She sighed. "Wayne would tell me I'm crazy, but I know better.

Something's going down, Momma. That girl's death weren't no accident. I can feel it."

She concluded her visit just like she always did, holding the family photo album in front of her mother's face, pointing at pictures as old as the day she was born. She always started on the first page, and her comments were always the same. "There's Wayne, Momma. He's your firstborn. Look at that rascal." She pointed to a baby picture, and then to another of Wayne in a cowboy uniform. "Remember this? He always did like guns . . ."

◆　◆　◆

Remembering the sheriff's warning not to spread information around before checking with him, Kerri decided to show him the postcard to see if he could decipher its meaning. She called soon after getting the mail, and a deputy promised she'd hear from him. But it wasn't until she was at work that the sheriff followed up on the call.

Kerri adjusted the oxygen mask over the little boy's mouth and nose. "It's OK, Tyler. Take some slow breaths. Breathe the medicine in."

The patient responded in a few minutes, and his wheezing lessened. He even loosened his death-grip on Kerri's right hand.

"Kerri," Gina Gearheart, the E.R. supervisor, summoned, "you have a visitor."

"I'll be there as soon as Tyler's inhaler treatment is done," she replied without looking.

"Kerri," Gina added with an urgent tone, "it's important."

She looked up and saw the large sheriff looming over the nurses' station counter. "Oh," she responded timidly. "Can you cover for me?"

Gina nodded at the uniformed man and whispered, "Are you OK?"

"I'm fine. I need to pass some info on to him, that's all."

"Here," Gina responded to the young patient with a smile. "Why don't you let go of Kerri and hold my hand?"

Kerri broke free and walked to the nurses' station. "Hi, sheriff. Thanks for coming by."

He held out his hand, and Kerri squeezed his meaty palm gently.

She wiped her hand on her smock without thinking as she led the officer to a quiet side-room.

She handed him the postcard. "I received this today. It's from Lisa Dale."

The sheriff read the small card without speaking.

Dear Kerri,

I am so afraid. I signed up for a research project as a paid volunteer subject. Now I think I'm pregnant, and I don't know how. I've kept our commitment—honestly, I have. The researchers will be upset that I've run. They want the baby. I know you will pray. I'll call you when I get to Deer Falls. I'm in deep trouble. I didn't know who else to tell.

Lisa

"You're sure this is the same girl? Do you know any other Lisas?"

"It's the same girl, sheriff." Kerri thought for a moment. "I can only think of one other Lisa offhand, and she lives in California with her husband." She shook her head. "It's from Lisa Dale all right."

He flipped the card over, then studied the postmark. "Seems to have been mailed from nearby. What does she mean, 'our commitment'?"

"It has to do with a program called 'True Love Waits.' We both signed a pledge last fall to wait until marriage to have sex. Ever since, whenever we were together and we saw a good-looking man, we would bring it up, almost as a joke. She would punch me and say, 'Remember our commitment!'"

The sheriff studied the attractive woman in front of him. She looked to be twenty, twenty-five tops, and she thought like his mother. What planet was she from?

"Any idea where she went?"

Kerri shook her head. "She didn't say. All day I've racked my brain. I remember her saying she needed to get some debts paid, but I had no idea she was so desperate." She looked at the sheriff soberly and raised her eyebrows. "I bet if you find out who was experimenting on her, you'll find out who ran her down."

The sheriff stiffened. "What are you thinkin,' ma'am?"

"Well, doesn't it seem a bit suspicious that Lisa was apparently in deep trouble and on the run from people who wanted her baby, and then she ends up here in Deer Falls dead?"

"I'd say this postcard indicates little more than she was greatly troubled and confused. She wasn't even sure how she got pregnant! Sounds to me like a strong case of denial." He shrugged, then added, "Maybe she was completely off her rocker, and in her crazed state she committed suicide by running out in front of a car."

"Lisa was not crazy!" Kerri shook her head firmly.

"All I'm sayin' is that the facts aren't necessarily connected. Sure, she might have been in some research project, and yes, she's dead after a hit-and-run, but in this case we have no link between the two."

"But if someone was upset with her, and she ends up dead, doesn't that look a little peculiar to you?"

The sheriff shrugged and studied the picture postcard a moment longer. The scene was identified as Pike's Peak.

"Look, I'll check with the universities and medical centers closest to this post office," he mumbled, touching the postmark. "I'll try to see what kind of research people are doing out there . . . see if she was enlisted in anyone's project." He put the card in his pocket. "I'll have to keep this. It may be important evidence."

"Can I make a copy first?" She smiled meekly. "It is *my* postcard."

The sheriff held up his hands. "Don't see how that would hurt."

Kerri took the postcard into a nearby office and returned the card to the sheriff, keeping two copies of the original note.

Wayne Boatwright stared at the card for a few more seconds. "If you think of anything else, let me know." He lowered his voice. "And as usual, I wouldn't be talkin' this thing up in the community. Let me know if you get any more mail."

The two shook hands, and Kerri excused herself to tend to her patient duties.

Sheriff Boatwright wiped his forehead. This was looking worse all the time. If he couldn't contain this soon, he'd have a real mess on his hands—exactly what he didn't need during this campaign.

He exited the hospital at a fast walk. By the time he reached the parking lot, he collapsed into his car, gasping for breath. He sat thinking for a few minutes while he regained his breath and his composure.

Why should I worry about this? Who cares what kind of trouble this girl was in? She's dead now. And for all I know, it was a simple hit-and-run, nothing intentional or complicated about it. But what about those two men and whatever they were doing at the Inn? Is it too much of a coincidence that she ended up dead after the two men visited her there?

He shook his head and comforted himself. Why worry about those guys? He certainly hadn't actually seen any suspicious activity. So what if this girl was involved in a research project? What she was involved in before her death was none of his business. She was dead, and it was a simple hit-and-run, nothing more.

He nodded his head resolutely. He pulled the postcard out of his pocket and slid it into the briefcase on the seat beside him. There was no use getting upset about this. It was too late to help Lisa Dale now anyway. He just hoped Ms. Barber could manage to stay quiet. He thought about the beautiful nurse for a moment and smiled. What a girl like that couldn't do for Lou Ellen!

◆ ◆ ◆

A steady rain fell as Seth Berringer drove toward Deer Falls. It didn't matter to him. Even sunshine wouldn't have improved his sour mood. He tried the radio and even played some of his favorite alternative music on compact disc. But nothing could drive the troubling thoughts from his mind.

How did Lisa Dale die? Why would someone use such an outdated mode of abortion when acceptable medical treatment options are available? Was it cheaper? Was the baby the product of some illicit relationship with a public figure, and this was their ignorant way of getting rid of the problem without anyone finding out? He shook his head.

Could it be that the abortionist didn't know modern techniques? No. Not in this day and age, and not in Deer Falls, with one of the newest modern hospitals in the state.

Could it be that she refused to seek an abortion, so her boyfriend forced this upon her? Or could this be the work of some sadistic killer—someone whose fantasies were darker than those of Berringer's patient?

The last option troubled the young doctor even more. Obviously, he had covered up the crime for someone—someone who was on the loose and could strike again. What if the killer raped or killed someone else, and the police could've stopped him if Seth hadn't thrown them off the track?

At least now the sheriff would find out the truth once Dr. Donovan reported his remarkable findings. Now everyone would know it wasn't a hit-and-run.

So why didn't Seth feel any better? Why did he still feel so guilty? Hadn't he done enough to straighten things out? He stared straight ahead, nearly mesmerized by his thoughts and the rhythmic thumping of his windshield wipers. He looked at the rain-slicked street and worried that even his feeble efforts to remedy his wrongs might have resulted in a fatal delay.

What if I've only helped a killer escape? What if he kills again? What if they would've caught him if I had left things alone? What if? . . . what if? . . . what if? The accusing words wouldn't stop. Seth Berringer wanted to be free. How could he have been so self-centered and stupid?

◆ ◆ ◆

That night, shortly after 2 A.M., Doc showed Bill how he got his nickname.

Once Bill unlocked the door from the inside, the Asian entered Baer Funeral Home. He kept his voice low, barely above a whisper. "How'd it go?"

"I've been hiding in a closet for four hours," Bill responded. "Don't ask."

Doc looked at the door, inspecting it carefully.

"Don't worry, I've already looked. There's no alarm."

Doc nodded. "Have they worked on our lady yet?"

"I heard them say they'll work on her tomorrow morning. Her funeral isn't until 4, so they have some time."

"Did you find the body?"

"Over there." He pointed to a stainless steel table in the center of a tiled floor. "In the bag."

"What? No refrigerator?"

"It doesn't matter what she looks like. They're going to cremate her." He chuckled softly. "Evidently they weren't any too happy about it, but the state's footin' the bill, and that's all they'll pay for. I heard the old man talking to his son about it." He shook his head. "Doing this all day long must get on his nerves."

Doc unzipped the bag. He wrinkled his nose. "Let's get started."

Lisa's body had undergone a full autopsy, including the cranium. Per protocol, she was put back together, sewn with coarse sutures. Doc looked at the torso, which had a large Y incision covering the chest and extending down the midline all the way to the pubis. It was closed with a thick, running suture, similar to a baseball stitch. He lifted the stitch near the pubis and clipped one end. He then pulled the incision wide open, revealing the now common thoraco-abdominal cavity. He lifted out the plastic bag that held the organs. "It should be in here."

Bill winced.

"Pathologists always leave 'em this way. All the organs should be here, even the brain. Everything is put in this bag and placed in the abdomen." He slit open the plastic bag and began lifting out the organs.

Bill put on a pair of rubber gloves and held up a small flashlight. "What does a uterus look like anyway?"

"Should be a little larger than my fist at this stage." He pulled out the liver, spleen, and two handfuls of small intestine.

"This is disgusting."

"What did you expect?"

Bill didn't answer. He really wanted some air. But when he tried to retreat, Doc demanded that he shine the flashlight onto a different area.

He put a small pear-shaped organ on the table. "This is the uterus, but it's been opened." He pulled apart the incision that ran the length of the uterus, then swore. "He's removed the baby!"

Doc frantically removed the remaining contents of the sack. "Shine your light in the bottom of the bag. This clone isn't going to be very big, you know." He held his finger and thumb an inch and a half apart. He looked in the bag again, then returned to the table where he'd laid out all the organs. He searched carefully—over and over. "It's not here." He directed Bill back to the body. "Maybe he threw it in here." He pointed at the abdominal cavity. It was empty. He whispered another curse. He picked up the uterus again. "My dilator is missing. No surprise there."

"Mr. Davis isn't going to like this. He's counting on those cells."

"Tell him to make another one," Doc snapped. He looked at the mess. "We've got to make this look like we were never here."

They hastily threw the organs back into the plastic bag and pushed it into the abdominal cavity.

"Aren't you going to sew it back?"

"With what?" He looked at the mess. "Naah. It just looks like it busted open. Help me get her back in the bag."

After the body was covered, Bill took a towel and wiped down the table and floor. "Let's get out of this place. I've been here too long."

"After you." Doc held out his hand.

They exited through the back door and walked two blocks south where their car was parked on a side street.

"Time to go see the medical examiner again," Doc said with a thin grin.

"You just want to talk to Tammy Lynn."

"Whatever." Doc allowed a smile to break his seriousness. "But we do need to find that tissue. And I'll bet that pathologist knows exactly where it is."

Bill nodded as the two got into the car.

Doc started the engine and drove along Main Street toward the center of town.

"Where are you going?"

"I'm hungry."

Bill paled. "After what you just did, you want to eat?"

Doc shrugged. "I hear there's a place where you can get breakfast twenty-four hours a day." He pointed to a sign on the right. "There it is."

"Clara's." Bill paused. "Maybe I could stand a cup of coffee. We have a long drive tonight."

◆ ◆ ◆

Seth Berringer didn't even attempt to sleep until midnight. He hadn't planned to stay up late, but he had taken the following day off to attend Lisa Dale's memorial service, so he wasn't uptight about getting to bed so late. In the early hours of the morning, he finally found a fitful sleep plagued with troubling dreams.

"Another rape victim in 5, Dr. Berringer." The nurse handed him a chart. "Better hurry, the waiting room's full."

The patient, already in stirrups, had her face covered by a sheet. Seth slid in a lubricated speculum, which ground firmly against a foreign body. The nurse looked over his shoulder and announced mechanically, "Another wooden spike. That makes four, doesn't it?"

The nurse assisted him through the exam and the collection of specimens, cultures, and hair samples. It wasn't until he finished that the patient's face turned into an exact likeness of Lisa Dale's. "It's all your fault!" She sobbed. "It's all your fault."

Seth wheeled his exam stool back against the wall.

The nurse shook her head in agreement. "You could have stopped this maniac, you know. If only you would have told the truth." She pressed her lips tightly together and frowned.

The patient attempted to stand up but quickly dropped back to the table, unresponsive and cold.

The nurse felt for a pulse. "There you go, doctor. You've lost another one. That should make Coast Care happy," she added sarcastically.

Seth screamed and jumped to his feet. He frantically attempted to reach his patient but tripped over a second body on the floor. When he looked up, tall grass covered the hospital floor, obscuring the second body.

"We need to get some help for these patients," he ordered.

The nurse shook her head. "We'll never find them in this grass. It's growing too fast. Better mark a trail or we'll never find them again."

Seth nodded and took off the victim's shoe. He placed it at the edge of the hallway. "Now at least we'll know what room they're in."

Seth ran through the emergency department yelling for help and tripping over bodies. Each body looked at him and recited a guttural plea: "Please don't run over me, Seth. I'm pregnant."

Seth rolled over, pushing his pillow to the floor. The dim light of his digital clock illuminated the rapid movements of his eyes behind the lightly closed lids.

Again asleep, he walked into a crowded chapel and slipped quietly into a seat on the back row. The funeral director began a eulogy on the life of Lisa Dale. When he finished, the mourners filed up one by one to view the body. Each one whispered a tearful good-bye.

"She was so pretty," whispered one.

"Such a beauty," responded another.

Seth forced himself forward, not really wanting to see the body in the long, silver casket. Slowly he moved ahead, until at last he stood face to face with Lisa's body. She was clothed in a formal white dress with her hands resting across her chest. Suddenly black tire tracks crossed her lower abdomen, and a crimson stain spread down to the hem of her gown.

"What have you done?" she whispered. The awful accusation shocked the doctor back to wakefulness.

He sat up and put his feet on the cool, hardwood floor. He ran his fingers through his hair and stared at the clock. Three A.M. He coughed nervously and sighed. Being awake and tired had to be better than being asleep and tortured by those terrible dreams.

He went to the kitchen and filled his coffeemaker. After a few minutes he sat at the counter and tried to read his unopened letters. He couldn't even keep his mind off the situation long enough to read his mail.

He closed his eyes, and the vision of the bodies from his dream returned. *Seth, you're losing your grip. She's a dead orphan, man. Quit torturing yourself!*

He poured a cup of steaming Colombian coffee. He tried to calm down, hoping Dr. Donovan's report would undo all the damage he'd done.

He dropped his head in his hands. Why couldn't he believe that?

CHAPTER
7

IN Wilson Davis's dreams, he held the weakened hand of his mother again. The deep yellow color of her skin contrasted with the white sheets, which his father changed faithfully every day. Wilson stood trembling at the bedside, a boy of twelve, watching his mother fight for breath, his private agony etched in his expression of horror. "Don't die," he whispered. "Please don't die."

Her expression didn't change. Mabel Elizabeth Davis closed her eyes to rest.

Pancreatic cancer pays little respect to its victims, slowly blocking the liver from its excretion of bile, turning the body yellow from the inability to rid the blood of the toxin. As the cancer advances, its message of pain spreads to other regions. For Mabel, the pain in her back, due to the cancer's growth into a plexus of nerves, stretched the limits of her tolerance. As she spent her final days in bed, her son fought to understand.

Day after day Wilson watched his mother slowly slip away. Day after day he prayed for a miracle. Day after day the jaundice deepened. Day after day a bitterness grew in Wilson's spirit, creating a watercourse for the flow of his life's ambition. *I will make Christians see what trusting in a dead religion will do. I will destroy their useless faith.*

When Wilson Davis awoke from his latest dream, the jaundiced hand he held was his own. The diagnosis of inoperable pancreatic cancer had been made only four months before. First his mother, and now him.

He rose and looked at himself in the mirror. He had to work fast. So many people had been misled. So many were leaning on a make-believe crutch. He shook his head. He didn't have much time. The project had to be finished. How else could he convince Christians of their stupidity?

He dressed and walked among the rooms of his winter home. His spent most of his time in the large front gallery, which housed an impressive array of biblical artifacts. The collection was the irony of his life. He seemed sure that a close examination of the sacred relics of the Christian church would eventually point out the fallacies in all man-made religion. He had long dreamed of discovering the bones of Christ and had financed several large digs to find them. What a telling blow to the idiot evangelicals that would be.

He grabbed the morning paper off the table in the center of the library. As he scanned the front page, he tried to imagine the headlines he would be creating. He was determined that Christian believers would see the idiocy of their empty religion, that they would finally understand what a fraud their leader really was.

He thought for a moment, then tossed the paper aside. He hurried to the kitchen where his housekeeper had placed a large glass of orange juice beside a steaming bowl of oatmeal and a half-dozen vitamin tablets. He ate without appetite, forcing himself to consume as many quality calories as he could stand.

He looked at his watch, anxious to return to the lab. His expectations of a special delivery from his harvest team made it difficult to think of anything else.

◆　◆　◆

Seth slipped into the sparsely populated room at Baer Funeral Home. Lisa's body had been cremated earlier in the day. The memorial services would be led by a volunteer chaplain in the front viewing room.

Long, velvet curtains hung from ceiling to floor, concealing the entire far wall. In front of the curtains, the director had placed a small table with a picture of Lisa and an urn containing her ashes. Padded folding chairs sat in rows with a single, central aisle. Venetian blinds covered the front windows, preventing onlookers from peeking in and funeral-goers from gazing out. The carpet was a deep maroon. The color of clotted blood, Seth thought as he took a seat in the back.

An unmanned upright piano stood in the corner. The room's music was canned, wordless, and New-Age.

Seth looked around the room. He recognized Kerri Barber, a nurse in the E.R., and noticed that she, too, was checking out the crowd. She smiled at him briefly and returned her attention to the front table.

Mrs. Barnum and Mrs. Fawley, the city librarians, were sitting in the second row. Lisa Dale had worked for them as an assistant.

Jamie Edwards sat alone in the front row, his head in his hands.

The rest of the people were unknown to Seth, who was beginning to wonder what he was doing there.

The chaplain, a seminary student, smiled and welcomed the crowd. He read from the Bible and spoke of heaven and the absence of suffering there. He smiled too much, in Seth's opinion. He was too plastic, like one of the stiffs in the next parlor.

While the chaplain spoke, Kerri Barber glanced around at the crowd. Apparently no relatives were there, not even a concerned uncle. The mystery man must have been after Lisa for some other reason. She tried to pay attention but found herself confused and angry about her recent conversation with the sheriff. She'd been right about her suspicions, and yet the sheriff blew her off, assuming Lisa's postcard had no bearing on her death.

From two rows back, Seth watched her. She seemed upset. He saw her look left and right again. Maybe she was a friend of Lisa's. He wondered if she knew Lisa was pregnant.

That thought led Seth to another question. Did the father know about the baby? Was the father there? The doctor scanned the room. The only virile men in the room were himself, the seminary student, and Jamie. The first two were definitely out, and Jamie was a long shot. In spite of his fantasies, he always seemed a bit afraid of a real relationship with a woman.

Seth looked up and then back at his shoes. *What about you, Seth? Are you afraid of a real relationship with a woman?*

The minutes ticked on until finally the chaplain asked everyone to stand. He prayed without notes and with full sincerity. "Holy God and Father of all, we humbly approach you, knowing that the way has been opened by your holy child, Jesus. I ask that you would comfort each person here—Lisa's friends who are saddened by her passing." He paused and opened his eyes, looking briefly at the crowd. Seth immediately closed his eyes, and the preacher did the same.

The chaplain continued, "I pray especially for the driver of the automobile that struck Lisa. I pray that you would hold that person in your arms and comfort him. Give him the courage to acknowledge his wrongdoing. Bring him forgiveness and healing."

Seth looked up again. *Was he looking at me?* He closed his eyes and listened as the chaplain prayed. *Why is he praying for me that way?*

"May your peace light the path to restoration for him."

Seth opened his eyes again, his vision now blurred with tears. *Come on, Seth. Get a grip.*

"Show him your love and tender direction."

This is for weak, old women, Seth. Not for you.

"Let him know the certainty of your grace and love."

Oh right, like God could love me after all I've done. He wiped his eyes with his sleeve, squinting hard. *You've been under too much pressure, Berringer. You're losin' touch, pal.*

"In Jesus' name, and by the authority of his blood sacrificed for us, Amen."

The chaplain laid a rose in front of Lisa's picture and dismissed the crowd.

Seth wanted to find the nearest exit—fast!

He slipped on his overcoat and walked to the front door and onto a broad, covered porch. He was about to descend the front steps when he felt a tug on his coat.

"Dr. Berringer?"

Seth turned to see Kerri Barber.

"Could I talk to you for a minute?"

The request took him by surprise. He shrugged. "Sure." He pointed to a row of rocking chairs lining the southern porch. "Is it too cold to sit?"

Kerri looked at the small crowd gathering on the steps and bit her bottom lip. "Maybe I could walk you to your car?" she asked, her voice barely above a strained whisper.

He shrugged again. "What's up?"

"I have a few medical questions, and I don't know too many of the physicians personally, but when I saw you—" She hesitated. "I thought maybe you could help me."

They began walking toward the parking lot. "I'll try."

Kerri drove straight to the point. "Could a medical examiner tell if Lisa was intentionally run down? I mean, would there be any signs the pathologist could pick up?"

Seth swallowed hard. "W-well, I, uh, I don't really know. I don't think he could tell the difference." He looked at her, his heart-rate accelerating. "Why are you asking me this?"

Kerri pulled a photocopy from the pocket of her dark wool coat. "I received this in the mail a few days after Lisa's death." She handed the copy to Seth and gave him a minute to read it. "It's obvious she was in trouble." She shook her head. "I can't imagine that her writing this letter, then ending up dead is a coincidence."

Seth looked at the signature. "The handwriting isn't very clear. Are you sure this is from Lisa Dale?"

Kerri nodded. "Believe me, it's from Lisa. The signature was smudged on the original." She looked at Seth, who appeared disturbed. "It was smeared with blood."

"It's postmarked here." He turned the card over. "From the looks of it, she bought the card somewhere out west but brought the card to town to mail."

"You're right!" She stared at the copy. "She must have mailed it the day she died." She thought for a moment. "But why would she have blood on her hands?"

"Maybe it was just juice."

Kerri shook her head. "I've seen enough blood spilled in the E.R. to know better. I suppose a forensics lab could tell for sure."

Seth nodded numbly.

"So, do you think the medical examiner's evaluation could tell if she was killed intentionally?"

"I—I don't know!" Seth responded a bit more forcefully than he'd intended. He lowered his voice. "What are you thinking? That someone killed her to get her baby?"

"I'm not sure of anything at this point. All I know is, I have a bad feeling about all of this."

"Who else have you showed this letter to?"

"I gave the original to Sheriff Boatwright." Her face reddened. "He made me so angry, Dr. Berringer. He—"

Seth interrupted, saying, "Call me Seth. We're not in the hospital now."

Kerri continued, "He downplayed the whole thing, like there was no connection at all. I went away feeling he thought I was overreacting. I felt stupid. But at the same time, I think I'm the one who's right."

Seth moved his feet nervously. Several other funeral-goers were climbing into nearby cars. "Look, Kerri, I—" He stopped, wondering how much he should say.

She looked at him and waited.

"Maybe I can shed some light on this for you." He waited as Mrs. Fawley and Mrs. Barnum climbed into a blue station wagon next to Seth's van. "Maybe we can find somewhere else to talk," he added in a quiet tone.

She studied his face for a moment, wondering what he knew.

"Clara's is right around the corner. How about a cup of coffee?"

Kerri smiled. "I'll meet you there."

Seth hopped into his van and pulled into the light Deer Falls traffic. Kerri followed in her Taurus.

A few minutes later Seth opened the front door of Clara's and allowed Kerri to enter.

They sat in the corner booth. The business was sparse except for a few college kids and an old man at the counter.

"What'll it be, doc?" Clara asked as she hurried toward the table. "Nice to see you."

"Hi, Clara." Seth managed a quick smile. "I'll just have some coffee."

Kerri looked up. "Hot chocolate for me."

"How about a piece of pie? Millie just made fresh shoofly."

"No, thanks," the two responded.

Clara shook her head. "Coffee coming up," she mumbled as she walked to the kitchen. "Kids! Never eat anything."

Kerri and Seth both began speaking at once.

"Sorry," Seth apologized. "You first."

"I wanted to tell you something I'd forgotten. On the night Lisa died, I was working the triage desk."

"Must have been after I left."

Kerri nodded. "It was." She glanced at him, impressed that he was so observant.

She continued, "A man came in, looking for Lisa. He showed me a picture and claimed to be her uncle. He said she was late getting home, and he was concerned." She shrugged. "Of course, he didn't know that I knew Lisa personally until I mentioned it. I'm certain she told me she didn't have any family here." She paused. "That's one reason I wanted to attend the memorial."

Seth squinted.

"I wanted to see if that man would come."

"And?"

"He didn't show. If he was her uncle . . ."

Clara delivered the steaming mugs. "Enjoy. Let me know if you change your mind about the pie."

Seth nodded again without speaking. Clara picked up some change from the next table and left.

Seth looked at Kerri. "So you're thinking—"

"I'm thinking it looks pretty suspicious to have some stranger looking for Lisa on the night she ends up dead in the street." She crossed her arms. "I told the sheriff about that, too."

"What did he say?" Seth sipped his coffee and studied Kerri's body language.

"He downplayed it. He told me that Lisa probably hadn't told me everything, that I was making something out of nothing. He warned me not to spread it around or I might risk raising needless suspicions about innocent people."

Seth sipped his coffee silently.

Kerri watched him play with his coffee stirrer. He seemed troubled. She leaned forward. "What did you mean about shedding light on this?"

Seth kept looking at his coffee. "I was with the medical examiner when he did the autopsy on Lisa's body."

Now Kerri leaned even closer. "And?"

He looked up, wanting to trust her, but not knowing how much to tell her. "Kerri," he began, "it looks like Lisa was dead before she was run over."

"What do you mean?"

"She bled to death from a botched abortion."

Kerri held her hand to her mouth. "Abortion?" She shook her head. "No! Not Lisa. She wouldn't do that." Her voice was low but strained. "We had talked about her feelings about abortion. She would never—"

"Kerri," Seth interrupted, "she had been brutalized. Her face was bruised." He hesitated. "The pathologist found a sharp wood branch shoved up through her uterus, through the cervix."

Kerri gasped.

"The medical examiner said he'd seen it before, but not for many years, not since abortion has been legalized. It's a technique for dilating the cervix to cause an abortion." He shook his head. "From what I saw, this was not an elective abortion. It looked like it had been forced all the way through the uterus. She bled to death as a result." He hesitated. Kerri looked pale.

"But the hit-and-run . . . the 911 call . . ." Kerri's voice trailed off.

Seth nodded. "All a hoax. It was someone's idea of disguising the murder to make it look accidental."

Kerri recoiled at his words. "What a sicko."

Seth looked down. If he said the wrong thing . . .

Kerri sat staring out the front window of Clara's Diner in silence. Finally she pulled the copy of the postcard from her jacket pocket. "Maybe someone really did want that baby . . ." She paused. "Now I guess the sheriff will believe me."

"Sure, he'll believe you. He should have the report soon. I wouldn't even be surprised if Dr. Donovan, the examiner, has called him already. He acted like the findings were significant."

She sighed. "I can't believe this. Right here in little Deer Falls."

Seth played nervously with his coffee stirrer. He changed the subject. "Where do you think they got that chaplain?" he scoffed. "Can you believe the way he prayed?"

"What do you mean?"

"He stood up there and asked God to show his forgiveness and love to the person who ran over Lisa." He sighed in disgust. "As if God could love someone like that . . . that sicko," he sneered, using Kerri's word.

She thought for a moment. "Well, it wasn't like the chaplain knew what you told me. He assumed the whole thing was an accident—like the guy freaked and left the scene after seeing what he did, that's all. It's not like he wanted God to bless some perverted sadist who kills young women. The chaplain didn't know who he was praying for."

Seth nodded. "True." *Truer than you know.*

Kerri sipped on her hot chocolate, now lukewarm. After a minute's silence she reached over and touched his hand. "I do believe God shows his love to all kinds of sickos. That's what's so amazing about him. He loves us in spite of everything we do to hurt each other and him. He just keeps on loving. It's his nature, Seth."

Seth's eyes clouded for the second time in an hour. "How can you believe that? It's a nice fairy tale. That's all."

"It's something I've experienced," she responded confidently. "And something I take on faith."

"How could God love someone who disguises a murder because of selfishness—someone who brutalizes a body even after death? That's low, Kerri."

"I don't understand how God could love someone like that. I just know it's true—based on the Bible, based on faith, and based on my own experience." She looked at Seth, who looked like a kid caught with his hand in the cookie jar. "No one's perfect, Seth. Not me. Not you. None of us deserves God's love. But that doesn't change the fact that God goes on loving us just the same."

Seth looked down and shook his head slowly. "I don't know, Kerri. I don't know."

"Can I tell you something personal, Seth?"

He looked up but avoided her eyes. He felt awkward, like a child who wants to cry but is afraid he's too old. "Sure. I guess so."

"I've been praying for you. I've watched you in the E.R., and I know you're one of the best doctors we have." She paused. "And I'm not the only one who feels that way. But you seem to be hurting, Seth. I think you're trying to be perfect or something." She shrugged. "I don't know exactly what I'm trying to say. Maybe just that I care and that I've been asking God to help you."

Seth didn't answer right away. Clara came and warmed up his coffee mug. When she left, he looked into Kerri's face. What was it about her? It seemed like she could see right through him. What was it in her that he wanted so desperately? Peace? She seemed so together, while he was falling apart. "I've never really thought much about God. It's not that I don't believe in him. It's just . . . well, I've never thought he cared about us. My dad never went to church, although Mom took me when I was little." He shrugged. "I grew up . . . well, thinking that as long as we try our best, everything will work out somehow." He sighed and shut his eyes for a few seconds to keep his eyes from tearing. "But my best hasn't been good enough lately."

"Can I tell you what I think?"

Seth smiled. He liked her spunk. She could charm a rattlesnake. "Could I stop you?"

"No." Kerri returned the smile. "Being acceptable to God isn't about being our best or being good enough. No one is good enough, Seth. We're all made of the same stuff, all in need of someone who can take away our evil desires and make us clean and acceptable to God again."

Seth nodded. "The blood—that's where this is leading, right?"

"Yes."

He lifted his eyebrows. "World Religions, Humanities 411. I took it my last year at Wake Forest."

"So you know the basics here." She pointed at his forehead. She looked him over. He seemed uncomfortable, but he wasn't running. "It took me a while, too. I knew all about Jesus' dying for me, about the blood. But I never really experienced it here. . . ." She placed her hand over her heart. ". . . until I was a mixed-up college freshman."

Seth shifted in his seat. "I can't imagine you that way—mixed-up, I mean." He looked away from the floor and glanced at Kerri.

She laughed. "You should have seen me." She looked down, away from his probing eyes.

"What will the sheriff do next?" Kerri asked to move the conversation away from the embarrassing emotion, a change she and Seth both appreciated.

"Probably launch an investigation. I wouldn't be surprised if he gets the state police, maybe even the F.B.I. involved."

Clara laid the bill on the table. She tried one last time. "Sure I can't sell you a piece of pie? Maybe a sandwich?"

Kerri smiled. Seth replied, "Afraid not, Clara." He left a five dollar bill on the tabletop to cover the two-dollar tab.

Kerri stood and looked at Seth without speaking.

"I guess I'd better go," the doctor stated.

She took his hand. "Thanks for the information, Seth. I meant what I said about you—about praying for you, I mean."

He cleared his throat. "I'll see you around the E.R., Kerri."

"Sure. When's your next shift?"

"Saturday night. When else? They love giving me the weekend crush."

They stepped into the parking lot, where their breath turned to fog. "You probably know that some of the nurses are threatening to change their shifts so they don't have to work with you." She smiled.

"That bad, huh?" He tried to smile but couldn't quite do it.

"They call you the misery magnet because so many sick people flock to the hospital when you're on duty." She laughed as she opened her car door.

He hopped into his van. *She's joking, but look at my life. I am a misery magnet!*

◆ ◆ ◆

That evening Connie Donovan, Eric's wife, picked up the living-room phone after the first ring. She hesitated saying hello so she could hit the mute button on her TV remote. In that fraction of time, Eric answered the phone in the bedroom.

"Hello," Eric said.

Connie held on to see if the call was for her.

"Hello, Eric." The voice was young and feminine.

Connie covered the phone with her hand.

Eric lowered his voice. "I asked you not to call me here."

"I always hang up if you don't answer," she replied softly. "Besides, I have news I want to share."

Eric looked uncomfortably over his shoulder, then pushed the door closed. "What's so important that you need to call me at home?"

"I'm moving out. Dr. Robinson finally convinced me to assert myself, to take control of my life."

Eric shook his head. "I thought we talked about that. It's not the right time. I'm not in a position to help—"

"Don't worry about me, honey. The money isn't a problem. Some cash came through, and I don't have to rely on Sonny for help anymore. I'm getting a place close to work so we can—"

Eric interrupted. "Look, I can't talk right now. I'll speak with you about this later."

Tammy Lynn frowned. "I thought you'd be happy."

He sighed. "I am happy, OK?" He paused. "You just caught me at a bad time."

When isn't it a bad time lately? Tammy Lynn bit her lip and nervously twirled the bottle of antidepressants in her hand. "OK." She put the receiver back in its cradle and began to cry.

Eric snorted and turned off his portable phone.

Connie was stunned. *Tammy Lynn is our daughter's age!*

CHAPTER
8

Doc tightened his muscular jaw as he listened. "Sure . . . OK." He held the cellular phone to his ear as he paced behind Deer Falls' only historical monument, dedicated to a forgotten Civil War hero. "Look, the girl changed the report, and she's not going to talk."

He listened again for a moment, squinting his eyes in the midday sun. "She assured me that no else knew, not even the sheriff. Only one other guy saw the autopsy—some guy named Berringer. We'll be on him this afternoon. I've got a hunch he might be our man. Why else would he have been so interested in the autopsy?"

He frowned at his accomplice. "Look, if the medical examiner has it, we'll get it." He shook his head. "No, the girl told me everything. She didn't send it to anyone." He shook his head again. "No chance for that. The body's been cremated, but I'm sure the tissue wasn't there."

He held the phone away from his ear and rolled his eyes. "OK, OK," he responded. He put his ear to the receiver one more time. Silence. He shrugged and pushed End.

"Not happy, huh?" Bill looked at Doc anxiously.

"He's worried about the medical examiner's report. I assured him that anyone who reads it won't know how the girl died."

"What about the pathologist? Won't he talk?"

He shook his head. "No. Not after I'm through with him." He sat down in the shadow of the concrete structure. "We'll use his secretary."

"Or money."

Doc smiled. "Or both." He looked around at the small, centrally located park, known to the locals as Mem. Park, known formally as Deer Falls Memorial Park.

A hundred feet away, children were chasing each other around a large wooden play structure. Squeals punctuated their delight as an exasperated teacher tried to gather them for a field trip picture beside the monument. "Over here, children," she yelled, pointing at the two men sitting beneath a statue of a Confederate soldier.

Doc stood and walked toward the parking lot. "I'm worried about the other fellow the secretary mentioned—that Dr. Berringer." He shoved his hands into his overcoat pockets. "Davis wants to know why he was so interested in the autopsy."

"So we'll talk to him."

"Right, and implicate ourselves by our interest." He shook his head. "Bad idea."

"Maybe it's no more than what Tammy Lynn said—professional interest by the girl's doctor."

"Maybe," Doc muttered. "But I have a funny feeling about this guy." He pointed at a public phone booth. "Let's look him up. I want to see what kind of vehicle this guy drives."

◆ ◆ ◆

Kevin Schwab carried himself more with the enthusiasm of a Little Leaguer than with the air of a prestigious scientist. Making the discovery of the century hadn't changed that. Being the most celebrated researcher in the public press only seemed to enhance his boyish charm. "The Computer Wore Tennis Shoes" stated a *Newsweek* headline. The subtitle referred to his research: "The scientist behind the shroud discoveries." *Time* took a reflective glance at the geneticist in a fall cover story: "Schwab Presents the Historical Jesus: Skeptics Examine Divine DNA."

To be fair, Schwab would point out, he had only built on the work of other N.I.H. scientists who had been granted a rare chance to reexamine one of the most treasured relics of the Catholic faith—the shroud of Turin. Long touted to be a fake, the N.I.H. scientists shocked the world with their declaration that the previous carbon dating of the shroud had been horribly inaccurate, missing the mark by over a thousand years because of bacterial contamination of the cloth. The new date, they concluded, was much closer to the actual birth of Christianity than anyone had ever imagined.

The Vatican responded by proclaiming that the Church owned the burial cloth of Christ himself, imprinted with the physical image of the Savior.

What followed was the most scrutinizing scientific evaluation possible. Schwab himself spent over a thousand hours staring into a scanning electron microscope, searching the shroud's surface. When it was all over, a small crimson stain overlying the left wrist attracted everyone's attention. Unlike the other reddish areas, this one contained human blood cells. The stain, only a few millimeters across, contained hundreds of red cells, confirming the nature of the new blemish. The real discovery came only after Schwab was able to locate a few white blood cells, the only blood cells with a nucleus, the central package containing DNA. Applying new extraction and reconstruction techniques, he mapped the exact genetic code found in that DNA.

The Vatican leapt to the same conclusion as the public media: If the shroud was the authentic burial cloth of Christ, then the stain represented the holy blood of the Savior, and thus examination of the DNA would reveal the physical characteristics of Christ's body!

Soon information from the DNA analysis trickled from the N.I.H. into mainstream newspapers. Reports on divine hair color, eye color, and skin color livened up the headlines. Christ's body build and height were reported. Slow and meticulous mapping of the DNA allowed scientists to render accurate physical drawings of the historical Jesus.

Millions accepted the new information as physical evidence of Jesus' reality. Thousands took a further jump and began to question the teachings of one who could no longer be considered a fairy-tale hero.

Now, months after the discovery and genetic mapping, Kevin Schwab's life had finally approached quasi-normality. He picked up a computer printout, the results of a DNA mapping project he had conducted on the side as a favor for an old professor and friend, Dr. Eric Donovan. He ran his hand over his two-day old stubble and fingered the bill of his Bluejays baseball cap. He picked up a day-old milkshake cup from a local Dairy Queen and tossed it in the trash. A strange foreboding gripped him. The nucleotide sequence in front of him looked too familiar. Was this some kind of joke?

He pushed back in his chair, a brown, padded one with a short back support and wheels. He launched himself in a straight line for the counter running against the opposite wall, lifting his feet and rolling the fifteen feet in less than two seconds. He tapped a series of commands on a computer keyboard, bringing up a long list of nucleotides that formed the central core of the fourteenth chromosome taken from the shroud's white blood cell.

Someone must have mixed things up pretty badly—unless he had gone completely mad. He shifted his weight and launched himself toward a phone on a corner desk, tracing a well-worn path on the wooden floor of his spacious office. What kind of tricks was old Donovan up to now?

Kevin grabbed an open bag of cheese-flavored snacks and looked at the clock. His waistline fortunately did not reflect his eating habits, which remained strictly Nickelodeon—adolescent garbage. Four-thirty. He wondered if Donovan still had that young secretary. He dialed and waited.

"Chief medical examiner's office. May I help you?" Tammy Lynn's soft, southern accent was alluring.

"Ms. Gaskins? This is Kevin Schwab from the N.I.H. May I speak to Dr. Donovan?"

"Hi, Mr. Schwab. I'll get him for you."

Kevin tapped his fingers to the hold music. In a few moments Eric Donovan picked up the extension in the back room. "Kev! How's life for the rich and famous?"

Kevin laughed. "Famous maybe, but I'm still driving the beach bomb."

Donovan shook his head and smiled at the memory of Schwab's V.W. Beetle turned dune buggy. "You jest."

"I'm serious." He wheeled himself across the room, stretching the phone cord to the limit. "I could never sell her. She's like family."

"Right." Donovan chuckled. "Did you get my specimen?"

"That's why I'm calling." He lowered his voice a notch. "Tell me where you got this again." He fingered his hat and coughed nervously. "Do you have any idea what you have there?"

◆ ◆ ◆

By the time Seth broke for lunch, he was forty-five minutes behind schedule. It wasn't even really lunch. Lunch, in Seth's view, included meat and bread. Peanut butter and crackers and a slice of blueberry pie brought in by a grateful patient didn't qualify.

The day seemed routine after that. Twelve scheduled patient follow-ups, six walk-ins with the flu, a newly diagnosed diabetic, and a high-schooler with a sprained ankle rounded out the afternoon.

At 6 P.M. Seth slumped at his desk and looked over his correspondence.

He flipped through the day's mail, puzzling over a small white envelope with no return address. He opened the envelope to find a thank-you note with flowery cursive lettering.

> To the best doctor in Deer Falls,
>   Have a great day! Thanks for the hot chocolate and for spending a moment with me. I'm praying for you.
>
>   Kerri

Seth smiled. He looked at the note a few moments longer, his mind filled with remnants of their conversation. His day had been busy enough to help him push his anxiety about Lisa Dale's death onto the back burner. Now, thanks to the note from Kerri, his thoughts returned to his misguided actions once again.

He thought about Kerri and what he had said to her. He hadn't lied to her. He just hadn't told her all that he knew. He couldn't admit to running over Lisa's body—not after she reacted the way she did. He looked at the note again. The cover had a single daisy held in the mouth of a bedraggled puppy. He thought of Kerri—her peaceful manner, her sincerity, her smile. He felt bad about misleading her. How long could he keep up this charade? He slowly reread the note. Some "best doctor" he was! Would the best doctor in Deer Falls desecrate the dead?

He hurried through the rest of his paperwork but fought the continual distraction of Kerri's note. What was it she'd said? "No one's perfect, Seth. Not me. Not you. None of us deserves God's love. But that doesn't change the fact that God goes on loving us just the same."

He pulled his coat off the hook behind the door. There was one thing he and Kerri Barber saw eye to eye—he didn't deserve God's love. He walked to the hall. Did he think God existed at all? Probably so. The body is too complex not to have a Creator. But a loving God who actually gives a hoot about what we do from day to day? He doubted it.

He looked up to see Mrs. Templeton, an African-American woman, mopping the floor and singing a hymn.

"Good night, Mrs. Templeton."

The woman put her hands on her ample hips. "Dr. Berringer, you look like you're carryin' the worl' on your shoulders. You need to do what I do, I'll tell you right now. You need to carry them burdens right to God and lay 'em down. That's what I do, for sure. He takes care of me, he does." She nodded her head in affirmation. "Yes, indeed."

He looked at the woman who was as old as his mother and shook his head. "That's what ever'body seems to be sayin' to me," he mumbled, unconsciously mimicking the accent he'd just heard.

"They're sayin' right," she called after him. "I know what I'm talkin' 'bout."

He turned around and lifted his eyes to the cleaning lady whom he'd known since he was a child. Envying her simple confidence, he couldn't speak again.

"You listen to me, doc. You need to pray."

Seth pursed his lips and nodded, then exited to the parking lot. Why was everyone talking about prayer? He walked a few steps further and stopped. *OK, God, I'll try it. Get me out of this mess!* He paused a few moments longer, then, not feeling any different, trudged on, half-embarrassed by his experiment.

Across the street, two shadowed figures sat in a BMW. "That has to be him."

"And look! He's getting into the maroon van."

"Sure looks familiar." Doc nodded and laughed.

"Looks like we've found our little hit-and-run artist."

◆ ◆ ◆

Kerri stopped at the Deer Falls Public Library before work and walked immediately to the local paper rack. There she carefully inspected the *Deer Falls Daily, The Daily Record*, and *The Coast Chronicle*.

This was odd. The autopsy report had been done for days, Lisa Dale's memorial was over and done with, and yet the public was still in the dark. Everyone still thought it was a hit-and-run. Why wasn't there anything in the paper about the autopsy?

She paged through the papers a second time before checking her watch and giving up. She thought about calling the sheriff's office but drew back when she recalled her last conversation with the sheriff about Lisa Dale. He would just think Kerri was off her rocker again. Maybe they were keeping things out of the media in order to get more information first; maybe they didn't want the murdering abortionist pervert to know they were on to him.

The last thought made her shiver. She walked outside into the cool air and headed for the parking lot. She hoped they'd catch the guilty party soon. She wouldn't feel safe until they did. She shivered a second time and gathered her coat around her. *God, put that pervert behind bars.*

She hopped into her car and nervously checked the backseat. She couldn't be too careful.

O God, protect me.

◆　◆　◆

Eric Donovan exchanged his lab coat for his overcoat and slipped a small specimen cup into his pocket. When he reached the front office, he saw Tammy Lynn sitting alone, concentrating on the dictation she was hearing on the headset. Quietly he slipped in behind her and embraced her neck.

She jerked her head violently, sending the headphones crashing to the ground. She screamed, then composed herself. "Eric, you scared me!"

He retreated sheepishly. "Sorry." He shrugged. "I guess I felt like celebrating."

She smiled. *He's glad I've moved out, isn't he? Maybe now we'll finally be able to—*

"Schwab from the N.I.H. told me some very interesting things about the specimen I sent him from the Dale case," he announced joyfully, interrupting her fantasy.

Tammy stiffened. "The Dale case? I didn't send anything out on that one—"

"Relax," he responded immediately. "I Fed-exed it myself. It wasn't official. Not one for the books anyway." He lowered his voice, even though they were alone. "I sent a sample of the fetus."

Tammy appeared uncomfortable. "Eric, I—"

"He's already doing some of the DNA mapping studies," he interrupted.

Tammy Lynn stood and faced him, then put her finger over his lips to stop him from talking. "Shhh." She clenched her teeth. "You won't have to tell anyone about this, will you?"

"What are you talking about?" He squinted with concern.

Tammy turned away. "You know I left Sonny."

The medical examiner sighed. "Yeah, but what does . . . Are we talking about the same thing?"

She nodded meekly. "I tried to tell you the other night on the phone.

I left Sonny because I can make it on my own financially now." She looked at Eric. "I mentioned that some money came through."

Donovan threw up his hands with open palms as if to say, "So?"

"It has to do with the Dale case."

Donovan sobered immediately. "Tammy, what's going on? You're not making any sense here."

She bit her lower lip. "Remember the Asian gentleman who wanted to assist with the autopsy?"

Donovan nodded.

"He came back. He offered me a lot of money if I would alter the medical examiner's report."

"Tammy, you didn't . . . !"

She began to cry. "I did it for us," she wailed. "Can't you see? I was afraid he would hurt me, or you." She looked toward the front windows. "I had read your report and had already typed it up. When he asked me to change it, to report that she had died from the hit-and-run injuries, I knew he must've staged the accident to cover for the way she really died. But when he offered the money, I couldn't resist. The girl was already dead—nobody could change that," she sobbed. She made eye contact with Eric. "I wanted to make a new start—with you."

"But he was covering up a homicide! I could lose my license if anyone finds out about this!"

Tammy cursed. "Is that all you care about? What about me? This is the break I've been waiting for—a chance for us!" She softened and draped her hands around his neck. "Besides, isn't it worth it?"

Donovan heaved a sigh and thought about the Dale autopsy. "What about that Dr. Berringer? He knows the truth."

"How will he ever learn what I've done? He's out of the loop. The sheriff has our report and will accept it verbatim. You told me yourself that he'd already made up his mind about the case when he came to see you before the autopsy."

Donovan shook his head. "I'm still concerned about Berringer."

"Don't worry," she responded softly. "The Asian wanted to know who else saw the autopsy, and I gave him Berringer's name. I'm sure they won't let him report the facts."

"I don't like this, Tammy."

She pulled him close. "You've been waiting for my freedom. You told me that yourself." She kissed him playfully. "Well, now I'm free."

Donovan pulled away slowly. "I—I need to think." He turned to the door. "I'll see you in the morning." He nearly ran to his Explorer, his head spinning.

What a strange twist. First, a call from Schwab to tell Donovan he was sitting on a gold mine, then the news from Tammy. Somebody didn't want anyone else to know about this baby—this gold mine.

He downshifted at the corner and turned the opposite direction from his residence, deciding at the last second to travel south toward Red Lake. If he played his cards right, he could end up with the money, his job, and Tammy Lynn. But first he needed to be sure no one else could capitalize on his fortune.

He flipped on his high-beams, illuminating the dark road ahead. The headlights danced across the pines bordering the roadway, their tall shadows casting an ominous appearance across the sandy fields beyond.

Alone with his silent greed, Eric Donovan embraced a shadowy scheme and vanished into the twilight.

CHAPTER
9

KEVIN Schwab couldn't shake the gnawing anxiety in the pit of his abdomen. He'd checked and rechecked the DNA from the specimen Donovan had sent him, and there was no denying the conclusion. Somebody somewhere had pushed a research envelope that should never have been attempted. Someone had accomplished a scientific monstrosity, and the growing trepidation he sensed propelled him closer to the only possible answer.

He scurried to his V.W., locking his opulent laboratory hours after all of his assistants had gone. The newly remodeled facility had been refurbished after a multimillion dollar gift by a private philanthropist. The way the contribution had been arranged hung heavy around Schwab's neck as he tried to understand exactly what was going on.

It wasn't until after he arrived home that the young biologist decided to call the only person capable of unlocking the present mystery—Ursula Baumgarten.

Knowing only the name of the city to which Ursula had quickly moved after the recent contribution, he called Information. The operator had the number.

In a moment Kevin heard the familiar husky voice. "Hello."

"Hi, Ursula."

Her recognition of her former N.I.H. associate's voice was immediate. "Kevin . . . So you've finally caught up with me."

"Yes," Kevin responded, his voice tense.

"Why are you calling? You said you'd never speak to me again. You told me that leaving the N.I.H. would end my career."

"Maybe I was wrong, OK?" He shifted his weight and began to pace.

Ursula smiled. "Of course."

"I need to know what you're working on now."

She raised her eyebrows. "You do? What would the great researcher want to know that for? I'm only working for a private company. You know that."

"Humor me, Ursula. It's important to me, that's all. What are you doing with the cells I sent to Davis?"

"It's a private company, Kev. You know I can't discuss our projects." She smiled again. "Besides, why should you care? You've got your new lab, and Mr. Davis has a few cells."

"It's an ethical issue, Ursula. Our code of conduct at the N.I.H. is strictly—"

A sharp laugh interrupted him. "You pious—"

"Look, Ursula, you have no idea what you're getting into—"

"You're the one without a clue!"

Kevin sighed and waited a moment, wondering whether she had hung up on him. "Ursula? Look, I didn't call to argue with you." He paused and heard no reply. "Ursula? Really, I'm concerned."

Ursula responded with questions of her own. "Why *did* you call, Kev? Why this concern all of a sudden? Have you had second thoughts about sharing your fame?"

"That's not it at all." He wondered how much to disclose. "Let's just say that I've gotten wind of your little project."

"Impossible. No one knows what we're doing. It's none of your business anyway. Mr. Davis handed you a contribution, and you were right to return the favor."

"I expected him merely to confirm the DNA mapping."

"Davis has a highly sophisticated lab. I wouldn't have left the N.I.H. to do high-school chemistry."

Kevin sighed again, frustrated at making so little headway in his search for information. "Look, Ursula, I was given a sample to evaluate—a piece of tissue taken from a girl who was murdered in Deer Falls. The DNA studies look surprisingly familiar."

Ursula jerked her head back. "What does that have to do with our research?"

"You tell me."

"Nothing. I have no idea what you're talking about." Deer Falls. Murder? Davis had said the surrogate died from an accidental hit-and-run. Kevin seemed to be the one who was misinformed.

"You're pulling my leg, right, Ursula? There are only a few people in the world who could have done this."

"What are you accusing me of?"

Kevin softened. "I'm not accusing you of anything. I only know what my sequencer is telling me."

"I don't have anything more to say. I don't know what you're talking about."

"You know exactly what I'm talking about."

"I work with scientists, not the Mafia, Kevin. You're letting your imagination run wild again. Now, unless you have more to say, this conversation is over."

"Be careful, Ursula. Watch your back. Maybe private research is as cutthroat as the N.I.H."

Ursula laughed nervously and cursed under her breath. She laid the phone down and shook her head. What was that all about? Murder in Deer Falls? Familiar DNA sequence? There was no way the tissue could have gotten back to Schwab! No way!

◆ ◆ ◆

Seth Berringer couldn't explain what was going on in his life spiritually. He didn't realize he was in the middle of a violent celestial war. All he knew was that he felt strangely torn. Unknown to him, he was being softly wooed by a gentle spirit on one front, tenaciously gripped by an evil one on another.

Part of the strangeness seemed to be the proliferation of God-talk around him. People who had never mentioned God before were suddenly telling him he needed to turn to him. Why would the chaplain pray for the driver involved in a hit-and-run accident at the memorial of the girl who had been killed? Why would Kerri suddenly speak to Seth about her concern and her prayers? Why would Mrs. Templeton choose to inform him of his need now? Was this all coincidence or something else?

Part of him wanted to run to the God whom Kerri had described in such loving terms. Another part screamed to resist such a decision; he had run his life fine so far without help from anyone else, his parents included. Why should he cave in now, just because of a single mistake?

Seth pushed his thoughts to the back of his wounded heart. He thought about Kerri, how peaceful she seemed, how beautiful she was. What wouldn't he give to have a woman like that? He shook his head as he looked at himself in the mirror and prepared to shave. She'd never go for a man like him. She'd want someone who thought about God the way she did. He sighed. Maybe he could change, accept her religion. No, he couldn't put on another charade, pretending to believe just to win her affection. He could never pull it off. She didn't really know him. She thought he was a sensitive, smart guy. She had no idea what he'd done to protect his image. She could never love the real Seth Berringer.

Seth shaved, showered, and drank a cup of black coffee, then emptied the rest of the pot into a large Wake Forest cup to take along on hospital rounds. His house was only ten minutes from the hospital, a location critical to Seth's selection of the old place. During the drive he listened to a local radio news program, amazed again at the lack of coverage about Lisa Dale. They still hadn't reported the medical examiner's findings. Wasn't that more important than a report on the campaigning sheriff visiting the local nursing home?

He turned into the parking lot, holding out his badge to activate the lifting of a gate restricting entrance into the closest physicians-only parking area. Wouldn't it be to the public's benefit to know that a murder had taken place? Seth reflected as he walked through a side entrance. Maybe Johnny Law was hot on this wacko-abortionist's trail and didn't want the media to get in the way.

Attempting to obey the first rule of patient rounds—never fight gravity—Seth started his rounds on the top floor, pediatrics, and worked his way to the intensive care unit on ground level.

He grabbed the chart of his first patient, a six-year-old whom he had treated in the past for ear infections and routine immunizations. He'd had an appendectomy the day before, so the surgeons were in charge of his care and Seth would be making more of a social visit.

"Hi, Brian," he said as he walked into the still, dark room. His mother, asleep on a cot before Seth's early arrival, sat up and squinted.

"Hello, Dr. Berringer. It's nice of you to stop by."

"Just covering the bases. How's he getting along?"

"Fine. He should get to go home tonight or tomorrow."

"Good. Good." He placed his stethoscope over the boy's chest. "Take a deep breath."

Seth looked over at the mother. "He sounds great." He glanced back at the patient. "Ready for a pizza yet?"

The boy wrinkled his nose.

Seth walked to the door. "Take care. His appetite will improve. I can see him in the office next week, if you like—check the incision, write out his excuse for school."

"That would be nice."

Seth walked down to the nurses' station and wrote a progress note, documenting his visit. He then progressed to the ortho floor to check on an elderly female with a hip fracture and pneumonia, got sidetracked with a family who wanted to talk about putting their father in a nursing home, checked on Mr. Jones, a diabetic with a deep venous thrombosis, Mr. Edwards, an angina patient in for a coronary catheterization, and Mrs. Henry, an obese woman with an infected foot ulcer. Finally, with only five minutes until he was due in his office, he entered the I.C.U. to see Mrs. Anderson, a patient he'd admitted with shortness of breath and cardiac failure the night before.

She was sitting quietly, reading a soft, well-worn Bible.

"Hello, Mrs. Anderson. You're looking much better."

"I feel so much better too."

He checked the catheter draining his patient's urine. "Looks like you've had a good response to the medicine." He pulled out his stethoscope. "Could you lean forward?" He placed the instrument over her lung bases. "Uh huh, you're sounding much clearer."

"Thank you."

"I'm going to start you on a new medication. It'll help your heart beat a little stronger." He walked toward the door.

"Doctor? I thought I was dying last night. I couldn't get my breath."

"You're going to be all right, Mrs. Anderson. You're not going to die any time soon."

"I'm ready to die, Dr. Berringer. When I die, I'll see the Savior." She clutched the Bible in her hands.

Seth nodded numbly and turned to leave.

"Doctor? I want to read something to you. I was reading it as you came in. Maybe it will bless you too." Her wrinkled hand moved to the passage in front of her.

"'He that covereth his sins shall not prosper: but whoso confesseth and forsaketh them shall have mercy.'"

She looked up. "I've only been a believer since Bill died. Now I'm ready to go." She pointed at the words in the Bible. "I confessed, and I found mercy."

What is it about me? Am I wearing a sign that says, "Preach to me" or what? Seth nodded his head politely. "That's nice." He didn't know what else to say. He just wanted to leave but dropped his patient list on the floor, then lost a pen out of his pocket when he bent over to pick up the list. Clumsily, he gathered the items and retreated again without speaking.

Mrs. Anderson closed her eyes tightly. *You were right, Lord. He's running, all right. Open his eyes to see the truth.*

◆ ◆ ◆

Connie Donovan sipped her coffee slowly and looked up as her husband walked into the kitchen. She accepted his kiss passively, then returned her interest to the hazelnut blend in her cup. After a minute, she cleared her throat. "You were out late."

"I went to the lake. I needed to think."

"I was worried."

"You worry too much."

Connie sighed. "You used to talk to me to work out your thoughts. Now you just turn to the solitude of that stupid cabin."

"That stupid cabin was your idea." He poured himself some coffee. "Only 250,000-dollar cabin on Red Lake," he murmured, "and all for a few weekends a year."

"I thought we would go there together, get away, be alone, put the spice back in our relationship."

Eric grunted.

Connie waited for a response. "Are you OK?"

He looked up from the paper and sighed. "I'm OK, I'm OK," he muttered. "Just some pressure at work. I needed some solitude."

Her eyes began to tear. "Eric, were you alone at the lake?"

He jerked his head up. "Yes." It was the truth this time. He didn't elaborate.

She composed herself and launched her assault. "You were with your secretary, weren't you? That Tammy Lynn who called you the other—"

"I was alone at the lake!" He raised his voice more than he'd intended. "And since when do you listen to my phone calls?"

Connie bit her lip. "I don't. I just happened to pick up the phone as you answered it, that's all."

Eric softened, stood, and faced his wife. He placed his hands on her shoulders, but she stiffened and withdrew. "Look, Connie, she's a young girl. She has a crush on me, OK? Is that so hard to understand?" He searched frantically for the right words, trying to minimize the damage he sensed. "She's a confused, young thing. She's depressed. She's seeing some sort of counselor to work through her poor self-image. She's on medication for it. She's—"

"She's as pretty as a model. I know how you love that type."

"Connie, listen to me! You can't be serious about this. I was alone at the cabin last night. You have my word." He decided to try humor. "Come on, honey. Have you ever seen Mr. Gaskins? He's as big as a house. He'd crush anyone who made a move on his wife."

Connie wasn't laughing. "I'm supposed to believe this is merely an innocent crush?"

He stood his ground and held up his hands. "You have my word."

She wrinkled her chin in an attempt not to cry. Eric gathered his wife in his arms, and this time she didn't resist. She desperately wanted to believe what he was saying. "Look, honey," he added, "let's go down to the lake ourselves this weekend. We both could use the break."

She laid her head against his chest. "What about the Nelsons? They've invited us to their daughter's wedding."

"Invite 'em along! She despises that boyfriend of Sally's anyway."

"Eric!"

He changed gears. "I'll talk to Lester. He'll understand."

Connie searched her husband's eyes, unsure what she was looking for. She felt like crying, hitting him, and kissing him all at the same time.

"It's going to be OK, Connie. You're going to be OK."

She placed her head against his chest again, wanting to believe but feeling a shadowy coldness she couldn't understand.

◆　◆　◆

By the time Seth's Saturday night E.R. shift rolled around, his anxiety about Lisa Dale's death had escalated to a new level. He had thought that certainly the autopsy report would straighten out any confusion he'd caused by tampering with the death scene. But so far he'd seen no evidence that anyone thought anything except hit-and-run. In fact, a news broadcast that very afternoon stated there was nothing new to report except that the sheriff's department was confident they would soon be able to apprehend the hit-and-run driver. *They shouldn't still be looking for a hit-and-run driver*, Seth thought. *They should be looking for a back-alley abortionist, or maybe a sadistic sex freak! When are they going to look at the medical examiner's report?*

A raucous college football crowd created a noisy backdrop as the staff tended to four students who had been injured in a celebratory brawl. One of the inebriated visitors threatened to punch Seth in the nose if he didn't soon pay attention to his wounded friend. A quick call to security and some fast backpedaling by the physician saved his face from the encounter. Although he hated the word *Gomer* (medical terminology popularized by the best-selling novel *The House of God*, for Get Out Of My Emergency Room), he mused that a few of his patients that night certainly fit the description. By midnight things were peaking, by 2 A.M. the crowd had thinned, and by 6 only two sleeping drunks were left.

Seth picked up his bag and headed out past the triage desk. Kerri Barber looked up. "You survived."

"Did you put out a flashing sign proclaiming free care or what?" Seth rubbed the back of his neck.

"You might think so."

Seth hadn't had a chance to talk with Kerri since right after Lisa's memorial service. "Thanks for the note."

"You're welcome."

He shifted his on-call bag to his opposite shoulder.

"Getting out of here?"

Seth nodded. "I need some sleep."

Kerri looked at her watch. "Care for some breakfast first? I'm out of here in two minutes."

"Oh, I shouldn't. I—"

"Come on, I won't bite. I've wanted to talk to you again. I was hoping I'd get the chance tonight, but we were so busy . . ."

Seth looked up. "The misery magnet theory, right?"

Kerri smiled. "Guess so." She made eye contact. "So, what do you say? Clara felt so bad the other day when we wouldn't order any food. We owe her a breakfast order at least."

"Well . . . OK." He looked at his wrinkled scrubs. "I need to change. Can we meet over there in thirty minutes?"

"I'll be there."

Seth headed for his van and made it home in record time. He changed, shaved, and pulled up to Clara's just as Kerri stepped out of her car.

It looked like a clear day, the temperature right at 45 as proclaimed by the digital sign at the Deer Falls Savings and Loan.

"It's beautiful out," Kerri said in greeting.

Just like you. Seth nodded. "Yeah."

They walked to the door. Seth pulled back before walking in. "Shouldn't you be going to church or something?"

She glanced at her watch. "It's only 7:30, Seth. I have plenty of time."

They sat in the same booth as on the day of Lisa's memorial.

Clara poured the coffee, this time for both of them. She smiled. "Don't tell me. No menu. Just coffee."

"No way. We've come for breakfast." Kerri looked at Clara. "My treat."

Seth looked at Clara and lifted his eyebrows. "In that case . . ." He laughed. "Bring me a number 1, scrambled."

"I'll take the french toast."

Clara winked at Seth. "Be right out."

When Clara left, Kerri wasted no time. "I'm bothered by Lisa's death. After what you told me, I've been watching the paper every day. They've hardly even mentioned it. They've certainly not reported the medical examiner's findings."

"I noticed that, too," he said soberly. "I guess they're keeping it quiet for some official reason."

"I've thought of that, but don't they have a duty to warn the public?"

"To let them know she was murdered?"

"The public ought to know about this. Someone covered up a murder with this scheme, and they aren't saying a word about it."

Seth shifted in his seat. "I've wondered the same thing, but I guess they have their reasons. I'm sure the truth will come out eventually."

Kerri shrugged. "I've been feeling out of sorts. I go outside, but I feel different—not scared, but . . . well, vulnerable. It's like the innocence of our little town has been lost or something." She looked out the window. "I can't really explain it. Maybe it's because Lisa was my friend. I've never had a friend die like that before," she continued, twisting her mouth as she said, "like that."

"Maybe you should talk to the sheriff's department. Ask them if they have any more information about Lisa's postcard."

"I've thought about that, but . . . well, I felt so stupid when I talked to the sheriff the last time. It's like they think I'm overreacting or something."

"But that was before the autopsy report. Come on, Kerri, your postcard plus the medical examiner's findings spell foul play from a thousand yards. Somehow Lisa got involved with some pretty bad dudes, and it backfired."

"That's not like her. She wouldn't willingly associate with someone like that." Kerri shook her head. "Whoever it is must be glad the news of the medical examiner's report hasn't gone public. Everyone is still believing the hit-and-run lie."

Seth coughed. "The hit-and-run lie should be debunked as soon as the autopsy report hits the streets."

"*If* it hits the streets. I'm beginning to wonder if the sheriff isn't hiding something himself."

Seth squirmed. How could she be so pretty, yet make him so uncomfortable? He looked up in relief as Clara delivered the food. Now at least they could talk about the chow. Anything except Lisa Dale.

Seth concentrated on the meal in front of him. Scrambled eggs, sausage, grits, and buttered wheat toast provided a wonderful aroma but failed to improve his waning appetite. He ate the eggs and grits but pushed the sausage around the edge of the plate.

Kerri cleaned up her french toast and drank two cups of coffee. She smiled. "That ought to keep me awake even if Pastor Dan gets long-winded."

"Where do you attend?" Seth wasn't sure he cared. He simply wanted to make conversation.

"Deer Falls Community Chapel—over on Harrison Avenue."

He nodded. "I've seen it."

"You're welcome to come with me."

"Me?" Seth clenched his teeth. "I don't think so. My beliefs are pretty private." He didn't know what else to say. He wasn't really sure what his beliefs were, but he was certain that whatever they were, they were pretty private.

"Can I ask you a question?"

He stared at her dark eyes. Eyes so deep and peaceful, he found himself drawn to her. Eyes so clear, he wondered if she would ever be capable of covering up anything. "Could I stop you?"

"Sure. Don't answer if you're uncomfortable."

He shrugged.

"What do you believe? What makes Seth Berringer tick? What makes you get up every morning?"

He smiled. "You said, 'a question.'"

This time she shrugged. "I couldn't help myself. I just want to know what's inside you, that's all."

You would hate me if you really knew me. I'm not even sure I like me anymore. Seth stalled, saying, "What do I believe? What makes me tick?" He looked out the window and sipped his coffee. "I guess I believe in God. Is that what you mean?"

Kerri nodded but didn't speak. She wasn't going to let him off the hook quite yet.

"I guess I would say he expects us to do our best—to help others where we can."

"What about man? What do you think? Basically good or evil?"

"Man, Kerri, I've talked to you two times, and you give me a philosophy test!"

"Come on, Seth. A man of your intelligence has to have worked through this stuff." She backed off, giving him more space. "Besides, I'm not grading the test." She smiled warmly, with her lips parted just enough so he could see her front teeth, the kind of smile that could disarm a charging bull.

"OK." He paused. "Let me think." He pushed his coffee mug away. "I think man is basically good. Look back over history. Consider what we've accomplished. I think that speaks of man's virtuosity, don't you?" He waited. "Well? What do you think?"

"Is that what you think about yourself?"

He wasn't sure he liked what he'd seen of his capabilities the last few weeks. Before then, he would have answered very differently. "Sure." He tried to sound confident.

"I hear what you're saying, and I do agree that man has accomplished a lot throughout history. But I think whatever good has been accomplished has come directly or indirectly from God's hand." She shrugged. "I think man, left on his own, is basically evil, with a bent toward selfishness. That's the whole problem that separates us from a perfect God."

That's exactly how I feel—separated from God.

"But I don't believe God leaves us without a solution, that he abandons us to our sins."

"Is this the way every conversation with you goes?"

She flashed another sheepish grin. "Maybe. Am I making you uncomfortable?"

Seth sighed. "I don't know, really. It's not you. I've just been trying to put a lot of things together lately." He shook his head. "And lately everyone's trying to tell me about God."

"More than just me?"

He nodded. "You, my cleaning lady, my patients, the chaplain at the memorial service. It's coming from everywhere."

"Maybe that's not a coincidence, Seth. Maybe, just maybe God is arranging all of this to draw you in, to convince you that he loves you enough to put crazy people in your path who will tell you the way to go."

"I—I don't know. I kind of think he's forgotten about ol' Seth Berringer. I'm doing pretty well on my own." He immediately looked down. He'd been telling himself that all his life. After what had happened recently, he knew it was a lie.

"You're no different than anyone else, Seth. We all need God. We all need to be restored, to solve the problem of our evil nature. You're not unique, Seth. We all need a Savior to make a way back to God."

Seth felt overloaded. Guilty and overloaded. Guilty, defensive, and overloaded. He threw up his hands. "Time out. This stuff is OK for you, all right? But for me?" He shook his head and looked at Kerri. For the second time in a week he felt close to crying, something he hadn't done since Jerry Quigmire had wrecked Seth's new ten-speed back in the sixth grade. "I look at you, Kerri, and you seem so together. You've got it all figured out." He looked at his hands. "I wish I could be like that, but I'm not, OK? I'm not sure I'll ever have things put together like that."

"I'm sorry, Seth. I'm pushing you too fast." Kerri studied his face for a moment before looking away. "I see a lot of good in you, Seth. You're smart. You care about people. I like you, OK?"

Seth sighed and stuck out his hand. "Friend?"

Kerri took it. "When's your next shift in the E.R.?"

A smile returned to Seth's face. "Not until next month."

"I guess I'll have to figure out some other excuse to see you." She smiled too.

"Can I call you?"

He'd call her after the way she'd come across? He had to think she was the pushiest woman in Deer Falls. Kerri's mouth dropped open slightly before she answered simply, "Sure." She scribbled her number on a paper napkin and pushed it across the table. "I'll try to control myself next time."

"Hey, I want you to be yourself." She was open, honest. At least he know where she stood. But she had no idea who he really was.

"I'd better run. I have to change before church." She walked to the cash register and paid the bill.

Seth stayed behind and drank another cup of coffee, thankful no one could read his thoughts. He felt exactly what Kerri had described—bent toward selfishness, separated from God. *It's like she sees right through me. But at the same time she has no idea who I really am or what I've done. Would she ever want to see me again if she knew what I did to her friend?*

CHAPTER
10

SETH Berringer wasn't the only one feeling remorse over Lisa Dale's death. Kevin Schwab had started to piece together the facts as he understood them—and he didn't like what he saw at all.

The N.I.H.'s eccentric biologist arrived at the lab harried and with a three-day growth of adolescent stubble on his chin. His first order of business was to personally incinerate the remainder of Donovan's tissue sample. If he knew anything, he knew that having extra DNA from that baby would potentially multiply his and the world's problems exponentially. Next, he would have to convince Donovan to do the same. He also wanted to clarify what Donovan knew about the way the girl carrying the baby had died. *Is he sure she was murdered? Maybe she died accidentally from the abortion attempt. Didn't he tell me she had been beaten?*

He sighed. If she was murdered to get the baby, responsibility could be traced back to him! But of course, he hadn't known what Mr. Davis would do. He couldn't be held responsible for that, could he? He rubbed the back of his neck and looked around his new laboratory. But no one would believe he didn't know all of that when Davis's money rebuilt his lab.

He picked up the phone on his lab desk. One of the reasons he hadn't called from home was that he only had cordless phones there, and he'd heard that calls from cordless phones can be intercepted and monitored with great ease. He wasn't being paranoid, he mused, just prudent.

He carefully dialed the number. Eric would have to listen to reason. They had to destroy that baby!

◆ ◆ ◆

Sitting in the silver BMW, William "Bill" Guessford and Jerry "Doc" Ling maintained their vigil with diligence. Their objective was clear, but their plan of action needed sharpening. "Find out what he knows. Find out why he's covering for us," Mr. Davis had instructed. But how?

"This is getting boring." Bill scratched his abdomen.

"Getting boring? I've been alone with you for days. Think how I feel."

"Very funny." Guessford looked across the parking lot of the Deer Falls Family Medicine Clinic. "I can't see how taking this guy out completely would hurt us any. We can get what we need from the pathologist and be on our way."

"Mr. Davis is worried about this guy. If he knows something and has shared it with someone else, his death would only warn the others," the Asian complained. "Besides, this case is getting too messy. Staying around after the girl died is risky enough."

"Her death was an accident, Doc. You were only completing the research she had consented to."

Doc rubbed the back of his neck. "Yeah, I know, I know. But then again, the original medical examiner's report said the spike went all the way through the uterus." He cursed. "I've never botched it like that before. Do you think the law would consider that anything less than murder?"

"You were doing your job, nothing more," Bill insisted. "It's like your medical practice back in China. You do your best, but occasionally there are complications. You can't expect every procedure to go perfectly."

"I know, but that was pretty bad. I must be losing my touch."

"Ridiculous. You're the best." He squinted to watch a patient enter the clinic. "That's what Mr. Davis told me." He nodded. "And believe me, he knows."

They waited in silence for a few minutes before Doc spoke again. "I think all this Berringer does is work. Work and sleep. Except for that babe he was with for breakfast the other morning, I'd say this guy is a complete loser."

Bill smiled. "That's who I think we should be watching. I'll take that assignment any day."

"You're old enough to be her father." He paused. "But then again, maybe she does know something. She's about the only person Berringer relates to outside the office."

Bill grunted. "Do you have any of those donut holes left?"

"No. You shouldn't eat in the car anyway."

"Then let's take a lunch break—maybe go over to that place the sheriff mentioned—Lanny's or Lenny's or whatever."

Doc shrugged. "OK. This guy never leaves before six o'clock anyway. Let's go."

◆ ◆ ◆

"So where do we stand, Clara? You been handing out those flyers?" The sheriff glanced at Clara's beehive hair before turning his full attention to the thick coconut cream pie in front of him.

"I've been handing them out. Don't worry."

"Great pie, doll. Tell Millie I said so." He wiped his generous mouth with the back of his hand.

"Know what I think?"

"How would I know what's in your pretty little head?"

"I think you should show up in some of the local churches, like Mr. Blackstock does. He's in a different congregation almost every Sunday, talking about family values and all that." She wiped off the next table with a moist rag. "Some of the folks who come in here think that standing up in church must mean you know what you're talkin' 'bout."

"Has he been over to the Catholic church?" Wayne eased out a quiet belch. "I used to go there."

"You?"

"Hey, I practically had my own pew."

She poked his abdomen. "I'll bet." She laughed. "He was there just last Sunday."

The sheriff snorted. "What about the church on the hill? Certainly Pastor Walsh wouldn't give up his pulpit just for—"

"Two weeks ago," she announced. "I heard him myself. He even prayed and everything. Then his daughters, Angie and Gayle, stood up and gave their testimonies, too."

"Oh great. I suppose you think I should take Wayne, Jr., with me. What would he say? 'Daddy bailed me out of trouble so many times, you should vote for him'?"

Clara chuckled. "Don't get me started on that boy." She slipped into the booth across from the sheriff and sat down. "Where's he been lately? He used to stop in after work."

Wayne Boatwright lowered his voice and shook his head. "He's up at Wellington Center again."

"Rehab?"

"Yeah, and he swears it's workin' this time. He hasn't had a fix in two months." He sighed and pushed the empty plate toward Clara. "I just hope he stays out of trouble until after the election."

He slurped his coffee, spilling a drop on his brown tie. He muttered under his breath. "Oh well, it won't show."

"I'm serious about this church thing. Ol' Blackstock might catch right up if everyone in those churches think he's the one."

The sheriff looked down. "People will say I'm a hypocrite, Clara. I can't just show up one time for their vote, can I?"

"Sure, you can. Tell them your religion is a very meaningful and private experience. Most of 'em could care less what you believe anyway. They just want to go right on with their comfortable little Deer Falls existence."

"I should make you my campaign manager." He smiled.

◆ ◆ ◆

With Kerri Barber, prayer was like breathing. Her prayers didn't seem to have a definite starting point and no precise end. She prayed as she dressed, showered, drove, and worked. She prayed as she ate, shopped, and jogged. With a sentence of request here or a thank you there, she enjoyed an ongoing, spontaneous consciousness of God's presence in her life that many believers yearn for.

She had the day off and used most of her time to clean her apartment, catch up on her grocery shopping, and type an E-mail to her mother. Throughout the day, her thoughts and prayers turned and returned to the handsome, young physician, Seth Berringer. It didn't take a master of divinity to discern his spiritual hunger—or his spiritual need for that matter.

She was captivated by him, to be sure, but she knew she would guard her heart with the strongest lock when it came to anything more than a casual friendship. Nonetheless, she would have had to be hormoneless and blind not to be attracted by his rugged looks and his caring attitude.

You are calling him, aren't you, Lord? Continue to soften his heart to your message.

Kerri jogged around the Deer Falls Middle School track. Ever since finding out how Lisa Dale really died, she felt uncomfortable running on her old loop around town. She looked at her watch, wanting to shave a few more seconds off her next mile. Seven minutes, fifty seconds. She frowned, knowing she should be able to do better.

She finished two more miles and walked back to her apartment. Faced with no desire to cook and tired of her cold cereal selection, she showered and headed to the mall. She'd get a salad at the food court, she promised herself.

As she drove, she prayed for Seth again. *Help him recognize the truth.*

◆ ◆ ◆

That evening Seth took a good look at himself in the mirror. He looked like death. He wasn't eating. He wasn't sleeping. He was just running from haunted memories of a murdered girl on a lonely highway.

Stepping on the scales, he was shocked. He hadn't weighed this little since high school. He thought about eating, but only because he thought he needed to. He really wasn't hungry.

You're killing yourself, man. You have to get on with your life. Forget Lisa Dale. Forget Kerri Barber. He waffled a bit on that last one. She would be difficult for any man to forget. Who was he trying to fool? Kerri wouldn't give him the time of day if she knew what he'd done.

Seth sat at his kitchen table and sorted through the mail, half-hoping to find another little note from Kerri. No such luck today.

He opened a box of generic cornflakes and poured himself a bowl. He had to eat something.

While he ate, his mind reviewed and re-reviewed the conversations he'd had with Kerri. She spoke about God like he was her best friend. It seemed to Seth that God was a thousand miles away—and yet close enough to point out his every fault. If God was a God of mercy, why did Seth feel so condemned? *God could never love me. I could never live up to his expectations—or Kerri's—or mine.*

His thoughts turned to his patient, Mrs. Anderson. Gently, the Holy Spirit goaded his memory with the verse she'd read. What did it say? If you cover your sins, you won't prosper? Why had Mrs. Anderson read that to him? He cringed at the memory of his clumsy exit from her room. He must have looked totally stupid. What was the rest of that passage? He couldn't remember. He glanced at the bookshelf in the next room.

He walked to it, leaving his half-eaten bowl of cereal behind. He ran his fingers over the books for a moment until he found an old Bible, one he'd used in a religion class in college. He thumbed through the concordance looking for the word "sins." There must have been a million references! He looked next at "covers" and found the Proverbs 28 reference under "covereth."

He that covereth his sins shall not prosper: but whoso confesseth and forsaketh them shall have mercy.

He read the words slowly, then slumped into a chair and mumbled a curse. *Confess? Confess to whom?*

Seth sat for a few minutes longer, his stomach in an angry knot. *Everywhere I go, every hour, I see Lisa Dale. It's been days since I've had an appetite, longer since I've had a night's rest.* He wiped his forehead.

He fingered the book in his hand. *Is this the reason Mrs. Anderson read me that verse—to show me what I need to do?* He shook his head. He'd been spending too much time with Kerri!

He paced around the house for another hour, his mind and stomach churning. He stared at his unmade bed, the dishes in his sink, and the clothes draped over the bedroom furniture. Somehow he just couldn't bring himself to clean up. Nothing seemed to matter. He had to do something to rid himself of his troubled thoughts.

He looked back at his bed. He couldn't face another night without sleep. He felt like he had to confess or die. He didn't know which would be worse.

Seth rubbed the back of his neck and coughed nervously. His mind was made up. He reached for his wallet and retrieved a small napkin fragment.

Carefully, he dialed the number.

"Hello."

"Kerri . . ." His voice strained at the words. "I need to talk—somewhere private."

"Seth?"

He looked around his house. His place wouldn't do—as if she'd agree to come to his home alone anyway. "Can you meet me in Mem. Park?"

"Seth, it's freezing out there!"

He felt stupid, but he had to go through with this. "I—I know," he stuttered. "Wrap up." He didn't know what else to suggest.

"I'll meet you in ten minutes."

"I'll be there."

Seth hung up before hearing her say, "What's wrong, Seth?"

CHAPTER
11

THE AIR was cool but the night clear, and thousands of stars peppered the sky. Kerri arrived a few minutes before Seth and stayed safely in her locked car until she saw him approaching. While she waited, she prayed—prayed and wondered about the man Seth Berringer.

She turned off her engine and got out as soon as she knew the man in the red parka was indeed Seth. She smiled. "You came prepared."

He looked at his parka. "Guaranteed to be warm at 15 below." He stopped and looked at her tensely. "Thanks for coming. I know it must seem crazy."

"What's on your mind? Is everything OK?"

"No." He looked past a wooden play structure in the center of the park. "There's a fitness walk over there." He paused. "I'm not sure I can hold still to tell this story."

She shoved her hands into her coat pockets. "Let's go."

"I—I don't know how to start. I've been feeling pretty bad lately about some things I've done. I've not really been honest with you. I haven't lied, but I haven't told you everything either."

Kerri could see he was hurting. He squinted his eyes and clenched his jaw between sentences. "You can tell me. It will be OK." She clutched the arm of his parka. "Really."

"It's about Lisa Dale." He glanced at her. There was no apparent reaction to his statement. "The night she died, I was the one who found her."

"Out by the Exxon station?"

"No. Before that. In the field out behind Lanny's Grill." He studied her again. She showed no sign of surprise. Seth was amazed at her apparent lack of reaction. "Look, what I'm going to tell you may make you hate me. But at least listen to my story, OK?"

Kerri nodded silently.

Seth continued, "I've been under a lot of pressure working for Coast Care. I've even been sued for malpractice." He shook his head. "The charges against me were finally dropped, but Coast Care was still on my case. They said I'd lose my job if there was any more trouble."

Kerri nodded again and wrinkled her forehead.

"Anyway, I had a patient—a psychiatric patient who always seemed harmless to me, even though he was continuously troubled by obsessions of violence and rape. Really, I always downplayed what he told me, and I'd always point out the fact that he'd never been a violent person, that his fantasies were exactly that—troublesome thoughts he could never act out." Seth kicked the gravel path with his feet. "Anyway, I faithfully recorded his obsessions in his patient record at the office." He stopped and looked at Kerri. He twisted his expression and continued, "My patient's fantasies were about Lisa Dale."

"Hmmm," Kerri responded, saying nothing more.

"The night she died, I worked the evening shift in the E.R. Jimmy was late, and I took care of a six-year-old who died in a bicycle/car accident."

"I remember. It was horrible."

"The boy's father practically assaulted me in the waiting room. He blamed me for losing his son."

"You did everything you could—"

"I knew at one level that it wasn't my fault, but I was devastated," he interrupted. "I hated losing the boy—losing him and knowing that Coast Care was watching—and that they were already reviewing my E.R. mortality figures." He sighed and started walking again. "So I did what I haven't done for years—I went to Lanny's and started drinking. I just wanted to forget it all. Everything I had worked so hard for seemed to be crashing in on me." He shook his head. "Then I saw my psychiatric patient in the bar drinking. I felt like a hypocrite. I'd counseled him not to do the very thing I was doing. By the time I left, the alcohol had done little to relieve my misery. In fact, I was in a worse funk than ever." He shook his head. "I didn't think the drinks would affect me so much, but . . . w-well," he stuttered, "I'm gettin' ahead of myself." He lowered his eyes and his voice. "I left Lanny's to find my car. That's when I cut across the field and stumbled across Lisa Dale's body."

"In the field behind Lanny's?"

"Right." He nodded. "I could see she had blood on her pants—blood between her legs. I thought she had been raped and killed. When I checked her wallet, I discovered who she was."

"And you thought your patient did it, right?"

"Exactly. And I freaked. All I could think was that people would check the medical records and see that I had a legal duty to warn her of my patient's homicidal fixation. All I could think of was losing my job, everything I had worked so long for." He stared at the ground. "All I could think of was myself!"

Kerri studied his face without speaking. Silently she prayed, for Seth and for her response.

"So I devised a plan to keep the authorities from finding out she'd been murdered. I had to get into Coast Care's records and remove my notes about my patient's obsessions. I know now that wasn't right, but I wasn't thinking too clearly at the time. I knew I couldn't get to the records until Monday. So . . . I moved her body to the road by the Exxon station and called 911 to report a pedestrian accident, but not before . . ." He looked at Kerri and bit his index finger. ". . . not before I ran over her body with my van."

Kerri's hand shot to her gaping mouth.

Seth studied her reaction for only a second. "I can't believe I did it, Kerri. I can't believe I thought it would work. The next morning, when I woke up, it was as if the whole episode was a bad dream." He shook his head. "I wish I'd never taken that first drink. How could I have been so stupid?"

Kerri stifled her revulsion. "You—you ran over her body."

Seth nodded.

"And then you left."

Again Seth tipped his head forward.

"You left, and they called it a hit-and-run." Kerri was nodding now.

"Right."

"So . . . you know who the murderer is, but you aren't turning him in because you're afraid you'll be implicated?"

Seth shook his head. "No. It's more complicated than that. I confronted my patient, but he didn't do it, Kerri. I was wrong. The guy was visiting his mother in the hospital, for pete's sake. He wasn't anywhere around when Lisa died."

"So . . . ?"

"So at that point I realized I'd better try to undo the damage I'd done. Somehow I needed to make sure the medical examiner didn't assume she'd died from the hit-and-run. I didn't know, of course, that she had died during an abortion, or perhaps at the hand of some sadistic pervert. I found that out during the autopsy. I just wanted to debunk the hit-and-run theory enough to get the authorities back on the right track."

"I see. And get yourself out of a guilt trip by undoing your little masquerade."

"Right." He slumped and sighed.

"OK," she responded gently, "I think I understand so far—except why all of a sudden you're telling this to me. What can I do?"

He shook his head. "It's not all of a sudden, Kerri. It's all I've thought about for days." He stuttered, "I—it's all so w-weird, really. I don't understand what's going on with me."

Kerri gripped his arm.

"I can't eat. I can't sleep. I'm tortured by the fact that I could have done this—desecrating a dead body . . . tampering with a crime scene . . . misleading everyone, including you." He looked up. "I'm not sure what it is about you, but I couldn't stand the thought of lying to you anymore."

She nodded.

"I know it sounds crazy, but I thought it would all go away as soon as the public found out the truth from the medical examiner's office. But it's as if no one knows any different—as if all my efforts to reverse what I've done haven't accomplished anything."

"So why are you telling this to me?"

"I don't know really," he responded slowly. "You've been telling me about God, about praying—you and everyone else, it seems." He paused. "A patient of mine read me an uncomfortably pertinent verse from the Bible—almost as if she knew what I'd done."

Kerri understood.

"I looked up the verse—something like, 'Hide your sins and you won't prosper. Confess them and you will find mercy.'" He shrugged. "I knew you were right when you told me about the condition of man, bent toward selfishness and all. It was as if you could see right through me. I don't know why, Kerri, but I had to get this off my chest. And I didn't know where else to turn."

"I understand, Seth."

They walked along for another minute in silence.

"Do you hate me—considering what I've done?"

"I don't hate you, Seth. I'm not condoning what you've done, but I understand." She pulled him around to look at her face to face. "You're under conviction, Seth. Do you know what that means?"

"I feel guilty."

"God has been speaking to you, calling you, wooing you through all the people around you who have been talking to you about him. Conviction is his way of getting you to see that you need him, that you can't be good enough on your own."

"I wasn't living up to my own standards or goals. And when I talked to you . . . well, I knew I didn't live up to what you would want either." He shook his head again. "Somehow I just wanted to be who you thought I was, not who I was pretending to be. You believed I was a concerned physician attending the funeral of a trusted patient. In reality, I'm just a man wanting to appease his own guilt by doing something right."

"It's deeper than that, Seth. It's more than you just wanting to live up to my expectations of you, or even your own. You're coming to see that you don't cut it before God, that you need him to straighten all this out."

Seth coughed, his breath a visible fog.

In the parking lot, a silver BMW drove by with its lights off. Seth turned to watch the car pause at Kerri's car and then his van before moving slowly on.

Kerri followed his eyes. "Who's that?"

Instinctively, he lowered his voice. "I don't know. Their lights are off, but maybe they just pulled out and don't realize it yet."

"The lot was empty when I arrived." She moved closer to him and touched the arm of his parka.

The car circled and drove on. In the moonlight the two friends could barely make out the dim image of the two occupants.

"They're leaving. Probably a couple looking for a place to be alone." She took a breath. "Look, Seth, I know you've probably heard this before, but let me say it just the same. Everyone stands guilty before God, separated from him because of our disobedience. Jesus died to pay the price for our wrong, to restore us to a right relationship with God."

He listened but didn't respond. He heard, but he couldn't quite believe it.

"Look, I know I've messed up . . . pretty badly, I guess . . ." He stopped. "What do you think I should do?"

Kerri thought for a moment. "Maybe you should talk to the sheriff. Tell him what you've told me."

"He'll arrest me, Kerri. It has to be against the law to move a body, to fake a hit-and-run like that. He'll probably put me in jail."

"What did you want me to say?"

He shuffled his feet. "I don't know. You're the only one, besides the medical examiner and whoever else has read his report, who knows how Lisa died. I guess I just hoped you'd have some idea how to straighten this all out—short of me going to the sheriff." He stopped and looked up at the stars. "Maybe I didn't really tell you this because I want answers. I told you because I wanted you to know the truth about me. I didn't want to live a lie in front of Kerri Barber anymore."

She nodded. "I'm honored . . . really." They walked around the path, soon reaching the beginning of the course again. "I think you've hit on the answer, Seth. You said it yourself."

He looked at her curiously.

"You said you don't want to live a lie."

He nodded soberly. She was right again. He wanted to be a man of truth.

◆ ◆ ◆

Bill whispered quietly, "Ten bucks says he takes her home. Just look at the fog they're raising."

Doc rubbed a circle in the clouded windshield. "Just look at the fog you're raisin' is more like it," he huffed. "You and your heavy breathing are making it difficult to see!"

"Just watch. He's going to take her home!"

"Control yourself, will you?" Doc shook his head. "Besides, she looks like a modern lady. She'll probably drive herself."

"What in the world are they doing out there anyway? The park closes at dusk."

"Maybe they want to be alone? Get a brain."

"I bet he can't wait to get her out of that ski jacket."

"Would you let it rest?" Doc rolled his eyes. "This whole scene bothers me. That Berringer guy knows something. Now he's meeting with this girl with no one else around to hear him. Something doesn't smell right."

"We should have taken him out a long time ago. I think Davis is wrong on this one. The longer we wait, the more chances we're giving this guy to talk."

"You might be right." Doc tapped the steering wheel, then widened the clear circle on the windshield with his glove. "But Davis won't let it go on forever. As soon as we get what we came for, we'll make sure Berringer won't be a loose cannon."

"He's walking her to her car!"

The two strained to see Seth open Kerri's car door. She entered the auto alone. In a moment a cloud of exhaust filled the air behind her vehicle.

"Let's follow her. Berringer will only be going home, unless they've decided on her place."

Doc shrugged. "It might be nice to know where she lives. It'll give us one more way we can hurt this guy if we need to."

Seth jumped in his van and brought it to life. He pulled out and turned left. Kerri turned right.

"What a loser!"

"Shut up. Let's see where the girl lives anyway." Doc started the car and waited until Kerri's taillights were barely visible.

Slowly, the BMW purred up the street, silently stalking the unsuspecting figure in the light blue Taurus.

CHAPTER
12

THE next morning Kerri awoke with a familiar burden to pray for Seth Berringer. She decided it was time to share the load and called Angie Blackstock, a friend she'd known since high school.

"Hi, Angie."

"Kerri!"

"You've been makin' yourself scarce. Out on the ol' campaign trail for your father again?"

She laughed. "Some. Gayle and I are the 'front men' these days. Dad says he wants people to see the family."

"Here's my trophy case," Kerri said in as deep a voice as she could muster.

"That's it!"

"Maybe you and Wayne, Jr., should square off in a debate for your fathers. But the thing is, Wayne wouldn't have a chance!"

"Girl, you're terrible!"

Kerri twisted her lips into a pout. "Yeah, I am."

"Are you going to the women's retreat?"

"I have to work. I'd give anything to hear Barbara Johnson though. She's a stitch."

"I guess I'll just have to room with Mary, or maybe Karen Bauer." She paused. "So, what's up?"

"I wanted to tell you about a friend and ask you to pray."

Kerri's redheaded friend grabbed a pen. "I'm all ears."

"It's one of the doctors at the hospital—Seth Berringer."

"Uh-oh. Another doctor pestering you for dates?"

"Not at all."

"Then you want him to ask you for dates—"

"Angie, quit interrupting! This isn't about dating. This is a real spiritual war thing. I can't share everything he's told me, but believe me, he's under the Holy Spirit's conviction if I've ever seen it. He's been asking the right questions, and he wants to work everything out for himself, but he's not ready to surrender—not yet."

"OK. What should I ask God to do?"

Kerri was used to this type of question. They both wanted their requests to be pointed and on target.

"His eyes need to be opened to the truth. He has a head knowledge of the Gospel but no heart experience. Pray that he will be strong enough to admit his error."

"His error?"

"Right. I can't be more specific—not yet."

"What else?"

Kerri shrugged. "I guess that's it."

"No, it's not." Angie shook her auburn hair. "I know this guy. I saw him when I had appendicitis last fall. If your heart doesn't melt around this one, well . . ."

"Angie!"

"Kerri!"

Kerri sighed. "All right, all right—pray for me too. My heart does a nosedive every time I look into his eyes."

"Atta girl. I'll hold you to it."

"Thanks. Let me know how the retreat goes."

"Sure. See ya."

"Bye." Kerri hung up the phone. *Good ol' Blackstock. She always hits the nail on the head, doesn't she?*

◆　◆　◆

For the next three days Seth Berringer sweated the inevitable. By Friday morning, he knew he needed to fess up to his ill deeds before the law. He felt better after getting the story out in the open with Kerri, but he knew deep inside that continuing to cover the affair up wasn't going to cut it with his own conscience. Even if the police figured out that Lisa was dead before the hit-and-run, they'd still be in the dark. Nonetheless, he picked apart the daily paper every morning looking for evidence that the authorities had a clue. Either they didn't or they just weren't saying. Either way, Seth had deceived them, and he knew he couldn't walk in a lie forever.

He worried about public opinion, he worried about Coast Care, and he worried about what his hospital comrades would think. In the end, the irony struck him. Coast Care would likely fire him for confessing to the very thing he'd done to save his stupid job in the first place! Now he was willing to do just about anything to restore his peace of mind and integrity.

Seth called ahead to the sheriff's office. He could see him at 2. The sheriff had an important luncheon first. In truth, he was eating greasy shrimp fritters at Lanny's Grill.

That afternoon as Seth climbed the concrete steps in front of the sheriff's department, he was sweating in spite of the cool air. He opened the door and followed a sign to the end of the hall. He stepped up to a counter, cleared his throat, and introduced himself to the young woman sitting behind the desk. "Uh, hi. I'm here to see the sheriff. I have an appointment."

"Dr. Berringer?" The woman smiled.

"Yes."

"You can have a seat on the bench. I'll tell Mr. Boatwright you're here." She poured a mug of coffee and knocked on a large wooden door behind her, opening the door a few inches. "The doctor's here."

Something was mumbled from behind the door that Seth couldn't hear. The young lady immediately disappeared into the office with the coffee.

After a few minutes she reappeared. "Mr. Boatwright will see you now." She lifted a countertop barrier. "This way."

"Thank you."

He followed her into an office suited for a man the generous size of Sheriff Boatwright.

The sheriff extended his plump palm and flashed a political grin. "Afternoon, Dr. Berringer. What brings you by? Has the county medical society decided to endorse my campaign?" He snorted at his own comment. "Have a seat." He pointed to a plush chair in front of an expansive desk. "Coffee?"

Seth shook his head. The last thing he needed was more caffeine.

"Donut?" The sheriff held up a half-empty box of glazed donuts.

"No, thanks."

The sheriff sat down. "What was it you wanted to see me about?"

"I'm here to talk about Lisa Dale." His heart wasn't nearly as calm as his words.

"The hit-and-run victim?"

"The so-called hit-and-run victim," Seth replied.

The sheriff raised his eyebrows.

Seth went on, "I guess you've seen the autopsy report."

Boatwright nodded and leaned forward, his elbows planted on the desk.

"I'm your hit-and-run driver, but . . . well, I have some explaining to do."

◆ ◆ ◆

Doc looked at his watch nervously. "I don't like the looks of this. He's been in there for thirty minutes. It's pretty obvious he's not just picking up a new city sticker for his car or something."

"He's a loose end." Bill cursed. "He knows something, all right. He knows how Lisa Dale died, and now he's talking to the sheriff's department."

"Maybe he's just worried that they know about his little cover-up."

Bill stroked his hair. "Hmmm. Could be they asked him to come in—to question him or something."

Doc nodded. "If he thinks his little secret is out, maybe he'll step into the open and reveal why he's covering for us."

The older man chuckled to himself. "Maybe the young doctor just has a secret fetish for dead women. I read about—"

"Shut up!" Doc flexed his jaw. "You're a sick man." He sighed. "Let me just remind you of the stakes, so you can focus your mind on the facts. Number 1, this guy is no dummy. He's a med school grad. Number 2, he alters the death of Lisa Dale so it looks like a hit-and-run. Number 3, he knows about the baby. He was at the autopsy, remember? And number 4, the baby is missing! All of that spells trouble with a capital T for Mr. Davis, and for you and me for that matter!"

"Ease up, Doc. I know all that. But I'd say our boy is either afraid that the sheriff has him figured out or that they're getting close. Why else would he be in there talking to them?"

Doc tapped the steering wheel with his thumb. "We'd better protect ourselves here. We need something to throw the suspicion away from us."

"What are you thinking? No one suspects us of anything."

"Not yet, at least as far as we know. But remember, the sheriff saw us at the motel on the night of the girl's death. That woman at the desk must have called him about the noise, remember? So, if the law figures out that the girl died from something other than a hit-and-run, we become suspects again, don't we?"

"But if they figure out that Berringer disguised the death scene to throw them off . . ."

"Then they'd suspect him of committing the crime in the first place."

"Of course." Bill nodded.

Doc chuckled to himself as he cracked the knuckles of his right hand. "Do we still have the girl's bloody shoe?"

Bill broke into an awkward grin. "I like what you're thinking."

Doc nodded. "We have a little evidence to plant."

◆ ◆ ◆

Lou Ellen Boatwright snapped shut the compact mirror she was staring into when the front doorbell sounded. She pushed up her large, gold-rimmed glasses and looked over the counter at a younger woman who looked like she ascribed to the same cosmetic theory as Lou Ellen: More is definitely better. Unfortunately, the effect had been long lost for Lou Ellen. For the younger woman, it made her appear nearly plastic, like a fragile china doll with rosy cheeks and hair that couldn't move under any circumstance.

"Hi, love." Lou Ellen smacked her gum. "Problem?"

"The furnace in number 14 isn't working. I'm wearing everything I own, and I'm still freezing."

"I called Glen over an hour ago. He's not been by?"

"No one's been by that had any interest in that furnace, Lou." She primped her hair. "Course, I can't blame anyone for that."

Lou Ellen ignored the comment. "I can move you to a different room."

The woman shrugged. "Gotta do something. I'll freeze to death if I stay in there." She looked around the lobby and eyed a plush chair. "Maybe I'll just stay here until Glen comes."

Lou really didn't want her decorating the lobby. Some things were easier tolerated if you didn't make them too obvious. "I'll put you in 211. Up the stairs on the right."

"Come on, Lou! I've got a bad back. Don't make me climb the stairs," the woman pouted. "Give me number 12. It's empty. No one's been in there for days!"

The older woman put her hands on her hips. "It's 211 or stay where you are. No one's going to use room 12."

"Why not?" She stared at Lou Ellen. "You're not savin' that one for—"

"I'm not savin' it for anyone!" She backed up and sat down. She opened her compact mirror and continued, "That room's bad news, that's all. Remember the hit-and-run girl?"

She shrugged. "Sure."

"She rented that room on the night she died." Lou pushed her lips into a pucker and applied a new coat of lip gloss. "I won't rent it to anyone, not until I can get the bad air out."

"Bad air?"

"It's cursed, OK? I wanted to get the priest down to bless it, but I opened my mouth in front of Wayne, and he nixed that idea. He don't want anyone findin' out she was at my place. He thinks that would look bad for him."

"Come on, Lou! Everyone knows about this place."

"Yeah, but no one's ever died here before. We're just a quiet little town secret. Nobody cares. Nobody gets hurt."

"She didn't die here, Lou. She was struck by a car. I read it in the paper."

"Something bothers me about that, Tracy. I even called Wayne about it that evening. I heard the girl screamin' in pain, and I asked him to check it out." She shook her head. "Ever since, I can't help thinkin' that I could have saved her life somehow. I keep thinkin' that the men who were with her that night had something to do with her dying."

Tracy pulled a thin gown across her shoulders. "I wouldn't torture myself about it. I'll take my chances with room 12, as long as the heater works." She held out her hand, expecting a key.

Lou shook her dyed hair. "No way. It's 211 or stay where you're at."

Tracy snorted. "Give me 211." She took the key and studied Lou Ellen for a moment. "Where do you buy your lip gloss?"

◆ ◆ ◆

Deputies Rick Zander and Todd Pheiffer watched across the one-way mirror as Seth made his detailed confession to the sheriff and a detective.

"Can you believe this guy?" Todd scoffed quietly. "Who does he think he's foolin'?" He caught Zander's eyes. "No one would be so stupid as to run over a dead body."

Zander's gut told him otherwise. For some reason, he found himself believing Berringer's story. He shrugged. "He was desperate. Afraid." He smiled. "And drunk." He folded his hands across his chest. "I seem to remember a certain intoxicated deputy at a Christmas party coming on to the sheriff's former wife—"

Todd shot him a look that said, *No more!* He diverted his eyes and huffed, "Zander two points, Pheiffer zero." He watched Seth from across the glass. "I don't know."

Zander stopped smiling. "I think he's tellin' the truth. He'd never make the same mistake sober."

"Come on, Rick. Even a drunk doctor would know he couldn't get away with fooling the medical examiner."

"I'm not so sure. My cousin's in family practice, and he doesn't have a clue about these things. They don't get any training in pathology, Todd." He paused. "And certainly none in forensics." He sighed. "The way I read this guy is that he's smart in his own little area, but outside that, he seems pretty naive."

Todd started to protest, but Zander continued quietly with his assessment.

"Besides, his going to visit the pathologist to make sure he found out the truth about the way the girl died goes along with his not knowing if the pathologist would be able to uncover the truth at all." He nodded his head at Seth across the mirror. "He just didn't know how much the pathologist could tell."

Todd shrugged and stood up. "It looks like our doctor is done spillin' his guts."

◆ ◆ ◆

"Is that it?" Detective Trainum looked at Seth.

"That's it. The whole story."

The sheriff reached over and snapped off the tape recorder. "Send for Deputy Zander."

Sheriff Boatwright looked at Seth, who was slumped forward with his arms resting on the table. "You're in a heap of trouble, son." He looked up when the deputy entered. "Ask Ms. Annie to give you a copy of the medical examiner's report on Lisa Dale and bring it to me. She'll know where it is."

The muscular deputy had short, blond hair and the constitution of a Doberman—loyal and fierce. "Yes, sir."

He scurried down the hall and returned in short order with the papers.

Boatwright snatched the documents and scanned them. "Hmmph. Just as I remembered." He cast a glance at Seth, who remained seated and quiet. He snapped his head to the left, pointing to the door with his forehead. The detective stood and walked to the door. "Stay with him," he snapped at Zander.

"Yes, sir."

The sheriff pulled the detective out of ear's reach of the room. "This guy's looney. None of what he says can be validated by this report." He slapped the paper with the back of his hand. "It's all just as I remembered it. She died from a crushed pelvis sustained in a pedestrian accident." He read further. "It even describes the girl's uterus. There is no mention of a baby or a spike driven through the uterus." He rolled his eyes. "The guy's nuts."

"What should we do?"

"I can't let him walk. This case already has the public eye. They want this case solved and solved fast. This is a chance for the department to shine." He thought the situation over. "He confessed to the hit-and-run. My hunch is that the whole experience just sent him over the edge. I can't arrest him without more evidence, but I can't just let a confessed criminal back out on the street either." He looked around and lowered his voice. "Especially now, when every move is being graded." He shrugged. "Besides, it's not safe letting this lunatic go free. There's no tellin' who he might run down next."

"So what's the plan?"

"Take Zander and Dr. Berringer to a holding room. We can legally detain him for two hours while I take my case to the magistrate."

"And?"

"I'll tell the judge about the doctor's confession, and I'll show him the medical examiner's report. That ought to be enough to convince him to order a three-day hospital psychiatric evaluation. If the doctors say he's crazy, at least he'll be off the streets. If they say he's OK, then maybe I'll arrest him for the hit-and-run."

"But he says he intentionally ran the girl over. If he really did, and the examiner's report says she died from the injuries, we can get him for something a lot worse than hit-and-run."

"I'll say. Either way, he's in real trouble." Boatwright looked back at the door. "It's too bad in a way. I've heard he was a good doctor. He even took care of Wayne, Jr., a time or two." He shook his head. "Pity to see him this way."

The detective nodded.

"Anyway, first things first. I'll go get my orders from the magistrate for the three-day hospital eval."

"Shouldn't we take him home to get some clothes or something?"

The sheriff shook his head. "Send a deputy to get what he wants. I don't want the smart doctor to slip out of our hands."

The sheriff lumbered off in the direction of the magistrate's office. Trainum turned to the door and wondered how the doctor was going to take the news.

CHAPTER
13

KEVIN Schwab was not enjoying his chairman's barrage of angry words. With the door to the plush office closed, at least no one else heard the fiery rebuke.

"Why didn't you tell me about this before? You have jeopardized the reputation of the N.I.H.!"

"I didn't think it was that important. They inferred that they only wanted to do confirmatory studies and that any new results could be funneled through our lab, as if we did the work ourselves."

"Did he actually say the grant wouldn't go through unless we gave him the cells?"

"Not exactly. He just inferred—"

Arnold Mayer interrupted and wiped his balding forehead with a hand-kerchief. "The Vatican will be furious."

"We don't have to tell them."

"But you yourself said that Dr. Donovan refuses to cooperate!" Dr. Mayer shook his head. "And even if Donovan destroys the tissue, how do we know they haven't been successful with other surrogates?"

"They don't have enough material, not from what I let them have. It's a miracle they've gotten this far."

"A miracle?" The chairman looked at Kevin sharply. "I thought a miracle was something phenomenally good." He shook his head. "You'd better see to it that Donovan changes his mind!"

Kevin sighed. "Once I convinced him of what he held, his perspective changed dramatically. All of a sudden he seemed determined to capitalize on the situation."

"Do you know what this will do? The Vatican will deplore this as a blatant attack on the Church. Ethicists everywhere will be appalled. We'll be under a microscope of scrutiny with every project we conduct for the next decade. If this research is carried to completion, half the Christian world will be in an uproar."

"Come on, the situation's bad, but—"

"But nothing! The very concept of Jesus' divinity will be challenged, which will cause a furor."

"You're an expert on theology now?"

Dr. Mayer pointed his index finger at the younger biologist. "You watch it, Kevin. If you weren't the media's favorite son, you'd be out on the street. As it is, you'd better make every effort to contain this situation before anyone else finds out what's going on. And don't make any more deals on the side just to secure grant money!"

Kevin looked at the floor. "Yes, sir." After a few moments he looked up. "We could tell the Vatican that some of the cells were stolen."

"No good, Kevin. We'd still come across as irresponsible. And what will happen if word of Davis's work hits the streets? He'll tell the world exactly where he got his material."

Kevin stood up and reached for the door.

"Where are you going?"

"To talk to Eric Donovan again."

◆ ◆ ◆

Seth backed into the corner of the holding room. The sheriff seemed even larger, his presence completely overshadowing the younger Berringer. "You can't do this to me! I'm a physician! I'm not crazy!"

Boatwright waved the paper in the air. "Just watch me, doc. This paper signed by the magistrate gives us the authority to confine you for evaluation!"

Berringer held up his hands. "Slow down. At least you owe me an explanation. I know what I did wasn't entirely rational, but—"

"Son," the grinning sheriff interrupted, "you're delusional. We can't substantiate anything you've said. Your facts are so distorted, you'd think the moon is made out of cheese!"

"Wait a minute! You asked for the medical examiner's report. It's all there! That will straighten all of this out."

"You're really fixated on this thing, aren't you?" Boatwright still had the examiner's report under his arm. "The whole story is right here, Dr. Berringer," he said, tapping the paper with his hand. "The problem is, it doesn't agree with your little fantasy at all!" He smiled. "In fact, if I didn't think you were crazy, I'd say you made all of this up to cover up something a whole lot more serious!"

Seth lunged for the report, only to have the sheriff pull it back with surprising agility. Two deputies forced Seth against a table, smashing his nose against the unforgiving surface.

"Show it to me," he seethed. "I want to see the report!"

The sheriff stepped away from him. "You're insane, Berringer." He shook his head, as if disgusted by the pitiful sight.

"You're wrong. I don't know what that report says, but I know what I saw." Seth's words were muffled against the table.

"Let him up."

The lawmen responded, though Deputy Zander kept a tight squeeze on Seth's left arm.

"Now, Dr. Berringer, you have a choice," the sheriff explained tensely. "You can go with us peaceably, or you can go in cuffs. It's your choice—but any funny stuff, and I decide."

Seth could see that his anger was getting him nowhere. He decided to plead instead. "Look, sheriff, you have to believe me. I'm not crazy. I know what I'm talking about." He dabbed the end of his nose with his sleeve and looked down. Blood!

The sheriff's patience was wearing thin. "The psych doctor will be the judge of that. It's only a three-day evaluation. After that, they'll decide whether you're fit for discharge or if we pursue a longer commitment." He was practically breathing steam. "Now, handcuffs or not?"

"No cuffs . . . please."

Boatwright looked at Zander. "Take his van home, and leave it in the driveway." He looked at the other deputy. "You're in charge of the patient," he said, with a sidelong glance at Seth. "Take Richardson with you. Make sure it's done by the book."

"You've got the situation all wrong," Seth cried. "It's not what you're thinking at all."

The sheriff's eyes were hard as steel. "Let's get it done."

"Don't I get to talk to an attorney or anything?"

"We talked about that earlier, before your statement, remember? You didn't see any need for it then, and you're not being arrested. This is a mental evaluation, nothing more. You don't need a lawyer for that." He turned to the deputies. "Take him."

Seth thought he was going to be sick. His mouth tasted metallic. The deputies nudged him toward the door. As he stumbled forward, he silently cursed his compulsion to confess.

At least he knew the psychiatrists at Chesapeake General. They should be able to get him out of this—he hoped.

◆　◆　◆

"Yes, I'm sure it was him! They led him away between two deputies and put him in the back of a police cruiser." Doc rubbed the back of his short, muscular neck. "A third officer carried a little suitcase. Wherever they're taking him, it's going to be for a few days at least."

"Could you follow them?" Wilson Davis inquired.

"Too risky. We did manage to follow another officer who brought the doctor's van back to his house."

"This doesn't look good for us," Davis responded, toying with the phone cord. "I'm afraid he's telling the law what he knows." He let out a disgusted sigh. "I've been expecting him to contact me, asking to be compensated for his silence. Maybe he's having second thoughts."

They paused for a moment before Doc added, "You know, Mr. Davis, Bill and I were talking . . . You don't suppose the girl could've been alive when he found her, and she told him something, do you? Maybe he's some kind of right-wing fundamentalist who wants to block the experiment or something."

"No. I've thought about that myself, but there are too many things against it. First, the autopsy sounds as if she was dead for a while. And besides, the guy's a doctor. If he found her alive, he would have taken her to the hospital."

"That's just what I was sayin' to Bill," Doc lied. "And besides, he threw her into that van like a sack of potatoes or something. That's why we figured she was dead."

"Besides, the girl didn't know enough to tell. Berringer couldn't have found out anything worthwhile from the girl even if she was alive."

"Maybe she had something on her body that alerted him—a note or something. Maybe some kind of information that along with the autopsy findings—"

"Ridiculous! You're reaching the edge, Doc."

Doc sighed. "Yeah, I guess I am."

"I think it's more likely we've had an internal leak. Maybe one of the scientists knew Surrogate Two would return to Deer Falls and asked Berringer to retrieve the tissue."

Doc cursed. "I hadn't thought of that."

"I may need you back here sooner than expected—to help find the leak." Davis squinted. He was nauseated and needed to concentrate on taking slow breaths to allow the feeling to pass. After a few moments he closed his eyes and continued, his words quiet but steady. "First concentrate on the pathologist. Find the tissue if it's still available. It sounds as if Berringer is going to be out of our hair for a while anyway."

◆ ◆ ◆

Kerri listened to the phone ring. Five . . . six . . . seven . . . eight. She hung up the phone and sighed.

She'd only really known Seth for a short while, but they'd shared so much. She'd thought he'd call her by now. Maybe he was confused, or even threatened by how much he'd told her. Maybe he thought she hated him now. *Lord, please don't let him think that!*

Kerri had tried to reach Seth every day since they'd talked in the park. She didn't want to come on too strong, but she did care about him, and she wanted him to know he could still count on her friendship. Her frustration grew each time she failed to find him at home. Maybe he was just pouring himself into work, although she thought he'd mentioned having this afternoon off.

She picked up the phone-book and looked up his office number. She dialed and waited.

"Deer Falls Family Medicine Clinic. May I help you?"

"I would like to speak to Dr. Berringer please."

"Dr. Berringer is out. Is this an emergency?"

"No. It's more of a private concern. I—"

"All of his patients are being covered by Dr. Sampson at Chesapeake Family Practice. If your concern can wait, I can make an appointment for Dr. Berringer late next week."

"No, I'm not a patient. I'm a friend. I just wanted to talk with Seth . . . uh, Dr. Berringer."

Seth? The attractive, young receptionist frowned. She called him Seth? Just who was this gal? "Dr. Berringer took the day off. Perhaps you can call him at home."

"I struck out there, but I'll try again later. Thank you."

She had his unlisted home number? "OK, Ms. . . ?" Getting no response, she added, "May I tell him who called?"

Kerri shrugged. "Sure. Tell him Kerri called. I'll reach him later."

"I'll leave the message." The nurse/receptionist put the phone down. In her mind she mimicked the soft, feminine voice she'd just heard, jealous of this woman she didn't even know.

On the other end, Kerri clicked off her cordless phone. She considered driving by Seth's house to see if his van was there. Maybe he was outside doing yardwork.

She felt a sudden apprehension. *Is Seth OK, Lord?*

She picked up her car keys. *Father, whatever Seth is facing, give him courage.*

◆ ◆ ◆

"Hey, what are you guys doing? The hospital's that way!" Seth looked back at Chesapeake General Hospital as it receded from view.

"We're not taking you there. The state doctors handle the three-day evals." The deputy chuckled.

"State doctors?"

"They'll take good care of you, doc." The lawman glanced in the rearview mirror at a pale Seth Berringer. "Besides, the magistrate's order mandates it. He didn't think your own fellow staffers at C.G.H. could give you an objective exam. You're going to Evergreen State."

"The state mental hospital? You've got to be kidding!"

Seth looked helplessly at the car door. He had a distinct desire to jump out, which he recognized as clearly irrational. Besides, a quick inspection revealed that the doors could only be opened from the outside.

His heart sank as the reality of the situation continued to dawn. The state mental institution was the home of mentally disturbed criminals!

Just then he saw a light blue Taurus approaching from the opposite direction. He recognized it instantly. He waved frantically and pounded on the window. "Kerri!"

The deputies noticed the attractive woman as well. She, however, passed on by, oblivious to the admiration of the officers or the anguish of her friend.

Seth continued to wave until Kerri was nearly out of view. He wasn't sure what he would have done even if she'd noticed him. Maybe he just wanted her to know where he was.

"Settle down, cowboy. That girl's too hot for you." The deputies enjoyed a laugh.

Seth Berringer slumped, defeated. The silence enveloped him as they approached the city limits. For a moment he thought he might be physically sick. He sighed and looked out the window, hoping to quiet the nausea. The cruiser slowed slightly to allow the car in front of them to turn into a gas station. Jake's Exxon!

It was the first time Seth had seen it since the night of Lisa Dale's death. The memory propelled his stomach into a knot. He leaned forward and emptied his lunch onto a plastic floor-mat.

The deputy cursed as the odor and sound of the doctor's vomiting penetrated the air.

Seth fell back against the seat. He could no longer suppress the tears. He glanced back a final time and saw the Exxon sign reduced to a red and blue blur.

If only I could erase that one night, everything would be so different. If only . . .

CHAPTER
14

ERIC! This is crazy!" Tammy Lynn walked onto the pier bordering the manicured lawn of Donovan's Red Lake resort house. "You really want to go fishing in the winter?"

"Why'd you think I brought you all the way down here?"

Tammy Lynn smiled and said nothing.

She watched Eric untie the bass boat. "I feel like I'm playing hooky or something."

He chuckled. "You're not skipping school—you're skipping work." He shrugged. "Besides, I'm the boss. I told you to come."

She rubbed her shoe against a wooden slat. "It still feels funny being down here with you—in the middle of the day and all."

"Get used to it." He untied the last rope. "Hop in. Besides, I finished the work on the Lynwood case. As long as we don't have any homicides, we're home free."

"What if someone needs you?"

"I have my pager." He turned the key, and his 150-horsepower Johnson engine revved to life. "And the cellular phone."

"What if Connie comes down?"

"Connie hates fishing." He threw up his hands. "That's part of the problem. She doesn't enjoy the things I love." He reached for her. "Like you."

She blushed and pulled away as he turned his attention to maneuvering the boat away from the dock.

"Now," he said, "will you quit asking me a thousand questions and just have a good time?"

"Just one more question?"

He suppressed a smile. "One more. Then I'll throw you to the sharks."

She stuck her nose in the air. "I know there aren't any sharks in there."

"Just ask the question."

"You said we're celebrating. What is it we're celebrating?"

Eric stared out over the lake. He shut off the engine and let the boat drift under a large overhanging oak tree, his favorite spot for bass.

"We're celebrating an opportunity," he responded. "The chance of a lifetime."

"Is that what Dr. Schwab said when he called again?"

"Not in those words exactly." He sighed. "Kevin Schwab is a research doctor—one of the best in the world, really. But he wouldn't know an opportunity to make a dollar if it bit him on the nose." He shook his head. "He's only told me enough to let me know that the Dale girl was involved in a most lucrative research project."

"She was rich?"

"Not her, exactly. But the baby she was carrying could be worth a lot of money to the one who put it there. Schwab hinted that someone would pay millions just to get it back."

"The father?"

"No. A research team." He shook his head. "The girl was a surrogate. The DNA of the baby was nothing like the mom's."

"Whose baby is it?"

Eric's eyes lit up. "Good question." He squinted in the afternoon sun, then smiled. "Hey, I only gave you permission to ask one more question."

She stuck out her tongue at him.

Eric answered the question anyway. "Schwab got real funny on me when he called back. He refused to reveal who had done the implantation. He even insisted that I destroy the fetus—and all that after he'd told me how valuable it was. I'm not sure what's gotten into him. He refused to answer any more questions, though he did say that if the researcher found out I had the tissue he wanted, he was sure he'd contact me."

"Is that your plan? Just wait to be contacted?"

"Basically, yes. I figure the man who paid to have my report altered has something to do with it."

"Are you mad at me about that?"

He shook his head. "Naah. It's probably best to leave the report as is. It might be prudent to let everyone think the girl died from a hit-and-run.

If I'm right and the same man who talked to you and me about the autopsy is the man who wants the tissue for his research, he'll be back."

"Eric . . ." she responded, biting her lower lip.

He looked up from his tackle box.

"Do you think we're in danger? I mean, think about how Lisa Dale died. If those guys did that to her—" Her voice trailed off.

"We need to protect ourselves from discovery. But are we at risk?" He shrugged, thought a bit more, then nodded. "Maybe so. It could be. We'll just have to be careful."

Tammy Lynn shivered. "I have some vacation coming. Now that I'm in my own apartment, I could use the time to do some decorating."

Eric nodded resolutely. "Maybe it would be best if you stayed out of the office for a while." He knew Connie would like that. He could invite her down to do transcriptions, just like old times.

"My place isn't far away."

Eric nodded his head and cast his line into the water.

◆ ◆ ◆

Kerri's level of alarm soared as she pulled up to the curb in front of Seth's house. In the driveway sat a police car with one officer in it. A second lawman was stepping from Seth's van.

She practically stumbled across the yard. "Excuse me, officer. Is anything wrong? Where's Se—, uh, Dr. Berringer? I've been trying to reach him."

Rick Zander looked up. "Hi, Ms.—" He paused. "I don't believe I caught your name."

"Kerri Barber. Is Dr. Berringer all right?"

The deputies, now standing next to each other, cast sideward glances.

"He's safe, if that's what you mean," Zander offered.

The second deputy silenced a snicker. "You can tell her. It will be public knowledge as soon as Bryson does his media report anyway."

"Dr. Berringer had to take a little vacation."

This time the second officer coughed to cover his laugh. "If you call being committed to the state funny farm a vacation."

Kerri looked confused. "What are you talking about?"

Rick Zander looked at his fellow deputy and shrugged. "Look, ma'am, Dr. Berringer showed up at the station this afternoon and admitted to being the driver in the recent hit-and-run. But the word at the station is that he concocted such a wild story, the sheriff had him sent down to the state mental institution for an evaluation." He shook his head. "That's all I know."

"Mental institution!" Kerri practically screamed. "He's not crazy!"

"Ma'am, I don't make the rules. All I know is that when the sheriff told the magistrate what he knew, they both agreed that the safest place for Dr. Berringer right now is under constant surveillance."

Kerri sighed. Great! He'd finally done the right thing, and they thought he was crazy!

The deputies excused themselves and drove off, leaving a bewildered Kerri Barber standing in the yard. She walked over to the front steps and sat down.

What was it about that sheriff? Certainly Seth had told him the same story he'd told her. She knew what Seth had done wasn't exactly rational, but it wasn't grounds for a forced psychiatric admission. *Lord, what is going on? Did he do this because of me?* Kerri hung her head in sorrow. She noticed the *Deer Falls Gazette* bundled tightly beside her. What had that deputy said? That it would be public knowledge as soon as some guy did his media report? *Please, Lord, protect Seth from evil!*

◆ ◆ ◆

The silver BMW slipped past Dr. Berringer's house without being noticed. The two men looked carefully at the van and its location in relation to the house and peered closely at the pretty brunette on the steps. Her head was bowed, and she didn't seem to detect their passing.

"That's the girl he was with the other night," whispered Doc. "See? That's her car by the curb."

"She's upset about something. Or sick."

"It's too early for a hangover."

"This must have something to do with her conversation with those two officers. Boy, I wish I could've heard what they said," Bill stated. "Let's circle around again. We should be able to see the girl's car from across the back lot. If she leaves, we can follow her. Maybe she'll lead us to wherever the doctor's being held."

Doc nodded and turned right at the first intersecting side street. They came up the next road and parked so they could see the light blue Taurus but not the front steps or Kerri.

They waited for five minutes, then watched as Kerri returned to her car and turned around in the driveway.

"She's heading the wrong way for her apartment."

"Come on, sweet thing, lead us to the doctor."

Annoyed at Doc's driving, Bill complained, "Don't let her get too far ahead."

"I can see her fine."

"She's turning at the light!"

"Relax. I can see her." Doc clenched his jaw.

After a few minutes of light traffic, Bill threw his hands in the air. "She's going to the sheriff's department. Unbelievable!"

"What is it with these two? First the doctor, now the girl," Doc huffed. "Five to ten, she stays in an hour and then is led away by the deputies."

"You're wrong this time. I'll bet she's going in to find out about the doctor."

Doc nodded. "Then she might lead us to him yet."

Bill looked around. "I'm hungry."

"You're always hungry."

"Can we go down to Lanny's?"

"We might miss the girl."

Bill cursed and rolled down his window. He pointed to the left, across from the brick office. "Pull in over there. We'll have a good view of the front door and enjoy the shade from the billboard."

They settled in after watching Kerri ascend the front steps.

Doc tapped out a tune heard only by himself. "At least we know where Berringer's van is."

"So?"

"You'll see. I have some plans for the girl's shoe."

Bill slouched down in his seat and pulled on the brim of his baseball cap. "I'm hungry."

"Of course."

"Shut up and watch the front steps. I don't want to miss the girl."

Doc smiled. "I don't want to miss her either."

◆   ◆   ◆

Kerri leaned over the counter and stared at the young woman at the desk. "I need to talk to Sheriff Boatwright."

"I'm sorry, ma'am, but if you don't have an appointment, I'll have to schedule you for next week." She barely smiled as she turned her attention to the appointment book in front of her.

"It's kind of an emergency. I've talked to him before, but I really need to see him today. Would you at least give him my name and ask him if he'll speak to me? You can tell him it's about Lisa Dale."

The receptionist sighed. "Your name, ma'am?"

"Kerri Barber. I'm the nurse he talked to in the E.R."

The secretary went to the coffeepot and filled a mug, adding three packets of sugar and a small container of creamer. She carried the cup over to the large, wooden door behind her desk and knocked rapidly. She opened the door a few inches and spoke quietly so Kerri couldn't hear. She then disappeared with the java and closed the door.

After five long minutes, she reappeared without the coffee. "He'll see you now."

The receptionist made no move to let Kerri through the counter barrier. Kerri spotted a hinge in the center section. She hoped Little Miss Hospitality hadn't treated the handsome doctor this way.

Kerri reached for the countertop just as the sheriff's door swung open. "Hello, Ms. Barber. Pleasure to see you again so soon." He extended his hand.

She took it and wasted little time on a greeting before going on. "Hello, sheriff. I'm here to talk to you about Dr. Seth Berringer."

The sheriff pulled back his meaty hand and raised his eyebrows. "I thought you came to talk about Lisa Dale." He cast a glance at the receptionist, who only shrugged.

"Lisa and Seth Berringer are connected now, aren't they?"

The sheriff exhaled loudly. "Just what is your business here, ma'am?"

"I want to know what's been done to Seth Berringer!"

A graying couple opened the door to the sheriff's reception area and walked to a position just behind Kerri.

The sheriff lifted the hinged countertop to allow his visitor to enter. "Perhaps you'd like to come into my office where we can talk *privately*."

Kerri followed without speaking.

"Now, Ms. Barber," the sheriff began, "you seem to know certain facts about this case, such as a connection between Dr. Berringer and Lisa Dale. Would you care to elaborate further?"

"I believe you know as much as I do. What I'm interested in is, what are you doing about it?"

"He told you his story then?"

"Yes. And although I didn't exactly tell him to confess it to you, he knew I would be supportive of his coming forward."

The sheriff looked at her and squinted his eyes, then walked around and plopped into his padded desk chair.

Kerri flinched. She was amazed the chair didn't collapse.

"Have a seat." He pointed to a hard chair across from his desk. "Let me get this straight . . . He told you that he ran down Lisa Dale on purpose, and you didn't report it?" He squinted. "You could be in some trouble yourself, you know?"

Kerri sat up straight. This was not the response she'd anticipated. "Wait a minute, sheriff. Seth Berringer didn't kill Lisa Dale. He found her dead body and made it look like a hit-and-run!"

"He's sold you on his story, has he? He's pretty slick, this arrogant, handsome—"

"He's not arrogant!" Kerri reddened, then, surprised at her intense reaction, tried to compose herself.

"Regardless of what you think of him, I had no choice but to seek a three-day psychiatric commitment for an evaluation of his sanity."

Kerri covered her mouth in shock. A three-day psychiatric commitment? Seth?

She attempted to keep her voice calm. "He's clearly depressed, but that's because of the extreme remorse he feels about misleading you. It doesn't take a psychiatrist to figure that out, does it? Certainly a man of your training can properly assess his condition, can't you?"

The sheriff nodded proudly. "The problem I had in this case is, none of the facts match up. The medical examiner's findings and Dr. Berringer's confession are at such odds with each other that—"

"Excuse me, sheriff, but if I may be so bold—"

"I doubt if I could stop you," he chuckled.

Kerri bit her lower lip and continued, "I think the facts fit together perfectly, including the postcard from Lisa Dale. She stated that someone wanted her baby. Then she shows up dead, and the medical examiner finds that she died because of some sort of primitive abortion gone awry or some other sick torture. Seth Berringer had nothing to do with all that." She forced herself to lean back in her chair.

"Hmmm. What you say is interesting, but unfortunately it isn't grounded in cold, hard fact. You have to understand that what Dr. Berringer told you about the autopsy and what was actually found are two entirely different things. In fact, the medical examiner's report confirms that she died from hemorrhaging associated with injuries sustained in the pedestrian accident."

"What!" Kerri's hand flew to her open mouth.

The sheriff nodded. "In fact, the way I'd put it—and please understand this is my professional opinion early in this investigation—Dr. Berringer's story is the product of a traumatized mind. You're a nurse—you've seen this before, I'm sure." He nodded at Kerri. "I'll go as far as to say that Berringer probably did hit the girl—whether he meant to or not has yet to be determined. Anyway, he hits her and then is so mentally traumatized by the event that he can't face what he's done. So a complicated defense mechanism clicks in, and he makes up a story so he won't have to take responsibility for killing poor Lisa Dale. He fesses up to a less serious offense, at least in his eyes, so he doesn't feel guilty anymore for killing her."

He leaned back, obviously impressed with his own ability to probe the psyche of the criminal mind. "The interesting thing about cases like this is, the defense mechanism is so strong that the person, in this case Dr. Seth Berringer, loses his grip on reality. I think he truly believes the story he told to me, and obviously to you." He nodded and smiled. "But I had the added information at hand that disproved his confession—namely, the medical examiner's report. You, of course, did not have that and thus were sadly taken in."

She shook her head. "But what about the postcard? What about the pregnancy?"

"As far as the postcard goes, the girl was obviously distraught. As I recall, she wasn't even sure she was pregnant. And as truth will have it, the medical examiner's report confirms that there was no pregnancy."

"And you're sure the report is correct?"

"Dr. Donovan has been a chief medical examiner in this state for fifteen years. I put great stock in what he says."

"Shouldn't you call him to confirm it?"

"I suppose I could do that. Wouldn't hurt, though I see no need for it."

Kerri sighed. Was the sheriff possibly right? Poor Seth! Had she been taken in by his good looks?

"Where did you take Seth?"

"The magistrate insisted we take him away from his own hospital for the evaluation. He was taken to Evergreen State."

The shock must have registered on her face.

"They'll take good care of him, Ms. Barber." The sheriff paused and admired the young woman, who even in her distressed state seemed refreshingly beautiful. "Could I give you one more piece of advice?" He went on without waiting for a response. "Lose the boyfriend. You obviously deserve better."

"He's not my—" Kerri stopped in midsentence and decided to let the sheriff think whatever he wished. "Thanks," she said sarcastically as she walked out of the office.

The sheriff watched Kerri as she left. She hesitated at the exit to let Deputy Zander enter.

"Hello again, Ms. Barber." He smiled.

"Oh, Ms. Barber," the sheriff called out, "I almost forgot. We've been looking for someone to claim Lisa Dale's things. She has no family, so if her friends don't want them, we'll just take them to the Salvation Army."

"Her *things*?"

He nodded. "After the funeral we found out she had an apartment over on Third Street. There really wasn't much there. She had apparently been away for a while. Looks like she really cleaned out the place before she left. Anyway, there are a few boxes in storage if you'd like them."

Kerri nodded. "That would be nice."

The sheriff looked at the deputy. "Zander, I'm glad you're here. Take this young lady over to the storage unit and let her have the stuff we took from the Dale apartment."

"My pleasure."

The sheriff snorted.

CHAPTER
15

THE SUN stood just over the horizon as the police car carrying Seth Berringer arrived at Evergreen State Hospital.

They drove up a long asphalt lane to a five-story, brick building with narrow windows. After they parked, Seth surveyed the area. He noticed the narrow windows, probably so no one could jump.

A few maple trees lined the entry, but Seth couldn't find anything to explain how the hospital got its name. There was nothing green around there, except maybe Seth after the forced ride.

A deputy strode around the car and pulled something from the trunk before joining Seth and the other lawman. "Here," he said, handing Berringer a basketball-sized cloth bag with a single snap at the top.

Seth read the words stamped on the side of the bag: "Chesapeake Correctional Facility."

The deputy could sense his confusion. "It's your stuff. The sheriff sent me out to your place while he talked to the magistrate."

Seth took a quick peek at the bag's contents—a T-shirt, his toothbrush, deodorant, and underwear. He eyed the deputy without speaking. *You rummaged through my underwear drawer? What else did you look at?*

Seth clutched the bag and walked between the two uniformed men. He climbed the front steps, pausing momentarily to inhale the cool air before entering. The sheriff had promised it was only a three-day evaluation. When he passed the test, he'd be a free man.

He turned around and looked at the clear sky, just beginning to show the orange hint of sunset. Would they let him come outside or just lock him up?

He scanned the grounds. Other than a simple chain-link fence, he didn't see any barriers.

"Come on, doc." The deputy tugged his arm. "Let's go."

Seth resisted for a few more seconds before walking inside. His thoughts were obvious.

They passed through an outer door into a small foyer facing a second set of doors. The deputies had obviously been here before. The taller of the two men pressed a buzzer and waited.

"Hello?" the intercom crackled.

"Sheriff's department. We've got a patient for a three-day eval."

An electronic sound signaled the unlocking of the door. The trio entered and were quickly greeted by a large, chatty orderly. The heavy door shut with an ominous thud, preventing a quick exit.

"Dr. Berringer!"

Oh great, somebody here knows me. Seth looked up to see the face of Ronny Templeton, the son of his cleaning lady. "Hi, Ronny."

"Doc, what are you doing here?"

"A mistake, Ronny. Someone's made a bad mistake."

Ronny, a large African-American man in his mid-twenties, pointed at the doctor as he told the deputies, "This guy fixed my knee last fall. It was messed up bad, too."

The deputies ignored the comments.

Ronny continued, "We gotta take him to check-in." He walked on ahead through a cool hallway laid with black-and-white checkered linoleum. He lifted a massive key-ring from his belt and unlocked the appropriate door. The door had a window, but like every other window Seth had seen here so far, it was covered with chicken wire.

Once they were inside, an elderly nurse stepped forward and handed Berringer a form. "Fill out the first two sections. Skip the part about insurance. Since you're here by commandment of the magistrate, the state will be handling the bill."

"Nice to see my taxes are being used so wisely."

"Don't get smart with me, Mr. Berringer," she snapped.

Seth had just arrived, but he'd already reached a snapping point. "*Dr.* Berringer to you!"

The deputies chuckled at the exchange but quieted down when they saw the nurse's cutting stare.

"Listen, I don't care if you're mister or a doctor or the President of the United States. You're in a state hospital now, and we do things by the book."

She softened. "You may use this pen." She handed him a twenty-nine-cent Bic. She looked at Ronny, sitting comfortably on the top of a small end table. "Make sure we get the pen back. It's on the forbidden list, you know."

Seth accepted the pen and began filling out his name. He wondered what else was on Nurse By-the-Book's "forbidden list."

The deputies watched as Seth filled out the form. When he was finished, the nurse inspected it and put it in a new file.

"Ronny, escort the deputies and our new patient to the fourth-floor nurses' station."

The three men waited as Ronny unlocked the door and let them into the hallway. They walked to an old elevator, also key-controlled. Ronny inserted another key into a panel beside the elevator door.

A loud, metallic screech emanated from behind the closed door. Ronny laughed at the expression of the two deputies. "Don't you worry 'bout that noise. It's sounded like that for years. Mr. Axel says it's nothing."

The door opened, and the deputies shrugged. They nudged Seth forward.

Once inside, the orderly turned another key and commandeered the elevator to the fourth floor. When they stepped off the elevator they were greeted by a door monitor, a young man in a white coat reading a large chemistry book. The area outside the elevator was only six by eight feet and felt very confining with so many people present. The door monitor looked at the orderly. "Hi, Ronny."

Ronny glanced at Seth. "Hey, Dr. Berringer, Lenny here is going to the university. He's going to be a doctor just like you."

The college student curled his upper lip at the suggestion.

Seth said nothing.

The monitor pressed a number sequence on a keypad on the wall, and the door unlocked with a click.

Seth watched the sequence but was lost after three digits. He knew that without Ronny's key-ring he couldn't go five feet without seeing another locked door or elevator anyway.

Again the deputy nudged him forward.

Ronny chatted on. "Just down the hall now, boys. We're almost home."

This isn't home!

Once at the nurses' station, Ronny handed Ms. Gardner the new patient chart. "Dr. Berringer, this is Ms. Gardner, head nurse."

"Hello, Mr. Berringer. You'll need to sit over here while I look over the orders." She looked at the deputies. "You may go now. Thank you."

Two other nurses were doing chartwork, and a social worker was handing out cigarette rations, which were kept, like everything else, carefully under lock at the desk.

The deputies disappeared through the door with the help of the monitor.

Seth looked around. Except for Ronny, who had plopped down next to him on an old couch, he knew no one. It seemed like Ronny had been assigned to be Seth's personal guard. He didn't ask why he needed a guard at all. He just wanted to go home.

"OK, Mr. Berringer," Nurse Gardner said, looking up from the admission sheet, "everything seems to be in order. Your room is 411."

Seth stood, clutching the gray bag housing his few belongings.

"We'll need to go through that, Mr. Berringer," she snapped, reaching for the bag.

"It's just a few toiletries and some underwear."

"Just the same, we'll have to look it over. I'll bring it down to your room if it passes inspection." She smiled curtly.

She looked back at the order sheet. "He's on suicide precautions, Ronny. You'll need to take the mirror out of his room."

She looked back at Seth. "I'll need your belt. And your shoelaces," she added, looking at his feet.

"You're kidding, right?"

He could tell by her face that she wasn't.

"My belt? My pants will fall down! I've lost some weight recently and . . . You can't be serious."

"It's on the forbidden list, Mr. Berringer. All patients on suicide precautions have to be prevented from having items known to be a hanging risk."

He reluctantly handed her his belt. His khakis felt uncomfortably loose. He feared they would fall to the floor with little resistance from his hips.

"This is crazy! I'm not going to kill myself!"

Ms. Gardner held up the chart. "Doctor's orders!"

"I haven't even seen a doctor. How can someone make such an assessment without even seeing me?"

"These are standing orders, Mr. Berringer. All three-day eval patients coming from the sheriff's department are placed on suicide precautions initially. If the doctor thinks it is unnecessary, the restrictions will be lifted after his examination."

"I want to see my doctor immediately!"

"He's off-duty—it's after six o'clock, you know. He'll be here in the morning." She pointed to the shoelaces. "Those too."

"My shoes are too loose without laces," Seth pleaded. He watched an older patient lope by. "He has shoestrings. Why do I have—"

"Because he is not on suicide precautions. Mr. Landry has been here for three years, and he's never shown himself to be hostile or suicidal. Give me the laces or I'll have Ronny take them away from you."

Seth looked at Ronny, who shrugged. "I gotta do my job, doc. I'm sorry."

Seth collapsed back onto the couch and unlaced his shoes. "This is barbaric. I thought this kind of stuff was left in the Middle Ages!"

"You will not be penalized for walking around in your socks until your laces are returned."

"How nice."

The nurse ignored his sarcasm. "OK, now empty your pockets!"

Seth held out his wallet, which was quickly snatched by the nurse. "We'll keep it locked up for you."

"The only other thing I have is some change and Chapstick." He proceeded to push the items back into his front pocket.

"Ah-ah, Mr. Berringer. The change is a choking hazard. You'll need to leave that with me as well."

He surrendered the coins.

She held out her hand again.

Seth ignored it.

"I'll take the Chapstick also."

"Why—"

"Mr. Berringer, Chapstick is considered a pharmaceutical. All pharmaceuticals must be dispensed by a nurse. If you need it, you may ask for it. It will be applied for you by a professional or—only with a doctor's permission, mind you—by yourself under direct supervision by a nurse." Her tone was mechanical. She'd obviously given this spiel and fought this battle before.

"This is outrageous! I am a physician!"

"We go by the book, Mr. Berringer! If you don't settle down, the doctor's standing orders have also included a tranquilizer. Do you think that will be necessary?"

Seth sighed heavily but didn't reply.

Ronny was uncomfortable with the exchange and began chatting nervously. "You know, doc, the same thing's true at Deer Falls Elementary, where my Alisha goes. They won't let *her* have Chapstick either. Oh no, that's a drug," he said with a deep authoritative voice. He shook his head and continued his nervous commentary. "But let her get to be twelve, and the same school system that takes away her Chapstick will give her all the condoms she wants! My mama almost had a fit when she heard that. This world is upside-down, that's what she says."

Seth nodded. This place needed more Mama Templetons.

The dejected doctor delivered his lip balm to the waiting hand of Nurse Gardner.

"Take him to his room."

Seth held on to his pants with one hand and carried his shoes in the other.

As he turned to go, the nurse gave him some final instructions. "Personal hygiene time is at 6:30 A.M. You'll not be allowed to shower without an orderly until your suicide precautions are lifted." She pursed her lips and sniffed the air. "I'd suggest that you take a shower tomorrow morning for sure. Breakfast is at 7. Group therapy is at 8. Your first testing session will begin at 10. Your physician should be able to see you in the afternoon."

Seth wanted to shut his ears. *Group? From the looks of these people, I'll bet that will be a scream. Testing session? Shower with an orderly? This is what I get for being honest?*

CHAPTER
16

THE DEPUTY pushed aside several wooden crates and pointed to the the corner. "Those two boxes marked 'Dale.' There's not much there. I helped clean out the place myself."

Kerri dropped to her knees and opened the top of one of the boxes. It appeared to be a hodgepodge of kitchen items, tableware, clothing, and a few books.

Going through the stuff was going to take time. Kerri looked up at the muscular deputy. "Is it OK if I just take both boxes? If there's anything I don't want, I can take it to a shelter or something."

"Hey, that's fine with me. You heard the sheriff. We've been waiting for days for some interested party to come by. You can have it all, for what it's worth."

She tugged at the edge of the first box. "This is pretty heavy."

"I'll get it for you. Where are you parked?"

"In the side lot. I'll pull around to the front."

"OK," he said impatiently. "I'll meet you on the front steps."

◆ ◆ ◆

"Wake up, Doc. It's the girl. She's alone."

"About time." The Asian started the BMW.

They watched as Kerri pulled out of the side lot, turned to the right, and pulled to a stop again in front of the building.

"What the—"

"She's getting something out of the trunk."

"No, that cop is putting a big box in there for her."

"Two boxes. Hmmm."

"Maybe it's stuff to take to Berringer."

"Maybe," Doc huffed. "But from here?"

"Beats me. Do we have to follow her? I'm starved."

"Let's just see where she goes. Then I want to visit Berringer's place again."

They waited until she was nearly two blocks away before following her. The sparse Deer Falls traffic made getting any closer too risky.

Doc bobbed his head and thumped his thumb against the steering wheel, keeping rhythm to a tune in his head.

"Would you cut that out? You're always pounding."

Instead, Doc began to sing the song he was thinking, and the car filled with a screaming monotone. "Fallin' into the night! There's no escape from my love! Carry me to the edge—"

Bill covered his ears. "OK, OK, bang the steering wheel all you want!" He lowered his window a crack and took out a cigarette. "There's no escape from your voice is more like it," he muttered. "Go ahead and pound—just don't sing!"

Doc quieted himself but kept tapping.

They moved through the streets of Deer Falls until they were a block from Kerri's apartment. They slowed down and pulled over, then watched as the woman struggled to get the two boxes out of her trunk.

"Looks like she's not going to lead us to the doctor."

Doc opened the car door.

"Where are you going?"

"Stay put. I can't stand to see a lady struggle."

"Maybe I should help, too."

"Don't be a fool. She saw you in the hospital. You're Lisa's uncle, remember?"

Bill nodded and sighed, then sat back and watched.

Kerri looked up to see a stocky Asian man with a dark mustache walking toward her.

"May I help you, ma'am?"

Kerri smiled. "Sure."

The man easily lifted the first box into his arms. "Quite a load here."

"I'll say. It's nice of you to help."

"Where to?"

Kerri pointed to the front door of the building. "Put it on the floor inside that door. My apartment is on the right just inside."

I know, baby, I know. Aren't you going to invite me in?

She waited by the second box, resting behind her Taurus. The helpful stranger was back in a jiffy. "You moving in?"

"Oh, no. This is just some stuff from a friend."

He grabbed the second box, which was even heavier than the first. Doc kept probing. "Your boyfriend must be giving you a ton of bricks."

Kerri laughed nervously. "No, it's not like that."

This gal was pretty tight-lipped, Doc mused.

"Just put it beside the other one," Kerri instructed as she held the door opening into a small entryway. "Thanks."

"I'd be glad to take 'em in for you. That's too much of a load for a lady."

"I'll be OK." Kerri didn't move from where she stood, holding the door open so the man could leave. "Thanks again."

"No problem." He paused and looked at her for a moment. She was even prettier close up—his type of woman.

Kerri was conscious of his inspection and backed away a few feet, instinctively letting the door begin to swing closed.

The man held out his hand and caught it. He slipped past her into the yard, brushing her arm. "Have a nice day," he added, turning his attention to the sidewalk. If he had his way, he'd see her again.

◆ ◆ ◆

Eric cradled the phone against his left shoulder with his head. He wiped the sweat from his forehead and tried to ignore the dull ache he felt behind his breastbone.

"I have the bridge luncheon to plan and all those invitations to address," Connie said with exasperation. "You know I can't come down there tonight."

He knew, but he had to ask. "It's probably just as well. I can get some work done on the boat tonight, so we can spend some time together this weekend."

"You're spending the evening there? I've made dinner."

"I'm sorry, hon. I broke away from the office early and rushed here to get a line in the water before dark. I should've called."

The line was silent.

Eric continued, "I'll see how the work goes. If it gets too late, I'll just sleep here."

"Suit yourself."

Connie the ice-woman! "I'll see you tomorrow."

Connie waited for a moment, then questioned, "I called the office this afternoon. Tammy Lynn wasn't there either."

Eric flinched. "She asked me if she could have a few weeks off." He gauged his words. "She says she wants some time away from the office. I told her to take as long as she needs. She left early this afternoon."

"Oh."

"I was thinking . . . Maybe you'd like to fill in while she's gone—like the old days."

"I'll think about it."

"You wouldn't have to work full-time—maybe just do some of the transcription. The temps always have a hard time with that."

"I said I'll think about it." She was irritated at his cheery little suggestion. He was ignoring her real question—was Tammy Lynn there with him? She was too tired for a fight and too afraid to risk an emotional letdown, so she let her suspicions drop.

"I'll see you tomorrow, Connie."

"Bye, Eric."

Tammy Lynn stood at the doorway to Eric's bedroom. He looked up from where he sat on the edge of the bed.

"Are you OK?" There was alarm in her voice. She moved to his side. "Eric, you're sweating. You're as pale as a sheet."

"I'll be OK. I have a bad case of indigestion, that's all. I'll just rest here a moment. Could you see if there's some antacid in the medicine cabinet?"

She studied him for a moment before mopping his brow with the sheet from the unmade bed. "Sure, honey. You lie down. I'll find something."

"I should know better than to eat while I'm on the boat," he chuckled. Lying always gave him indigestion.

◆ ◆ ◆

"That's as tight as I can get it," Doc said angrily.

"Don't put it against anything that moves or it'll fall out."

"It's hard to see under here. Do you want to do it?"

"No."

A dog barked nearby.

Doc edged his way out from under the van. "This clunker leaks oil. You'd think a doctor could afford something better."

"Let's get out of here."

Even in the light of the moon, Bill could easily see the grease stain on Doc's forehead. "You're a mess. Let's get cleaned up so we can eat. I'm hungry."

"You're always hungry. Keep your voice down."

◆ ◆ ◆

One item at a time, Kerri spread the objects out on her living room floor—a few clothes items, a frying pan, a few pots, an old coffeemaker, several books. Lisa hadn't accumulated much in the way of earthly goods.

Kerri began sorting Lisa's things into two piles—"clothing/books" and "kitchen." She looked over the items and picked up a small cross-stitch picture of a kitten playing with a ball of yarn. The initials "L.D." in the corner indicated it had been a personal project by Lisa. Kerri held it to her chest for a moment. She would keep this. The rest was pretty much junk.

She unloaded the books from the bottom of the second box. There were a few school texts. The cover of an economics book bulged with papers. Kerri flipped open the front cover. It was mail! The deputies must have just shoved everything in there.

From the look of things, Lisa hadn't opened her mail for months. It was a wonder the Postal Service kept putting it in her box. Perhaps she'd asked her landlady to put it in her apartment for her.

The most recent letter was postmarked only three days before Lisa's death. Why hadn't Lisa opened her mail once she was back in Deer Falls? Perhaps she'd been staying somewhere else. Or maybe her killer got to her before she could get home.

Kerri turned to the last letter, a personal one with a handwritten return address in Lakeland but no name. With her curiosity pricked, Kerri opened the envelope. She felt guilty about prying into someone else's private correspondence but reasoned that since Lisa was dead, it was all right. Besides, maybe she could find a clue about her friend's last days. The sheriff sure hadn't seemed interested in searching for the truth, but Kerri was.

The letter was handwritten in blue ink with tight, small lettering. It was written on Chesapeake University stationery.

Dear Virgie,

I'm home safe and back to work at my old job at Zano's Place. The pay sure isn't what they promised me at the institute, but at least it's reliable. Let me know when you get back to the area.

I wanted to phone you, but the information operator said your line was out. Maybe you're still at the institute? I forget when your sampling date was to occur. Can you believe they rejected me? I was mad at first, but I guess it's better this way.

They've taken the ad out of the Student Center, so I suppose you must have been the best guinea pig yet.

Give me a call when you get back.

                                                    Sue

A small smiley face had been drawn next to the name "Virgie."

Virgie? Wasn't this sent to Lisa? Kerri turned the card over. It must have been some sort of nickname. What institute was Sue talking about? Evidently they both had been volunteers in some sort of research project— just like the postcard said!

She reread the note several times. It apparently contained references that Lisa would have understood but that left Kerri uninformed. "Sampling date"? "Rejected me"? From what? Kerri had to talk to this girl! Perhaps she knew what kind of research Lisa was involved in—and who was doing it and who might have killed her!

Kerri studied the return address. Without a last name, she couldn't just call Information. She'd have to go to Lakeland to find this Sue, or write and hope she'd get back to her.

Lakeland was between Deer Falls and Evergreen State Hospital. Maybe she could drive up to see Seth and ask his opinion on trying to find this girl who just might hold the clues they needed to unlock the truth about Lisa Dale. And then maybe Kerri could discern what was true and what wasn't in Seth's story as well.

O God, what is the truth? Was it possible the sheriff was right? Was Seth suffering from the trauma of the event so much that he'd lost touch with reality and was—how did the sheriff put it?—using a subconscious defense mechanism to suppress the guilt of murdering Lisa Dale?

Kerri shook her head. The sheriff's theory didn't ring true. If Seth was in denial about killing Lisa, why would he feel so guilty about altering the death scene and running over her body?

And what about the postcard Kerri had gotten from Lisa? What about Lisa's fear that someone was after her and wanted her baby? And what about the autopsy evidence indicating an abortion attempt? Or maybe the sheriff was right—Lisa wasn't even sure she was pregnant, and in her distressed state of mind she was just being paranoid.

She heaved a sigh as another thought leapt at her. She told Seth about the postcard when they were at the funeral home, and he told her about the autopsy shortly afterwards at Clara's. She wrinkled her forehead. If Seth made up the autopsy findings to correlate with the postcard, he had to do some pretty fast thinking to come up with such an elaborate scenario.

The questions and suspicions wouldn't leave her alone. Could Seth be deliberately lying to her? Was she being won over by his appearance and personality?

That, too, seemed unlikely to Kerri. She had sensed that the Holy Spirit was calling Seth, gently nudging him to consider his need for a relationship with him. Seth seemed open but not ready to receive the message. He definitely didn't seem like someone who was trying to twist the truth. If that were the case, why would he tell her what he did at all? She certainly wouldn't be drawn to him because he ran over a corpse!

The issue became clearer in Kerri's mind. Either she could believe what the postcard implied and what Seth confessed, or she could believe the medical examiner's report that the sheriff had referred to. Only one or the other could be true.

She decided that the following day she would confront Seth and make up her mind.

O God, can I handle the truth?

CHAPTER
17

GETTING up by 6:30 the next morning was no problem for Seth. He'd been awake since 4, when a housekeeping cart rattled up the hallway. From 4 to 6, his racing thoughts and the antique mattress prevented him from returning to sleep. At 6 he summoned the nurse and waited for his orderly escort so he could shower. The orderly followed the spirit of the law rather than the letter and "watched" Seth shower from outside a thin, hospital-green curtain.

Breakfast was cold, runny scrambled eggs, link sausage, and hard biscuits. Seth knew the staff watched everything closely, so he forced himself to eat. His new resolution had been firmly formulated the night before, after his humiliating introduction: play their game by their rules. He hoped his plan would be enough to secure a release after his three-day evaluation.

Next on the morning agenda was "group," the shortened nickname for a group therapy chat session where patients were encouraged to share their feelings about their progress. Seth was obliged to introduce himself but fortunately didn't have to share anything else, having just arrived.

While the others discussed their therapy, Seth found himself guessing their diagnoses. *She's manic . . . He's depressed . . . He's schizophrenic . . . She's probably schizo-affective.*

After he figured out everyone else's problems, he thought again about his own. Other than the stuff he'd have to tell the psychiatrist to convince him he wasn't delirious, he'd have to put a lid on discussing Lisa Dale with anyone. And from the looks of the trouble he was in, he'd need a good attorney.

After the group session, Seth was singled off and given a battery of psychological tests by a clinical psychologist. The test results would be reviewed later by his psychiatrist. He took an M.M.P.I. (Minnesota Multiphasic Personality Inventory), an ink-blot test, and a second personality test, followed by a mental status examination by the psychologist.

For the latter, he was forced to subtract serial sevens starting at 100, remember three unrelated items to test his short-term memory, and interpret simple sayings such as "People in glass houses shouldn't throw stones." He was also asked who the President of the United States was and what year it was.

Seth had actually used the mental status exam, or M.S.E., many times during his own psychiatric rotations as a resident. He understood the point of each of the questions. By the end of the test he was tired of it all. So when asked whether he ever had the feeling someone was controlling his thoughts, he quipped, "No, I've never had any signs of thought insertion or thought broadcasting." The psychologist was surprised by Seth's knowledge of the test and wisely retreated.

By the time lunch rolled around, Seth was actually relieved to be out from under the psychologist's scrutiny, even if it meant dining with "the group." The meal consisted of grilled cheese sandwiches and vegetable soup. Again, Seth forced himself to eat and sat quietly with two other patients who looked like they hadn't seen the sun in months.

That afternoon Seth met the psychiatrist assigned to his case, Dr. Peter Interman. He was a balding man with a gray beard, looking a little too much like Sigmund Freud for Seth's comfort.

Dr. Interman asked Seth to sit down while he reviewed the file. Seth was glad he could observe the doctor's first reactions as he studied the magistrate's order and a form filled out by the sheriff, followed by Berringer's check-in data, psychological tests, and mental status exam, and finally the nurse's notes since his arrival the evening before.

"Hmmm." The psychiatrist sorted through the papers. "Ah hah." He paused and turned another page. "Oh."

He finally looked up and extended his hand. "Dr. Berringer, I'm Peter Interman."

Seth smiled quickly. Other than by the orderly, it was the first time he'd been addressed by the title "Doctor" since he arrived. He shook the psychiatrist's hand firmly.

"This all seems to be a big mistake," Seth opened.

"That's what I'm here to figure out, isn't it?" Interman pushed the papers aside. "Let me see how much you understand about what is happening to you." He leaned forward and put his skinny arms on the desk. "What can you tell me about why you are here?"

Seth twisted in his seat uncomfortably.

"Why don't you start from the beginning and tell me the whole story? This information is entirely confidential. The only thing the state wants from me is a determination of your sanity. In other words, are you capable of telling the difference between what is real and what is fantasy—are you psychotic or are you thinking rationally?"

Seth told the whole story from start to finish, beginning long before he found Lisa's body—the pressures he felt from Coast Care, the malpractice hearing, and the death of the little boy in the emergency department, ending with his conversation with the sheriff the afternoon before. He included a detailed description of the autopsy he'd witnessed and talked about how guilty he felt for desecrating Lisa's corpse and for misleading the police and the community.

Dr. Interman listened quietly, nodded, and typed notes onto a laptop computer. After Seth had completed his story, the psychiatrist closed his computer, pulled out the sheriff's report, and stared at it again.

Finally the doctor stood, checked his watch, and held out his hand. "Thank you, Dr. Berringer. That will be all for today. I'll be in tomorrow to talk with you further."

Seth shook Interman's hand but felt compelled to vocalize his burning thoughts. "That's it? Aren't you going to ask me some questions? Perhaps clarify some of the issues in the story or ask about the discrepancies in the medical examiner's report?"

"No. I'll have some questions for you in the morning, after I've reviewed all your psychological tests."

He turned to leave, but Seth didn't want him to go so quickly. "What about lifting the suicide precaution orders? I'm not about to kill myself. You can see that."

"I think that decision would be premature. I've not had a chance to fully evaluate all the data, and I can't take the risk of releasing the restrictions until the entire assessment has been completed."

Seth stood up, allowing his pants to droop pitifully low over his hips. "Come on, Dr. Interman, I look ridiculous! I can't walk anywhere without holding my pants up! At least tell them to give me my belt back," Seth pleaded.

"You're a doctor. You understand legal risk. I could be sued if you tried to hurt yourself and I had allowed it to happen."

"You're even more paranoid about malpractice than I am!" Seth regretted the words as soon as he said them.

"That may well be," the psychiatrist said tensely. "But I'm not the one under evaluation here, am I?" He looked at Seth's pants, hanging precariously off his buttocks, revealing three inches of his boxer shorts. "Besides, you shouldn't worry about your pants. It's the style. All the kids are wearing them that way." He chuckled at his own joke and departed before Seth could reply.

Seth plopped back into the chair, not bothering to pull his pants back up. *Way to go, Seth! Alienate the one guy who can set you free!*

◆ ◆ ◆

Sheriff Boatwright tossed the newspaper aside. "How come Blackstock's gettin' all the media attention around here?" he protested. "If I see his smilin' face on the front of the paper one more time, I think I'll puke!"

Deputy Richardson cringed at the thought and picked up the discarded paper. "Maybe you should attend more of these barbecues or church functions, like Mr. Blackstock."

"I suppose I could, if I didn't have to work, but someone's got to keep this department running." He placed his hand on his stomach. "What I need is some public interest in what this department is accomplishing to make our community a better, safer place to live."

The deputy nodded.

"We need to wrap up this Lisa Dale case, that's what we need to do. Put a cap on it, and let the media know how efficiently we did it. That ought to impress the voters."

"I thought you had that case pretty well figured out, now that the doctor confessed. The paper said you were confident of solving the problem."

"It depends on the doctor's evaluation up at Evergreen State. If they let him go, the community's going to be in an uproar, I can tell you that, especially after the media suggested the hit may not have been accidental."

"Where did they get that idea?"

"From our press release. We simply stated that the doctor had confessed to intentionally running over Lisa Dale's body and that his claims that she was already dead were not substantiated by the medical examiner's report.

We'll have to make sure we get him off the street, even if it's for his own protection."

"Will the magistrate issue an arrest warrant?"

"It depends on the charge and on the case we have against him." The sheriff scratched his expansive abdomen. "I guess we'd better get on with confirming as much of Berringer's story as we can."

"What do you have in mind?" Richardson asked.

"Get the proper warrants to search Berringer's vehicle. Zander parked it in his driveway last night. If he really did what he said, there should still be some evidence in his van. If his van's clean, we'll have to scour up some other leads." The ambitious sheriff wished he could talk to the two gentlemen who visited the Inn the night Lisa Dale died.

The deputy nodded.

"I'll call the medical examiner's office. If they mixed up the paperwork on this one, we'd all come out looking stupid. I'll have to confirm that the copy we have is correct."

"I'll go on out to Berringer's place."

"No, bring his van here. But get the proper paperwork first. I want this done by the book. The media's going to be watching."

◆ ◆ ◆

The sheriff wasn't the only one disappointed with the morning paper. When Kerri read it, she wanted to cry. There on the front page of the local news section, complete with a picture of Seth Berringer, stood an article on the progress in the Dale case.

LOCAL DOCTOR CONFESSES TO HIT-AND-RUN

Dr. Seth Berringer of Deer Falls turned himself in to the sheriff's department yesterday for the hit-and-run occurrence that killed Lisa Dale. "Berringer confessed to running over the body," reported a spokesperson for the sheriff's department. Inconsistencies in the evidence have raised serious questions about the doctor's mental competence and resulted in his committal to the hospital for an evaluation. Sheriff Boatwright called the confession a real breakthrough, praised his department's handling of the case, and promised a quick resolution.

Troubled and angry, Kerri threw the paper in the back of her Taurus and headed for Evergreen State. She looked at her watch. She had just enough time to get there for visiting hours.

The drive took a little over an hour, including a five-minute delay because of a wrong turn. When she arrived at the hospital, it appeared older than she'd remembered from her only previous visit there as a nursing student. The building itself stood alone in the middle of a field. The closest other buildings were part of a strip-mall over half a mile away.

After she rang the buzzer, an orderly escorted Kerri to the office. There she approached a petite woman wearing a pink volunteer coat.

"I'm here to visit a patient."

"Name?"

"Kerri Barber."

The volunteer searched the patient list. "I'm sorry. We don't show a patient by that name here."

"No, I'm sorry," Kerri responded. "That's my name. I'm here to visit Seth Berringer. He came in yesterday afternoon."

"Oh yes, I remember. Fourth floor." She nodded. "I read about him in the *Chronicle*."

Kerri smiled sweetly. So had everyone else. Seth's excellent reputation was undoubtedly ruined.

The volunteer continued, "I don't believe they've processed his approved visitors application yet. These things are highly regulated here, you know. We protect the patient's rights. Unless you are immediate family or your name was listed on his initial admission paperwork, we'll have to wait until we get his approved visitors list."

Lord, I have to talk with Seth. Please, Lord.

The volunteer worker scurried into the office and came back a moment later shaking her head. "Well, I'll be!" She pointed to Seth's admission paperwork. There he had penned a single name: "Kerri Barber."

Kerri smiled. *Thank you, Lord.*

The volunteer called Ronny to escort Kerri to Seth's room.

Her eyes widened as they traveled up the old elevator and past the hall monitor and yet another locked door.

Finally they paused in front of room 411. The orderly knocked rapidly before pushing the door open. "Dr. Berringer, you have a visitor." Ronny motioned for Kerri to enter.

Seth was seated on the side of the bed in a drab room with pale green walls and containing only a desk, a wooden desk-chair, and a single bed. He brightened when he saw her. "Kerri!" He stood to greet her.

She bit her trembling lower lip before speaking. "Oh, Seth, I'm so sorry."

Ronny left and let the door close behind him.

Seth held up his hands and attempted a weak smile. "I'm glad you . . ." His voice trailed off. He looked at her, discerning an expression of surprise and pity. Or was it revulsion? "How did you find me?"

"I was worried about you, so I went to your house, and a deputy parking your van told me what had happened. Then I talked to the sheriff about it too." She sat next to him on the bed. "Why didn't you tell me you were going to talk to them? I could have gone with you."

"I wanted to go alone. I had gotten myself into a mess, and I wanted to get myself out."

She studied him for a moment, instinctively reaching out to his unshaven cheek. He caught her hand in his and held it for a moment before letting it go. "Like it?" He lifted his chin. "It's the new Suicide Precaution look. They won't let me shave. I can't be trusted with sharp objects, you know."

"Suicide precautions? You?"

He rolled his eyes. "Standing orders on all three-day evaluation patients from the sheriff's department." He stood up and did an about-face in the middle of the small room. "They've confiscated my belt and my shoestrings, so I can't hang myself." He pulled out his empty front pockets. "They even took away my Chapstick. All *medication* must be given by their nursing staff."

"Oh, Seth."

He sat back down, his little parody completed. Not knowing what to say, he added sarcastically, "And how was your day?"

"Seth, I feel horrible about this. You confessed because of me, didn't you?"

He shook his head. "No. I mean, yes. I mean, no." He looked at her, his eyes pleading. "I'm not sure what I mean. You helped me understand that I didn't want to live a lie anymore. That's what we said that night in the park, right?"

She nodded.

"We just didn't know it would turn out like this, did we?" He slapped his knee. "That Boatwright is such a jerk! I suppose he told you why I'm here?"

"Yes, but I want to hear your side."

He took her hand. "You've heard my side. I told you everything when we were in the park."

"But what about the medical examiner's report—how do you explain what the sheriff said about that?"

"I don't know. As soon as I get out of here, I'm going to call Dr. Donovan. I need to know how this thing got so fouled up."

"Maybe I should call him before you get out. Perhaps there's been some sort of mix-up in the reports. Maybe he could talk the sheriff into canceling your evaluation."

"Boatwright? Now there's a man who listens to reason!"

Kerri squeezed his hand gently before letting it go again. "He's not malicious, Seth. He may be incompetent, but I think he's trying to do his job."

Seth rolled his eyes.

"He thinks you were so traumatized by running over Lisa Dale that a defense mechanism kicked in, and you came up with a cover story so you wouldn't have to face the guilt associated with killing Lisa."

"Oh, that's rich. Psychiatrist Boatwright gets me committed." He looked back at Kerri. "What do *you* believe?"

"I believe you, Seth. I believe Lisa was killed or died as a result of someone trying to get her baby. I believe she knew something was desperately wrong and was scared. That's what the postcard indicates. I think the autopsy proves that Lisa's worst fears came true."

Kerri stood, walked to a narrow window, and looked out at the overcast sky. "Why did you confess, Seth?"

"It's hard to explain. I felt guilty. I had a crazy thought that maybe what my patient said was more than a coincidence, that maybe there is a God who's interested in what I'm doing with my life and maybe he's been trying to break through. I thought the right thing to do was to obey the verse I told you about and not hide my wrongdoing any longer."

"You did the right thing, Seth. You're on the right track. God *is* interested in you. I believe he's working all of this out, no matter how it appears right now, so you'll come to trust him."

Seth sighed. "It hasn't worked out very well yet." He hung his head. "The hospital staff called Coast Care this morning. They've hired a temp to replace me. Just like that. One day I'm taking care of my own patients, and the next I'm not." He shook his head. "I doubt I'll come out of this with my job intact."

"I'm so sorry, Seth."

"The ironic thing is, I was trying to protect my job by doing all this foolishness in the first place. And it's the very thing I'll end up losing."

Kerri nodded as she sat in the wooden desk-chair. "I have some other news."

Seth lifted his head.

"The sheriff gave me a few boxes of stuff from Lisa Dale's apartment. I found this in one of them." She handed him the letter from Sue.

He read the letter slowly.

"Hmmm. Sounds like they both volunteered for the same research project."

"That's what I thought. I want to find this girl, Seth. She may have some information that will lead to Lisa's killers."

He looked at the envelope. "How will you find her?"

"I have the address, and Lakeland is only fifteen miles from here."

"It's worth a look."

"Something else bothers me about this. This was just one letter in a small stack of mail dating back a few months. I can understand not opening your mail if you aren't home, but the postmark on the postcard I received indicated she was back in Deer Falls."

"Which indicates she wasn't staying at her own place or she died before checking her mail."

"Hmmm."

"Hmmm what?"

"You've made me think of something. Lisa was kind of a loner. I was about the closest friend she had. I don't think she was staying with anyone."

"So maybe she was at a motel."

"The only thing we have in Deer Falls is the Deer Falls Inn."

"It's worth checking into. The motel clerk should have a record of the people who stayed there. Somebody might have seen her or talked to her."

"Maybe I can find a clue to what happened in her last hours."

"It's a long shot, Kerri. She was on the run, and whoever wanted her got to her before she arrived at her apartment. But it can't hurt to check around."

"We may never know what actually happened." She shoved the letter back into her jeans pocket. After a few moments of awkward silence, she asked, "How are they treating you here?"

"Other than my exciting wardrobe modifications, you mean?" He smiled.

You look great, Seth, even without shaving.

"They made me take some personality tests this morning, and I talked to a psychiatrist this afternoon. I pretty much told him the whole story. The problem is, the sheriff's report counterbalances what I'm telling him. Hopefully, he'll have sense enough to know I'm not a danger to myself or others and will let me out of this place."

A knock came at the door. "Dr. Berringer?" It was Ronny. "Time for supper."

Kerri stood to leave. "I'll be praying for you, Seth. I'll talk to the medical examiner, and I'll try to find Lisa's friend."

"Thanks for coming."

He reached for her, and she rested for a moment in his arms. Her eyes blurred with moisture. "I didn't want to cry."

He smiled. "It's OK."

"Can I call you?"

"I'm not sure. I don't have a phone in the room."

Ronny, who had been watching from the doorway, explained, "There's a pay phone at the end of the hallway, Doc. You can call the pretty lady after supper every evening."

"Do you know my number?"

Seth nodded.

"I'll be seeing you."

She exited under the large arm of the orderly.

Seth watched her go. He hoped her prayers worked better than his had.

CHAPTER
18

KERRI slowed the Taurus to a crawl and studied the numbers on the front of the apartment building. When she saw 1210, she pulled into a space between two rundown station wagons. She glanced at the envelope in her hand. The return address was 1210 Oak Street, apartment B.

Brown, grassless paths criss-crossed the lawn, and two tricycles, a plastic slide, and a Bigwheel littered the front sidewalk. Kerri shoved the envelope into her pocket as she stepped around the toys.

She opened the door and climbed to the second floor. The light was out in the stairwell, and the air carried a stale odor of smoke. The dull throb of a bass guitar competed with the squeals of playing children. Apartment B was on the left, at the top of the stairs. Kerri pressed the doorbell but couldn't hear a ring. After a minute she pounded the door loudly.

She heard the dead-bolt turn. The door opened, and a young girl, about age four, greeted Kerri from the other side of a chain lock.

"Is your mother home? I'm looking for Sue." Kerri smiled.

The girl ran out of sight. "Mommy!"

In a moment the little girl was joined by a woman dressed in shorts and a T-shirt in spite of the cool temperature. Her hair was brown and her face wrinkled with worry. She wore no makeup and had a large quilted hot-mat in her hand. "Yes?"

"I'm looking for Sue."

The woman made no move to remove the chain. "What is your business here?" The tone was matter of fact and slightly suspicious.

"I'm a friend of Lisa Dale's."

"I don't know where she is." She pushed the door shut and turned the dead-bolt with a click.

Kerri was taken aback by the sudden action. She could hear the woman calling to the little girl. "Taylor, get in the back room! Now!"

Kerri knocked again. This time there was no answer.

She looked at the door, which had a peephole at eye level. She hoped someone was watching. "Please talk to me. I have a letter from Sue." She pulled the letter from her pocket. "I'm a friend, or was a friend, of Lisa's. She was killed. Did you know that? I'm trying to find out what happened. I may need your help."

The latch turned again, and the door opened an inch against the chain. "Give me the letter."

Kerri handed it to the woman through the crack.

"How did you get this?"

"The sheriff down in Deer Falls gave it to me along with Lisa's other belongings. She didn't get a chance to read it before she died."

"She's really dead?"

"Surely you heard about it in the papers or on T.V."

"I don't have a T.V." The woman, in her twenties, let out a curse. "How did she die?"

Kerri stood back a bit. "Can we talk without . . . " She paused. ". . . without this door in our way?"

"You're not from the institute?"

"No. But I'd like to know what the institute is."

"Show me some I.D."

Kerri opened her wallet to her driver's license and held it up. "It's not a very good picture."

The woman studied it for a moment, then opened the door. "Come in. You can sit there on the couch. I'll be right back—I have something on the stove."

It was quieter inside the apartment. Evidently the bass guitar was in apartment C.

"Tell me about Lisa," the woman said as she reentered the room.

Kerri leaned forward. "My name is Kerri Barber. Are you Sue?"

"Yes. I'm sorry about before." She waved her hand at the door. "When you mentioned Lisa, I thought you were looking for her too."

A high voice cried from the back room, "Mommy!"

Sue excused herself for a moment. Almost as quickly, she reappeared with a baby in her arms and the little girl on her heels.

"Have other people been looking for her?"

She nodded. "Two men. A week or two ago. They returned twice, as if they didn't believe I didn't know where Lisa was. They scared me plenty. I thought you must be looking for her as well."

"No. Lisa was killed shortly after you wrote this letter."

"Killed?"

"Yes. The paper reported it as a hit-and-run, but they don't have all the facts."

"How did she die?"

"The medical examiner's findings seemed to indicate that some sort of wooden spike had been driven through her uterus, evidently in an attempt to cause an abortion."

"No!" She gasped loudly. "Not Lisa!"

Sue balanced the baby in one hand and looked at the little girl. "Why don't you go play in your room, honey. Mommy needs to talk."

The girl, dressed in a worn sweatshirt and brown pants, frowned but walked away obediently.

"Why did you come here?" Sue used her free hand to dab the corners of her eyes.

Kerri sighed, wondering where to begin. "It's a long story. For now I'll just say I think the sheriff's department is on the wrong track in its investigation into Lisa's death. I personally think that how she died is somehow tied to a research project she was involved in. I was hoping you could tell me more."

"I can tell you that you've already got it wrong, or at least the medical examiner does. Lisa is the last girl in the world who would need an abortion. She was a virgin." She scoffed. "That's why they kept her in the stupid study in the first place." She shook her head. "No one would do that to her. Not to Virgie," she muttered.

"You called her Virgie?"

"It was a nickname. You know—virgin?" She rolled her eyes. "You'd have understood if you were at the institute." She laid the baby, a little boy, on a blanket on the floor and handed him a rattle. "We signed up to be volunteers in a research project. They were studying a new birth control pill. The plan was to put us on the pills and do biopsies of our uteruses or something. The thing was, you had to be a virgin to qualify. I thought I could sneak into the program, but somehow they knew." She wrinkled her nose, and for the first time Kerri saw a hint of a smile. "I guess when they have you in those stirrups, they can tell. Anyway, they dropped me from the study like a hot rock. Lisa stayed there. I thought she was the lucky one. That's what I called her—the lucky virgin. Eventually I just shortened it to Virgie." She lowered her eyes to the drab, apartment-beige shag. "She's really dead? I can't believe it. I was hoping we could get together. She seemed like such a good gal—fun to be around, know what I mean?"

Kerri took out the photocopy of Lisa's postcard and handed it to Sue. "She sent me this right before she died. I didn't receive it until after she was killed."

Sue read the card and cursed again, then apologized. "Excuse my French." She shook her head. "Pregnant? She thought she was pregnant?"

"What can you tell me about the institute you mentioned? Is that where the research was conducted?"

Sue nodded. "Yeah. It was all done very secretively. They picked us up at the airport outside Denver—paid our way there and everything. Then they shuttled us to their research facility in a limo with tinted windows. No one knew exactly where we were by the time we arrived. It took a good hour and a half from Denver, I'd say. They put us up in their own hospital rooms and gave us our meals. They regulated everything."

"Didn't you think it was odd—I mean, no one knowing exactly where you were?"

"I guess, sort of. But the reimbursement was so generous, we didn't think about it. Plus they told us that they needed to do things that way because the pharmaceutical industry is so cutthroat. They said they relied on the strictest security to be sure they kept ahead of the competition."

"Who was doing the research?"

"I'm not sure. After they examined me, they said I couldn't be used for the study."

"Do you remember the name of the company?"

"Genetic Concepts or Genetic Concert or Gene Conquest—something like that."

"How about the researchers' names?"

Sue shook her head. "One of the women in the lab had a foreign name, and she talked with an accent. Ursa? Ursula?" She shrugged. "I'm sorry, I'm just not sure."

Kerri looked back at the postcard copy. "Does this make any sense to you? Could they have inseminated her or something?"

Sue's face took on a smirk. "Gag!" She shook her head. "I don't think so."

"How did they do the research?"

"They said they would have to do several exams. They called them speculum tests, I think." She leaned forward and picked up the rattle her son had tossed aside. "I only had one before they discovered my little secret." She paused. "I guess I really don't know what they did after that." She shook her head. "But we certainly didn't sign up for anything other than taking medicine and submitting to the exams and biopsies."

"What do you make of her fear that someone wanted her baby?"

Again Sue shrugged. "I don't know. I really wasn't there long enough to know most of the people. Lisa was the only person I talked to much at all."

"Mommy!" The cry came from the back room.

Sue disappeared. When she returned, she had an armload of old children's books and her daughter on her heels again. "You may look at these here, as long as you're quiet."

The little girl nodded.

"Did you say some others were looking for Lisa?"

"Yes, two men. They made one excuse after another for asking about her. I'm almost positive they were from the institute."

"What did they look like?"

"One guy looked Chinese and had big muscles, dark hair, and a mustache."

Kerri shivered as she remembered the man who helped her unload Lisa's belongings.

"The other guy was older and taller—kind of thin, with gray hair."

"Hmmm." That could have been the man who was looking for Lisa at the E.R. the night she died.

"Does any of this help?"

Kerri nodded. "At least I know she really was in a research project and that it had something to do with birth control." She shrugged. "If it wasn't for the medical examiner's report, I'd say she was just confusing the effects of the birth control pills with pregnancy. Apparently somehow someone made her pregnant."

She thought for a moment, then added, "Did they ever use anesthesia with any of the exams?"

"They told us they would need to use a local anesthetic for some of them, I think."

Kerri sighed. She couldn't think of anything else to ask. "Can I call you if I think of more questions?"

Sue shrugged. "I guess so."

Kerri pulled out a pen. "What's your last name, Sue?"

"Bergy." She reached for the pen and wrote her name and phone number on the bottom of the postcard copy.

"Thanks. I'm not sure if I'll ever get to the bottom of this, but I'll try." Kerri smiled and looked at the little girl. "She sure is pretty."

Sue looked at her children. "I just wanted to make a better life for them. That's why I wanted the job at the institute." She shook her head. "They promised us a place to stay and all our meals plus twenty thousand dollars for up to four months of work."

"Wow."

Sue opened the front door.

Kerri slipped into the hall. "Thanks again." The low throb of the bass guitar greeted her once more.

As she stepped onto the stairs, she heard the rattle of the chain returning to its slot and the click of the dead-bolt sliding into place.

◆ ◆ ◆

Seth scuffed up the hallway, holding his shoes on by curling his toes. He had tried going in socks only, but the cold floor discouraged that. Ronny sat at the nursing station reading a local paper. "Can I have it when you're finished?" Seth asked.

Ronny pushed the newspaper aside. "Sure. Take it. I've got to make lock-up rounds anyway. Check out those Deer Falls Blazers. I think ol' Coach Smith has the team he's been prayin' for all these years."

Seth grunted in gratitude, then took the paper to his room and quickly scanned the front page. So far, so good. He turned to page 2. Still OK.

He flipped to the local section, and his heart sank as he read the title, "LOCAL DOCTOR CONFESSES TO HIT-AND-RUN." As he looked through the article, he became angrier and angrier. *They can't say this! I didn't confess to the hit-and-run occurrence that killed Lisa Dale! I said I ran over a dead body!* He continued to read and sighed with deep grief. Great! Now the whole world knew he'd been committed for a psych evaluation. He'd probably lose all his patients. He shook his head. He might as well resign and avoid the humility of being fired by Coast Care.

He threw the paper in the trash and slumped onto the bed. He held his head in his hands. How had things ever come to this?

God, do you really care about me at all? Kerri seems so sure. So why did confessing my evil deeds put me here? I was trying to do the right thing. Isn't that what you wanted from me?

And yet he knew he couldn't blame God for the mess he'd made for himself. God wasn't the one who dragged Lisa's body into the street. Confessing his sins meant accepting he was ultimately responsible. *I have only myself to blame.*

Seth stood up and stared out of the small window. There were a few lights on the building itself, but only darkness beyond. *I'm so alone, God. I've made such a mess of things.*

He thought about the article in the paper. The sheriff promised a quick resolution, did he? Seth blew his breath against the cold window pane. If anyone was going to bring this case to a truthful resolution, it looked like it would have to be him.

Seth walked out into the hallway and down to the end of the corridor, where he found the pay phone just as Ronny had said.

He waited a few minutes for another patient to finish a call, then dialed in his calling card number and called the Chesapeake General Hospital. "Operator, this is Dr. Berringer. I need the chief medical examiner, Dr. Donovan. Can you page him for me?"

"He prefers to be called at home at this hour. I'll be glad to ring his home for you."

"Thanks." Seth tapped his foot, slapping his loose shoe against his heel.

After two rings Eric picked up. "Dr. Donovan here."

"Dr. Donovan, this is Seth Berringer. I'm the physician who came down to see the Lisa Dale autopsy."

Donovan cringed. "Yes, I remember."

"I'm in a difficult situation, sir. I need to go over the autopsy report with you and would appreciate your contacting the sheriff's department to set the record straight."

"Set the record straight? What are you talking about? Hey, didn't I read that you're in the hospital or something?"

"If you can call it that, yes. Basically I'm here because I confessed to the sheriff that I was the one who ran over Lisa's body. Remember, you pointed out to me how she was dead before she was run over? Well, you were right. I was the one who found her. I thought one of my patients had killed her. And, well—" Seth stopped himself. He wanted to be careful about what he said. "What's important is that the sheriff seems to think she died from the hit-and-run, not from the uterine perforation you showed me. My story and your report were so different, the sheriff thought I'd flipped or something. The next thing I knew, he had me committed to a mental hospital for an evaluation."

Donovan raised his eyebrows. "You're calling from a hospital?"

"Evergreen State. You know the place."

"Of course." He paused. "You say that the girl died of a uterine perforation?"

"Yes. You showed me how the cervical dilator had penetrated the uterus and lacerated the uterine artery."

Donovan clenched his teeth. "That girl's pelvis was so smashed, you couldn't tell what was what." He hesitated. "I'm not sure what you remember, but she was pretty messed up from that hit-and-run."

Seth raised his voice. "Hit-and-run! She died from a botched abortion! You told me that yourself!"

"Dr. Berringer, I see hundreds of cases a year. You can't expect me to—"

"This wasn't that long ago! Think! You've got to talk to the sheriff and tell him how she really died. You remember, she was pregnant! You sent some tissue to your friend, Dr. Schwab!"

A nurse walked down the hall and placed her hand on Seth's shoulder. "Mr. Berringer, calm down. I'll have to ask you to hang up the phone now. I can't have you getting so worked up." Seth pulled away from the nurse and lowered his voice, but the strain was still evident. "Come on, Dr. Donovan, you remember!"

"I have no memory of a pregnancy. Certainly I would remember that. An abortion attempt? No . . . I remember now. She died from a pelvic injury sustained in a hit-and-run accident." Berringer was a nice guy, and Donovan hated to put him in the middle of all this. But Seth was young and would certainly have other chances for success. For a man the age of Eric Donovan, however, an opportunity like this might come only once.

"You're lying!"

Donovan rubbed his left arm, noticing that dull ache again.

The hospital nurse called for Ronny. "I need an orderly—now!"

She put her hand on Seth's shoulder once more. "Mr. Berringer, I must ask you to hang up."

Seth whirled around and faced the nurse. "Please," he pleaded, "I'll be done in a second. Dr. Donovan, please talk to the sheriff. He thinks I'm psy-

chotic because I told a story quite different from your report. Please clear
this up."

"Mr. Berringer, please." The nurse spoke in a firm but gentle tone.

"I'll review my report, Dr. Berringer. That's all I can do. Good night!"

Seth slammed the phone down. "I can't believe this! His report is a lie!"

To the nurse, the patient seemed awfully paranoid. She'd have to report
this to Dr. Interman.

"Mr. Berringer, perhaps you'd like a sedative to help you sleep."

Seth ignored the suggestion and walked back to his room. He wished
he knew what was going on.

◆　◆　◆

Eric Donovan hung up the phone and immediately dialed a long distance number.

"Kev, I was hoping I'd catch you."

"Eric? Unless you've changed your mind, I have noth—"

"Hear me out, would you?" He wanted to select the right words. "Do
you have any record of the tissue I sent you?"

"I told you, I destroyed it. I urged you to do the same, remember? And
I didn't formally log it as a specimen since you asked me to look at it on the
side as a favor to you."

"Good. Let's keep it that way. I've changed my mind about the situation. I'll destroy what I have. The specimen is history—a rumor—it never
happened, if you get my drift. It's better that things like this never get out.
I don't know what I was thinking."

Kevin Schwab breathed a sigh of relief. "Thanks, Eric." He shook his
head. That was one less worry he'd have about protecting the integrity of
the N.I.H.

Eric smiled. "As far as I'm concerned, I never saw the baby." He chuckled. "And the mother was cremated days ago." It would be better if no one
knew that records had been altered.

"Is that it?"

"That's all. I just wanted you to know that I've come to my senses."

"Thanks for calling, Eric."

"Bye."

Oddly, Dr. Donovan was grateful to Seth Berringer for reminding him
of another possible source of confirmation of his version of the Lisa Dale

case. Without the medical examiner's verification and without Schwab's record, who would ever believe Berringer over Donovan?

Now Donovan just needed to wait until the real creator of the baby came forward. For the right price, the examiner was sure he could remember where he put the fetus.

CHAPTER
19

THE next morning Arnold Mayer looked across the yard at his van, already running in preparation for church. He cradled the phone on his ear and whispered to his wife, "Give me a minute. It's Kevin."

His wife rolled her eyes and pointed at her watch.

The N.I.H. chairman nodded and held up his hand. He turned back to the phone. "You've managed to dodge a mighty big bullet this time, Kevin." He sighed. "I'm not sure how you did it, but thanks."

"I'm not sure how I did it either. Ol' Donovan had me worried there for a while. It seems as quickly as he lost his mind, he regained it."

Mayer squinted. "Are you sure Davis doesn't have other clones on the loose?"

"Highly unlikely. He's sophisticated, but I doubt he has enough to repeat the experiment."

"As long as Donovan didn't send a sample to anyone besides you, there shouldn't be a problem." He stared out of the window. "You don't suppose Davis would stoop to exhuming the surrogate—"

"Not possible. She was cremated."

"Good."

"Donovan destroyed what he kept, and I've destroyed what he sent me. There shouldn't be evidence of any misdeeds anywhere."

Dr. Mayer chuckled. "I can't tell you what a weight that is off my shoulders. I can't imagine the public outcry if he'd been successful."

Kevin nodded soberly. "Really."

The chairman tapped the side of his receding hairline with his index finger. "How about meeting somewhere for lunch? This news deserves a celebration. Have you tried that new Indian restaurant on the corner?"

"Mighty tempting there, boss, but I have two peanut butter and jelly sandwiches with my name on them in the lab refrigerator," he responded with truthful sarcasm.

Working on Sunday? Mayer couldn't believe it. Didn't this guy ever quit? "Suit yourself."

Kevin put his Bluejays baseball cap back on, twisted the bill around to the rear, and smiled. "Thanks for the offer."

Dr. Mayer watched his wife climb into the van as he added, "And, Kevin, no more cell donations to anyone, regardless of the size of their pockets."

"Don't worry—I've learned my lesson."

◆ ◆ ◆

The sheriff was talking at the garage in the sheriff's department with Roy Williams, who had spent his morning combing the undersurface of Seth Berringer's van. "This had better be important, Roy, since you interrupted my first church appearance in three years," he said with a truthful sneer.

"Here's where we found the shoe," he said, pointing just inside the front right wheel.

"Does it match the girl's other one?"

Roy nodded. "Definitely. We've sent it to the state forensics lab for a confirmation on the blood type."

"The medical examiner still had her clothes?"

"Yes. Everything's in order. We sent samples of her bloody jeans to get a blood match with the shoe and fragments of the purple jacket to confirm a match on the fabric."

"The fabric?"

"Gary didn't tell you?"

The sheriff shook his head.

"We found some thread and small fabric samples on the undersurface toward the rear of the van. I bet it'll match the girl's coat. You can almost tell without the microscope."

"Good, good. So far it looks like our doctor was telling the truth, at least about running the girl over."

He squinted at the sun, straining to remember the story as Seth Berringer had confessed it. "Hmmm. I seem to recall his telling us that he took the girl's shoe off to mark the location of the body. And now you find it under his car." He nodded thoughtfully. "Seems like his story is breaking down a bit." He chuckled softly.

Boatwright walked around grimacing at the bottom of the van. "Any sign of the accident in the front of the van?"

Roy shrugged. "Seems clean. If the girl hit the front of the van, it sure didn't do much damage.

"Hmmm."

"I would have expected to see something, especially if she was hit at a speed high enough to cause death."

"She could have tripped and been on the ground when he struck, or perhaps even diving to get out of the way."

Roy nodded. "You mean like this guy intentionally ran her down?"

The sheriff unintentionally lowered his voice and nodded. "Something just doesn't sit well with me about this whole thing, Roy. I've got a doctor who says he intentionally ran over a body, a body he claims was already dead, and I've got a medical examiner's report that says she died of injuries sustained in the hit-and-run." He sighed. "There are only a few ways to put this together. Maybe he intentionally killed her and was afraid of getting caught, so he confessed to a lesser evil."

The two men backed away, and Roy lowered the van back to the garage floor.

"Did you check out the inside?"

"Yeah. It seems clean."

"Any evidence that Berringer's story about putting the girl in the back could be true?"

"Not really, though the inside looks like it's been thoroughly scrubbed, and the carpet in the back is missing. Other than that, it looks okay."

The sheriff nodded. "Good work, Roy."

"Glad to be of help."

"Say, would you like some lunch? I thought I'd head down to Lanny's Grill."

"No thanks. Mabel always makes a pot roast on Sundays."

"Some other time then. Lanny makes great shrimp fritters, though."

The sheriff slid his thumbs inside his belt and raised his pants an inch.

"If you find out anything else, just call the station, Roy."

He nodded and watched the sheriff's car sink as the large man boarded. Roy chuckled to himself and rolled his eyes behind the lawman's back. The last thing Boatwright needed was greasy shrimp fritters.

◆ ◆ ◆

The staff's weekend wrap-up discussion took place in the fourth floor conference room, the only room with carpeting, vintage 1970. It was lime green and actually matched the thin yellow and green striped curtains that could no longer filter out the winter sunshine. Wood paneling covered the walls, and two pictures of sailboats provided the only decorations. The center of the room was dominated by a large table with a shiny veneer finish.

In spite of a state regulation, half of the attendees smoked, choking the atmosphere with carcinogens. Dr. Interman took charge and, as usual, presented his thoughts first and took comments and questions afterward.

"In summary," he concluded, "I find Dr. Seth Berringer to be very interesting indeed. I do not believe he is psychotic. Certainly, parts of his story are a bit unbelievable and, as I understand it, aren't supported by other objective evidence. Nonetheless, none of our studies have shown him to be anything less than firmly connected with reality." He looked carefully at the group, made up of Sally Gardner, the head nurse, David Tompkins, a clinical psychologist, Barbara Scot, a nurse, and Henry Opperham, a social worker. "Any comments or questions?"

Sally spoke first. "So we can release him?"

The psychiatrist shook his head. "No. Not until the three-day evaluation is up anyway. Some points still have to be clarified."

"But we can take him off suicide precautions?"

"Yes. Give the poor doctor his belt back." He laughed.

"He seems so angry," Barbara commented. "I caught him practically yelling into the phone last night. I, for one, must express concern, not that he's in danger of hurting himself, but that he might be angry enough to act dangerously toward others."

"He does seem to be angry, but if his story can be substantiated, perhaps that isn't totally inappropriate response," Interman responded.

"And if it can't be confirmed?" The staff nurse folded her arms.

"At that point I would entertain the possibility of excessive paranoia. But," he added, exhaling a smoke ring, "unless paranoia is associated with disassociation with reality, it's not something we can confine him for, especially against his will."

Dr. Interman looked at the psychologist. "Dave, what are your comments, based on his testing?"

He shrugged. "I'd go pretty much with what you said. I do think he has a few areas worth exploring. He seems to be carrying an excessive amount of guilt."

"I picked up on that, too," Henry added.

Tompkins continued, "He also scores pretty high on a modified hostility scale. He definitely feels set up—not paranoid really, but definitely angry."

"He seems to have so much anger directed toward himself," the social worker mused.

Ms. Gardner tapped her pen against the desk, impatient and irritated at the smoky atmosphere. She coughed and fanned the air in front of her face with her hand.

"Is everyone in agreement?" Interman inquired. "Take off the suicide precautions, and I'll deal with the hostility and guilt issues later today. Tomorrow we'll see how he's doing. I'm not going to promise him a discharge, just in case something else comes up."

Everyone but Barbara nodded.

The staff nurse shook her head. "I'll let you know if he has any more outbursts." She rolled her eyes. "This one scares me. He really does."

"I'll note that in the report," Interman quipped. "Now, I'm sure you all have work to do." He stood, signaling the end of the discussion.

◆ ◆ ◆

Later that afternoon Seth shifted in his chair and wiggled his toes, enjoying the feel of his tightly laced shoes.

"I want you to know I've found no evidence that you are out of touch with reality. However, we do have two ongoing areas of concern about you, Seth," Dr. Interman confided.

"According to our testing, your story didn't grow out of psychotic delusions. That leaves us with one of two conclusions." He stroked his gray beard and locked eyes with Seth. "Either you are telling the truth or you are willfully lying."

Seth remained quiet.

"But what you say seems to carry inordinate hostility and guilt, neither of which are considered healthy responses."

Seth responded with a shrug. "That seems fair to say."

"I personally feel your guilt arises from your remorse over the hit-and-run. What isn't entirely clear to me is the role your anger plays. Could it be that your accident wasn't so accidental?" He watched Seth for a reaction. "I would expect your self-blame to be much greater if you intentionally ran this girl over than if you had an accident. That would explain your self-recrimination."

Seth sighed and stifled any impulsive reaction. He knew the psychiatrist was testing him. "I felt guilty because I recognized just how low I had gone to protect my own interests. I realized that regardless of my station in life, I basically function as a selfish person." He paused, returning his examiner's serious gaze. "I'm telling the truth, doctor. I didn't accidentally hit Lisa Dale. I found her already dead and made it appear that she died of a hit-and-run."

The psychiatrist nodded. Berringer was certainly sticking by his original story.

"OK, let's say you're telling the truth. Let's deal with the guilt you feel. Once you realize that this emotion is totally self-generated and self-defeating, you should be able to logically and calmly lay it aside."

"Self-generated?"

"You impose a standard upon yourself, you don't meet it, you feel guilty." The psychiatrist nodded resolutely. "It's that simple."

"It's not that simple to me. Maybe it's been that way for me in the past, but . . . I'm beginning to think it wasn't merely a self-generated standard I violated. I think I let God down, not just myself."

"Ah, yes, you've let God down, have you?" He chuckled. "Now we can talk about delusions, doctor."

Seth stayed quiet.

Dr. Interman continued, "You are an intelligent man, Seth. God is a concept, a crutch if you will, that people create to serve their own emotional needs. You were bad, so you invent a God to punish you. Your own guilt becomes the evidence that he exists." He lit a cigarette. "Certainly you've seen the same phenomenon in your own religious patients."

Seth twisted in his seat uncomfortably.

"Guilt is a useless emotion that you inflict upon yourself. As soon as you realize there are no absolute standards of behavior inflicted upon you by a deity, the sooner you can abandon the guilt feelings you have for not reaching those standards."

Seth nodded, less from agreement than from his desire to appear agreeable. "Hmmm."

"Anger and hostility tend to be negative emotions as well, but they can be powerful motivators and tend to make some people very productive. Overall, too much of anything is bad." He reached into his pocket, pulled out his business card, and handed it to Seth. "We may want to explore some of these emotional imbalances at a later date."

Seth brightened. "Does this mean I can go home?"

"Not yet. Tomorrow will end your three-day evaluation. Unless we get other instructions by the sheriff's department, a decision will be made by tomorrow afternoon as to whether we can safely dismiss you."

"The sheriff's department?"

"If I declare you to be competent, they will certainly entertain whether or not you will be arrested on other charges. That's up to them." He shrugged.

Seth sighed. As that baseball guy once said, "It ain't over till it's over."

CHAPTER
20

O<small>N</small> Monday morning Kerri debated between a phone call and a face-to-face visit with Dr. Donovan. A phone call would be quicker, but an in-person confrontation would likely give her more information. She finally opted for a visit to the chief medical examiner's office.

The office was in Gleason, twenty miles south of Deer Falls in southern Chesapeake County. She covered the distance in just under forty minutes. After she arrived at the correct building, a modern brick structure with Williamsburg overtones, she was directed down a long hall ending with a doorway marked "Chief Medical Examiner." Beneath the title, Eric Donovan's name was emblazoned on a gold plaque.

She pushed the door open and glanced around. It looked just like her insurance agent's office. This was no place for autopsies.

Two painted metal doors stood on the other side of the spacious office, which was partitioned by a series of gray, chest-high dividers. The office was quiet except for a radio and the soft, rapid clicking of a computer keyboard.

An attractive woman with gray hair and a slender build stood to greet her, quickly removing a headset. "I'm sorry. Have you been here long? Thanks to the radio and my concentrating on this transcription, I didn't even hear you come in."

Kerri smiled. "No problem. I just arrived. I was wondering if I could speak to the medical examiner."

"He's busy with a case," Connie Donovan responded. "Could I help you?"

"I was hoping to speak to him personally about an autopsy report he did on the body of a hit-and-run victim by the name of Lisa Dale."

"I remember reading about that case in the paper." She walked to a tall file drawer. "Maybe I can find the report."

Connie looked for a moment, then pulled out a manila folder. She stopped on her way back to the counter that separated them. "You're not a reporter, are you?"

"No. I was a friend of the deceased."

"Oh," Connie responded with genuine sympathy. "I'm sorry." She opened the folder. "Maybe something in the report will answer your questions. I guess since you're a friend, it's okay for you to read it."

Kerri studied the document. Just as the sheriff had said, the report indicated that Lisa died from hemorrhagic shock from a pelvic injury sustained in a pedestrian accident. There was no mention of an injury due to a foreign body piercing the uterus and no mention of her pregnancy.

Kerri frowned.

"It must be terrible losing a friend this way," Connie responded.

"No . . . I mean, yes, it is. But that's not why I'm frowning. You see, my friend, Dr. Seth Berringer, witnessed the autopsy, and what he saw is different than what is reported here."

"Different?" Connie retrieved the paper and slid it into the file.

"Well, for one thing, Seth said the girl's exam revealed that she was dead long before the vehicle struck her. She had died from an abortion attempt."

Connie winced. "I'm sure that Eric . . . uh, Dr. Donovan would have reported that. Are you sure this friend of yours hasn't mixed up his cases?"

She shook her head firmly. "No." She paused. "It certainly would help if I could talk with the medical examiner."

"Well, this does seem to need his explanation, doesn't it? I'll see if I can find him." She disappeared through the back doors.

In a few minutes Dr. Donovan, clad in surgical scrubs and a plastic apron, marched out with Connie on his heels.

"Hello. I'm Dr. Donovan." He stripped a rubber glove from his hand and held it out toward Kerri.

Kerri shook it. "I'm Kerri Barber. Thank you for taking time to talk with me." She found the gray-haired pathologist intimidating, though she wasn't sure why.

"My secretary indicated that you felt my report was inaccurate in some way."

"Not exactly, sir. It's just that it doesn't correlate with the memory of

Dr. Seth Berringer, who was present at the autopsy. Your report makes no mention of the abortion attempt or the pregnancy."

Donovan stiffened and rubbed his left arm. "Give me the report, Connie."

After she retrieved the file, he scanned the document and shook his head.

"I have nothing further to say, Ms. Barber. Number one, as mandated by the state office, we give out information regarding autopsies only to next of kin. Number two, my signature is on this report, and that authenticates it. I can neither add nor subtract from this legal document without serious legal implications."

"Do you recall the pregnancy?"

Donovan continued to side-step. "There is no mention of pregnancy here."

Kerri sensed his insecurity. "Surely you would remember—"

"Ma'am, I do thousands of cases a year. I'll stand by my official record. If it doesn't mention pregnancy, she wasn't pregnant!" His voice was becoming louder, and Connie gently held his arm.

"Eric, settle down."

Kerri felt compelled to take a bolder stance. "I'm sorry, but I don't believe you. I have proof of her pregnancy—in a letter! Why are you covering up the truth, Dr. Donovan?"

Donovan paled. Seething with anger, he attempted to cap the volcano threatening to erupt. "I do not need to put up with this. How dare you insult my integrity! Perhaps you should recall that Dr. Berringer, not me, is the one committed for psychiatric evaluation because of his delusions. I answer to the state, not to you!"

Kerri's voice was steady, belying the fright she felt. "You will answer to God, Dr. Donovan, and to him alone."

The pathologist stormed through the back doors.

Connie stood with her mouth agape. What was going on? Was Eric in trouble?

Kerri shook her head, amazed at her own boldness but invigorated by her fight against evil. *O God, deliver us from the darkness!*

◆ ◆ ◆

Wilson Davis dipped a Q-tip in hydrogen peroxide and cleaned the exit site of the tube in his right upper abdomen. A radiologist had inserted the tube three weeks before to divert his obstructed bile. It was merely a palliative effort to relieve the jaundice that occurred when his pancreatic cancer blocked the common bile duct leading from the liver. He cursed his fate every time he cleaned the tube.

A rapid knock came at his office door.

"Just a minute," he called. He used a safety pin to secure the bile bag back underneath his shirt, covered the tube with a small dressing, and tucked in his shirt again. "Come in."

"Mr. Davis, you asked to see me?" The scientist wore a long white lab coat over a navy dress.

"Yes, Ursula, I did." A body spasm accompanied a painful-sounding cough. Ursula winced. "I want you to contact your friend Kevin Schwab. It seems that our retrieval team has been unable to get the tissue we need."

He sat down in a soft office chair. "We have little choice without the surrogate harvest but to go back to the single cell stage."

"Do you think I can talk Dr. Schwab into giving us another supply? In my opinion—"

"I have known you to be very persuasive in the past."

She smiled thinly at the compliment but also remembered the last conversation she'd had with Kevin Schwab. "He won't help us anymore."

"Why not? He did before. Perhaps you should approach him on a personal level. We'll fly you out there. You can visit old friends, take Kevin out to a nice—"

"I'm sure he won't deal with us any further, Mr. Davis," she interrupted. "He called me a few days ago, trying to find out exactly what we are doing. He claimed to have gotten wind of our project—"

"Did you tell him?"

"Of course not. I told him that was impossible."

Davis sighed. "How could he have a clue?"

Ursula waved her arms. "He said he was sent some tissue to analyze—a specimen from a murder victim in Deer Falls. He told me it looked awfully familiar."

"Deer Falls? Why didn't you tell me about this before?"

"I didn't think it was important. Besides, he said he was analyzing tissue from someone who'd been killed in a murder, not a hit-and-run victim like our poor Lisa. And besides," she added, "there's no way on earth that Schwab could have received the clone."

Davis didn't regret not having told Ursula everything. She couldn't possibly keep it all in perspective. "What did he mean, it looked familiar?"

"He didn't explain. He just kept pressing me to tell him what we're doing."

How dare she not tell him these things! What else had she let slip? Had she leaked information to Seth Berringer? Was that why he was covering for them? He had to find out if Schwab had any contact with the medical examiner, Dr. Donovan.

"Hmmm." He tapped the desktop with his pen. "It still might be worth a trip to see Schwab."

"Trust me—he's not in a cooperating mood."

He looked at the researcher and sighed. "That will be all, Ursula."

Taken aback, she quietly stepped away from his desk and into the hall.

Behind her, Davis reflected on the worsening situation. Ursula had no idea of the seriousness of what she'd told him. Somehow Schwab had gotten a sample of that baby! And if that was so, the medical examiner hadn't destroyed it. And by now he likely knew exactly what a treasure he had in his hands.

He walked to the window and gazed at the clouds lying above the snow-covered Rockies. He placed his hand against the cold double window pane. Murder? That had to be their girl from Deer Falls. Ursula didn't know how Lisa had died because Davis had only told her she died in a hit-and-run. It was better that way. He rubbed the back of his yellowed hand.

It wasn't like they'd wanted her to die. She shouldn't have run. They had no choice.

He thought further about the news Ursula had brought him. A sudden smile spread across his face. The tissue was still available! He would instruct his men to talk with Donovan again.

But what about Berringer? They still hadn't figured out why he was protecting them. If he knew about their little project, he would likely want to contact them.

Perhaps Berringer had even taken the clone himself and disguised the body so no one would find out about the pregnancy.

"OK, Berringer," Davis whispered, staring at the mountains, "it's your move."

◆　◆　◆

Seth took an extra long shower just to savor not being under observation. After that, he ate breakfast, endured "Group," and met with Dr. Interman.

During his session they covered little ground, and Seth was pleased to find out that the sheriff's department had not left any instructions. Seth would be free to go at noon.

Seth almost ran from the session to the pay phone. He entered his calling card number, followed by Kerri's number. *Please be home!*

She answered on the third ring.

"Hi, Kerri." His voice was anxious.

"Seth! I was hoping you'd call me."

"I tried last night, but you must—"

"I was at work," she interrupted. "Will you be released today?"

"Yes. That's why I'm calling. I was wondering if you could pick me up. I understand if you can't make it. I can take a cab or—"

"Seth, slow down! I want to come get you, OK?" She smiled. "Man! Let a guy out of a mental institution and he goes manic on me." She giggled.

"Thanks a lot, girl." He sighed. "Listen, I'm free at noon. Is that a good time?"

"Perfect. I go to work at 3, so that'll give me plenty of time. I need to tell you about my visit with the medical examiner."

"You talked to Donovan?"

"That's a polite way to put it. I got a little carried away, to be honest."

"He's a jerk, Kerri."

"Seth!"

He lowered his voice and scanned the hall for any nursing staff. "I talked to him on the phone." He looked up and saw a nurse walking toward him. "Maybe we'd better talk about this in person."

"OK. I'll be there at noon."

"Bye."

Seth hung up the phone and smiled at the nurse. It was time to pack his bags.

◆ ◆ ◆

Sheriff Boatwright entered Lanny's Grill and removed his overcoat. "Morning, Lanny."

"Morning, sheriff. Cold enough for you?"

"This temperature ain't nothin', Lanny. I used to go barefoot on days colder 'n this." He moved to his corner table. "How 'bout a couple Cokes with extra ice?"

Lanny shook his head. "Coming right up."

He placed two frosty bottles in front of the sheriff. "You want the usual?"

"You know, I think I'll just have a burger today. Do you still make that bacon burger with jalapeño cheese?"

Lanny nodded.

"I'll take two."

"Any fries?"

He patted his abdomen. "I'd better not."

Lanny squinted. "Too bad about ol' Doc Berringer. Sounds like he really snapped."

The sheriff nodded. "I'm kind of glad to have that case coming to a close."

"I heard Coast Care dropped him. Just recently I called his office for an appointment. He'd been after me to come by to get my cholesterol checked. I'd been puttin' it off—don't know why." He chuckled. "Anyway, when I read about his trouble in the paper, I figured I wouldn't have to wait as long for an appointment as usual. But when I called, they offered me a checkup with a guy named Rotinski." He shrugged. "I told 'em to forget it." He shook his head. "I like Dr. Berringer."

The sheriff grunted.

"You know, he was in here the night he hit that girl. He even bought a few drinks." He stared at the front windows. "I don't believe he's ever had a drink in here before."

The sheriff took a sudden interest. So Berringer had indeed been drinking that night, just like he'd told them. So some of his story could be verified, like his drinks at Lanny's and his running over the girl. But the other stuff he'd told them was out of this world!

The sheriff didn't share his thoughts. "Yeah, he seemed like a nice guy."

Lanny left to fix the burgers, and Boatwright pulled out the morning paper. It would sure be nice to have this hit-and-run solved. Too bad it had such a devastating impact on the doctor, but . . . He slurped his first Coke straight from the bottle and wiped his mouth with the back of his hand. He supposed he'd flip out too if he hurt someone like that. Maybe it was even harder on the doctor—a man who'd devoted his life to helping people get well, then killed an innocent victim with his car. No wonder he snapped.

He wouldn't mind having a name to pin on the crime, even if he had to squelch his conscience to do it. With the election coming up, he didn't want too many unsolved cases hanging around.

He wondered how the doctor's evaluation was going up at Evergreen.

◆ ◆ ◆

Eric Donovan knocked softly on the door, then used his own key for Tammy Lynn's apartment. Tammy walked into the front room as he entered. "Eric . . . shouldn't you be at work?"

He shook his head. "We have to talk."

His look made her heart sink. "Not about us." She shook her head. "I'm not ready to hear this." She bit her lip.

"It's not about us, Tammy." He leaned over and kissed her cheek before he sat on the front edge of a flowered couch. "It's more serious than that."

Her face tightened. "Now that you're working with Connie, you probably don't need me around. She always was a breeze at transcription."

"This isn't about you, and it isn't about Connie. It's about the autopsy report on Lisa Dale." He wrung his hands. "Someone else knows."

"Someone else—"

"Berringer's been spouting off. He called me on the phone and accused me of lying." He rubbed his neck. "The next thing I know, some girl, Kerri Barber, evidently a friend of both Lisa Dale and Berringer, comes to the office and asks me why I'm covering up the truth. If he's told this girl, who else is in on the information?"

"So what? Let them ask their questions. The dead girl's an orphan, so no one cares how she died."

"Tammy, Seth Berringer called me from a state mental hospital. The sheriff had him committed after he confessed to the hit-and-run. My report and his version of the story were so different, they thought he was psychotic or something."

"I read about it in the paper. They didn't say why they thought he was crazy." She sat beside him and placed her hands in his. "Hey, it's unfortunate that this has happened to Berringer, but he brought it on himself. Why did he run over a dead body in the first place? We certainly didn't intend to hurt him." She squeezed his hands and locked eyes with his desperate gaze. "We did this for me, for us, remember? I'm sorry he got stuck in the middle, but don't we deserve to look out for ourselves once in a while? A chance like this doesn't come every day. Without the money I'd still be stuck with Sonny. You know that."

The pathologist sighed. "I guess you're right."

Tammy Lynn pulled away and put her hand on her chin. "You don't suppose Berringer botched an abortion on this girl, do you? Maybe that's why he disguised the death."

"Hmmm."

"Maybe he's working with the guy who asked me to change the report. Obviously *he* didn't want anyone to know about the real way she died either. I'll bet you Mr. Moneybags paid the doctor to do his dirty work for him—"

"—and when she died from the procedure, he panicked and tried to make it look like she'd died some other way."

"But why come forward now?"

"Maybe his conscience just got the best of him." He shook his head. "I don't know." Eric coughed nervously. "I just wish we'd never started this lie. It's getting worse all the time, like quicksand. People are starting to get suspicious. If they can prove we changed the report, I'll lose my position."

"It sounds like maybe Berringer isn't the only one with a guilty conscience around here." She touched his shoulder. "I wouldn't let them do that, Eric. I'd swear I was the only one who knew. I won't let them blame you. You can say you don't remember or something. If one of us has to go down, let it be me. I have less to lose."

"Tammy . . ." His eyes searched hers. "I can't let you do—"

She put her finger over his lips. "Shh. No one is going to find out, Eric." She shrugged. "And if they do, I'll take the fall. I'm the one who got us into this."

He nodded resolutely.

"Besides," Tammy offered, "who would you believe—the chief medical examiner or a physician who has no training in forensics—a doctor just released from a mental hospital?" She nodded and stood up. "It'll work, Eric, it'll work." She walked to the kitchen. "Now, would you like some lunch?"

❖ ❖ ❖

Tracy sulked in the lobby of the Deer Falls Inn. "I need a different room, Lou. My back is killin' me."

"We've been over this, honey," Lou Ellen moaned. "The heater in your old room will be fixed next week. You've got to put up with the stairs for another few days."

She rolled her eyes and sat on the couch next to a large blue glass ashtray. Every few minutes, she exhaled an irritated sigh and pulled hopelessly on her leather skirt in an attempt to keep it from riding too high.

The front doorbell clanged and diverted her attention to a striking young woman.

Kerri approached the desk, her face serious and unsmiling.

Lou Ellen looked up. "May I help you?" She pointed to a stack of papers on the counter. "Fill out your name and address. Rooms are $44.50 plus tax."

"I'm not here to rent a room." She pulled out a newspaper photograph of Lisa Dale. "I'm trying to put together some information about my friend. Do you recognize her?"

Lou Ellen stood and put aside the mascara case she was holding. She studied the photograph. "Where'd you get this picture?"

"From the *Deer Falls Gazette*." She paused, studying Lou Ellen's face. "This girl was killed, and I'm trying to find out what happened. She had an apartment in town but hadn't been living there. I thought she might have been staying here."

Lou Ellen twisted her face. "This isn't funny." She sat back down. "Did Wayne put you up to this?"

"I'm not sure what you mean." Kerri wrinkled her forehead.

"Is this a test? Of course I know her. She was staying in my motel—room 12. Things like that are hard to forget."

Tracy stood up and walked to the counter. "Can I see the picture?" She inspected the photograph. "Oh, she's pretty. What was her name? She looks like an April. I knew an April once. She was beautiful too."

Lou Ellen stood up again. "Didn't you know her? I thought you knew all the new girls."

"Oh, lands, Lou, she wasn't with us. I'd remember her."

Lou Ellen cursed under her breath.

Trying to understand what was happening, Kerri looked at Lou. "So she did stay here? What did you mean about things that are hard to forget?"

"Yeah, she was here—just one night. Well, not even the whole night, really." She suddenly changed her expression. "If you're working with Wayne, he should have told you all this."

"I'm not working with Wayne . . . whoever that is."

"The sheriff. I just assumed, since he's always the one investigating things around here . . ."

"I'm not working with the sheriff. I'm just a friend of Lisa Dale. I think she was murdered. Her autopsy showed that she didn't die from the hit-and-run like the paper said. She was long dead before her body was run over."

Lou Ellen paled and put her hand to her mouth.

Tracy looked at her and gasped. "You're white as a sheet, Lou. You'd better sit down."

Lou Ellen looked at Kerri. "You're making this up, aren't you? Wayne told you to say this, didn't he?" She shook her head. "He knew I felt bad about that girl. This isn't funny. It's not funny at all."

"I don't know what you're talking about, ma'am. No one has put me up to talking to you."

"Oh, my. My, oh, my," Lou Ellen blubbered. "This is just awful." She dabbed at the thick blue mascara that bordered her eyes.

Tracy put her arms around Lou's massive trunk. "There, there. What's got you so upset?"

"I just knew that room was cursed. I told you so, Tracy." She waited for a minute, blowing her nose and pulling out her compact mirror to inspect her eye shadow. "Wait a minute," she responded. "Wayne indicated that the medical examiner was sure she died from a hit-and-run."

"The report is wrong," Kerri said confidently. "Lisa most likely died at the hands of someone who was trying to perform an abortion." She watched Lou Ellen as she cleared her nose again. "Why did you feel bad? You said that Wayne knew you felt bad about that girl."

Lou Ellen composed herself. "No one likes to lose a customer." She turned to Tracy. "Please tell me you knew her."

"Sorry, Lou. I'd never forget a face like that one."

Kerri didn't understand. "Why is it important that she know her?"

Lou squinted. She couldn't tell Kerri what she thought about her friend. And she definitely couldn't admit that she'd let two men in to see Lisa on the night she died. Lou waved her hand. "It doesn't really matter. I just thought Tracy knew everybody."

Kerri decided to try a different angle. "Was Lisa alone? Did anyone come to visit her?"

Lou played ignorant. "How should I know? She might have had visitors."

"I believe some men were looking for her. An older man with gray hair and a younger Asian man with a mustache." Kerri studied Lou's response.

The motel owner bit her lip, leaving red lipstick smeared on her front tooth. "Listen, I get a lot of people in this place. I can't always remember from day to day . . ."

Kerri frowned. "Did she leave anything behind in her room?"

"No. I'm sure of that. I've been over the room myself. It's clean."

"And available," Tracy sulked. "Lou here won't let anyone stay in there since the girl died."

"Did you feel responsible?"

"Of course not," Lou Ellen snapped. "The room's bad luck though. You can't just let someone else stay in the room where somebody was staying on the night they were struck by a car. You might pick up their bad luck."

"It wasn't bad luck," Kerri countered. "She was murdered."

"That's your story," Lou stated more calmly than she felt. "My Wayne would have told me if that was true."

"Your Wayne doesn't have all the facts," Kerri responded, trying to interpret Lou Ellen's gaze.

Lou Ellen grunted and looked away.

Kerri softened. "Look, I'm sorry if I've upset you." She wrote her name and phone number on a registration paper and pushed it toward Lou. "Please call me if you remember anything. Something she said, where she was going, if someone came to visit—anything."

Lou shrugged. "Why are you doing this?"

"I'm not sure. I think I owe it to a friend to see that her killers don't get away scot-free."

Lou Ellen nodded soberly.

Kerri shrugged and walked to the front door. "Thanks."

Tracy watched her go. "Nice figure." She pulled at her leather skirt. "She probably does those aerobics or something. I used to do them, until I hurt my back."

Lou rolled her eyes. "I need to talk to Wayne about this. I had a bad feeling about that girl."

"You really think she was murdered, Lou?" Tracy leaned against the counter. "I need to get more insurance."

"The girl was hit by a car. You read the paper. That doctor admitted doing it himself."

"The lady said she died from an abortion. Where'd she get that idea? Did the medical examiner say that? I didn't read that in any paper." She moved back over to the lobby couch and pulled her skirt down as she sat. "The closest place you can get an abortion is over in Lakeland."

Lou raised her voice. "That girl don't know what she's talkin' about! My brother tells me about these things. She's a mixed-up kid who's upset about losin' her friend, that's all," she insisted with more confidence than she felt.

Tracy nodded her head. "I hope you're right, Lou. I can't afford any more insurance."

Wayne had better be telling her the truth about this! She felt bad enough knowing Lisa Dale had stayed in her place. Now she knew Lisa didn't work with Tracy. And she'd let those men have her key! She tried to stop her lip from trembling. If that girl was right . . . *O Lord, I've never tried to hurt anybody. Honest!*

CHAPTER
21

SETH nearly ran down the front steps of the hospital when the attendant opened the front door. Kerri smiled and hurried along behind. "Seth, wait!" She jumped the last two steps. "I parked over there." She pointed in the opposite direction.

"Oh." He smiled sheepishly. He thanked her for the fifth time for coming to get him.

"Would you stop it already? You're welcome, all right?" She grabbed his hand.

They walked along, not noticing the cold wind. "I've never been so glad to be outside."

"Did they let you out at all?"

"Not even once." He shook his head and glanced back at the formidable brick structure. "Alcatraz would have been nicer."

She laughed. As they approached the car, she slowed to a stop. "Seth?"

He looked over at her, noticing how nice she looked. *Easy*, he chided himself, *anyone would look nice to you about now.*

"Why did you ask me to come?"

He shrugged. "Who else?"

"I don't know. Your parents? A relative? Another physician?"

He shook his head. "My dad's dead." He shook with nervous energy. "My mom's in Florida—I haven't seen her for three years. I was an only child, and I don't have any close relatives. Another doctor?" He laughed. "I don't really want any of them to see me like this."

"But why me?"

He thought, then swelled with the exhilaration of freedom. "You're the prettiest—"

"Seth, be serious!"

He squinted at her. He *was* serious. He was really enjoying seeing her again. "You're the only one who knows the truth about what I've done whom I feel I can trust." He leaned against her Taurus and looked back at the hospital. "I told my psychiatrist the truth, but . . ."

"Did he believe you?"

"I'm not sure." He shrugged. "At least he realized I wasn't a danger to myself or others and that I'm not overtly psychotic."

"That took three days? I knew that."

"How long did it take you to figure it out?"

She smiled.

"Don't answer that!" he interrupted. "I don't think I want to know."

"Suit yourself." She put her nose in the air.

"Let's get out of here before they decide to keep me any longer." He shook his head and jumped into the passenger seat. "I half expected the sheriff to arrest me on another charge."

"Really?" She started the car.

"Really." He stared straight ahead. "The psychiatrist made it sound like he expected that too. I guess they need to figure out what I really did and indict me appropriately."

"They already know what you did." Kerri turned left at a stop sign.

"Correction. They know what I *said* I did. Unfortunately, it doesn't agree with the medical examiner's report."

"That guy's way off base."

Seth lifted his eyebrows. "Tell me about your visit. You actually went down and talked to him face to face?"

Kerri nodded her head rapidly. "I have a lot to tell you. I've been doing my share of snooping."

"I'm all ears."

"Are you hungry?"

"Are you kidding? You should see what they feed you at that place. And for the first two days, the only thing they gave me to eat with was a spoon." He sulked and imitated the high voice of the nurse. "Doctor's orders, Mr. Berringer. It's safer this way." He let out an angry sigh. "Have you ever tried eating ham with a spoon?"

Kerri's laugh slipped out in spite of her attempts to contain it.

"What's so funny?"

"You cutting meat with a spoon." She laughed again.

Seth suppressed a smile. "See if I ever ask you to pick me up from a state mental hospital again."

She laughed harder. So did he. A deep, emotion-releasing laugh.

Kerri weaved up the road like an inebriated teenager.

"Up there . . . Mom's Diner," he gasped.

Her face was red as she made the turn and parked the car. "I'll see if they have forks." She snickered before losing it again.

◆ ◆ ◆

Wayne Boatwright didn't like loose ends. He wanted everything tied up neat and tidy. All cases solved. All criminals behind bars. Chesapeake County—the safest place to live and raise a family, all because of Wayne Boatwright.

But that's not how he felt at the moment, and he worried about the election-year consequences. It didn't take the intelligence of a rocket scientist to pinpoint the source of his anxiety: Seth Berringer and the Lisa Dale case. Things weren't adding up to a characteristic Boatwright solution.

He stared at the file in front of him. What should he do now? A confession by the driver—evidence on his vehicle—a dead orphan. Why couldn't he put it all together?

Why would Berringer make up such a tale, saying he intentionally ran over a dead body? Was his story a product of his defense mechanisms? Or was it part of a sinister cover-up of another crime? Was Berringer covering for his own vehicular manslaughter?

Wayne looked at the clock on the wall opposite his massive desk. The three-day evaluation was winding up. It was time to talk to the psychiatrist about this Berringer guy.

The sheriff's door to the front office was cracked open a few inches. He could just see his secretary that way. He had an intercom but rarely used it. "Deb!"

She walked over and opened the door.

"Call Evergreen State Hospital and find out the name of the doctor responsible for Seth Berringer's evaluation. Get him on the phone. It's about time they get back to me on his workup."

She turned around.

"Oh, and could you get me some coffee? Three sugars and one creamer."

She mouthed the words as he said them. She'd heard them a thousand times before. She rolled her eyes and whispered, "I'm not stupid."

In less than four minutes she placed his coffee on his desk, intentionally avoiding his outreached hand. "I have Dr. Interman on line 2."

"Thanks." He watched her walk out before he reached for his coffee and picked up the phone.

"Dr. Interman? Sheriff Boatwright here. I'm calling about Seth Berringer. Can you give me an update on your workup?"

"Ahh, sheriff, I'm glad you called. Dr. Berringer is an interesting case."

The sheriff laughed. "Yeah, a real nutcase, huh?"

The psychiatrist bristled at the comment and shook his head. "Not exactly, sheriff. He's a deep thinker, that's for sure, and very hostile, and carrying a lot of guilt. But he's certainly not psychotic. He knows what he's doing. He's very capable of distinguishing reality from fantasy."

"So what are you sayin', doc—that Berringer is tellin' the truth?"

"I didn't say that. That's for you to judge. The purpose of the evaluation was to assess his mental competency, to determine whether he was capable of rational thought or was psychotic." Interman stroked his gray beard.

"That's it?"

"That's what the state asks me to do, yes."

Boatwright sighed. "You're not makin' my job any easier. Now I've got to figure out what to do with him." He paused. "Are you sure he didn't make the story up as a part of a protective defense mechanism because he was so upset about runnin' the girl down?"

"Not possible. Our testing showed no signs of that."

The sheriff cursed under his breath. "I guess I'd better come up there so I can question him some more." He couldn't just let this guy get away. The media would make Boatwright look soft on crime. But what could he charge the doctor with? Hit-and-run? Vehicular manslaughter was a serious charge—first-degree murder.

"Don't come looking for him here. He's been released."

The lawman looked at the clock. "But his seventy-two hours aren't up!"

"His evaluation was complete. We didn't have any instructions beyond the evaluation, so I let him go." He tapped on his desk, sensing the sheriff's frustration. "He doesn't seem to be a dangerous man to me, sheriff."

Boatwright's eyes simmered with anger. "You say he's feeling guilty and hostile?"

"I can't really pinpoint the source. But yes, he scores pretty high on those scales."

"I have to run. Can you get me a formal report anytime soon?"

"I'll fax you a copy by tomorrow."

"Great. Thanks, doc."

The sheriff slammed down the phone. If Berringer wasn't crazy . . . How could Boatwright piece all this together? The suspect must be intentionally lying.

He drummed on his desktop. Maybe they should polygraph him. But first he had to contact the chief medical examiner and make sure there hadn't been a huge mix-up. If Donovan confirmed his suspicions, he'd make sure he discovered what Berringer was trying to hide.

◆ ◆ ◆

While Eric Donovan enjoyed his long lunch hour, Connie's anxieties grew. At a few minutes after 1 P.M., the pathologist reappeared, popping an antacid tablet as he came through the office door.

"Hi, Connie. Any messages?" He slipped by her desk, not expecting a positive response.

His wife wrinkled her brow. "Just one. The sheriff from Chesapeake County called. He wanted to verify the results of the autopsy on Lisa Dale."

Eric grunted but didn't verbalize a reaction. Instead, he rubbed his left arm and unwrapped another antacid tablet.

Connie followed him to the back. "Do you mind telling me what's going on?"

He exchanged his sport coat for a long white lab coat. "What do you mean?"

"The call from the sheriff—the visit by that Barber girl—why all the attention on this case?"

"It's nothing really," he lied, shaking his head. "I guess that family doctor up in Deer Falls got into so much trouble, he started telling stories to get himself out."

Connie didn't drop the subject as he'd hoped. "He came down for the autopsy, right?"

"Yes. Maybe that was a mistake. I shouldn't have let him come." He picked up a thick file, opened it to the first page, and sat down. He obviously wanted to go on to other business.

His wife sighed. "Eric, I don't want to nag you. I want to help. I can see this thing is bugging you—why not tell me what happened? Getting it out might help." She began to massage his neck.

He closed his eyes and shut the file, sighing deeply. "I guess I shouldn't let it get to me. Dr. Berringer calls down here before the autopsy and tells me he thinks something is fishy about the case. He thought I should look beyond the hit-and-run. Then he comes down for the autopsy, and after it's all over, he runs to the sheriff's office and confesses to the hit-and-run, but also claims that the girl was already dead and that someone else had killed her." He hesitated as he carefully constructed a convincing lie. "It's almost as if he wanted me to believe there was foul play, so I would raise the question in my report."

Connie continued to work magic on her husband's neck and moved to the sides of his head. "I see. Maybe like he can't quite stand the fact that he killed her with his car?"

"Or worse." Eric started to relax a notch. Connie's gentle touch felt incredible. If she'd have stayed down here in the trenches with him instead of running off to fulfill her social calendar, he wouldn't be visiting Tammy for lunch.

"I think you'd better clue the sheriff in on your thinking."

"I'll give him a call in a few minutes." Or in a few hours, if she kept this up. "I just hope Berringer stops this absurd talk about the autopsy. He's only going to hurt himself. I have it all here in a black and white report." He chuckled. "And we're certainly not bringing the girl back for an exam."

Connie moved her hands to his shoulders and massaged him gently for another minute. She ended with a squeeze and pulled his head back against her. "Is that all that's bothering you?" She waited a moment. "Because if it's me or something about us . . . don't you think we can work things out?"

Eric stiffened. "I—I don't know what you mean. I've been under a lot of stress lately, that's all." He reached up and touched her hand. "I've enjoyed having you back down here. It's almost like old times."

"It can be that way again."

It could never be that way again. He'd gone too far, told too many lies. Connie deserved better.

The ringing of the phone startled her. "I'd better get that." She walked to the front office. "Call the sheriff, Eric. I left his number on your message board."

◆ ◆ ◆

Just being around Kerri seemed to help Seth relax. Or maybe it was getting out of the hospital, or his thought that things couldn't get much worse. Whatever, he felt better, and his appetite showed it for the first time in days.

Kerri looked at his plate incredulously. "Didn't they feed you in that place?"

Seth's lunch special of meatloaf, mashed potatoes, fried okra, and brown beans were history before Kerri could finish her Caesar salad. He shrugged and pushed back the empty plate. "I wish I had room for pie. This stuff was great."

Actually, Seth's finishing before Kerri had more to do with the amount of talking she'd done, explaining in detail her encounter with Sue, her discussion with Lou Ellen Boatwright, and her visit to see Eric Donovan.

"I wish I could've seen his face," Seth responded, shaking his head. "You actually told him he was going to answer to God for his actions?"

She nodded her head.

"Why doesn't that surprise me?" He smiled. She'd basically told Seth the same thing.

Seth's whole face changed when he smiled. As if all the anxiety just melted away. And his eyes—they were the first thing she noticed about him. Eyes that could stop her heart from beating with just one soft look.

"Hello?"

Kerri came to.

His voice softened. "What were you thinking?"

She blushed. "That you look younger when you smile," she responded truthfully.

He studied his hands. "I haven't felt so young lately." He looked up. "But I do feel younger when I'm with you."

"Would you tell me about your family, Seth? I don't seem to know much about your life until a few weeks ago." She touched his hand across the table. "I didn't know about your parents."

He shrugged. "I guess my recent problems have kind of gotten in the way of you knowing anything else about me."

"I'd like to hear it all—about you, I mean." He suddenly seemed self-conscious, but cute in a boyish sort of way.

"Not much to hear, really." He shrugged. "I grew up with my dad. My mom left us when I was twelve—ran off with her boss, a big insurance man in our town. Dad was a builder. He held things together pretty well until I left for college. Then alcohol took over his life. It was like he became a different person." His eyes met hers.

Was he going to cry? His eyes were wet.

"He died when I was in medical school. Cirrhosis." He exhaled slowly. "My mom and I send each other Christmas cards. That's about it."

Kerri reached over and took his hand. "I'm sorry, Seth."

They sat quietly for a minute longer before she spoke again. "Why did you go into medicine?"

A smirk lightened his face. "I've been asking myself that question lately. Anyway, I've wanted to be a doctor ever since I was a kid. When my best friend was hit by a car, I went to see him in the hospital every day for a week. His doctor showed me around, showed me my friend's X-rays and everything. I thought it was neat." He shrugged again. "I guess I never stopped thinkin' it was neat."

She nodded. A waitress delivered the check, and Seth grabbed it.

"My treat. It's the least I can do after all you've done."

Kerri nodded her acknowledgment. "I want to help." It was the truth, as corny as it sounded. "What will you do next, Seth?"

"I've been thinking about that. I guess I need to gather my defense. It's only a matter of time before the sheriff figures out that the psychiatrist said I'm not crazy. Then he'll have to hold me accountable for my actions. I'm sure it's not legal to tamper with murder evidence."

"But he doesn't believe she was murdered. He thinks you killed her in a hit-and-run."

"That's why I need evidence that my story is true."

"But with Dr. Donovan's report—"

"Dr. Donovan isn't the only one who knows about the autopsy findings. He was so intrigued by finding the baby that he sent a sample to the N.I.H., to one of his buddies—a Dr. Kevin Schwab. Ever heard of him?"

"Kevin Schwab, Kevin Schwab," she repeated. "Why do I know that name?"

"The shroud of—"

"The shroud scientist. Of course! I've read all about him! It's really fascinating."

"Yeah, well, putting all that aside, Donovan said he was going to send him some tissue to analyze. He said he owed him a favor."

Kerri looked puzzled.

"Don't you see? If this guy did DNA studies on a baby Lisa was carrying, we can prove it was her child by the DNA match." He paused. "So, all I need to do is find that baby, and my record will be cleared."

"Then they'd know you're telling the truth."

Seth nodded.

She looked at her watch. "We'd better get going. I need to be at work by 3."

Seth paid the bill and followed her to the car. Once they were on their way, he took advantage of her attention on the road to study her profile.

Her hair was full and short, but it framed her face in a perfect compliment of soft, brown wisps. A turtleneck shirt hid her slender neck. A dainty silver earring dotted each earlobe. Her face certainly didn't need any work, and the application of eye-liner and lipstick revealed her minimalist makeup philosophy.

How had she ever got mixed up with a man like him? She was so lovely. And it was more than just the way she looked. She seemed so together, so . . . pure and innocent.

Kerri cast a glance out of the corner of her eye. "OK, Mr. Quiet, what are you thinking?"

Busted!

"I was wondering about you," he responded. "You've never told me about your family."

"Fair enough. I come from a big family by today's standards." She adjusted her rearview mirror. "We're a typical modern family, I guess. My oldest brother, Doug, lives in Greenville, Rod lives in Lincoln, and Jean lives near Asheville. I'm the baby. My parents live over in Buck County. My dad still runs a country store there."

Seth noticed that when she talked about her family, it was impossible for her to suppress a hint of a smile. And when she smiled, her cheek dimpled. He fought the urge to reach for her face. "Why did you go into medicine?" he asked, mimicking the question she'd asked him.

She wrinkled her nose. "Genetic flaw?" She looked at him again.

He rolled his eyes. "I knew it."

"It was just natural, I guess. My parents were constantly reaching out to others, always helping others, even when they didn't have much themselves. I saw nursing as a way I could do the same thing." She shrugged. "And I like the action. The E.R. has always fascinated me."

They rode along for a few more minutes, talking about their interests and their favorite colors, foods, sports, music.

When they arrived at his home, Seth found himself wishing the drive could have been longer. He looked over at her, their eyes meeting for a moment that seemed to solidify the bond they felt between them. "Thanks."

He began walking to his front door.

"Seth, you forgot something!" She reached over the seat and retrieved the drab gray bag. She opened the door and handed it to him.

As she did, their hands touched, and Seth paused again. "Thanks again," he added, leaning toward her. When she didn't flinch, he continued forward until their lips met in a soft, raptured moment. A friendly kiss that wanted more and yet held back a flood of emotions seeking release.

Kerri surrendered briefly and leaned forward before slowly pulling away.

"Bye, Seth."

He tried to swallow. "Bye," he whispered quietly.

CHAPTER
22

THE first thing Seth did was change clothes and head to his office. He knew his appointments had all been postponed until the following day. But he knew the paperwork would still be piling up, so he wanted to sort things through before arriving the next morning.

It puzzled him to see so many cars in the parking lot. Patients' cars? There wasn't anyone here to see patients. He walked in the back way, and he could tell by the response of his nurse that she didn't expect him.

"Dr. Berringer!"

He squinted questioningly. "Hi." He walked past an exam room. Work was definitely in progress. He decided against opening the exam room door and retreated instead to the door of his office manager, Barb Sullivan. He knocked, then pushed the door open.

"Dr. Berringer!"

"Hi, Barb." He sat down. "What's going on around here?"

She stared at him for a moment and leaned forward, wrinkling her brow. "You really don't know?"

He shook his head.

"Have you read your mail?"

"No." He shrugged. "I came straight to your office after I saw that things were obviously going on without me."

"Hmmm, I see. Well . . ." She coughed. "I guess that really about sums it up. Things are going on without you, I mean." She tensed her jaw. "You'd better check your mail."

He straightened. "You've obviously heard the news. Why don't you just share it with me? It's not like I didn't really expect it."

"You've been replaced." She pulled out her copy of a letter written from Coast Care to Dr. Seth Berringer.

"They can't just fire me because I had a mental evaluation, Barb. Besides, the evaluation proved I'm not crazy, if anyone would like to add that to the gossip mill around here."

"They didn't fire you for that, Dr. Berringer. They cite a clause in your contract that says you can be dismissed without cause with a two-week notice."

"Hmmm. Well, it hasn't been two weeks. I could still work for another ten days or so."

She shook her head. "You had vacation coming, Dr. Berringer. They'll keep you on salary until the end of the month. They asked me to inform you that you should clean out your office so Dr. Rotinski can move in his things as soon as possible."

"Great," he muttered. "Just great." He sighed deeply and collapsed back in the chair. "All my life I worked for this." He shook his head, not knowing how to respond. After a moment he looked up. "What do you suggest?"

Barb looked up and lowered her voice. "Why don't you get a lawyer? If you can prove they've treated you unfairly—"

"It's not likely to do any good, Barb. It's all within the rights of their contract, just like you said."

"What are you going to do?"

"I'm not sure, but I'll tell you one thing—I'm not going to lay back and let my reputation be completely destroyed without a fight." He knew he'd have to come up with some solid evidence that he was telling the truth.

He stood and walked to the door. "Thanks, Barb. Tell your new doctor I'll clean out my stuff afterhours." With that, he turned and left. He didn't want to talk to anyone else. Not yet.

He had to talk to Kevin Schwab.

◆ ◆ ◆

When Kerri arrived at the E.R. a few minutes after dropping Seth off, she tried to throw herself into her work. Fortunately, her assignment was on the non-acute side, so she didn't have anything too serious to deal with. Chronic bronchitis, back pain, menstrual cramps, and constipation failed to capture her attention. Not that anything would have. She plugged along from patient to patient, alternately thinking how wonderful she felt experiencing Seth's embrace, and scolding herself for letting her heart go.

He's so manly, but so vulnerable, in a boyish sort of way. I love his self-effacing manner, and those eyes . . . just touching his hand . . . I can't believe he—

"Earth to Kerri!" Laurie stood with an outstretched chart in her hand.

Kerri looked up from her seat at the nursing station.

"Sore throat, room 8."

She accepted the chart. "Thanks."

She checked her watch. Only 4:30? It was going to be a long night.

◆ ◆ ◆

When Lou Ellen arrived for her weekly visit, she found Janet Boatwright slumped in her Geri-chair. Lou put her things on the hospital bed and struggled for a few minutes to get her mother a bit further back in the chair. Then she retied the sheet around her mother's waist to hold her there.

She deftly tied a bib around her mother's neck and unsnapped the lid to the Tupperware bowl filled with applesauce. "Open up," she coached. "There, it's good, isn't it? . . . OK, swallow . . . Good . . . There."

Lou kept up her running commentary of encouragement and instruction for only a few bites before launching in on her story of Kerri's visit to the Inn earlier that day.

Her story lasted through the applesauce, fixing Janet's hair, and the application of her makeup. Actually, the story was relatively short, but Lou Ellen's commentary and personal agonizing over the situation flowed in a continual stream.

"I knew something was going on with that girl. She seemed so scared."

Janet sat without speaking, just as she had for the past eighteen months since her last stroke.

"Do you think Wayne had something to do with this? Maybe he's just trying to upset me. He knows I think that room is cursed. Maybe he's just makin' fun of me. That would be just like Wayne."

She brushed her mother's thinning, white hair.

"So why should I let it upset me?" She paused to blow her nose, sending a rhythmic snort into the hallway. "It just doesn't make sense. But if Wayne's not behind this, why would this girl make up such a story? And if this Lisa girl wasn't working with Tracy, what was she doing at the Inn? And why would she stay at the Inn if she had an apartment in Deer Falls? All these questions really disturb me, Momma."

Lou Ellen sniffed again and dabbed the corner of her eyes with a tissue. "So why did those two men ask to get into her room if she wasn't working with Tracy? And why did they pay for the services?"

She wrung her hands. "It's blood money now, isn't it, Momma? I shouldn't have taken it. But how could I have known?"

Lou continued babbling until her own eye shadow began to mix with the rouge over her ample cheeks. "I had a bad feeling about that girl all along. I don't know why—I just did."

She looked at the family photo album, yet unopened. "Do you want to see pictures, Momma?" She sniffed again. "I don't feel much like it somehow."

She opened the first page anyway and stared at the aging photographs of years gone by. Another happy lifetime when Wayne, Lou Ellen, Janet, and Harold Boatwright were together. Dysfunctional for sure, but together and mostly happy nonetheless.

She looked at a picture of little Wayne. "Doesn't he look like a character, Momma? It'd be just like him to convince that girl to tell me a story just to get my goat. He knew I was upset about her death and all."

Lou Ellen nodded again and dabbed her eyes. "That's it, isn't it, Momma? The girl was lyin' just to get my goat. Wayne put her up to it just to upset me. And there I go, getting all distressed just like he—"

"Miss Barber is telling the truth."

The voice was Janet's.

Lou Ellen jerked away and flailed her hand into the mostly empty applesauce bowl, causing it to clatter to the floor. Her eyes were wide, and her mouth hung open.

"Momma?" She stared at her a moment, then reached out to touch her mother's face. "Momma, you talked!" Lou's face took on a wild appearance of wonder and terror. Her eyes narrowed into a fine squint. "Momma? Say something to me."

Janet maintained a lost gaze, an unfocused attention on the far wall, just as she had for months. Had it all been Lou Ellen's imagination, the work of an overwrought emotional state? She couldn't accept that.

She knew she'd heard her mother's voice—a message for her daughter! She backed up and stumbled quickly into the hall, calling for a nurse. "Somebody come quick! Momma talked! Momma talked to me!"

CHAPTER
23

KERRI sat at the far corner table of the hospital cafeteria. She was dressed in her green scrubs with a white lab coat on top, the requirement of anyone leaving the E.R. while on duty. Although it was 8 P.M., it was her supper break. Eating any earlier made her shift seem inordinately long. Angie Blackstock sat across from her with wide eyes, having responded to Kerri's plea that she come by during her supper break to talk.

"You kissed him?"

"*He* kissed *me*."

"Kerri."

"OK, OK, I kissed him. We kissed. Whatever!" Her words were hushed but emphatic.

Angie shook her head. "I can't believe you." She smiled. "After all your talk about never dating a non-Christian—"

"It's not like we're really dating. I just went to pick him up."

"And you kissed him, Kerri. You don't kiss a mere friend." She paused and squinted at her. "You kiss your boyfriend."

"But I didn't plan it that way. It happened so fast."

"Nothing happens that fast, girl. I've listened to you talk about Seth before. It's pretty obvious that your feelings didn't spring up all at once. You've been nursing this one for a while." She shook her head when Kerri started to protest. "Just listen to yourself. The way you describe the moment is something out of a fairy tale."

Kerri sighed. She had to admit it—she had handed over her heart. "I didn't plan to fall for him." She played with her tossed salad.

Angie looked at her friend. "I'm not blaming you, Kerri. I just want you to see what's happening. That's what you called me for, right? We help keep each other on track."

Kerri nodded and looked at her plate.

"He *is* awfully cute. And he's a great doctor, and he really cares for people. I can see how you'd get tangled up so quickly."

"It can't be wrong to like him."

"Of course not." Angie raised her eyebrows. "I just want you to be careful. Make sure you're not just rescuing a lost puppy. He needs you, for sure, but what about you? What do you need?"

"He's so sensitive—"

"Right."

"And so handsome."

"I can't argue with you."

"And he doesn't focus on money like so many—"

"Be careful, Kerri," Angie interrupted. "He's not a believer. You need someone who can stand beside you in your faith."

She sighed again. "I know. That's why I called you. I've been fighting with myself ever since I first felt attracted to him. I find myself wanting to be with him, so energized when he's around, but feeling frustrated, knowing I shouldn't give my heart away when he can't share the most important thing in my life."

"How does he feel?"

She shrugged. "We haven't really talked about it. We've just been friends—until he kissed me," she added.

"Are you sure he feels the same? I mean, a lot of people offer a simple good-bye peck, and it doesn't mean anything. Maybe you're just reading a little too much into—"

"I can tell the difference, Angie. He kissed me like . . . well, you know . . . like he wanted me," she admitted with a blush.

They sat quietly for a moment before Angie responded. "I guess you know what to do."

"Talk to him."

Angie nodded.

Kerri played with her salad. Angie always had a way of making her face the truth.

◆ ◆ ◆

Seth stopped at the grocery store prior to heading home. He picked up cereal, milk, some fruit, a bag of potato chips, and some Oreos before looking at the meat. He picked up a steak and fingered it briefly before setting it down again. Maybe he should start watching his food budget. He didn't know how long he'd be unemployed.

He walked the aisles for a few moments looking for something for supper. Several people watched with interest, and he thought he heard an older lady whisper his name. Was all of Deer Falls watching him? He smiled thinly at the checkout girl. He'd seen her a hundred times before. Most of the time, she'd called him by name. Today she only nodded.

"Sixteen sixty-two."

Seth handed her a twenty. "Nice evening."

The girl nodded again. "Three thirty-eight in change."

"Paper or plastic?"

Seth looked up to see the bag-boy shoving his cereal into a plastic bag. "Plastic will be fine," he responded with a shrug.

He walked out without speaking. Maybe it would be best just to move away and start over.

He slipped into his van. It wouldn't be right not to set the record straight. He was getting the shaft, and someone was covering up the truth. "I'm not leaving Deer Falls until I can leave without running away from Lisa Dale," he muttered to himself.

He passed Chesapeake General and thought for a moment about trying to see Kerri in the E.R. He rejected that idea, however, when he thought of the attention he would attract just by showing up. He wanted to tell her about Coast Care's decision, but that would have to wait until he could see her outside the hospital.

He stopped at the mailbox and retrieved two bills, a Land's End catalog, and a letter from a physician recruiter. He looked at the letter reflectively. Coast Care must have told them he'd be looking for a job. He surveyed the opportunities in Alaska, Montana, South Dakota, New York City. He pulled forward and stopped his van in the driveway. In minutes he was sitting down to his supper of Cocoa Puffs and milk.

As he ate, his thoughts vacillated between losing his job, restoring his reputation, discovering the truth about how Lisa Dale died, and Kerri

Barber. Mostly he just thought about Kerri—her smile, her face, her laugh, the tender touch of her hand in his, the soft warmth of her mouth.

He shook his head and tried to focus on a plan to clear his name. Focusing was difficult with Kerri on his mind. Whatever else came of this, at least he'd stumbled into a relationship that looked like it had some promise. But what she saw in him after all he'd told her, he was sure he'd never know.

He pushed the cereal box away from him and put the empty bowl in the sink. He paced around the old farmhouse talking to himself and grasping for clues. His eyes lit upon the Bible he'd used to look up the verse his patient had quoted to him. It sat on the end table in the living room, next to an overstuffed lounge chair.

That's what had started his trouble, wasn't it? If he wouldn't have felt so guilty after reading that Scripture, he wouldn't have confessed the whole mess to the sheriff, or to Kerri for that matter.

He put the Bible back on the shelf. Maybe Dr. Interman was right. Maybe God was an imaginary projection, created out of our own need to punish our guilt. Seth walked out onto his back deck, a large wooden structure he'd built himself the year after moving to Deer Falls and buying the old house. The evening had turned to night, and a chill hit him immediately after opening the back door.

He gazed into the expansive sky. Was God imaginary? Then why did he seem so real to Kerri? How could she seem so normal and yet talk about God like he was right beside her? And why did it seem so right to follow the Bible's instruction to confess?

He wrapped his arms around himself to ward off another chill. His thoughts turned to Kerri again. He knew her well enough to know that she could only love a man who shared her personal faith.

He shook his head. He doubted he could ever believe like that, even if it meant that Kerri would want him the way he wanted her.

Why was Kerri so sure about what she believed? Could anyone really know that God cares about us like she said? Or was she just falling into a giant psychological trap like Dr. Interman described? That didn't set right with Seth either.

The crisp, cold air was doing little to clear the confusion that clouded his mind. He shivered again and slipped back inside his home.

He knew what Kerri would suggest. She'd say he should pray. He snorted at that idea. He remembered the last time he'd tried that, right after

Ms. Templeton told him to. He'd asked to get out of this mess and look where that prayer got him—in Evergreen State, out of a job, and under suspicion by a sheriff who was probably chomping at the bit to have him charged in the death of Lisa Dale.

He sat in his recliner and gathered an old afghan around his shoulders. "OK, God," he whispered, "I don't really know where else to turn. I don't even know if I believe in you. Even if you're real, like Kerri says, I'm not sure why you'd listen to me, after all I've done to foul up my life." He shook his head. "But . . . help me find the truth."

His words seemed to bounce off the ceiling, mocking him for his weakness. *Just look at you, Seth. You're just doing this so you can tell Kerri you prayed.*

He closed his eyes and tried to shut out the accusations.

"Help me, God. Show me the truth."

The silence screamed. The house seemed cold. And Seth felt totally alone.

◆ ◆ ◆

Doc struggled to remember the name he had used the last time he spoke to Donovan. "Dr. Donovan? Uh, Dr. Yamatsu here."

Eric Donovan clenched his teeth and lowered his voice. He thought Connie was in the kitchen, but he spoke into the phone in hushed tones just in case. "Yes, Dr. Yamatsu, I've been expecting your call."

"You have?" Doc nodded at Bill, who was sprawled out on the motel room floor, stretching his back. "Does that mean I won't need to tell you want I need?"

"You need the clone."

"How did you find out?"

"The tissue was analyzed."

"But only a few could have recognized it."

Donovan bit his lip. He didn't want to betray Schwab, as he had promised to pretend he knew nothing about the fetus. "It doesn't matter how I know. I've read the current genetics journals. The code isn't exactly a secret," he lied. "I know I have what you need." He tried to sound tough. "It's not going to come cheap."

"We are prepared to give you a fair price."

"What do you have in mind?" Donovan tried to calm his racing heart. A dull pain had returned in his left arm, and sweat beaded his forehead.

"Fifty thousand."

The pathologist laughed. "You don't seem to understand the stakes here. I know it's more valuable than that."

"I'll need to check with my source. I've not been authorized to do more."

"You are in no position to argue, Dr. Yamatsu. Tell your source I hold the evidence that could get you convicted of murder. You know that as well as I."

"If you bring that out, you'll implicate yourself as well. Don't be a fool. You'd lose everything you've worked for."

"I'm ready to quit anytime. I'll not be losing anything."

The look on Doc's face showed anger and desperation. "What do you want?"

"Five million." He rubbed his arm. "Any less and I'll forget what I did with the specimen forever."

"You're insane."

"I know your source can afford it. He's paying you well, isn't he?"

Doc cursed. Bill looked at him and stood up, concerned over the younger man's lack of composure. "Don't tick him off," he whispered.

Doc grunted. "I'll talk to my employer and call you back."

"I'll be waiting."

Doc slammed down the phone. "That arrogant—"

On the other end, Eric gently put the phone back on his desk. In the kitchen, Connie held her breath and pushed the off button as soon as she heard Eric disconnect.

What was her husband doing? It was a whole lot more than an immature fling with his secretary, that was for sure.

◆ ◆ ◆

Lou Ellen paused briefly to catch her breath as she stood beside Lanny's coatrack. Smoke and the aroma of fried seafood thickened the air. Thirsty customers lined the bar, and the clink of tall glasses and tableware punctuated noisy conversations. With her brow knitted, she scanned the large front room. She had rushed from the nursing home to the sheriff's office, to Wayne's home, and back to the nursing home again to check on her mother's progress.

Janet appeared just as she had for months—her stare distant, her expression displaying no meaningful recognition. No amount of prodding or talk could entice her into speaking again. Finally, after an exhausting hour, the nursing home staff asked the exasperated daughter to leave so they could put Janet back in her bed.

Wayne wasn't to be found at the office or at his home. Since his divorce and even for months before, if the truth be told, Wayne could be found at suppertime in one of a few eating establishments around town. Lanny's should have been Lou's first stop, not her last, but with her mind racing, sensible behavior was out of the question.

She spied him at his favorite large table, surrounded by the mayor and several other men in dark suits, as well as two of the sheriff's off-duty deputies.

She pushed her way forward, weaving between the crowded tables, her large pocketbook striking more than one irritated customer during her progression. She arrived at Wayne's table in a state just short of panic, looking like she had dashed off in the middle of removing her eye shadow.

Blue, matted makeup had thickened into an irregular streak beneath her right eye. The left looked better, but a quick glance revealed what appeared to be a smudge extending toward her left ear, as if she had repetitively wiped the corner of her eye with a moist rag.

"Wayne, we have to talk." Her breathing was erratic.

The sheriff choked on a shrimp fritter. The mayor dodged a flume of fried batter.

"Lou Ellen, what are you doin' here?" He coughed again into his napkin.

"Momma talked—that girl was murdered. Momma told me so. Oh, lands, I knew somethin' bad was going on! She spoke, I tell you, she—"

Wayne stood and grabbed his sister's arm. Now was not the time for pleasant introductions. Lou was out of control and spilling a stream of misinformation in the wrong crowd. "Let's talk private."

When she tried to pull away, Wayne clamped down harder. "Try to calm down, Lou. Let's go somewhere else to talk," he hissed through clenched teeth.

She yielded to the searing pain just above her left elbow. When she began walking with her brother, the sheriff loosened his grip.

Behind them, the mayor could barely contain an incredulous laugh. The deputies just looked at each other and grinned.

Lou stumbled into the parking lot behind a rapidly moving Wayne

Boatwright. Once they were clear of the door, he turned to examine her in the moonlight. "Lou Ellen, what's gotten into you? You look horrible!"

The shock of the statement and the pain in her arm brought Lou Ellen to tears. "Oh, Wayne!"

He rolled his eyes and ushered her into his car, then started the engine and turned on the heater. He handed his sister a handkerchief and winced as she emptied her sinuses with a deep, sonorous snort.

He tried to keep his voice low and steady. "Can you tell me what this is all about?"

Lou stumbled through the story of Kerri Barber's visit to the Inn and her own visit later in the day to see their mother.

"It's an omen, Wayne. You've got to talk to that girl. Momma's givin' us a message."

"Try to look at this rationally. Did you actually see Momma's lips move?"

"No, not exactly. I was pointing to the picture album," she responded. "But it was her voice, Wayne. Just as clear as mine is now."

"You were upset by the girl's visit. She was way out of line, torturing you like that. She's fixated on this wild story Berringer told her. But the story is a lie, Lou. None of it matches the autopsy results. I verified that myself with a phone call to the medical examiner just this afternoon."

"Maybe Berringer's the killer then. Maybe he killed her and came up with this story to cover it up." She fumbled with the strap on her pocketbook. "I've had a bad feeling about this all along. Now with Momma indicating that it's a murder and all—"

"Come on, Lou Ellen. Momma hasn't spoken a word since—"

"Since five o'clock. You weren't there, Wayne. I heard her myself. I think she knew I would tell you and wanted to help you out." She sighed. "You know the truth is gonna come out sooner or later. Berringer must be tied to those other creeps who came to the Inn."

"If Berringer murdered her, why would he dispute the medical examiner's findings?"

She sniffed. "I don't know. This whole thing doesn't make sense." She stared at the front windshield, fogged over from her heavy breathing. "Maybe he tried to run her over and is just trying to throw you off the track with a stupid story." She rubbed her finger against the window. "Why would Momma say the girl was tellin' the truth?"

The sheriff looked at his sister. If she really thought their mother had said something, maybe he should send her to Evergreen State.

He shook his head. "What did you tell Miss Barber?"

"I don't remember. I was so upset."

"Think, Lou Ellen! This is important! Did you tell her the girl was working at the Inn?"

"No." She shook her head resolutely. "She wasn't workin' there, Wayne. Tracy said she didn't know her."

"But what about those men—"

"They was after her, Wayne! Don't you see? And I let them into her room!" She started sniffing again and caught her breath in rhythmic gasps.

Wayne cursed. "Don't cry. You didn't know. It's history." He looked out the fogged window. "You told me the men paid you to visit her. So she must have invited them. Just because Tracy didn't know her doesn't mean she she wasn't cutting in on their business."

Lou Ellen sighed and tried to compose herself. She retrieved a compact mirror from her pocketbook. "Oh, dear, I look a wreck!" Gasping at her appearance, she busied herself with wiping off the eye shadow. Several times when she hit a resistant smudge, she moistened her finger with her tongue and transferred it to her cheek, then rubbed even harder with a tissue. "I can't believe the mayor saw me like this!" She looked at her brother. "Oh, Wayne, I hope I didn't embarrass you. I'm so sorry."

"Forget it. The mayor's a big supporter of mine. You know Bob—he's never offended."

"I feel terrible."

"I know, I know." He flipped on the defroster. "Listen, I know you're upset about this, but please don't mention it around town. I'll handle the investigation. If there's a problem around here, I'll get to the bottom of it." He studied her a moment longer. "I don't know why this has upset you so. You've always just let people go their way in the past. As long as they stayed out of your way, it didn't matter to you what they were doing."

"Don't you see? She paid me for a room—a *safe* room, Wayne. And I let her down. I let someone in her room—someone who might have killed her."

"OK, Lou, that's one possibility. But leave the investigatin' to me. And don't spread this kind of news around town. It wouldn't be good for your business." It wouldn't help his reelection bid either.

She blew her nose again. "I'll try."

"Why don't you get cleaned up and come in and eat. Have a drink to calm yourself down." He nodded toward the door of the restaurant. "Lanny has a nice new ladies' washroom. He showed it to me himself."

"I need to go home—I'm a wreck. I've embarrassed myself enough for one day. I don't think I could face seeing those men again right now."

Wayne shrugged. "Suit yourself. I'm going back in to eat."

Lou Ellen headed to her car. "Thanks, Wayne. I'll be seein' you."

The sheriff watched her go. Their mother talked? A message? An omen? He rolled his eyes. Then again, was it possible Lou was on to something? Was Berringer linked to the two men the sheriff talked to on the night of Lisa Dale's death? Did he intentionally run her down and make up the abortion story as a cover-up?

He rubbed his chin. The postcard Ms. Barber received did make it sound like Lisa Dale was afraid of someone coming after her.

And why would the psychiatrist say Berringer was so full of guilt and hostility unless he was hiding a crime?

Boatwright walked back into Lanny's and deeply inhaled the fried seafood smell. He would need more calories if he was going to figure all of this out.

CHAPTER
24

KERRI'S shift ran long, so she arrived home at midnight. She had been pulled from the non-acute side to help out with an elderly male patient who had come in with congestive heart failure. His breathing had been severely labored, and he had to be sedated before being put on a mechanical ventilator to assist his breathing until the fluid in his lungs could be removed by medications. Because he was so ill, she stayed with him until his transfer to the cardiac intensive care unit.

Once that experience was behind her, she wanted only to escape the busyness of the E.R. and seek the solitude of her apartment. It always took her an hour to unwind. Lying down before that guaranteed insomnia.

She hung her coat in the closet and glanced into the kitchen, noting with some disappointment that her answering machine was not blinking. Seth hadn't called.

She rubbed her hands for warmth since the trip from the hospital was not long enough to benefit from her car heater. After microwaving some water, she sat down at the kitchen table to make a cup of decaffeinated tea and read the day's mail. An electric bill and a seed catalog. About as exciting as her answering machine. Kerri looked wistfully at the clock. It was too late to call Seth, though she was anxious to know how he was doing.

She carried her tea into her small den and sat on a flowered couch. As she sipped, she prayed, her thoughts repeatedly drawn to Seth and their new relationship.

You know I want to do what you want, Lord. And you know how much I've fallen for Seth. I can admit that to you. I've always wanted a man who knows you, someone who can share my love for you. So how did I ever get mixed up with Seth like this? I know he's not a Christian. But he's so caring, Lord. And so vulnerable—so open—so handsome.

Her thoughts drifted from her prayer to the good-bye they'd shared earlier that day. It had felt nice to have him reach for her that way.

She sighed. *I'm sorry for drifting off, Lord. I know I sometimes push ahead of where you want me to be. Forgive me. I know Seth is seeking answers. Please help him find the truth. Show him how much you love him. And help me to know what to do about him.*

She thought for a moment, then added, *And help me uncover the truth about Lisa Dale. She was my friend. I owe her that much. In Jesus' name, Amen.*

She sat for a moment longer, feeling lonely but not alone, full of thoughts but empty of answers. Silently she rose and prepared for bed.

Maybe she'd see him tomorrow. But would she be able to tell him how she felt? How could she tell him he had to be a Christian to be her boyfriend without sounding high and mighty?

She stretched out on her bed and pulled the quilt up to her neck. *What if he doesn't really care about me like I think? Maybe to him a kiss is not such a big deal. Maybe he was just so happy to be out of Evergreen . . . No, that wasn't how he kissed me. What did I see in his eyes? Love or just passing infatuation?*

She tried to sleep. She scolded herself for sounding more like a naive schoolgirl than a woman who knew about true love.

And yet somehow she knew he'd felt what she'd felt. She smiled at the thought and fell quickly into needed slumber.

◆ ◆ ◆

The next morning Seth awoke early, long before the sun rose over the bay east of Deer Falls. He spent the first hour organizing everything he knew about Lisa Dale, including notes on his memories of the night she died, her autopsy, and his conversations with Eric Donovan and Sheriff Wayne Boatwright. After an intense hour his hand grew weary, and his thoughts focused on the fact that all he had was his memory. Other than Kerri's copy of Lisa's postcard, he had no hard evidence to convince anyone that his story was anything more than a fabrication.

He had to find Lisa's baby! If Donovan had told him the truth, the baby was sent to Kevin Schwab and wasn't cremated with Lisa. If Seth could find that child, the DNA studies would prove that the baby was Lisa's and that the autopsy report was a hoax. Then he could clear his name and . . . And what? Get his old job back? Was that what he wanted? To practice medicine as dictated by Coast Care?

He shook his head no in response to his own question. But at least he could hold his head up in the community again. And armed with the truth, he could stand up to the sheriff. It was just a matter of time before Boatwright would come after Seth with more charges, and this time the doctor wouldn't be rescued by apparent insanity. He sighed deeply, then stood up to make some coffee. He put five overflowing scoops of coffee into a filter and let the first drippings fall straight into his favorite mug.

Seth sipped the resulting brew, which neared Herculean strength. As he drank, his mind focused on a plan. Since Donovan obviously wasn't cooperating, Seth's first contact would have to be with Dr. Kevin Schwab himself.

He made more than a dozen calls to Information. Schwab's home phone was unlisted, as expected. Seth decided to ask about common names in hopes of locating a relative but came up only with a number for a Bill Schwab in a town a hundred miles from the N.I.H. He then asked about the N.I.H.'s directory and obtained numbers to six different departments Schwab might be involved in.

He called the Center for Biologics Evaluation and Research, the National Center for Research Resources, the National Library of Medicine, and the National Center for Human Genome Research before reaching a secretary who acknowledged that Dr. Schwab worked in her building. She transferred him to another secretary, who forwarded his call back to a DNA sequencing lab. A lab assistant there denied checking in any specimen from Dr. Eric Donovan within the last two weeks.

Seth sighed and again called the secretary who had at least admitted to being in the same building as Schwab. After talking with two additional secretarial staff members in the National Center for Human Genome Research, he came to the conclusion that he needed to speak directly to Kevin Schwab in order to get any meaningful information. He left a series of messages and waited—and waited—and waited.

It wasn't until he used Donovan's name that he got any response.

◆ ◆ ◆

Per usual, Kevin Schwab tossed one phone message into the trash after another. Since his popularity had exploded, he had become relentless in protecting his own privacy and rarely returned messages from strangers unless the agenda was clearly one he shouldn't decline.

The first message, quickly delivered to the circular file, simply stated, "Call Dr. Seth Berringer" and gave a number but no message. The second repeated the first but added, "About outside specimen DNA analysis." The third caught his eye with its additional sentence, "Please call today regarding fetus sent up for analysis by Dr. Eric Donovan, Deer Falls."

Kevin mumbled nervously to himself. "I thought Eric said he wanted to pretend this never existed." He stared at the message. Who was this Dr. Berringer anyway? He dug through his trash and retrieved the two other messages. This guy was persistent. What did he know about Eric Donovan and the specimen he'd sent?

Irritated at having to deal with a situation he'd thought adequately buried from the public eye, he picked up the phone and dialed Seth's number.

After one ring Seth picked up. "Hello."

"I need to speak to Dr. Berringer."

Seth's heart-rate quickened. "This is he."

"This is Kevin Schwab, returning your call. You had some questions for me?" Kevin carefully avoiding mentioning Eric Donovan.

"I'm looking for some information concerning a patient of mine in Deer Falls. I believe our medical examiner, a Dr. Eric Donovan, sent you a specimen from her autopsy to analyze."

Schwab shifted in his seat and launched his rolling desk chair into the middle of his lab. "Can you give me the patient's name?"

"Lisa Dale. I'll hold while you check your records."

Seth shuffled his notes during the uncomfortable silence.

Finally Schwab was back. "No luck, Dr. Berringer. I'm afraid we have no official record of a specimen being sent from a Dr. Donovan," he replied truthfully.

Seth shook his head as he looked at his autopsy notes. "I remember Dr. Donovan telling me the state wouldn't pay for an expensive analysis. He intended to ask you for an off-the-record opinion, just out of scientific curiosity. He said he knew you well from your training days and that you owed him a favor."

Kevin bit his lip. "I'm afraid I can't help you." He pushed himself nervously around the center of the lab. "Do you remember what kind of specimen it was?"

"A baby—a fetus. The patient was pregnant. He sent you the baby for genetic studies, I believe."

Berringer knew more than Schwab had hoped. Donovan was supposed to keep this information to himself! "No," Schwab responded hopefully, "I'm sure I have no evidence of a specimen like that around here." He shrugged and tightened his grip on his conscience. He was telling the truth, technically.

"Look," Seth said with a sigh, "I'm in a real bind over this. It's a long story, but I need that specimen in order to confirm important information about the way this patient died. The official word is that she died in a hit-and-run accident, but that isn't right at all. This girl was murdered, and someone is going to get away with it unless I can prove it." He paused. "I think she was killed by someone who wanted her child. And unless I find that baby, there is little I can do about it." Seth wasn't sure what to tell the N.I.H. scientist, but he wanted to stress the urgency of the situation without giving away too much detail about his own involvement in the case.

Schwab felt his gut churn. What was going on down there? Donovan had told him the tissue was from a murder victim, but how would finding the baby help catch a criminal? Schwab shook his head as the seriousness of the situation began to dawn on him. Did her carrying the clone have something to do with the reason she was killed?

"L-look, Dr. Berringer. I'm r-really sorry. But I don't have any records to indicate that your medical examiner sent me anything on that case."

"If you find something or remember anything that might help, will you give me a call?" Seth paced across his squeaky hardwood floor. "It's important. I can't stress that enough."

"Uh, sure," Schwab muttered. "I'll do what I can."

Schwab hung up and cursed his luck. He hadn't put two and two together before. The surrogate may have been killed precisely because she was carrying that baby!

He put his head in his hands and stopped the movement of his chair by putting his feet flat on the floor. If he told the truth now, everyone would knew he'd sold the shroud blood cells in exchange for the biggest donation in N.I.H. history. He gripped his hair tightly in his fists. And yet, if Berringer was right, something more sinister was going on than Schwab had ever imagined.

◆ ◆ ◆

Seth slumped into his easy-chair. Everywhere he turned, he met a dead end. How could he ever convince the sheriff he was telling the truth? How could he ever clear his name unless he found that baby?

◆ ◆ ◆

Sheriff Boatwright pushed aside a stack of his campaign pamphlets and looked across his expansive desk at Deputy Zander. "With this Barber girl out there spreadin' rumors about our hit-and-run case bein' a murder, we're going to look pretty stupid if we can't explain our actions."

"Explain to who?"

"The voters, idiot," Boatwright huffed. "The media love stuff like this."

"I've been watching the paper. They haven't mentioned a murder."

"And they'd better not. We've got to keep this girl from talking to them."

"What do you have in mind?" The young deputy placed his hands on his thighs and tightened his chest.

"Nothing really. Maybe I should just talk to her—let her know an investigation is underway and we don't want to tip anyone off with her rumors."

"Good idea." The deputy nodded. "What are you going to do with Berringer? I heard he's a free man again."

"I've been talking to the magistrate about that. I haven't quite convinced him to give me a warrant for his arrest."

"We can get him on involuntary manslaughter and leaving the scene of an accident. Show the magistrate the evidence we found on Berringer's car. We should be able to arrest him this afternoon."

"That's not exactly the warrant I'm looking for."

"I don't follow."

Boatwright raised his eyebrows. "Berringer admitted to intentionally running over the body, right? And the pathologist says she died from injuries sustained in the accident, right?"

The deputy nodded.

"And the psychiatrist reported that Berringer is holding in an extreme amount of hostility and guilt—more than you'd expect of a person who did something accidentally."

"What are you saying? That we pick him up on a murder charge?"

The sheriff shrugged, then stood and walked to his door, nudging it shut with his elbow. "Not yet. But what I smell is pretty fishy."

"Why not just pick him up on what we can prove already? Maybe we can convince the magistrate to set the bail out of reach, so we can keep Berringer in the hoosegow until we get more evidence."

"I'd rather not. If we pick him up on another charge, then change it, I'll look wishy-washy. I'd rather have an airtight case before he's arrested."

Zander was tempted to say something about the voters running the investigation but held his tongue.

"There is something else I haven't told you," the sheriff said with low-ered voice. He sat back at his desk, clearly glad to be in control of the con-versation. "I can't prove it yet, but I believe the girl was working as a prostitute. I suspect that our dear town doctor got involved in a risky situ-ation he didn't want anyone to know about. Then, to cover it all up, he runs the girl down and reports it as a hit-and-run."

"But if it was murder, why did he try to sell us on the idea that she was already dead?"

"I spent a lot of time going over this last night," he responded with a nod. "I think maybe the good doctor got involved with this girl and—how should I say it?—things got too rough. Maybe he killed her accidentally." He lowered his voice even further. "So he takes her out and runs her down, to make it look like a hit-and-run. Then he has second thoughts and fears that the medical examiner will figure things out, so he makes up the story he told us."

"Not realizing that the medical examiner hadn't picked up the real cause of death." Zander finished the sentence for him.

"Exactly." The sheriff nodded. "It's just a theory, but if my initial thought about Berringer being crazy isn't accurate, then he must be cover-ing for something, and the most logical thing is his own guilt for murder."

"That's going to be hard to prove. After all, we don't have a body to examine."

"I know. That's why we need more evidence—a witness—maybe even a confession." He thought about telling the deputy about the two men he saw at the Inn on the night of Lisa's death but didn't. He suspected that somehow the two men were privy to the murder—if not as participants, then as witnesses. After his conversation with his sister, he'd also thought long and hard about what she'd said about their mother's speaking. Though initially waving it off as impossible, he now wondered if Lou was right. Maybe his mother *was* sending them a message.

"What makes you so sure it was murder?"

Boatwright decided against telling him the details about his mother's condition. "Just something my momma said." He left it at that.

Zander let it drop. "So what do you want us to do?"

"Leave the Barber girl to me. You keep an eye on Berringer. We won't seek an arrest warrant, not yet; but be sure Berringer sees you watchin' him. If he's guilty, he won't like it. And the pressure might just scare the rabbit into a run."

"Or a confession."

"Exactly."

◆ ◆ ◆

Connie looked up from her desk as Eric Donovan returned after another long lunch hour. He skirted her desk, dodged the large bank of filing cabinets, and hit the large metal door leading into his lab. It swung open with a thud.

"Hello," she offered weakly as he disappeared without a greeting.

She looked at him with consternation. Her mind was filled with both fear and curiosity. He was hiding something, and this might be the time to find out what. She picked up a Post-It and carried it to the back.

"I took a phone message for you." She held out the paper, not offering to read it for him. On the note she had written, "Dr. Yamatsu will be coming by to talk about the deal."

She studied him for a moment as he read the message, then crumpled the paper and threw it into the trash. There was no facial reaction.

Reluctantly she inquired, "Eric, what's this all about?"

"It's a meeting—that's all. When is he coming?"

"He called over an hour ago. I told him you were eating lunch." She hoped that was really where he was. "It sounded as if he wanted to see you as soon as possible. He wouldn't leave a number."

He sat down, hiding his apprehension. He pulled his microscope forward and went to work, hoping his wife would leave. Connie didn't budge. She stood over his desk and watched.

"Eric, I'm concerned. What's going on?"

He sighed and pushed back from the desk.

"I heard you talking to him the other day—you were talking about money. You sounded like you were threatening him."

He didn't answer for a moment, and when he spoke, his tone was fatherly. "There are some things about my job," he began gently, "my job as a medical examiner, that you don't know anything about, Connie. Sometimes the things I discover constitute important criminal evidence. They have the potential of getting certain people in deep trouble."

"Stop talking down to me, Eric. I know what you do, OK? But I heard you asking for money. What is going on?"

Eric tapped a pencil against the desk, formulating his next thought. "Remember the message you left me from the sheriff?"

She nodded.

"I'm cooperating with a little sting to bring the guilty parties into the open. Sometimes the evidences I gather mean little unless the law can associate them with a motive." He paused and sighed again. "It's nothing you should be worried about, Connie. I don't think you should be brought into this. The sheriff insists on very tight security. I'm not even supposed to tell you this much."

This time Connie sighed. She wanted to believe him, but she still had nagging doubts. First he'd told her his secretary had an innocent crush on him. Now he was involved in a sting operation with the sheriff's department? Was she being too suspicious—or too gullible?

Eric rose and put his arms around his wife. She stiffened momentarily before surrendering and placing her cheek against his chest. "Don't worry, it's going to be OK." He stroked her hair. "You're going to have to trust me on this one."

She wanted to believe him. But a gnawing anxiety pulled her back.

"OK," she whispered.

He held her at arm's length and looked into her eyes. "Hey, isn't this your bridge night?"

She bit her lower lip and nodded.

"Why don't you take the rest of the day off? Go get ready for your club. I'm not going to do any dictation this afternoon anyway."

She shrugged. "I really should get some of the filing done and—"

"Go on home. It will do you good. Really, I want you to go."

She softened. "I *could* use the time to fix some food."

He sat back down and slid toward his microscope. He cast another glance at Connie. "I'll see you about 7:30. I need some time to finish another case."

"Sure." She felt a strange letdown. She had come ready for a fight and hadn't anticipated Eric's disarming her so easily.

She walked away, and Eric watched her go. He hated lying to her but justified it by telling himself that he wanted to keep her from sharing in the guilt of his misdeeds.

He felt a sudden wave of nausea. Cold sweat beaded his forehead, and a dull ache radiated beneath his sternum and into his neck. He took a deep breath and searched his top drawer for an antacid.

In a minute the feeling passed, and he returned his attention to the microscopic slides in front of him. His concentration, however, was continually bothered by the memory of his wife's concern.

Maybe he should get out of this deal before it was too late. He shook his head. He wouldn't turn back now. He'd never been so close to a big break—and a new start.

He looked up when he heard someone in the front office. Probably Dr. Yamatsu. It was time to make a deal.

CHAPTER
25

KERRI leaned her head against the window pane overlooking the small manicured grass court in front of her apartment. Her first thought that morning was identical to the last one she'd had the night before—her growing attraction to Seth Berringer. She sighed and cast a furtive glance at the phone. Why hadn't he called? He couldn't just kiss her like that and then ignore her, could he?

She paced around the small apartment and tried to make sense of her thoughts. *It's only been a day, Kerri. It's not like he's ignoring you. And it's not like he doesn't have other worries. He's probably already back at the office seeing patients. Maybe you'll see him in the E.R. tonight, if he's called in to admit one of his patients.*

She started a load of laundry and swept the kitchen floor. Her mind, however, was elsewhere. Finally, she gave in and called his office. It couldn't hurt to tell him she was thinking about him.

"Deer Falls Family Medicine Clinic. May I help you?"

"I'd like to speak to Dr. Berringer."

"He's not in. If you have a medical question, I can put you through to a nurse."

"No thanks, I really need to speak to Dr. Berringer." Kerri looked at her watch. Maybe he was at lunch. "Will he be in this afternoon?"

"No, ma'am," the sweet southern voice intoned. "But if you need to speak to a physician, I can see if Dr. Rotinski is free."

"Dr. Rotinski?"

"Yes." The receptionist sighed. She had obviously explained the situation a hundred times already. "He's Dr. Berringer's replacement. Dr. Berringer is no longer an employee of Coast Care."

"What? No longer an—"

"That's right. Now, if I can help you in any way, perhaps Dr. Rotinski will be able to—"

"No!" Kerri said more loudly than she'd intended. "No," she repeated in a softer tone. "That won't be necessary. Thank you."

Kerri hung up the phone, the receptionist's words echoing in her ears.

"O God," she whispered earnestly, "what's happened to Seth?"

She picked the phone up from the receiver. Her hand quivered slightly as she dialed his home.

Busy! The busy signal greeted her and frustrated her.

She had to talk to Seth!

◆ ◆ ◆

Seth put down the phone in frustration. Why didn't the medical examiner's office answer the phone in the middle of the day?

He called the hospital operator and asked to have Donovan paged to Seth's home number. He waited fifteen minutes, and when the page went unanswered, he shifted to plan B—call Dr. Donovan's home. He found the unlisted number in a medical directory available only to hospital staff from Chesapeake General.

Connie picked up on the second ring. "Hello." Her voice was cheery.

"Hello. I'm trying to reach Dr. Donovan."

"He's not here right now. May I take a message? If this is work-related, you should be able to reach him at the medical examiner's office."

"I've tried that. There's no answer there."

Connie began to frown. "Well, that's where he's *supposed* to be," she stated with a hint of suspicion.

Seth sighed. "Look, if he comes in, could you have him call Dr. Berringer?"

She dutifully took down his number. "If he's busy, he might be ignoring the phone. I don't think he has a front office person working this afternoon." That must be it. He's just occupied.

"Maybe I should just go see him at his office."

"I'll tell him you called. Can I leave him a message?"

"He knows what this is about." Seth didn't care to spill the details.

Connie recognized the physician's name from Kerri's visit. She waited a moment, then found herself talking before she could stop. "Is my husband in trouble, Dr. Berringer?"

Seth seemed taken aback by the question. "I—I'm not s-sure, Mrs. Donovan. I'm not sure of much anymore."

Connie exhaled slowly. "I see."

"Thank you, Mrs. Donovan."

As soon as Seth hung up the phone, it rang.

"Hello."

"Seth!" The voice was unmistakably Kerri's.

"Hi, Kerri."

"I've been trying to reach you," she said with obvious exasperation. "I heard about your termination."

"Courtesy of the hospital grapevine, I'm sure. I suppose the old rumor mill is just about busting by now. First, I get forced into Evergreen. Then I lose my job—"

"Seth," she said urgently, "I didn't find out at the hospital. I called your office to see how you were. I thought after yesterday, you might call."

"Well, I—" Seth paused. "I wanted to tell you last night. Really, I did. I thought about stopping by the hospital, but I was afraid everyone would start gossiping."

"What happened?"

"Coast Care laid me off."

"Just like that? What reason did they give?"

"Basically, they invoked a clause in my contract that says I can be terminated anytime without reason with two weeks' notice. They decided I'm on vacation for the next two weeks."

"Can't you fight it? They can't just fire you!"

"They did, Kerri. They've already hired a replacement." He sighed. "But, yes, I'll fight it. I'm sure it has to do with this whole flap with Lisa Dale and my mental competency evaluation." He shook his head. "Now, more than ever, I need to uncover what's going on around here. If I can just prove to the sheriff that I'm telling the truth . . ."

"What are you planning?"

"I need to get to the bottom of the revised autopsy report. I'm beginning to think that whoever wanted Lisa's baby must be behind this. Why else would Dr. Donovan be acting so strangely? Somebody must be paying him to make me look guilty."

"Do you really believe that?"

"Why else would Donovan be so adamant about his report being correct? Why would he want to cover up the facts about Lisa's pregnancy?"

"Are you sure he's lying? Maybe he just doesn't remember, and now he's too proud to admit that his report is inaccurate."

"Is that what you think?"

Kerri sighed. "No." She paused. "I feel the same way you do—something smells fishy around here."

"It's more than fishy. It's rotten. And I've been stung by whatever or whoever is behind it."

Kerri looked at herself in the mirror as she held her cordless phone. She frowned as she pulled out a gray hair. "So what's next?"

"I talked to Kevin Schwab this morning. Like Donovan, he doesn't know anything about a specimen, doesn't know anything about a pregnancy, or about Lisa Dale for that matter."

"Do you believe him?"

"No. But I have no evidence that he's hiding anything."

"So—"

"I know," Seth interrupted, "what's next? I need to talk to Donovan again—jog his memory. I think I'd better do it face to face this time. Maybe I can get more out of him if I go down to his office."

"Do you want me to go with you?"

"No. I think I'd better do this on my own. You had your shot at him, and he's not likely to open up if he sees you again."

Kerri wrinkled her nose at the memory of her encounter with Donovan. She giggled nervously as she remembered telling the medical examiner he would have to answer to God someday. "I think he had it coming."

Seth chuckled too. "Oh yeah."

"When are you going to see him?"

"Today. I was just getting ready to leave when you called."

"Oh." She remained quiet for a moment. "Seth?"

"Yes?"

"I . . . Well, I . . . Be careful, OK?"

"I'll call you when I get back."

"I start work at 3."

"I'll call you after I confront Donovan."

Kerri let out a tense breath. "Thanks. I'll talk to you later. Bye, Seth."

"Bye."

◆ ◆ ◆

Kerri hugged the phone against her for a moment as a distinct uneasiness chased away the delight she'd felt while talking with Seth. *I need to pray. Something's not right. He's stepped on someone's—something's?—toes.*

She opened her mouth to whisper her request when a sharp knock followed by the doorbell sounded. She placed the phone on her bedside table and walked to the front door. Peering through the peephole, she could see the sheriff's profile, appearing even more round due to the distortion caused by the small optical channel.

She opened the door. "Sheriff, I didn't expect you—"

"Hi, Ms. Barber. Maybe I should've called."

"It's OK. What can I do for you?" Kerri smiled cordially but stood her ground in the doorway.

The sheriff moved his feet anxiously. "Would it be possible for us to talk inside?"

Kerri's feeling of uneasiness heightened. "Sure." She stepped out of the way and backed into her apartment. She pointed to a couch. "You may sit over there if you like."

"Thank you. I won't take much of your time."

She sat on a footstool and faced him, her hands knotted in her lap.

"I want to talk to you about Lisa Dale," he began. "I've spoken to Lou Ellen from the Deer Falls Inn. She told me you were by to see her."

Kerri stiffened and held her tongue.

"I'm sure you know she's my sister."

"It's a small town, sheriff," she responded with a nod.

"She was quite distressed by what you told her."

"I'm sorry to have upset her. That wasn't my intention."

"Just what was your intention, Ms. Barber?"

Kerri shifted in her seat and concentrated on maintaining her composure. She felt as if she were on trial. "I am simply seeking the truth about my friend's death, Mr. Boatwright."

The sheriff chuckled. "Well, I thought we knew all about that. We've got pretty conclusive evidence that she was involved in a hit-and-run, if that's what you mean."

"I think you know what I mean, sheriff. With all due respect, I happen to believe what Dr. Berringer told you, and I'm beginning to wonder why your department is so reluctant to look into his claims."

Boatwright stiffened. "Why, Ms. Barber, I don't think you understand my position. We *have* looked into his claims. So far I've found nothing to convince me he's telling the truth." He focused a steely gaze on Kerri's face. "And if he's not crazy, then why is he lying? What does he have to cover up? Maybe your friend has told you something you'd like to tell me."

"That's ridiculous. He's not hiding anything. If anything, his *honesty* is what's making him suffer."

"Are you protecting him, Ms. Barber? Just what is your relationship with Dr. Berringer?"

Kerri flushed. "That's really none of your business."

The sheriff could see he was unnerving her. "Listen, before you believe everything he tells you, you need to know that I've already caught him in a lie. If you're so concerned about finding the truth, you ought to begin by examining the smooth lines he's been feeding you."

"If you are referring to the autopsy report, I know about that. I think the report is false."

"I wasn't referring to the autopsy report. There are other inconsistencies in his story."

Kerri challenged his stare with unmoving eye contact.

The sheriff softened. "Look, I can't go into all of the evidence, but I will tell you one thing—we obtained a search warrant to look over the doctor's van. We found the victim's shoe, Ms. Barber, the one your boyfriend claims to have removed and placed beside the road. It was lodged under his van. And the lab has given me a positive blood match on the victim from a sample taken from that shoe."

Kerri shook her head. "Maybe it was the other shoe. That doesn't mean he's—"

"The other shoe was on the victim. And I had a team out at the roadside for half a day searching the place where Berringer says he placed the shoe." He shrugged. "It's not there." He sighed. "He's lying, Ms. Barber. Lying to me and . . ." He paused. "I hate to tell you this, but he's lying to you as well."

"But—" The words lodged in Kerri's throat. Her voice tightened into a knot.

"I'm afraid this guy might be dangerous. I really only came by to warn you and to ask you to stop forwarding rumors in this community that might be damaging to our investigation."

"He's not lying. I know he wants to do the right thing, sheriff. I'm basically the reason he came forward and confessed this whole thing in the first place. He told me the story, and I encouraged him to get things out in the open."

"It's nice you feel this way, but honestly, I think his confession was a smoke screen. I think he felt threatened in some way. Perhaps he felt that we were close to discovering his other misdeeds and came forward with this confession to throw us off."

"Other misdeeds? What are you talking about?"

"He's obviously covering up something." The sheriff sighed and stood up. "Look, I've said too much already. I really have no business doing anything but warning you to stop talking about this case in public and to be very careful about your interactions with Seth Berringer. He's very smooth, Ms. Barber, very smooth. A man like that can convince some people of anything."

"Just what do you think he's done, sheriff?"

"I'm really not at liberty to say. But I can say the evidence we have does not confirm his testimony."

Kerri wanted to speak but could only exhale in frustration. This didn't seem right at all. Seth had confessed because he felt convicted by the Holy Spirit, not because he was trying to conceal something!

The sheriff captured her gaze again. "Can I count on you not to speak again in public about this matter? I can assure you that my department is investigating every lead to the fullest extent, and I don't want the community getting stirred up unnecessarily."

She thought carefully about what to say. "I really don't think Seth, uh, Dr. Berringer is trying to mislead you, sheriff. He—"

"Just the same, Ms. Barber, be careful. I think he has you under a spell. What a pretty young woman like you would see in a man like that is beyond me." He shook his head.

Kerri felt her face redden, and not from embarrassment.

She walked to the front door of her apartment. "Thank you for the warning." She opened the door, and this time she didn't attempt to smile.

The sheriff replaced his broad-rimmed brown hat. "Good day, Ms. Barber."

Kerri shut the door and walked back into her living room. Once there, she melted onto her couch. *What is going on, Lord? Is Seth a liar, dangerous, a smooth talker?* She bit down gently on her index finger to suppress a sob. It didn't add up. Seth hadn't lied to her, had he? The sheriff seemed so sure and sincere. Was he merely misinterpreting the evidence?

Why is the truth sometimes so hard to see?

◆ ◆ ◆

A Chesapeake County patrol car pulled into the Deer Falls Gas Mart just behind Seth Berringer's maroon van. Deputy Zander walked up and engaged in small talk with the physician as he filled the tank with regular gasoline.

"Sure is gettin' cold, eh, doc?"

Seth looked up, eyeing the uniformed man without contempt, but with more than a little suspicion. "Huh? Oh, sure," he grunted before looking back at the numbers spinning by on the gas pump much faster than he'd have liked.

"I heard old Ned Thompson shot an eight point buck this morning over by the Springston farm. Heck, that's only a stone's throw from the city limit." He shook his head and leaned against the van driver's door. "Herd's too thick, really. It's a wonder we don't see more trouble here in town."

Seth nodded and focused on the pump.

The deputy continued, "We've had no less than four deer killed by cars on Route 728 alone." He walked around to the front of the van. "Ever see what a deer can do to a car?" He shook his head again and took off his hat. "It can flat total a car, especially those little import jobs." He studied the front of the van, then lowered his voice, even though they were alone. "Say, doc, forgive me for askin', but why didn't that girl you hit leave a mark on your van?" He ran his hand across the old chrome. "From the looks of things here, you didn't even scratch the bumper." He hesitated, hoping to get a rise out of Seth. "Pretty strange, if you ask me."

Seth grew impatient. "I didn't ask you. But if I had to explain it, I'd refer you back to the story as I explained it to the sheriff. I ran over a dead body, one that was lying on the ground. I didn't strike anyone standing up. In such circumstances, I wouldn't have expected to see anything on the front of the van, would you?"

Zander shrugged. "Hmmm."

Seth straightened and pulled the nozzle out of his tank. "Come to think of it, maybe I should bring that up to the sheriff. Maybe if he'd do an inspection of the van, it would prove my story."

The deputy chuckled. "I don't think so."

Berringer raised his eyebrows.

"They already searched the van, doc. I assumed you knew that. The magistrate issued a warrant to search the van soon after you were taken up to Evergreen."

Seth glared at the deputy. "And?"

Zander shrugged. "I don't guess it will hurt to tell you. You're going to find out sooner or later anyway."

"Tell me what?"

"They found the girl's shoe jammed under your van."

"Her shoe?" Seth shook his head. "Her shoe was still on the body."

"The other one, doc—the one you said you used to mark the body's location." He nodded his head in a confident, patriarchal manner. "Seems to me like that kind of blows your little story." He leaned forward. "Maybe you should come on down to the station and tell us what really happened."

"I have work to do." Seth bit his tongue to keep from exploding. He walked toward the cashier.

"Think about it, doc."

Seth kept walking.

"I'm sure if you'd come clean, everyone would look kindly on your cooperation."

Seth paid the bill and returned to his van. The deputy leaned against the front of his own vehicle, now running, until Seth hopped in and pulled away.

Using the rearview mirror, Seth watched the patrol car pull out behind him. Great! He wondered how that shoe got under his van? Maybe the deputy just said that to get him spooked. He shook his head and wondered if anyone would ever believe his story.

Not in this town—not without finding that specimen.

Seth made a left turn and headed south toward the medical examiner's office.

The patrol car did the same.

CHAPTER
26

Doc was stern and unsmiling. In addition to his medical education, he'd been trained to interrogate, and his specialty was the incremental introduction of painful stimuli. Today he wouldn't use such means. Today he wanted only cooperation. Today he was Dr. Yamatsu, concerned only about the recovery of a valuable lab specimen.

He shut the briefcase slowly, to be sure Eric Donovan appreciated the amount of cash it carried.

Donovan saw it all right and tingled with excitement. Instinctively, he reached for the case.

Doc pulled it away. "Not so fast." He cast a glance at his taller associate, a bearded man who appeared older but solid, a man he had introduced as a lab assistant, Mr. Collins. "This is only a deposit. Once we have the specimen and have confirmed its authenticity, we will wire the remaining balance to your bank."

Donovan coughed as he felt his heart racing beneath his sternum like a runaway train. He wiped the sweat from his forehead as a dull ache settled into his upper abdomen and lower chest. "I don't have it here."

The taller man stepped forward with his right fist clenched. Dr. Yamatsu grabbed his arm. It was a show of force, an intimidation tactic they'd used several times in the past. "What do you mean?"

"I was worried about the concern over my autopsy report. If someone found the specimen, they could prove the report was a fabrication."

"Concern over the autopsy?" Doc's eyes narrowed. "What are you talking about?"

Were they are unaware of the suspicions voiced by Dr. Seth Berringer?

"Dr. Berringer observed the autopsy and raised questions with the sheriff when my report didn't correlate with the physician's memory."

Doc had a flash of understanding. Was that the reason Berringer went to the sheriff? But why did he cover for them to begin with? Just how much did this Berringer know? Maybe he was after the specimen too. He tried to refocus on the business at hand. "But you do have the fetus, right?"

Donovan's breathing quickened, making him unable to talk without gasping between sentences. "I have it. I can guarantee it's what you want." He fought for breath again. "I'll need the money in the bank before I give it to you." He sat down on his desktop.

"Are you OK?" The words came from the taller man. "Doc, he's awful pale!"

"I—I don't feel so good." The examiner struggled for composure. "You agree to the five million figure, then?"

Doc shook his head in rising frustration. "Only after the specimen is in our lab." He looked at the pathologist, who had now shifted around and was sliding into his chair.

Donovan's head ached and spun. Overwhelmed with a sudden, violent nausea, he was barely able to grab his waste can before vomiting.

Bill moved away and cursed in disgust. "Man, that's foul. This guy is sick."

Donovan heaved again and laid his head on the desk.

Doc grew impatient. "Who else knows about the specimen?" He started to enumerate. "Berringer, your secretary . . ."

"That's all," Donovan whispered. "That's all. I swear it."

Pain gripped the pathologist's chest. "I need help. I'm having a heart—" He stood and reached for the phone, but dizziness prevented him from picking it up.

His cardiac muscle, now starved for oxygen, began a fatal rhythm known as ventricular fibrillation. In a moment Donovan knew only darkness. His body pitched forward, his right hand closed in a fist over his chest, and he fell as his legs buckled.

Bill leapt forward to catch him but only slowed his descent to the floor. Donovan's body collapsed in a free fall, slipping out of the reach of his interrogator, his head snapping back violently as his forehead struck the corner of his desk.

Doc cursed loudly and ran to the pathologist's side. Blood oozed from a jagged forehead laceration. The Asian's fingers slipped naturally into a position lateral to Donovan's trachea. He cursed again. "He's dead!"

"Do something!" the older man shouted as he picked up the phone. Doc slammed his hand over his associate's.

"What are you doing?"

"Calling 911!"

"Idiot! We can't let anyone know we were here!" He looked back at Donovan. "Besides, there's no saving him. He was dead before he hit the floor."

Bill swore and stared at the dead man's pale face. "You're the doctor," he mumbled. He snapped himself from his self-imposed trance. "Let's get out of here."

"Not so fast."

The older man's eyes widened, his face in an angry snarl. "Come on! We don't want to be found in here with him!"

"Think, idiot!" Doc cursed again. "Let's look for that specimen."

"No way I'm stayin' around he—"

He was stopped short by a firm grip on his forearm. Doc released his grasp slowly. "Don't you see? Finding that specimen will keep anyone else from discovering the truth about the way the girl died."

Bill's expression remained blank.

"Think! If they find out she really was pregnant, it's only a matter of time before that sheriff figures out we had something to do with her death. He knows we were in her room."

"He doesn't even know our names. There's no way he can—"

"Shut up! I'm not taking any chances. Besides, if we get that specimen, maybe we can get some of the money Davis would have paid Donovan." He pulled a pair of rubber gloves out of a box on an exam table. "Here," he said, tossing some gloves to his partner. "Put these on." He looked around. "Did you touch anything in here?"

"Just the doorknob as I came in."

"Wipe it down. Then help me look." He pulled open a metal cabinet and began sorting through plastic containers. Each had a label with a name and a series of identification numbers. He cursed. "There must be a thousand different containers in here!"

In a moment he was joined by his partner. Together they rifled through three separate cabinets, finding nothing with Lisa Dale's name.

"It's not here." Bill wiped the sweat from his forehead. "I don't like this. Someone's bound to come in here. Where's the secretary?"

Doc shrugged. "I don't know. Keep your voice down. She might be back out there, for all we know."

"Donovan said the fetus wasn't here." Bill brightened. "Then again, maybe we don't need the specimen to get Davis to fork over some of the money."

"What do you mean?"

He lowered his voice. "Well, what if Davis doesn't know the medical examiner died? Maybe he'll give us the payoff to give to him anyway."

"No way. Davis said we needed the specimen before he gave the guy any more money."

"We can tell him Donovan wouldn't budge—that we had to make a deal or lose the specimen forever."

Doc stiffened and worked his mouth into a frown. Then he slowly nodded his head. "It could work. Donovan was never very cooperative. It could be believable." He looked around. "But how are we going to prevent him from figuring out he died?"

"We'll hide the body. Then if Davis finds out he's missing, we just tell him Donovan told us he was going into hiding for a while, but that we know how to contact him."

"What do we do with the body?"

"Who cares? We can bury it or maybe throw him in the bay with a few cinder blocks tied to his belt."

Doc shrugged. "How do we get him out of here in broad daylight?"

They looked around for a moment before spotting a silver, zippered body bag lying on a metal table in the center of the room.

Bill nodded. "We'll put him in there. I'll bet everyone's used to seeing bodies come and go around here."

Doc touched the bag with one extended finger. "This one's in use." He walked to the back of the room and opened a heavy latch on a silver door. He slid out a long tray, obviously designed for a body. "Hey," he called out softly, "I've got a better idea. Rather than risk taking him outside, let's just stash him in the freezer. No one will look for the pathologist in here." He smiled. "Besides, all we need is a few days to convince Davis to release the big money to us."

The older man laughed. "Let's tell him Donovan held out for the full five million and insisted on cash."

Doc looked around the lab. "Straighten up his desk, and wipe that blood off the floor."

Bill grabbed a handful of paper towels from above a large sink, cleaned the floor, and threw the towels into a trash can, then helped lift Donovan's body onto the long tray and slide it back into the refrigerator unit.

"There," Doc laughed. "They won't find him for a week."

Bill surveyed the scene. "Let's get out of here." He began walking to the front.

"Not so fast. We need to get rid of the bloody trash." He pointed at the container on the floor. He opened the cooler again. "Just throw that stuff in with the doctor. Once they find him, it will be all over anyway."

Bill had just started tying up the trash-liner when they heard a voice from the front office.

"Dr. Donovan?" The voice was male.

Doc scanned the room. In hushed tones, he cursed and motioned for his partner. "Come on! Let's go out the back."

Bill threw the trash bag on top of Donovan's body and slammed the door, not realizing the bag was caught in the latch. The door bounced open behind the rapidly retreating man.

Doc eased open the back door and, seeing no one, slipped into the early afternoon winter air with his associate right on his heels.

"Do you have the briefcase?"

"Right here," Doc responded with a sigh of relief. "And now it's all ours."

◆ ◆ ◆

"Dr. Donovan?" Seth called. He sighed with frustration. "Is anybody here?"

He shook his head. Everywhere he turned he met another obstacle. No one believed him. He'd lost his job and his reputation, and the law was watching his every move. Could things be any worse? He approached the counter and rang a small silver bell before sitting down on a hard wooden bench to wait.

That deputy must have followed him for ten miles! What was it he said? "Maybe you should come on down to the station and tell us what really happened." What did they think happened? They were acting as if Seth had killed Lisa Dale!

He waited for a few minutes, then checked his watch impatiently. Where was everybody? Seth stood and paced back and forth in front of the counter. Unable to wait any longer, he quietly approached the door leading to the back lab and knocked. "Dr. Donovan?" Maybe his wife had warned him that Seth called, and now he was avoiding him, knowing Berringer wanted some answers about Lisa Dale's autopsy.

He pushed the door open a few inches and raised his voice again. "Dr. Donovan, are you here?"

Seth stepped into the large room and quickly surveyed the situation. The lights were on, and several cabinet doors along the near wall hung open. There were plastic specimen containers scattered on the floor in apparent disarray. He whispered to himself as he carefully stepped over the containers. "What's going on around here?"

"Dr. Donovan . . . It's me, Seth Berringer," he said at low volume. "I need to talk to you about Lisa Dale's autopsy report."

He looked around to confirm he was indeed alone. He stepped back to the heavy metal door leading from the lab and opened it. There was still no one in the front room. He pulled a metal trash container over and propped the door open so he could hear anyone entering the front office, then turned his attention to the back room. *I might as well look around. I might find out something about Lisa Dale if I look hard enough. Can't hurt*, he mused.

He walked back to the desk, quietly pulled open the side file drawer, and looked through the few folders he found. Nothing. Where did Donovan keep the records of the autopsies? Seth opened the first drawer of a tall gray filing cabinet. There he saw hundreds of case files, each labeled with a number. He should've known they'd be stored by number instead of name. He looked back toward the door. Maybe he could access the computer records.

He pushed the file drawer closed and glanced at the far wall. Along it loomed a large refrigerator unit, its contents hidden by a dozen thick, silver square doors. The closest one, Seth could see, was ajar.

Curiosity drew him, and he glanced back toward the front room. He was alone. Moving swiftly to the refrigerator door, he pulled it open. There he could easily see a man's body—a man in a white lab coat! He gasped in horror as he recognized the man's face. Donovan!

Instinctively, he pulled his hand back from the door. "Oh, man," he groaned softly to himself.

He slowly eased his head forward so he could see the top of the body. There was blood on the face and in the hair. Seth touched the cheek with the back of his hand. The body was cooling, but not cold. The deceased obviously hadn't been there too long. Berringer watched the chest carefully.

There was no movement. He leaned his own face close to Donovan's nose and mouth. There was no breathing. He was beyond resuscitation.

Donovan was dead. Had someone killed him? Had he killed himself? Seth went to the counter, picked up a pair of rubber disposable gloves, and put them on so he could do a better exam. He slowly slid out the long, silver tray holding the pathologist's body. Had he shot himself while lying in the refrigerator? Seth looked for a gun. There was no weapon, and the dead man's hands were at his sides. Seth looked closely at Donovan's scalp. The wound was superficial and definitely not a gunshot wound. Possibly it was a laceration from blunt trauma since the edge was irregular. Or maybe he'd been struck in the head and died from an underlying brain injury.

Seth slid the body back into the refrigerator and returned the door to its partially closed position.

The gravity of the situation began to dawn on him. Should he call the police? He began to pace. This could look bad for him. The police already suspected he'd done something wrong. And now the very man the sheriff knew Seth had a serious disagreement with was dead. Seth thought back to his last interaction with Donovan and winced. He'd really lost his temper with him on the phone back at Evergreen. Did the nurse know whom he was talking to?

Seth shook his head. He couldn't call the police. It would be better if he were a long ways away from here by the time someone found the body. He thought momentarily about shutting the door to the refrigerator and tidying up the scattered containers. But that was out of the question, considering what had happened to him since he'd altered Lisa Dale's death scene. He was in enough trouble—he needed to get away from there as quickly as he could. Get away and find Lisa's baby!

He sighed. No one would believe his story without proof, and now the only other person who'd witnessed the autopsy was dead. His only chance was to find that tissue!

Seth snapped to attention. He looked at his hands. He decided he'd better keep the gloves on until after he left the office, to avoid leaving any more fingerprints than he already had.

He practically ran from the office. Once in the hallway, he slowed to a walk and tried to appear calm. As far as he knew, no one witnessed his exit. He climbed into his van, his mind spinning. Had anyone see him come? He tried to recall the events of his arrival just a few minutes before. What about the deputy? Seth winced. He turned around a few miles back, didn't he?

The frightened physician pulled onto the highway and headed north. "No one saw me. No one saw me," he whispered to himself, but his troubled mind refused to accept the comfort. He worried that he was forgetting some crucial detail. Something important. He pounded the steering wheel.

Who knew I was coming? Kerri—that's all, right? She's OK.

His next thought struck him with sickening anxiety. *I told Donovan's wife I was going to see him! Great!*

I need to get out of town.

I need to find the truth.

I need to find that baby!

◆ ◆ ◆

Connie Donovan was happy to have the afternoon to prepare for her bridge party, though she felt quietly uncomfortable with the enthusiasm her husband had shown over her leaving. What was going on with Eric lately? He'd been so distant. And now this talk of a sting. What was she to make of that? And did it really take Eric an hour to grab a bite to eat from the corner cafe?

She rubbed a water spot off the side of a wine glass using a soft cloth and thought back to her early days with Eric Donovan. There had been a time when he would sneak away at lunch just to see her.

She reflected on her conversation with Seth Berringer. He'd sounded so discouraged. What was it he said when she asked whether her husband was in trouble? She paused, then picked up another glass. "I'm not sure." That was his response, but there was something in the way he said it. A hidden worry perhaps?

She shook her head. Why wasn't Eric answering her calls? He didn't have any new autopsies to keep him away from the phones.

Connie finished setting a small side table on which she would display her hors d'oeuvres. She arranged some dried flowers as a centerpiece. Impulsively, her suspicions again moving her to action, she called Eric's workplace. She listened silently to eight rings. Perhaps he was out of the office, but why? And where? He'd said he had an important meeting. Could it be with Tammy Lynn?

Should she call her husband's secretary? She shook her head. What could she say? "Are you and my husband having an affair? Could you stop it? You're ruining my life!"

She sighed and rotated the center arrangement a quarter turn. Frustrated by her lack of answers to her nagging questions, she slumped into her favorite chair and opened a romance novel. She quickly escaped into an artificial world filled with lusty excitement. Why couldn't her life be like that?

◆ ◆ ◆

Davis smiled at the news and victoriously shook his closed fist in the air. "You're sure he has it?"

"That's what he claimed, sir," Doc replied, gripping his cell phone with one hand and drumming the dashboard nervously with the other. He lowered his voice. "There's just one problem."

Davis's smile was short-lived. "Problem?"

"He wants the money first."

"No way! He can't do this to me! He doesn't know how much this specimen means—"

"But he does know," Doc interrupted. "And he wants to play hardball."

Davis sighed. He was running out of time, and he needed that specimen!

Doc shifted in his seat nervously and stared straight ahead to avoid looking at Bill. He tried a new angle. "If you'll get me a partial payment, I think I can force him to deliver."

"Force him? How? I don't want anyone else getting—"

"He has some action going on the side with his secretary. We've watched him long enough to know, believe me. Let me offer him a fraction of the total, in cash, in return for the specimen. Otherwise, his wife just might find out about his outside interests."

"Will he go for it?"

"I'm sure of it."

"We can't have anymore foul-ups. This tissue harvest has turned into a nightmare." He sighed. "Do what you have to do."

Doc clenched his jaw. "I'll need money."

"Talk to him first thing in the morning. Make an agreement first. Then he'll get his payoff." Davis shook his head. "I'm not going to play on his terms."

"Right. I'll call you after I talk to him tomorrow." He clicked off the phone and looked at Bill. "He'll make a cash deal with Donovan."

Bill Guessford smiled. "Let's just hope no one finds that body."

Doc laughed. "Don't worry. No one would look in the fridge for a missing person." He chuckled at the apparent security of their position.

◆ ◆ ◆

Kerri gently but firmly restrained the small infant so the pediatrician could complete a fever workup. The procedure, a spinal tap, would determine whether the baby was suffering from meningitis, an infection of the layers surrounding the spinal cord.

Only moments before, Kerri had ushered the parents into a crowded waiting room. She had explained what needed to be done and the need to restrain the child. Although the mother had wanted to stay and help hold her baby, Kerri assured her it would be better if the mother played the role of the rescuer. "Let me hold the child down during the procedure. That way, I'll be the bad guy in the little fella's mind," she added, looking at the baby nestled in his mother's arms. "Once it's over, I'll come right out to get you, so you can comfort him again." Reluctantly the parents relented, and Kerri busied herself setting up the lumbar puncture tray for Dr. Gearing, a pediatrician.

The afternoon had been particularly hectic in the emergency room. A motor vehicle accident resulting in four victims had filled the trauma bays. A flu epidemic had contributed six other patients with fever and cough. A depressed college student had overdosed on Tylenol. A high schooler had sprained an ankle at basketball practice. And two stretchers in the hall were filled by a young girl with possible appendicitis and a chronic alcohol enthusiast recovering from a binge.

In the midst of the onslaught came the baby boy with a fever of 104 and a stiff neck, a telltale sign of meningitis.

The baby squirmed as the physician painted the infant's back with an antiseptic. "You'll have to hold him a little tighter," Dr. Gearing instructed.

"I'm trying. He's a wiggly one."

"Try to curl him up more, with his head pulled forward to his chest."

Kerri complied, and the baby squealed.

The doctor introduced a small amount of local anesthetic, followed by a longer spinal needle into the lower back. In a moment drops of turbid spinal fluid slowly emerged at the hub of the needle. Gearing carefully collected several test tubes of the infected fluid for analysis in the lab.

"Oh, man, I can make this diagnosis with my naked eye," he responded. He sighed and bemoaned the fact that he'd seen three cases of meningitis in the past month. "You'll have to start an IV—D5 with quarter percent saline with twenty milliequivalents of potassium chloride."

Kerri nodded and stayed quiet. Now it would be her turn to torture the child. She hated this part of her job. Adults were one thing. They understood. Kids were another ball game altogether.

She summoned another nurse to help her, then started her search for an appropriate IV site. The baby had been vomiting prior to arrival, and the subsequent dehydration would make Kerri's job more difficult.

"Try the scalp," Deb Blackwell, a veteran E.R. nurse, offered. "Let's put a rubber band around the forehead. That might enable us to see a vein."

Outside, an impatient surgeon bellowed, "I need an exam room. How can you expect me to see patients out here in the hall?"

Deb looked at Kerri and rolled her eyes. "We're too busy to put up with that egotist."

Kerri stayed quiet and rubbed the baby's scalp with an alcohol swab. "There," she muttered. "I think this will do."

Mr. Bailey, the intoxicated patient lying just outside the first trauma bay, alternatively dozed and screamed for attention. Just when everyone else seemed occupied, he demanded a urinal—now!

The two-way radio at the desk announced, "This is rescue unit 4. We're en route with a sixty-two-year-old male with substernal chest pain."

The surgeon started checking the exam rooms. "There has to be a place for me to see my patient. You call this a hospital?" He pulled back the curtain in Kerri's cubicle just as she finished securing the IV.

The surgeon looked at the trio. "I need this room. Move the baby to the hall—"

His eyes met the fiery gaze of Deb Blackwell. "Take a number!" she ordered.

The surgeon huffed and moved on.

Mr. Bailey, the alcoholic, tried in vain to throw his leg over the stretcher rail. "I gotta go!"

The radio squawked again. "Chesapeake General E.R., I need permission to start the lytic therapy protocol. We have some impressive EKG changes here that haven't changed with nitroglycerin. I've transmitted the rhythm strip. Can I get a physician OK?"

The E.R. secretary looked for a doctor. Of the three covering the department, none were to be found. She pressed the intercom. "I need a doctor at the desk, stat!"

John Alcorn, R.N. picked up the transmitter. "Our physicians haven't seen the strip. Continue oxygen and nitroglycerin, and we'll get back to you."

A harried E.R. physician exited the first trauma bay. "We need a stat head C.T. for trauma 1." He looked at the ward clerk, who immediately looked back at John Alcorn.

"Dr. Nicholson, Rescue 4 is seeking permission to begin a lytic protocol for an acute M.I. Can you look at this rhythm strip?"

"Get Dr. Blevins to look at it. I'm covering trauma." He focused his attention on the ward secretary. "Let's order that CT scan right now!"

The nurse threw up his hands.

Deb Blackwell ran toward Mr. Bailey with a urinal. "Sit down, Mr. Bailey. You're going to fall!"

The surgeon heaved a sigh and started examining his patient in the hallway.

Kerri held the baby boy in her arms and tried to soothe him. "There, there."

"Where's Dr. Blevins?" Alcorn raised his voice.

The unit secretary used the intercom again. "Dr. Blevins to the desk. Dr. Blevins."

Just then Seth Berringer stepped into the emergency room, entering through the back entrance. He surveyed the commotion, looking for Kerri.

Alcorn spotted him and shoved the EKG strip in front of him. "Dr. Berringer, what do you think of this?"

Seth was startled by the sudden attention. "Huh?" He looked at the strip of paper. "What lead is this?"

"Lead 2. It's from Rescue 4."

Seth mumbled his response, still looking for Kerri. "Acute ischemia, likely an inferior M.I."

He walked toward the first exam room, hoping to get a glimpse behind the curtain.

Alcorn called after him, "Shouldn't they start the lytic therapy protocol?"

Joe Blevins walked up, snatching the EKG strip from John's hand. "He doesn't work here anymore!" He scowled. "Stay out of this, Berringer!"

Seth shrugged his former associate off and looked behind the curtain.

He saw Kerri handing a crying infant back to his mother. He caught her eye just as Deb Blackwell called, "Kerri, move the infant with meningitis to the back hall. We need that room for the new chest pain patient coming by squad."

Seth and Kerri moved into the hallway. "I need to talk to you." Seth's eyes communicated urgency.

Kerri waved at the commotion. "I'll have to call you when I get out of this zoo."

An E.R. physician emerged from the first trauma bay again. "Forget the head scan. Call the university helicopter. This guy's right pupil just blew. He needs a neurosurgeon yesterday!"

The girl with appendicitis vomited on the examining surgeon's shoes.

The mother of the baby with meningitis touched Kerri's arm. "What did the test show?"

Blevins ordered the lytic therapy, instructing the paramedic in loud tones via the radio transmitter.

Deb looked at the mess on the floor and paged housekeeping on the intercom.

Kerri looked at the mother. "Your baby has meningitis. Dr. Gearing will talk to you in a moment. Would you mind waiting with your baby back here? I'm sorry, but we need the space for a heart patient." She pointed to a chair in the back hall.

The young mother bit her lip and nodded.

"This patient needs a gram of Mefoxin. And get the mother to sign a permit for an appendectomy," the surgeon added, shoving a clipboard into Kerri's hands.

"I need to leave town," Seth said in a hushed tone as he caught Kerri's eye.

"Can we talk later? I'm underwater here. I'll call you if I get a supper break."

"I'll be on the road." He exhaled sharply and held her arm. "Something's happened to Donovan."

"To Donovan? What—"

The surgeon interrupted, "I called the O.R. They're waiting for you to get a permit!"

"Chesapeake General, this is Rescue 4. We're two minutes away."

"Dr. Nicholson," the ward secretary shouted, "I have the helicopter service on the phone. They're grounded due to weather."

Nicholson cursed his misfortune and looked up to see Kerri standing with Seth Berringer. "We'll have to do a burr hole to relieve the pressure. Set up a tray in trauma 1." He looked at Seth, avoiding actual eye contact. "Now!" he emphasized to Kerri.

Kerri glanced back at Seth, who grabbed her hand for a final squeeze.

Kerri disappeared into the first trauma bay, and Seth retreated through the automatic double doors just as Rescue 4 arrived.

Seth paused for a moment, looking back into the confused scene. He felt isolated, helpless, alone. He sensed a strange foreboding as he sniffed the cold air. He wondered if he'd ever work in this place again.

CHAPTER
27

As Seth drove north, he formulated his next step. He would contact Kevin Schwab in person, just as he had planned to confront Donovan. Somewhere somehow someone was hiding the truth. And now, more than any time before, he knew he had to acquire direct proof that would improve the credibility of his word.

It had been no secret that he'd had a major beef with Eric Donovan. Now, with Donovan dead, he was sure to be on the sheriff's short list of suspects. Seth sighed as he drummed his hands on the steering wheel. Who knew about that fetus? Just Donovan and him? No, there were a few more. Schwab should know, unless Donovan had lied about knowing him. Could it be he said that just to impress Berringer? The thought of that possibility added to the knot in Seth's gut.

Who else knew about the pregnancy? Only Kerri, because he'd told her. But did even she believe him? He thought back to their first discussions about the case and the postcard from Lisa. Of course, she believed him. Why shouldn't she? Why would he make up such a story? And why would Lisa have written that she thought she was pregnant in the first place?

He shook his head. The only reason he was in so much hot water was because Donovan changed his medical examiner's report and made him look like an insane fool.

No, that wasn't entirely right, he admitted with a sigh. He wouldn't be in such trouble if he hadn't tried to change the perception of the truth. *I was only trying to protect myself and my job—and look how that ended up! I've spent my whole life relying on my own intelligence. I certainly should be able to figure a way out of this mess.*

Relying on yourself is what has gotten you into this mess.

Seth blinked and jerked his head up a notch. Where did that come from?

He drove on, lost in his thoughts, desperately formulating a plan. As he neared Washington, D.C., the traffic thickened and slowed. Road construction and rush hour combined to weave the traffic pattern into a troublesome snarl.

He hoped no one would find Donovan before morning. By then Seth would have alibis that would place him far away. Besides, the authorities wouldn't be sure exactly when the examiner had died.

If they found him too soon, a good pathologist would be able to nearly pinpoint the time of death, which certainly wasn't too long before Seth was present. Donovan wasn't even room temperature by the time the physician arrived.

Seth hoped to interact with someone soon—someone who would remember him. He needed to check into a motel, maybe eat out, get the names of people he met. He could use his credit card so there'd be a record.

You're still running from the truth, Seth.

This time Seth verbalized a response to the thought that had intruded on his consciousness. "I'm *seeking* the truth! That's what I'm doing! I'm trying to find evidence that will validate my story and restore my credibility." He snorted, then stopped and shook his head. *Maybe I'm losing my mind. Now I'm arguing with . . . ?* He shrugged. *Who am I arguing with?*

After another hour, Seth exited the interstate and headed for Rockville, Maryland. Arriving after the N.I.H. had closed for the day, he checked into a Howard Johnson motel for the night. He was served at the registration desk by a pleasant woman with gray hair and medium stature wearing a name tag—"M. Stevens."

Seth asked her about the N.I.H., commented on her beautiful silver hair, and asked her about local Chinese and Mexican restaurants, all in hopes of making the conversation one she'd remember. When he reached his room, he carefully recorded their conversation and wrote down her name.

He looked at his watch. Kerri wouldn't be home until midnight. He needed to tell her about Donovan. He thought for a moment longer, then decided to go ahead and phone Kerri's apartment, hoping a call from his room would further confirm his alibi.

After two rings Kerri's machine picked up, "Hi. You've reached Kerri. Please leave a message after the beep."

"Hi, Kerri. It's Seth. I'm in Rockville, Maryland. I'm here to talk to Kevin Schwab at the N.I.H. I'll call you later." He paused, then added, "Please pray. I, uh, well, I know I just saw you, but . . . I really miss you."

He hadn't really intended on leaving a personal message, but hearing her recorded voice prompted a flood of emotions.

What's happening to me? Asking for prayer? He shook his head. *Hopefully Kerri's prayers work better than mine.*

He collapsed back on the double bed to rest a moment before heading out to find a place to eat. Oh, how he wished Kerri was there.

◆ ◆ ◆

Tammy Lynn carefully wrote down the psychic hotline number displayed on the T.V. screen. The testimonials and the promises were so convincing. "Do you need advice about love and relationships?" That was her, all right. She wanted to know if things were going to work out for Eric and her.

She set the number aside, distracted by the glamorous tennis bracelet advertised on the home shopping channel. She'd have to tell Eric about it. It was such a bargain, too. Just four easy payments of $24.95.

She walked to her front window and looked toward the street. Where was Eric anyway? He'd told her at lunch that he'd come by after work. Connie would be busy with her bridge club and wouldn't miss him.

She smiled thinly at the thought of Connie and her friends. What a bunch of high-class snoots! She'd love to see her face when she learned that Eric was spending more time in Tammy Lynn's arms than in hers. He had promised to tell her soon.

She looked at the phone. Maybe she should call the office. If Connie answered, Tammy Lynn could hang up. As she listened to the endless ringing on the other end, she carried the phone into the bathroom. She hoped everything was OK. He'd been having indigestion again at noon.

She finally put the phone down, confident Eric had left for the day. Deciding to freshen up, she applied more lip gloss. Eric was on his way!

◆ ◆ ◆

Connie's frustration at Eric's absence melted as she drank, ate, and grumbled with her girlfriends. The more they played, the more they realized that the cards were just an excuse to relish their common plight—the social worries of the upper class.

Soon the conversation transitioned to the medical staff and eventually to the gossip surrounding Seth Berringer.

"I heard he lost his job with Coast Care. They've already replaced him," reported Janet Sullivan.

"I heard he decompensated after striking that girl. His whole life fell apart. They had to put him in a hospital somewhere," Barb Netter added.

"Decompensated? That's what you call a nervous breakdown if you're being politically correct, huh, Barb?" Sally Bixby laughed. She put her nose in the air, looked through her half-glasses, and said the word again with a throaty emphasis, "Decompensated!"

"I went to him for my blood pressure," said Janet with a coy smile. "It was all I could do to keep my pressure in line, just looking at that fine young man."

Connie didn't find that comment to her liking. She didn't smile but simply noted, "You could be his mother!"

Janet shrugged her shoulders. "You haven't seen him then."

"I've talked to him," Connie replied. "Just today."

"He's not in the hospital?" Barb looked surprised.

"He's not crazy, Barb. He was only trying to reach my husband. I suspect he wants to talk to him about that girl he hit." Connie shook her head. "Evidently he's obsessed over the case or something. Eric told me a little about him. He came down and watched the autopsy and everything."

"Eric let him watch?"

"He didn't know that Dr. Berringer had anything to do with her death, of course. He just thought he was interested because he was her doctor." Connie took a sip of wine, which further loosened her tongue. "Now he seems to have some disagreement with Eric about the findings." She shrugged and continued, "A friend of his came in the office the other day and accused my husband of altering his records—created quite a scene."

"The nerve of some people! Eric's the best medical examiner this county's had for a dozen years," Sally added, patting Connie's hand.

"Fifteen," Connie corrected.

"Has it been that long?" Barb shook her head. "I'm gettin' old."

"Not me," Janet countered.

"Me neither," Connie added. "I married an older man."

"Smart woman." Janet laughed. "You won't have to put up with him as long."

"Janet!" Barb scolded.

Sally snickered.

Connie shrugged and ate a slice of cheese.

"I was only kidding. Besides, Eric runs around like a man half his age."

"Deal the cards. Didn't we come here to play?"

◆ ◆ ◆

Kerri worked nonstop for three hours after Seth's mysterious visit. The acute M.I. patient was admitted to I.C.U., the infant with meningitis was sent to pediatrics, two of the trauma victims were sent to the orthopedic floor, and one was transferred to the university hospital by ground transport. Mr. Bailey's son came by after work and took his belligerent father home. Dr. Perkins, the impatient surgeon, cleaned his shoes and did an appendectomy.

Finally, near eight o'clock, Kerri and her coworker, Deb Blackwell, made plans to slip away to the cafeteria for a bite to eat.

As they walked away from the desk, Dr. Frank Nicholson put a gentle hand on Kerri's shoulder. "I saw Seth Berringer earlier." He looked down. "Things were so hectic, we didn't speak. I—well, I hope he's doing OK."

Kerri looked at the physician and attempted a smile. "I suppose you're employed by Coast Care as well?"

"Who isn't? They bought just about everyone."

Joe Blevins butted into the conversation. "I suppose you're blaming Coast Care for Seth's problems?"

This time Kerri didn't smile. "I didn't say that. But I would hope that we who know Dr. Berringer's excellent clinical reputation wouldn't be too quick to toss aside our loyalty to a colleague."

"He was committed to a state mental hospital, Kerri," the man countered.

"He underwent an *evaluation*, was cleared, and was released, Dr. Blevins. Believing rumors will only keep us groping blindly for the truth."

With that, Kerri spun on her heels and walked away.

Behind her, Blevins punched his associate in the arm and lowered his voice. "Ol' Seth must have done some smooth talkin' to convince a feisty babe like that to believe him."

Once they were down the hall, Deb turned and gasped. "Way to go! It's about time someone put that guy in his place." She giggled and imitated Kerri's last statement. ". . . groping blindly for the truth." She shook her head. "Why can't I say something like that?"

"I was only giving the facts."

They walked on in silence for a moment, entered the cafeteria, and made their selections. Once at a small table, Deb questioned Kerri again. "What was Dr. Berringer doing in the E.R. tonight anyway?"

A line of concern wrinkled Kerri's forehead. "I'm not exactly sure. Something was bugging him, I could see that much."

Deb brightened. "You've been seeing him, haven't you?"

Kerri allowed a little smile. "Believing rumors will only keep us groping blindly for the truth." She couldn't say it with a straight face.

"Come on, I saw you light up when he came in."

"We've been out a few times." Kerri thought about her admission. They weren't exactly dating, but they had eaten out together.

"I thought so. John told me he saw you two at Clara's." With a smile, she added, "I think that's great. All of us have been wondering who would be the first to grab his attention. I know I'd wilt for the chance."

Kerri pushed her salad around the bowl with her fork. Thinking about Seth brought up a river of emotions. She wanted desperately to do the right thing, to follow the Lord, not just her heart.

"You're being pretty quiet."

Kerri looked up and wrinkled her nose. "Just thinking, that's all."

Deb stayed silent.

Kerri thought, then opened up. "You know, you're right—I do like him." She turned a lettuce leaf over with her fork.

Deb prodded, "But . . ."

She shrugged. "I don't know—I guess I don't want to move too fast. I don't want him to like me just because I've been supportive when others have written him off."

"Get a grip, Kerri. There's little worry in that." She extended her hand, holding an imaginary object. "Have you looked in the mirror lately? A girl like you can have anyone you want."

"That's not the way I want it." She looked up, wanting to watch Deb's response. "I want to meet a man who believes the way I do—someone who has the same Christian faith."

"I'd convert to Buddhism if Seth Berringer would look my way."

"I'm being serious."

Deb looked down. "Your religion is pretty important to you, huh?"

She nodded.

"What does Seth think about your requirement?"

"It's not like that. I would never put a prerequisite on our friendship," she said slowly. "Seth's changing. He's been through so much lately. I think he is still trying to figure everything—"

The hospital intercom interrupted with an urgent report of cardiopulmonary arrest. "Code blue, emergency room. Code blue, emergency room."

Kerri stood and quickly carried her tray to a conveyor belt. "We'd better go. Sounds like we may be needed back in the pit."

Deb shook her head. "Nice supper, huh? Let's go."

◆ ◆ ◆

Tammy Lynn's patience was growing thin. She waited, reapplied her lip gloss, called the psychic hotline, waited some more, ordered a set of collapsible plastic containers from the home shopping channel, and waited some more.

She looked at her watch. Where was he? Certainly he would have called if he'd had an emergency.

She waited for another fifteen minutes before leaving the house to find Eric Donovan. Within a few minutes she was driving by his house, inching along slowly to see if she could spot his sport utility vehicle. He wasn't there. Just Connie and her ritzy friends.

She drove on past and decided to check his office. Once there, she saw his Ford Explorer parked in the farthest slot.

He was just working late. She smiled. Maybe she should go back to her apartment and wait. She hesitated, then pulled into the parking lot. She'd go in and surprise him.

The front door was locked, but she quietly let herself in with her key. She walked down the front hall, hoping the sharp clipping noise of her heels wouldn't alert Eric to her coming. He'd be so surprised. She couldn't wait to tell him what the psychic advisor had told her about their future!

She opened the door to the front office. All the lights were still on. Quietly, she eased open the door to the back lab. Immediately sensing that something was wrong, she quickly glanced around the room at the disarray. She put aside her idea of surprising Eric and timidly called out his name. "Eric . . ." She paused. "Are you here?"

She walked to his desk, instinctively running her fingers along the edge as she examined his desktop. Once she reached the desk's corner, she pulled her hand away and rubbed her fingers together. Something sticky was drying there. She inspected the desk and her hand. Blood!

Could one of the technicians have gotten sloppy with a case? No, Eric would never tolerate that!

"Eric?" Anxiety seized her. "Eric, where are you? Eric, come out! You're scaring me!"

She turned and slowly scanned the far wall. Her eyes were drawn to the open refrigerator door.

"No," she whispered softly, squinting to see beyond the door. "No!"

Reality settled in as she recognized the white linen coat. She stepped toward the large, silver unit, her eyes fixated on the now-visible body. "Eric! No!" She touched his face only momentarily before pulling her hand away in horror. His skin was pale and cool, and she could see the blood on his forehead.

She sank to her knees. "No. No. No," she sobbed. "It isn't supposed to be like this. Noooo!!!"

She ran from the room, stumbling over a formaldehyde container as she fled from the death behind her. Once in the front office, she concentrated on trying to calm down. She talked to herself as she collapsed into her chair. "I have to tell someone. I have to get help. They need to find the person who did this to Eric—the person who did this to me!"

She dialed 911.

"This is 911 emergency. How may I help you?"

"Someone has murdered Eric Donovan!"

CHAPTER
28

SHERIFF Boatwright pulled out the long, silver tray with a gloved hand. "It's Donovan all right. I'd bet my lunch on it."

The deputy nodded and kept his thoughts to himself. His lunch? He *must* be sure. "Think it's a suicide?"

"I'm not ruling anything out yet, but from talkin' with that secretary, I get the distinct feelin' that she didn't drop by just to catch up on transcription. I'd say we have a lover's triangle here. And judgin' by that gash in his forehead, I'd doubt he did it himself." He shook his head. "A shame, really." He looked back at a detective who was taking notes on an open laptop computer. "Get the county medical examiner down here. And I want the evidence technician down here pronto to get some prints." He looked at a deputy standing with another young man holding a camera. "Hey, Bucky, get a shot of the corner of the desk."

The deputy was still processing the first order. "But, sheriff, he *is* the medical examiner."

"He's the *chief* medical examiner," the sheriff explained, "the boss of the county medical examiners."

"Oh." He went to his radio to relay the message.

In another hour the office and laboratory of the chief medical examiner were a bit crowded. Two evidence technicians collected fingerprints, the medical examiner did an initial scene evaluation, and a photographer recorded everything.

Dr. Robert Wright, the county medical examiner, spoke in hushed tones to the sheriff. "I can't really tell if it's suicide or homicide. I suppose he could have overdosed, then fallen and hit his head, but it seems odd there's no blood between the desk and the refrigerator unit. That's assuming, for the time being, that he hit his head on the desk and that is indeed his blood over there."

"From what I've seen of the trash contents thrown on top of him, it looks like someone was awfully concerned about cleaning up the blood." The sheriff pointed at the plastic trash bag, now lying on the floor.

"He'll have to go over to the central chief medical examiner for an autopsy," Wright added. "There's no obvious external cause of death except for that forehead gash, and that doesn't appear to have caused an external bleed-out."

The sheriff looked at another deputy. "Get the contents of this trash to the lab. I want to know if all of this is Donovan's blood."

He looked over at Detective Dave Trainum. "How'd things go with the girl?"

He shook his head. "She's not making a lot of sense yet. She's focused on some astrology charts or something." He shrugged. "She says Donovan was supposed to be working this afternoon, alone, with his wife covering the front office. He doesn't have a large staff. He evidently only has help available to process specimens when he needs it."

"Has she clarified her relationship with Donovan?"

"Yeah, but she wants it under the table. She says they wanted to break the news to his wife in the near future."

"Right," Boatwright muttered. "Is she able to identify any suspects, assuming he didn't do this to himself to escape his problems?"

"She's pretty uptight, Wayne. I think she's hidin' something. That's my gut feeling anyway. I don't think she did it though. I don't think she has the physical strength to put him in that refrigerator." He thought it over. "I don't know why, but I don't trust her. She's not telling the whole story."

"Did you ask her opinion?"

"I always do."

"Well?"

"She figures Berringer did it. She says he argued with the examiner about the Lisa Dale autopsy. And we all know he was just released from the state mental hospital."

"Berringer?" Deputy Zander spoke up. "I followed him down Route 11 north of here not three, four hours ago."

The sheriff looked at Dr. Wright. "How long you figure he's been dead?"

"Can't be sure, but from the gross inspection I'd say two to eight hours tops.".

"Hey, Robbie, any luck on the prints?" The sheriff looked at the evidence tech.

"I've got a great one here on the refrigerator door. Looks like a thumb. We'll send it to the state lab. Should have an answer in twenty-four hours."

Boatwright cursed. "Can't we run it against the stuff we've collected locally, just in case we get a match?"

"We can, but it won't stand up in court unless we have a certified expert do the analysis."

"We'll get the certified analysis—don't worry about that! I just want to eyeball the best print you have against one in our stock. Then you can send it to the state expert. I want a fast turnaround so we can strike before this trail has a chance to cool."

He looked at Zander. "Go dig up a copy of Seth Berringer's fingerprints. We have 'em on record from his recent workup."

Zander nodded. "Yes, sir."

"If you can get an unofficial match, talk to the magistrate right away. Berringer had a motive—he claimed Donovan was lying about the Lisa Dale case. If the print belongs to Berringer, the magistrate will certainly give us an arrest warrant."

"I'm on it."

"If we get a match, I want that guy locked up before morning."

He touched Detective Trainum on the arm. "Let's go visit Ms. Donovan. We've got some news for her. Besides, I'd like to see if she can verify where she was for the last eight hours."

"You think she may have wanted to get even with her husband?"

"Doubtful, but it's always good to have an open mind."

The two men walked out to the parking lot. Yellow crime scene tape kept back a small crowd of newspaper reporters.

A light rain had begun to fall, and a news reporter in a rain poncho called out to the sheriff who was quickly exiting the scene, "Any word on the victim's name, sheriff?"

"Not until we notify next of kin."

"Has it been ruled a homicide?" called another.

"We have our suspicions, but no facts yet."

"Any suspects?"

"Again, only suspicions. We are working rapidly to notify next of kin and are followin' up on some fingerprint analysis. I'll have more to say after that."

With that, he strode off to his police cruiser with his detective on his heels.

In another five minutes they pulled up to Donovan's home, where a social gathering was apparently still in full swing.

"Either she hasn't missed him yet, or she knows he's dead and decided to throw a party," chuckled Dave Trainum as they walked up the front steps.

He rang the doorbell and stepped back next to the sheriff. Both men were in plain clothes.

After the second ring, a well-dressed woman with a glass of wine in her hand came to the door. She spoke to the two men using an intercom, though she could clearly see them through an oval window in the top half of the door. "Can I help you, gentlemen?" Connie asked.

"We're from the Chesapeake County sheriff's department. I'm Detective Trainum," the taller man reported, holding up his badge. "This is Sheriff Boatwright."

Connie opened the door while calling into the other room to her friends, "It's the police!" She then turned to the two men on the front steps. "You may come in out of the rain. Has there been some sort of trouble?"

She suddenly remembered the sting operation her husband had told her about. Connie clutched her glass with white knuckles. "Tell me Eric's OK," she added, her eyes pleading.

"Maybe we should sit down, ma'am," the sheriff offered softly.

Immediately, Connie's friends surrounded her. "What's wrong, officer?" Barb demanded.

The sheriff and his detective exchanged glances.

"What's going on?" Connie asked again.

"There's been some trouble down at the medical examiner's office," the sheriff began. "Maybe you'd better sit down."

Connie nodded, the knuckle of her right index finger now pressed against her front teeth. Connie and her three friends moved as a group to a small couch in a front sitting room.

The sheriff remained standing. "Your husband's dead, Ms. Donovan." He thought it best to take a direct approach when delivering bad news. "A secretary found him just over an hour ago. She saw the lights on afterhours and went in to investigate." When no one said anything, he added, "We're just beginning our investigation, and we'd like to ask a few questions. We haven't ruled anything out yet, but my first thought is that we are dealing with a homicide."

Connie sat quietly for a moment, completely stunned by the news. The detective watched her carefully. The emotion seemed genuine.

"It was the sting, wasn't it?" she sobbed quietly. Her eyes bore down on the sheriff's face. "This is your fault, isn't it? Your little sting backfired on my husband!"

Trainum locked eyes with the sheriff, who appeared as clueless as Trainum felt.

"Ma'am, with all due respect, I'm not sure what you're referring to." The sheriff showed gentle compassion in his voice.

"You don't have to pretend. Eric told me he wasn't supposed to tell. He was meeting with Dr. Yamatsu."

"He was scheduled to meet with someone this afternoon?" The detective opened his laptop computer.

"Yes." She looked at them, hoping to see confirmation in their eyes. "Eric told me he was involved with a sting operation with your department. All I know is that it had something to do with evidence he'd discovered that had the potential to get someone into trouble."

The sheriff's beeper sounded. He looked at the message. It was the office. "May I use your phone?"

Connie nodded numbly. Sally showed the sheriff to the kitchen extension.

The detective prodded further. "Was anyone else at your husband's workplace this afternoon?"

"No. I was there until around 2. Then I left him alone."

"So, let me get this straight—he was alone but planned to meet with someone by the name of Yamatsu?"

"That's right. I think I left a message for him on the desk. I set up the meeting for him myself."

"Did he have any other meetings planned?"

Connie shook her head. She was pale, her hands trembling, as the obvious truth began to dawn. "Are you saying that the sheriff's department and my husband weren't working together in a sting operation?"

The detective shook his head. "I'm sorry, ma'am."

She sat quietly for a moment in frozen silence.

"Was anyone else planning to see him for any reason?"

Connie began to shake her head, then stopped suddenly just as the sheriff returned from his phone call with the department. "Wait . . . I did talk to that doctor who was in the news—Seth Berringer. He called the house this afternoon looking for Eric. I told him he was at the office. I think he might have been planning to visit him."

The deputy looked up and made eye contact with the sheriff. "I talked with Zander," Boatwright reported. "He's got a 99 percent positive I.D. on the fingerprint on the refrigerator door."

The detective stood.

The sheriff bit his lip in a show of sympathy. "We're deeply disturbed to give you this news tonight, Ms. Donovan." He looked at the floor. "And I'm sorry we had to ask so many questions." He paused. "Would it be OK if we came back in the morning? It should be a better time for all of us."

She nodded as Boatwright placed his hand briefly on her shoulder. Then, as quickly as they'd come, the duo left again, striding down the front steps and jumping into the patrol car.

Once inside, Trainum asked, "It was Berringer's print?"

"The one and only."

"Did Zander get the warrant?"

"The magistrate didn't hesitate." The sheriff put on the blue lights and pressed the accelerator to the floor.

"Call for backup. I want to make this arrest myself."

◆ ◆ ◆

By the time Sheriff Boatwright arrived at the Berringer farmhouse, Deputies Zander and Pheiffer had been on the scene for fifteen minutes.

"He's not here," Zander reported, shaking his head. "There's no sign of his van, and no one has taken in today's mail."

The house was dark. The sheriff squinted his eyes at the windows. "You're sure he's not in there watching? He could be sleeping."

"We tried the phone, just to see if he would answer. He's not home."

"Maybe you two should stay in the neighborhood. Watch for his maroon van. Dave and I will pay a visit to his girlfriend's place. If he's running, maybe he told her something."

They all nodded and walked toward their cars.

As the sheriff reached his vehicle, he turned and called out to Deputy Zander, "Go ahead and issue a statement to the press. Release Donovan's name as the victim, but don't tell them Berringer's an official suspect yet."

"Yes, sir."

After a short drive, the sheriff knocked on the door of Kerri's vacant apartment. "No one here either."

"Let's check the Chesapeake General emergency room. You said she's a nurse over there, right?"

The sheriff looked at his watch. It was 11:30. He shrugged. "It's worth a try."

◆ ◆ ◆

Kerri was hoping to head home by midnight. Then the sheriff arrived in the E.R. Though her shift ended at 11, she was not free to go until she had given the oncoming nurse a report on all her patients.

As she handed the last patient clipboard to Barry Newsome, R.N., she saw the sheriff approaching.

"Ms. Barber, may we have a word with you?" The sheriff's manner communicated urgency.

Kerri thought back immediately to their last conversation, when the sheriff had warned her about Seth and asked her not to speak of Lisa Dale's death as a murder. She disliked his implication that Seth was lying to her then, and she didn't anticipate enjoying anything the sheriff would tell her now. She decided to take an assertive stance. "Sheriff, I've had a very stressful shift, and I'd like to go home. If you're here to continue our conversation about Lisa Dale, I can assure you I've not spoken publicly of it since."

Boatwright looked around. "It's not that." He hesitated. "Is there anyplace private where we can talk?"

Kerri sighed and started walking toward the back hallway. "We can use one of the empty patient cubicles back here."

She walked into the room, which was empty except for supplies and two stretchers. She looked at the two men without speaking.

"Please sit down. I'd like to ask you a few questions," the sheriff began.

"I'll stand." She looked at the second man and held out her hand. "I'm Kerri Barber. I don't think we've been introduced."

The detective privately enjoyed the way she pointed out the sheriff's lack of social graces. "Dave Trainum. I'm a detective with the sheriff's department."

"Is there a problem?"

"We need to talk to you about Seth Berringer."

Kerri paled. "I . . . Is Seth OK? He's not hurt, is he?"

"Nothing like that," the detective responded.

"There's been some trouble, and we think Seth may know something about it," the sheriff explained.

Kerri's alarm quickly turned to suspicion. "Trouble? What kind of trouble?"

"Dr. Eric Donovan was found dead," he reported bluntly. "Just a few hours ago."

"Dead?" She pulled a closed hand to her chest in shock. "Dead," she repeated. "How?"

"That's what we're trying to find out, Ms. Barber." Boatwright paused for effect. "Do you know where we can locate Mr. Berringer?"

"Seth?" Her eyes widened. "What does he have to do with this?" Kerri thought back to Seth's mysterious visit to the E.R. only hours earlier. Something was definitely bugging him. What had he said? The alarming words came back clearly: "Something's happened to Donovan." She'd asked him what, but he didn't answer because they were interrupted. Kerri stared into space, lost in her memory, oblivious to the sheriff's voice. What else had he said? "I'll be on the road." O God, *what has happened to Seth?*

"Ms. Barber? Ms. Barber, are you OK?" Dave Trainum touched her arm.

Kerri focused. "I—I'm sorry. Yes?"

"We have reason to believe that Mr. Berringer may have been present when Dr. Donovan died."

Kerri shook her head, unwilling to believe the implication. "Wait a minute," she said slowly. "You're not saying that you think Dr. Berringer had something to do with it, are you?"

"I'm not here to debate with you, Ms. Barber. I'm merely trying to find Mr. Berringer so I can question him."

"Is he under arrest or something?"

Dave Trainum tried to explain. "No. He has to be present to arrest him, but we do have a warrant—"

The sheriff's eyes bore down on his detective as he interrupted, saying, "We're just lookin' for Mr. Berringer."

"I don't know where he is," she said mechanically. "Seth wouldn't hurt anyone. Why do you think he—"

"Look, Ms. Barber, you're letting your heart do the thinkin' here. You're too close to this friend of yours to be objective. He and Donovan had a significant disagreement, one that has potentially ruined Berringer's reputation. He certainly would have been angry about that, don't you think?"

"Sure, but he wouldn't—"

Boatwright sighed heavily, upset at himself that he was actually arguing over evidence and motives with a suspect's friend. "Look, we have a fingerprint match that places Berringer at the scene, OK?" He waited, his eyes unmoving from Kerri's delicate features. "I've told you more than I should have. Now please, I've not held anything back from you, so can you extend me the same courtesy?"

Kerri stumbled backwards and sat on a stretcher. "I don't know what to tell you. I'm not holding anything back. I don't know where Seth is."

"Did you talk to him today?"

"Yes. On the phone." She hesitated. "And once tonight when he stopped by."

The duo looked at each other with raised eyebrows. The detective prompted her further. "What did he want?"

Kerri shook her head. "I honestly don't know. He wanted to tell me something, but we were really busy here . . . Our conversation was interrupted."

"Did he say anything, where he was going—anything?"

"I told him I'd call him after work. He said he'd be on the road."

"On the road? That's it?"

Kerri nodded. "That's all. I don't know where."

Dave Trainum looked at Wayne Boatwright. "Sounds like our man is on the run."

The sheriff nodded. After a moment he looked back at Kerri, who sat unmoving on the padded stretcher. "He'll probably call you. I'm sure we can count on you to help us bring him in."

She didn't reply.

The two men turned to go. "We'll be in touch. Thanks for your help."

Kerri sat alone for a few minutes, trying desperately to put the last few minutes into focus. Seth wanted for murder? She shook her head. *I know I haven't known him very long, Lord, but I know him well enough to know that he's not capable of that. Don't I?*

Her mind raced, trying to determine whether Seth was perhaps radically different than she'd thought. She knew how she felt toward him, and her heart wouldn't allow her to believe the worst. She put her head in her hands and began an earnest prayer with a personal admission: *O Father, I'm in love with a wanted man!*

CHAPTER
29

SETH looked out from the private beach, his back warmed by the sun, his toes imprinting the white sand as he walked.

"The water is so beautiful," she said.

He looked at her, the one whose hand he held, and longed to tell her his feelings—feelings he had locked inside for so many years. But now, with his heart so near the bursting point, he found himself holding back, unable to fully communicate the love he desperately wanted to shower upon her.

"Yes, it is," he responded, admiring her for a moment before turning away. *Why am I so afraid to tell you how I feel?*

The sun cast sharp shadows on the sand in front of the couple, outlining the woman's every admirable quality, yet not able to reveal the inner strength that allowed her to walk unencumbered and free.

Seth looked at his shadow beside the woman he adored. He could not see manliness reflected there. He could see only darkness—darkness that threatened to overtake him completely. *How can one so pure and lovely find satisfaction with me?* he wondered. *I am so stained.* To him, his shadow appeared hideous, distorted, disfigured.

She broke his gentle grasp and giggled as she ran along the water's edge before lying down on a towel in the sand. Her hair danced with the breeze, highlighted with the sun's kiss.

He lowered himself beside her, longing to accept her love, longing to give in return. But this time he couldn't meet her gaze, couldn't look into the eyes that seemed so full of love. *Why do I feel this way? I am innocent, am I not? Why does your loveliness challenge me so? Why can't I tell you, "I love you"?*

◆ ◆ ◆

Seth rolled over on the sagging mattress and looked at the clock. It was still too early to call Kerri. He pulled a second pillow close to him and closed his eyes. He'd try to grab a short nap before Kerri got home from work.

His busy mind surrendered to his need for slumber, and he tossed fitfully as his unspoken fears filtered through his consciousness.

◆ ◆ ◆

Seth groped for the light switch, unable to find his way without stumbling in the darkness. He was alone in the hotel room but was suddenly transported outside to a deserted field. With his vision still hampered, he held his arms out in front of him, moving slowly, one foot at a time, into the darkness.

Suddenly he was falling, hurling headlong, having tripped over an object in the tall grass.

Not wanting to look but unable to resist, he parted the tall blades of grass to see the pale face of Lisa Dale.

He stood to walk away but seemed unable to go on. He surrendered to the compulsion to look again upon the dead face, which now bore the likeness of Eric Donovan.

He pulled away from the gaze of the dead man, horrified at the image of his pale, bloodied flesh.

"I have to get away!" he yelled. "I have to run away!"

Above him loomed the expansive image of Wayne Boatwright's smile, a billboard image, yet full of life and calling after him, "Why are you running, son? What are you hiding?" Boatwright emitted a hearty laugh.

"I have to find evidence of the truth!" Seth yelled, holding his fist up to the yellowing sign, which now mocked him with unmoving silence. "I can do it. I've succeeded in the past. I'll find the truth my own way!"

"You're running from the truth, Seth. Relying on yourself is what got you into this mess."

◆ ◆ ◆

Seth awoke as God's Spirit again troubled him with the undeniable fact of his spiritual need.

"I've always trusted myself," he whispered into the dark room. He sat up, trying to focus on his hands. The only thing visible in the blackness were the red numbers on the clock radio: 12:25. *What's happening to me?*

He flipped on the light above the bed and reached for the phone. Since he'd left the earlier message, he'd called Kerri twice more, each time getting the recording, each time hanging up without talking again.

This time Kerri answered after the first ring, "Hello."

"Kerri!"

"Seth!" Kerri gushed in a near-sob, unprepared for the almost overwhelming flood of feeling that came when she heard his voice. "What's going on?" she cried.

As he heard the choked emotion in her voice, tears flooded Seth's eyes. He wanted to compose himself, but Kerri continued, her voice rhythmic as she spoke through her tears, "Seth, I talked to the sheriff. He—he th-thinks you killed Eric Donovan."

"It's not true, Kerri," he responded with more calm than he felt. "Tell me you don't believe him!" Suddenly nothing else mattered. He needed only to hear that she was still on his side.

In her heart she had always believed in his innocence. Now, hearing the longing in his voice, her mind believed it too. "Of course I don't believe him." She bit her bottom lip. "Tell me what happened."

"I don't know what happened. That's what I came to tell you at the E.R. I went down to see him, just like I told you. When I arrived, everything was in disarray—containers everywhere, as if someone was searching for something. I looked around for a few moments, hoping to see something, anything that might be a clue to Lisa's case." He halted, thinking back to the scene in the lab. "I kept calling out Dr. Donovan's name. That's when I found him—that is, his body. Someone had put him in the large morgue refrigerator. The door wasn't completely shut, so I could tell there was a body inside. When I got close, I could see it was Donovan."

"But why did you run off? The police think you're guilty. They want to arrest you!"

Seth sighed. "I knew they wouldn't believe me. I'd talked to a deputy earlier in the day. He practically accused me of murdering Lisa Dale and covering it up! When I found Donovan's body, I knew they'd think I was lying. So I ran away. I hoped they wouldn't find him until I'd had a chance to collect enough evidence to convince Boatwright I'm telling the truth." He paused. "My only thought was to talk to Kevin Schwab in person, in hopes of convincing him to come forward about the specimen Donovan sent him." He hesitated again, listening for Kerri's response. "I only hope Donovan didn't lie about that as well."

"Oh, Seth, come home. We'll talk to the sheriff together. We can get you a good attorney. You have to tell them you're innocent!"

"I—I can't, Kerri. Boatwright will have me behind bars so fast . . . Kerri, I have to prove I'm telling the truth. If he locks me up, who else will believe me enough to locate that specimen?"

"What will that demonstrate, Seth? Only that you told the truth about the autopsy, not that you didn't kill Dr. Donovan."

"Don't you see, Kerri? These things must all be connected somehow. Someone killed Donovan, but why? And why now? Could it be related to Lisa's death in some way?" He shook his head. "I can't believe it's circumstantial."

Kerri wiped her eyes. "I'm not sure I'm following you."

"It must have something to do with the research she was involved in. Someone was after that baby. That's what she said in her postcard. And apparently Lisa died in the process of someone's attempt to end her pregnancy. I'm beginning to think it isn't any coincidence that one of the only people who knew the truth about the way she died has ended up dead himself."

"But if you run, the sheriff will think you're guilty."

Seth sighed. "Kerri, I know what you're saying is true, but I'm not sure the sheriff or his department is playing above the board."

"What do you mean?"

"I can't be sure yet." His words were slow and studied. "This afternoon the deputy told me something that shows that either the sheriff's department is involved in something dark or . . ." He hesitated. "Or whoever is responsible for Lisa's death is going to great lengths to keep the sheriff's department confused and me looking responsible."

"What did he say?"

"He told me they'd found Lisa Dale's shoe under my van."

Kerri nodded as she remembered her conversation with the sheriff. "The sheriff told me they'd caught you in a lie."

"I wasn't lying. I left that shoe on the side of the road to mark where I could find the body. There is no way that shoe could have ended up stuck under my van unless someone planted it there."

"Or someone in the sheriff's department is making up a story," she responded, completing his thought.

"Exactly."

"Hmmm." Kerri sighed and sat down on her couch with her portable phone in her hand.

"Which is one reason I'm not ready to surrender to Mr. Boatwright."

Kerri was quiet for a moment, then spoke cautiously. "I don't know, Seth. I'm not a big fan of Boatwright or his department, but I don't get the sense he's deliberately trying to frame you. He may be misguided by facts that don't add up, but I think he's sincere. I think the other option is more likely—that whoever killed Lisa Dale is setting you up and taking advantage of the natural cover you've given them."

Seth shook his head. "I never dreamed it would turn out this way."

Kerri sat silently, not knowing what to say. She felt empty, drained of emotion.

"I wish I had the opportunity to live that one night over. Everything would be different."

"Look on the bright side." Kerri smiled. "I'd have probably never talked to you."

"I think I would've liked to try and meet you some other way, thank you very much," he responded, his voice hinting at a smile for the first time.

"I'm serious. Maybe it's all working according to plan."

"You're not suggesting that God created this trouble just to let us spend some time together—"

"No, Seth," she said gently. "But I do believe God uses unusual circumstances in life to remind us of our need for him."

"I don't know. I've been pondering these things a lot lately, particularly since we've been talking. I've even tried to pray. But I end up feeling stupid, like I'm talking to the wall or something. And usually I end up worse off than before." He paused. "But there are other times when a thought will hit me out of the blue—almost like someone speaking to me."

Kerri sat up and raised her eyebrows. "What do you mean?"

"Today as I drove up here I was determined to calculate my way out of this mess. I've relied on my own determination and intelligence for a long time and . . . Well, before all of this . . . Anyway, I felt like I was getting

along just fine, building my own life, listening to my own heart." He hesitated, wondering how much to tell. "I was thinking about all that when suddenly the message came to me that relying on myself is what caused my
problem. It was w-weird. I c-can't really describe what happened without
sounding crazy, but the thought didn't seem to originate with me."

"Maybe you should listen, Seth. Maybe, just maybe, it was the Lord
prompting you, guiding you."

They were quiet for a moment before Kerri spoke again. "What will you
do next?"

"I've had plenty of time today to think about that. If Schwab can't help
me by giving me the specimen Donovan sent, maybe I should try to contact the researchers who set up the whole project."

She thought for a moment. "What makes you so sure that finding the
fetus will prove anything? If Donovan's report says nothing about the
pregnancy, there'll still be a discrepancy. Boatwright will just say the baby
wasn't hers."

"I've thought about that. All we need is a DNA analysis of the baby
and of Lisa to prove her motherhood."

"OK, but even if you find the baby, where do you get DNA from Lisa
Dale? She was cremated."

"There should be serum stored in the state lab from her medical examiner's autopsy. They keep all of that stuff for later court analysis if needed."
He scratched his head. "Everything hinges on me finding the baby, or at
least proof that the baby existed. Then I can prove I was telling the truth
about Lisa Dale. That in turn would show I was subjected to a needless psychiatric examination, and then my reputation will at least have a shot at
restoration."

"But what about Donovan?"

"If I find the baby, whoever wanted it is likely to be pretty upset." He
considered his words. "If someone really wants that specimen and comes
forward, I'll bet we'll find the person responsible for Lisa's death, and possibly Donovan's. Think about it. The examiner lied and changed the
autopsy report. What would motivate him to cover up the real cause of
Lisa's death? And then I find *him* dead." He shook his head. "There's bound
to be a connection."

"I don't know."

"Do you have any better theories?"

Kerri shook her head. "No," she replied meekly.

Seth yawned. "Look, I need to get some sleep. I have to be thinking clearly tomorrow. Wish me luck."

"No, Seth, I'll pray."

He nodded. "Thanks, Kerri." He wanted to say more. "Thanks for believing me. That means a lot."

"Of course." Sniff. "Seth? You know I . . . Well, I care about you."

"Now I'm starting to worry about your judgment."

"Stop."

There was silence for a moment.

"Call me tomorrow?" she asked, knowing his response.

"Sure. Right after I talk to Schwab, I'll—"

Kerri interrupted, remembering the sheriff's last statements to her. "Don't call me here. I'm sure the sheriff will be looking for me, wanting to know if you called. I can't lie, Seth. I just can't." She hesitated. "But if he doesn't know where to find me, I won't have to tell him what I know. Call me at Angie Blackstock's. He'll never go there, especially since her father is running for sheriff. I don't have to work, so I'll go there first thing in the morning and stay until I hear from you."

He carefully copied the number. "Thanks, Kerri. Wish me . . . uh, pray for me, will you?"

"I never stop, Seth. I never stop."

◆ ◆ ◆

Kerri heaved a sigh and flopped back on her bed. Could she avoid the sheriff's department so she wouldn't have to tell them what she knew? Was it right to keep information from them while they were doing a murder investigation?

But they were searching for the wrong man! Kerri closed her fist in frustration.

And what about Seth's suspicion that the sheriff's department might be intentionally deceiving them? She shook her head. That didn't ring true.

What about the shoe they'd found on Seth's van? For that shoe to end up there, someone had to know where Lisa died and whose shoe it was. The only ones who knew where Seth found the body were the folks at the sheriff's department—and her killer!

Could the person responsible for Lisa's death have seen Seth's van? Were they watching over her body? The thought chilled her.

Or did they look for her, recognize her shoe, and plant it on Seth's van after the newspaper reported he was the driver in the hit-and-run? But why?

The possibilities made her head spin.

O God, what is the truth?

CHAPTER
30

Early the next morning, Detective Trainum held an extensive interview with Connie Donovan.

Though she was not officially a suspect, they told her she could have her attorney present during the questioning. She had politely declined and said she'd help them any way she could. She just wanted to find the truth, and the sooner the better as far as she was concerned.

Dave Trainum shifted in his seat. As many times as he'd done this, he didn't like making people talk about their private lives. "Ms. Donovan, I need to ask you a few personal questions," he continued softly. "I'll apologize in advance if they make you uncomfortable."

She nodded. She appeared to be a model of composure. She wore a dark blue suit, a white blouse, and small pearl earrings, a gift from her late husband.

"Do you have any reason to believe your husband was suicidal? Had he been depressed, distraught, drinking a lot—that sort of thing?"

She shook her head. "No. If Eric had a fault, it wasn't depression. He thought too much of himself to be depressed." She paused. "Did he drink?" She shrugged. "On occasion, socially, but nothing heavy." She thought for a moment longer, then confessed, "He had seemed a bit withdrawn lately." She looked down. "Things weren't going so well between us."

"What do you mean, Ms. Donovan?"

She looked at him squarely. "He wasn't very good at communication. Never was, I guess. But lately he seemed to be preoccupied. He said it was work. I suspected more."

"Did he have any other relationships?"

Connie rephrased his question. "Was he having an affair?" She nodded. "I've certainly had my suspicions." She wrung her hands. "I think he was seeing his secretary."

"Tammy Lynn Gaskins?"

She nodded and bit her lip. "I've known about it for a while, I guess," she added. "I just didn't want to believe it was happening again."

"Again?"

She looked up at the detective, her eyes moist. "He did the same thing with me, when he was married to his first wife. You'd think I would've seen it coming . . . It was going to be different with me."

Trainum sighed. He hated to see her pain.

"Can you tell me more about the meeting your husband was to have yesterday afternoon?"

"I don't know much really. A few days ago a man—a Mr. Yamatsu—called. I overheard his conversation with my husband. They talked about a deal. He wanted something from my husband, and in return Eric asked for money." She looked at the detective, then added, "A lot of money."

"What did he want from your husband?"

"A clone. That's what he said. I don't know what it was all about—genetic duplication or something." She shrugged. "Anyway, I don't think Mr. Yamatsu was happy, and I heard my husband say he had information about a murder—something like that. I don't know any details, but I got the feeling that my husband thought he was in a position to hold out for a lot of money in return for this clone."

"And his silence?"

"I guess."

"Did you ever ask your husband about the deal?"

"Yes, but he didn't want to tell me much, and I didn't want to push. I just wanted to close my eyes to it all. I knew something wasn't right. I mean, if it was all above board, he'd tell me, right?" She shook her head. "I was afraid I'd lose him. Before I met Eric, I was a business school dropout. I feared I wouldn't be able to make it on my own again."

"Did you ever see this man, Yamatsu?"

"No. I talked to him on the phone and listened to him conversing briefly on the telephone with my husband, that's all." She paused. "I think he's Chinese."

Trainum knew Yamatsu was a Japanese name but kept quiet. After a moment he asked, "Do you think this man had a motive for murdering your husband?"

"Possibly." She shrugged. "Eric may have been in over his head. What I overheard that day sounded like he was threatening Yamatsu. He told me that sometimes during his job as a medical examiner he made discoveries that serve as evidence in criminal investigations. I told him to stop talking down to me. I let him know that I'd heard him ask Yamatsu for money, and I wanted to know what was going on."

"What did he tell you?"

"That's when he claimed he was part of a sting operation with the sheriff to bring the guilty parties into the open."

The detective nodded. "I see." He waited a moment, then shifted his questioning. "What about Seth Berringer? What was his relationship with your husband?"

"He was a professional colleague, that's all. I don't recall Eric ever mentioning him until he did the recent autopsy on that hit-and-run case. Evidently Dr. Berringer came down and viewed the autopsy, then later confessed to the hit-and-run. Am I right?"

Trainum nodded.

"According to what I saw, Berringer remembered the details of the autopsy differently than my husband, and that made Berringer look bad." She shook her head. "It's all very confusing to me. I knew little of this until a friend of Berringer's, Kerri Barber, came barging into the office accusing my husband of altering the record, claiming he would have to answer to God for his lies."

The detective's eyes lit up. "Was she angry?"

"She was that day."

Trainum made a note on the pad in front of him. "Hmmm. What about yesterday—what was your conversation with Dr. Berringer?"

"It was quick. He called in the afternoon, looking for my husband. He said he had called the office and there was no answer. I told him my husband was probably busy." She shrugged. "Anyway, he didn't want to leave a message. He just said my husband would know what he'd called about." She hesitated. "I don't know . . . There was something in his voice—maybe just tiredness, maybe frustration. I felt sorry for him. I remember asking him if Eric was in trouble, and he responded, 'I'm not sure.' Then I believe he said something to the effect of, 'I don't know much of anything anymore.' His voice was really more sad than mad or vindictive."

"Did he tell you he planned to go to your husband's office?"

"I think he mentioned it. I don't remember his exact words."

Trainum sat pondering his notes for a moment longer. He needed to tell Boatwright about this Yamatsu guy. He might be the one they needed. He straightened his papers, reading Kerri's name on the last page, and thought about meeting her in the emergency room the night before. Maybe this girl was more complicated than they'd thought. Could she have helped make Donovan "answer to God"?

"Ms. Donovan, I think you've answered all my questions for now. We'll contact you as soon as we make some headway."

They stood and shook hands politely.

Another deputy escorted Ms. Donovan down the hall to the exit, while Trainum gathered his work and closed his briefcase. He looked up just as the sheriff filled the doorway.

"Any insights from Ms. Donovan?"

"A few. She told me more about this supposed sting operation. It had something to do with a specimen Donovan was selling to a man named Yamatsu."

The sheriff nodded. "Hmmm. That's consistent with what the secretary told me."

"How'd your interview with Tammy Lynn go?"

"Very interesting. I mentioned the Yamatsu name Ms. Donovan gave us last night, and the sweet young thing broke down completely."

"What did she say?"

"I'll tell you the full story later." The sheriff sighed. "Suffice it to say that her theory bears some looking into. She thinks this Yamatsu guy was working with Berringer." He shook his head and nodded at the door across the hall. "She's a wreck. Now that Eric Donovan's dead, she's afraid she'll be next. She said she won't be safe until Berringer is behind bars."

"Do you believe her?"

"I haven't made up my mind. But I think she needs to be watched. She says she won't go home without police protection."

Trainum rolled his eyes.

"I want you to send our second car out to her apartment. Just tell Pheiffer to chill out, watch her place, and stay put."

"But we could use him for—"

The sheriff cut off his protest. "Just do it, Dave. If this Berringer is half as weird as she says he is, she may indeed be in danger."

◆ ◆ ◆

"This stuff is unbelievable." Kerri rolled her eyes and pointed at the page of the *Deer Falls Gazette*. She quoted from the article: "The sheriff promised swift action in the case of the county's latest homicide. Although the official word from the sheriff's department is 'No comment,' unofficial sources reveal that Dr. Seth Berringer is being sought for questioning."

"How does the paper get their information?" Angie asked.

"I'm not sure. Obviously someone in the sheriff's department told them about it." Kerri paced to the front window of the Blackstock home, then back to the kitchen, where Angie sat at the counter sipping coffee. She linked her fingers behind her head and walked toward the front room again.

"Would you stop pacing? You're making me nervous."

Kerri wrinkled her nose. "Sorry." She looked at the phone. "I wish he'd call."

"I wish you'd sit down."

She complied, plopping down in an overstuffed chair.

Angie studied her for a moment. "You've really fallen for him, haven't you? I haven't seen you this concerned about a guy since—"

Kerri shot her an icy stare, cutting short her comment.

Her friend smiled at a memory. "OK, OK. Well, it's been a long time anyway." Angie sighed. "Are you sure you're right about him? I mean, what if he's as smooth as the sheriff says?"

"He's not like that, Angie. I know it." She sulked for a moment. "I can't believe you!"

"I'm only trying to show some objectivity—something you have obviously lost, dear."

Kerri shook her head and exhaled slowly.

"Come on, Kerri, look at you. You're hiding out, not wanting the sheriff to talk to you, just so you can protect this man."

"He's innocent."

"How do you know?"

"I watched him for a long time in the E.R. before all this mess started. He's always treated people with compassion. And later, when he came to me and told me what he'd done to Lisa Dale . . . Well, you should have been there. He was brutally honest with me, even knowing I might reject him for what he'd done." She made eye contact with her friend. "You need to talk to him, then you'd know. To think he is so smooth that he'd deceive me with a series of lies . . . Well, it goes against everything I've observed. And lately, in the middle of all his trouble, I've watched him take a few small steps toward Christian faith." She shook her head.

"And where is your heart in all this?"

"Don't ask me that." Kerri folded her arms around her knees, which were drawn up to her chest.

"Kerri . . ." Angie drew out her name.

"I know I need to come to terms with how I feel. I have to talk to him about us." She looked at the floor and rocked herself gently. "I understand I can't give my heart away as long as Seth hasn't committed his life to the Lord. I know about being unequally yoked," she added referring to a biblical principle they'd both held dear. "But it's not wrong to love him, is it?"

"You're talking in circles."

"I'm thinking in circles," she countered. "We just haven't had a chance to talk about our feelings. Everything is happening so fast around us, and to us, that our communication has been consumed with the trouble he's in."

"It may be your trouble, too."

Kerri looked up, her brow wrinkled with a question.

"Think about your last visit with Dr. Donovan. You told me about it yourself. Did anyone witness you telling him he'd answer to God?" She made quotation marks in the air.

She nodded. "There was a lady in the office." Kerri's eyes widened. "His secretary, I guess."

"Don't you think that will come out in the investigation?" She paused. "I think you'd better hope they find the real guilty party soon, and not just so they can clear your friend's record."

"You don't really think I could be a suspect, do you?"

"Not realistically. You probably have a host of witnesses as to your whereabouts during the time of death."

"I can tell your father was in police work. You think like an officer yourself."

"Must be in the genes." Angie sighed. "Look," she added, "why don't we pray about this? We can't just sit around worrying. This problem needs to be placed in God's hands."

Kerri nodded. She knew Angie was right. She also knew how hard it was going to be for her to let go of this one.

◆ ◆ ◆

Todd Pheiffer watched Tammy Lynn walk up the front steps of her apartment. "I'll park right here, so it'll be obvious to anyone going in."

She nodded and trudged solemnly into her apartment.

Once inside, she continued mulling over her present situation. She fretted about her safety. She worried that she'd told the sheriff too much, that he wouldn't believe her, and that she would be in trouble for her own confession. She worried about the future. She was afraid she'd go to jail. She agonized about a life without meaning, a life without Eric Donovan.

She lowered the venetian blinds and peeked at the patrol car. The officer, a young man with blond hair, was sipping coffee.

"It's all my fault," she sobbed softly to herself. "Oh, Eric, I'm so sorry." She slumped onto a worn love seat, leaning forward to pick up a small picture frame. The recent snapshot of Eric standing beside his boat on Red Lake only added to her painful memories.

"We were going to be together," she sobbed. She threw the picture aside with a sudden, violent fling.

As her remorse, fear, and anger came to a boil, she went to her purse and removed a small bottle labeled "Elavil," an antidepressant medication she'd been taking under the instruction of a local clinic. Motivated by a second, dark impulse, she walked into her bathroom. She opened the medicine cabinet and found a pain reliever she'd obtained after spraining her ankle the summer before.

She shook the bottle in her hand. She figured the Darvocet-N100 would be enough to take care of her suffering for a long time.

She went to the kitchen and took out a cold diet soda, then swallowed a handful of Darvocets and the remainder of her Elavil. She walked to the front window again and peeked through the blind. *Thanks for protecting me, officer.*

She sat on the love seat until she became dizzy. She stumbled into the bedroom and collapsed onto her bed. She thought momentarily about writing a note but decided against it when a second wave of dizziness hit her.

She felt so sleepy and so alone. The room seemed to darken with each minute. Suddenly fear gripped her. She had to get help. What had she done?

She crawled from her bed and into the little hallway. There she lay down for a moment. She had to make it out to the officer. Maybe if she rested for a minute, she'd feel better.

She inched forward, stopping just inside the front door. There she managed only to reach up and flip off the lock before lying down again. She surrendered to her desire to sleep and quickly lapsed into a deep coma. After a few minutes, too deeply unconscious to protect her own airway, she vomited into her lungs.

In another eight minutes Tammy Lynn Gaskins was dead from asphyxiation, drowned by the very fluid her body sought to vomit away.

An hour later, Deputy Rick Zander knocked sharply at her door, intending to inform her he was taking Mark Pheiffer's place for a while. He stood in the common foyer tapping his foot. It sure was quiet in there. Maybe she was sleeping. He knocked again. "Ms. Gaskins?"

He twisted the doorknob, surprised to find it unlocked. If she was so afraid, why didn't she lock her door?

He pushed the door open gently. "Ms. Gaskins?"

The stench of human vomit hit him first. Sensing alarm, he pushed the door further, striking her body on the shoulder.

Rick dropped to his knees and assessed her airway and pulse. He grabbed his radio and called for help, then gave her a quick breath using mouth-to-mouth resuscitation. Repulsed by the feel of her cold mouth, he turned his head and spat on the floor. He quickly wiped out her mouth with his finger and wrinkled his face in distaste before giving her another breath.

Her chest rose slowly as he forced air into her lungs. He felt again for a carotid pulse prior to starting chest compressions. He continued a one-man revival effort until a rescue unit arrived. "One and two and three and four and five and . . ."

Steve Lambert, the rescue team leader, recognized the deputy. "What's going on, Rick?"

"I don't know. I just came in to check on her. I found her here, just inside the door. No pulse. No breathing."

"Great," he muttered, slipping a mask over her face and using an ambu bag to begin ventilations. He looked at a team member. "Get her on the monitor, Sue. Let's see if she has any rhythm."

As she attached three EKG leads, he inserted a tube into her trachea. "Oh man, it looks like she's aspirated," Steve announced. "We need to get her to the truck so we can suction her lungs."

The monitor screen showed a flat green light. "We've got nothing here, Steve." Sue looked at the deputy who was continuing cardiac compressions. "How long do you think she'd been down?"

"One of our deputies saw her go in the apartment about an hour ago."

Steve shone a light in her pupils. "Fixed and dilated. She's dead, Rick. She was dead before you started."

The deputy sighed. "Great. Just great!" he said sarcastically. "She dies right here under our watchful eye!" He stopped the useless chest compressions. "Let's call the county medical examiner." He shook his head. "Sheriff Boatwright's going to love this—"

"Tell me what I'm going to love, deputy!" Boatwright's frame filled the hallway.

"Sheriff!"

The emergency medical technicians and the deputy stood speechless for a moment.

"I heard your distress call. Now, will someone explain to me what's going on around here?"

"She's dead."

"I can see that."

"I don't know what happened," Zander began. "I took Todd's place and just thought I'd let her know that. I knocked on the door and got no answer, so I tried the doorknob. I found her right here, with the door unlocked. She didn't have a pulse, and she wasn't breathing, so I started CPR and called for help."

"She's way beyond resuscitation, sheriff. I'd say she's been dead for a good while."

The sheriff cursed. "Well, isn't this dandy! She comes to my office this morning, implicates a suspect in a murder case, we put her under protective surveillance—and she dies under our watch!" He shook his head. "Wait 'til the media hear about this!"

Steve and Sue boxed up their supplies. Rick Zander pointed at the endotracheal tube sticking out of her mouth. "Leave that in, guys. The medical examiner will want to know exactly what we've done." He looked at her pasty appearance and grimaced. "Do you think she killed herself?"

"Maybe. Perhaps she was an epileptic or something. Call the medical examiner. Let him figure it out."

While they waited, Rick examined the area, noticing the two empty pill bottles in the kitchen. "Hey, sheriff, check this out." He pointed at the bottles.

"Don't touch 'em. We'll get the evidence tech to dust 'em for prints." Boatwright paced around the small apartment, bemoaning the loss of a key witness and desperately wanting to save face for his department (and his election). He muttered under his breath, "So help me, Berringer, you're not going to get off this easy."

A few minutes later Dr. Robert Wright arrived. He carefully and quickly recorded the room temperature and the temperature of the fully clothed body—88 degrees. She hadn't been dead very long. He finished a gross inspection of the body within a few minutes. "There aren't any obvious traumatic injuries. Her throat was full of vomit—same as on the floor," he added, pointing to a small puddle beside her face. "There are pill fragments," he reported, scraping a sample into a plastic bag. "We'll have them analyzed to see if they match her stomach contents and the labels on the bottles you found."

"So it looks like . . ."

"Suicide, clearly. But we'll ship her over to the central chief medical examiner's office for an autopsy. I assume you'll want one?"

"Of course." The sheriff looked at the efficient physician and added a question of his own. "Have they reported anything on Donovan's autopsy yet?"

Dr. Wright straightened. "Oh, no. I bet we won't hear anything on that one for a week, maybe ten days—what with their office handling our work plus theirs for a while. He asked me not to send the body up until first of the week."

Boatwright assumed an incredulous expression. "So where is he . . . er, his body now?"

Wright smiled. "Right where we found him—in the morgue refrigerator."

"You left him there?"

He nodded. "Sure. What do you think that unit is made for?"

Zander snuffed a laugh. "How convenient."

"In fact, after the scene photographs we'll probably take Ms. Gaskins's body on over there, too." Dr. Wright was a practical man.

The deputy couldn't resist. "Won't that be cozy! The pathologist and his cute little secretary chilled out there together. From what I understand about these two, they'd probably like it that way."

That was bit too much even for the sheriff. "You're a funny guy, Zander."

"I knock 'em dead, right, sheriff?"

"Stop it." He paused. "I'm serious. I want a cap on this from you two. I don't want any reporters getting wind of this. It will look bad on the department if we don't keep complete control over how this gets out."

Dr. Wright and Deputy Zander nodded dutifully.

Outside, however, Steve Lambert was standing by the rescue vehicle giving the whole story to a radio reporter who had been monitoring a police scanner and had come to investigate.

By noon, the word would be all over Deer Falls.

CHAPTER
31

SETH moved slowly up Old Georgetown Road, bordering the seventy-acre campus of the National Institutes of Health. When he saw Lincoln Drive, he turned left and entered the grounds. He pulled into the large multilevel parking complex on his right and locked his maroon van. He studied a large sign's confusing map of the campus and finally decided to start looking in the large hospital building known as the Warren Grant Magnuson Clinical Center. After a ten-minute walk, he entered the modern building and tried to orient himself again. The front of the building contained a huge lobby, decorated tastefully and containing multiple seating areas, each hosting a large central aquarium. He thought back to the drab lobby of Chesapeake General Hospital. He was amazed at what government money can buy.

He found an information desk and picked up a campus map. He studied the building names but couldn't find anything labeled the National Center for Human Genome Research. He found a bank of pay phones along one wall of the lobby and pulled Kevin Schwab's phone number out of his wallet. He looked around as he dialed. The place resembled an airport.

After two rings he heard a friendly, female voice. "National Center for Human Genome Research. How may I direct your call?"

"I need to speak to Dr. Schwab."

"I'm sorry, but Dr. Schwab is in a meeting. May I leave him a message?"

"This is Dr. Seth Berringer. It's very important that I talk to Dr. Schwab. When will his meeting be over?"

"That's hard to say. May I give him a number where he can reach you?"

Seth sighed. "I'm at a pay phone." He paused. "Would it be possible for me to come to his office and wait? It's really important."

"I'm sorry, sir, but Dr. Schwab's schedule makes that impossible. He has to pre-approve all his personal meetings."

Seth stared at the map in his hand. "What building are you located in?"

"We're in the Lister Hill National Center, sir, but you can't just come up to Dr. Schwab's office. The security here is very efficient," she added.

"I need to see him today," Seth urged. "I'll call again in an hour."

"May I at least tell him what this is about?"

"I'm afraid not. But you can tell him it's urgent. I'll call back later. Thank you."

He hung up the phone and carefully searched the map. Building 38A was the Lister Hill National Center. He decided to go there and see what he could find out.

Seth walked at a brisk pace, partially to keep warm and partially because he found it impossible to relax. In a few minutes he stared up at a huge, modern building adjacent to the National Library of Medicine.

Inside, an African-American female of about twenty-five greeted him. Her outfit clearly identified her as part of the security force. "May I help you, sir?"

Seth decided it couldn't hurt to try. "I'm here to see Dr. Kevin Schwab."

"Name?"

"Seth Berringer."

She typed something on a computer keyboard, then looked up. "I'm sorry, sir. You'll need an appointment to see Dr. Schwab."

"It's very important," Seth protested.

"If you're seeking information, perhaps our tour beginning at 1 this afternoon would help." She pointed at a sign to her right.

"No thanks." Seth dropped his eyes to the floor and turned around.

He walked over to the library, passed the security desk, and browsed through the largest medical library of its kind in the world. He checked his watch every five minutes. When an hour had passed since his last contact with Schwab's office, he called again, this time from a pay phone in the lobby of the National Library of Medicine.

Again a cheery voice greeted him.

"This is Seth Berringer. I'm calling back to see if Dr. Schwab is available."

The secretary sighed. "Look, Mr. Berringer, I don't know what this is about, but Dr. Schwab specifically told me I am not to set up a meeting for you. You may leave a message if you like, and I'll pass it on to him."

Seth was ready for her response. "OK, here's the message. Tell him this is not a threat but a warning. Are you writing this down?"

The secretary rolled her eyes. "Yes, Mr. Berringer."

"OK. Tell him Eric Donovan has been killed, and he may be in some danger himself. I need to talk to him today. This is a matter of critical importance."

The secretary raised her eyebrows. "Let me get this straight. Eric Donovan is dead—"

"Eric Donovan has been killed," Seth interrupted, raising his voice.

The security officer looked over at Seth, who immediately turned away.

"OK, Mr. Berringer, I have it."

"Tell him to call me within five minutes at this number." He slowly read the number off the pay phone.

"Understood."

"If I don't hear from him within five minutes, I'll leave this location and call him from the lobby of the Lister Hill National Center."

"You're here, on our campus?"

"Yes." He sighed. "Please have him call."

The security officer eyed Seth suspiciously. He'd better keep an eye on the questionable visitor.

◆　◆　◆

The sheriff heard the news broadcast just after arriving back in his office.

"There has been another death in Chesapeake County. The body of Tammy Gaskins has been identified by the sheriff's department. She was found in her apartment just this morning. The details are sketchy, and an autopsy has yet to be performed. Ms. Gaskins was employed by the chief medical examiner's office and was a close associate of Dr. Eric Donovan, the medical examiner who was found dead of a homicide only yesterday. Ms. Gaskins was evidently under the protective surveillance of the sheriff's department when her death occurred."

The sheriff punched the intercom. "Get Deputy Zander in here right now!"

"Yes, Mr. Boatwright."

Minutes later, Rick Zander pushed open the door. "You wanted to see me, sheriff?"

"What's the idea of talking to a reporter?"

Zander stiffened. "I don't know what you're talking about."

"You'd better not," he warned. "Somehow the Gaskins story is already on the street, along with the information that she was under our protection when she died!"

The deputy blanched. "I—I didn't talk to anyone. I swear it," he added.

The sheriff slapped the desktop with his meaty palm. "It must have been that doctor then."

"Dr. Wright? I don't think he—"

"Well then, who? No one else—" He stopped as he recalled the scene.

They made eye contact as the same thought hit them both. "The ambulance crew."

Boatwright cursed. "I hate ambulance-chasin' reporters!" He stood and paced. "Our department is going to take a beating over this. First, I let a prime suspect for Lisa Dale's murder out from under our nose when that maniac Berringer walked out of the hospital in spite of the psychiatrist's warning that he's angry and guilt-ridden. Then it looks like he killed Dr. Donovan. And now the girl dies while we watch!" He snorted, then blew his nose in a large white handkerchief "How am I ever going to convince the voters I'm worthy of their trust?"

"We can still save face, sir." Zander shrugged. "No one can keep someone from committing suicide. Our duty was to keep someone else from harming her. The public won't hold you accountable for that."

"But that's not what they reported on the radio," he countered. "They said her body was found and an autopsy has yet to determine the cause of her death. We'd better do some quick damage control and issue a bit more information to the press."

The deputy nodded. "That should take care of the Gaskins problem." His eyes met Boatwright's. "As far as Berringer being a blemish on your record, there's one sure way of remedying that."

The sheriff nodded. "I'll make sure he never sees another free day again."

◆ ◆ ◆

Seth paced back and forth, staying close to the pay phones in the lobby of the library.

After five minutes, he sighed and turned to go. Just as he reached the front doors, the phone rang. He did an about-face and practically knocked over a young lady carrying a stack of books.

"Ooof! Sorry, ma'am," he exclaimed as he sprinted to the phone.

"Hello. Dr. Schwab?"

The security guard walked a few steps closer and pretended not to be listening.

"Dr. Berringer? I got your message. What's this all about?"

"I hoped you could tell me."

"Is Eric Donovan really dead?"

"Yes, and I don't believe his death was an accident. I think it has something to do with the murder of Lisa Dale."

The security officer raised his eyebrows.

"Listen, Dr. Berringer, I told you before, there's nothing I can tell you about her case. I don't know why you're calling me—"

Seth interrupted, saying, "You may be in danger too. Think about it! Donovan knew the truth about the way she died, right? I think you know it too." He sighed. "Even if you don't, his killers might think you know something."

Seth listened uncomfortably to the silence. *God, persuade him to talk to me.* Suddenly he thought of another argument. "Look, you're a scientist. Truth has to mean something to you. For some reason the facts in this case have been very difficult to detect. I think you can help in their discovery, Dr. Schwab."

"You actually think I may be in danger?"

"I don't know, really." Seth sighed. "I'm in deep trouble over this, Dr. Schwab. My whole career has been ruined. It's a long story. If I can spend some time with you, I'll try to put the story in perspective."

"OK, I'll talk to you." He paused. "But not in my building." He certainly didn't want anyone to overhear this conversation.

"I'll meet you anywhere."

"My secretary says you're on campus?"

"That's right."

"OK. Meet me at the Fogarty International Center. It's an attractive stone building on the hill—just up Center Drive from the Lister Hill building. Do you know where that is?"

"I think so."

"Meet me in twenty minutes on the patio facing the Lister building. I'll be sitting in a metal patio chair. I'll have on a Blue Jays cap." His voice carried overtones of fear. "Given the temperature, we'll probably have the place to ourselves."

"Thanks, Dr. Schwab. Thanks a lot."

The line went dead. Seth checked his watch, smiled at the security guard, and walked out into the cool air.

Twenty minutes later Seth walked up Center Drive toward the Fogarty International Center, which he'd located on his N.I.H. map.

True to his word, Schwab was sitting alone at an outdoor metal table.

"Dr. Schwab?"

He nodded. "Have a seat."

Seth held out his hand. Schwab didn't stand but accepted a quick handshake. "Seth Berringer."

"Now, what is this all about? Someone killed Dr. Donovan?"

Seth nodded. "I discovered his body myself, only yesterday." He shoved his hands into his coat pockets. "It's a complicated story. When I talked to you before, I told you I needed to find a specimen that I think Dr. Donovan sent to you."

Schwab nodded but made no reply.

Seth took a deep breath and poured out his story—how he'd discovered Lisa's body, disguised the death scene, watched the autopsy, confessed to the sheriff, had an evaluation at Evergreen State Hospital, and found Eric Donovan's body at the medical examiner's office. He filled him in on what he knew of Lisa Dale, the postcard, and the conversation Kerri had with the other girl who'd been with Lisa at the research institute in Colorado.

"So you think if you find this specimen, this fetus, it will prove to everyone that you're telling the truth, that you're not crazy," Kevin said soberly.

Seth nodded. "Yes."

"What makes you so sure that finding such a specimen would convince anyone you were telling the truth?"

"DNA studies would prove that Lisa was the mother. Then people would know I didn't make up her pregnancy."

"And how does this relate to Donovan's death?"

"This whole thing is too closely related in time *not* to be related. I mean, he was one of the few who knew the truth about Lisa's death. If the killer thought Donovan was about to speak out, killing him would be the best way to silence him forever."

"You sound like a desperate man, Dr. Berringer. I've been trained to think scientifically all my life. There are several holes in your theory. First, even if you found a fetus and could prove it was Lisa Dale's, no one could prove she was pregnant at the time of death. One could claim she'd had an abortion months before she died and that the autopsy report accurately stated she was not pregnant when her life ended."

Seth's countenance fell. He hadn't thought of that. He'd spent so much time focusing on the need to find that baby . . .

His thoughts were cut short by Schwab's continuing analysis. "Secondly, Donovan could have been killed for any number of reasons other than the one you've mentioned. The events may have been connected, but it's a bit difficult to see the link."

Seth shook his head. "You may be right." He lifted his eyes and stared over the seventy-acre campus of the N.I.H. "My reputation is shot. My career is in ruins." He looked at the scientist, wondering if there was any appeal he could make that would make a difference. "For all I know, the police consider me the prime suspect in Donovan's murder. Maybe it's too late to restore my career, but maybe, just maybe, I can hang on to a little self-respect if I can solve the mystery surrounding Lisa's death. After what I did to her, I owe her that much." He considered another question. "Can you honestly tell me Donovan didn't send you a specimen from her autopsy?"

Schwab looked at the physician in front of him. Seth sat with his shoulders pulled forward, his head bent toward the ground. He was a broken man—and it wasn't entirely his fault. Schwab knew that in a way he was responsible for the whole mess. If he hadn't have given those cells to Wilson Davis, Lisa Dale would be alive, and Berringer would never have stepped into this swamp. And if Berringer was right and Donovan was dead because of Lisa's autopsy, Schwab was responsible for his death too.

The N.I.H. scientist's mind was spinning. For all he knew, Donovan changed the autopsy report just because Schwab had told him it would be best if no one ever knew about the clone. He'd had no idea anyone else knew and would get in trouble by contradicting Donovan's report.

I should help you, Berringer, but I don't want anyone to know that I gave away the cells from a sacred cloth in return for a multi-million dollar contribution to my lab.

Schwab sighed. He words were guarded and slow. "He sent me a specimen."

Seth looked up.

Schwab continued, "But I truly have no record of it. And the specimen was destroyed. There is no physical evidence that your suspicions are correct."

"So you know she was pregnant?" Seth's countenance brightened for the first time since their conversation began. Maybe the sheriff would believe Schwab.

He nodded. "But the proof you're seeking isn't there, Dr. Berringer. She was pregnant, all right, but DNA studies would never prove she was the mother."

"Sure, they would! Maternity is established by DNA analysis all the time."

"Not in this case." He shook his head. "Trust me—I analyzed it myself."

"But the mother's DNA—"

"She wasn't the biological mother of the baby she was carrying."

Seth jerked his head back. "You mean—"

"She was a surrogate mother. She was merely housing the baby. No one analyzing that child could prove Lisa had anything to do with it." He paused. "Your sheriff won't be convinced by that data one bit."

Seth wanted to curse. "How do you know?"

Schwab weighed his words carefully. "Let's just say I recognized the pattern as something that would have been impossible for Lisa to produce. That's all I can say."

Seth sighed in defeat.

"Maybe there *is* one more way you could find the truth about Lisa Dale—maybe even some of the evidence you're seeking." He looked up, making eye contact with Berringer again. "You could contact the researchers responsible for her baby."

"I have no idea who that is. All I know is the state."

"Maybe I can help you. There's a research facility—outside Colorado Springs, I believe. I know one of the researchers there. I think Lisa Dale was involved with them somehow. I'll call them for you—see if I can convince them to help you." He just hoped the truth could come out without the world finding out where that baby came from!

Seth nodded his approval.

"Where can I reach you, Dr. Berringer?"

"I'm staying at the Howard Johnson in Rockville."

"I'll call you—hopefully within the hour."

Seth stood. He hadn't quite figured out Schwab's role in the whole story. "Dr. Schwab?"

The scientist stood.

"Why did you deny knowledge of the specimen when I called before?"

"I only said I had no record of the specimen." He shrugged. "That's true, actually."

"But why the need for so much secrecy?"

Kevin Schwab's eyes rose above Seth's head to the outline of the N.I.H. campus. He couldn't look at him anymore. "There is something very special about the child Lisa was carrying. Something very special—and something very hideous."

He shook his head. "That's all I can tell you. If the researchers tell you more, fine. But even if they do, I don't want anyone to learn I ever knew anything about this," he pled, his lower lip trembling slightly. "I never knew about it, never wanted to know about it. Understand? I refuse to bear any responsibility for the existence of that baby!"

Seth's questions were multiplying, but he held his tongue. Probing further would only risk shutting off his last chance of getting to the bottom of his problems.

Kevin Schwab began walking downhill toward the magnificent building that housed his renovated laboratory. "I'll call you in an hour. And forget this conversation, Berringer. I'll deny we ever had it."

With that, he was gone, and Seth stood alone staring after him.

◆ ◆ ◆

"There goes the deal," Doc moaned as he slapped the front page of the *Deer Falls Gazette*. "It says his secretary found him."

"It figures she would be the one out looking." Bill managed a weak smile. "What I can't figure out is this Berringer character. Does it say why he's a suspect?"

"No." Doc smiled. "But it sure was nice of him to take the rap for us again."

"I'll say." Bill paused. "Didn't Donovan say something about him raising concerns over the autopsy report?"

Doc nodded. "The police must have something else on him. I don't think they'd name him in the paper just for that." He shrugged.

"You don't suppose we could keep this news from Davis and go through with the deal, do you?"

"No chance. This story might even make the AP wire." He paced around the small motel room. "I'd better call him before he hears the news."

Bill nodded.

Doc unfolded his cell phone and dialed. He explained the situation to Wilson Davis, who insisted that Doc read the article to him word for word.

"I've had a bad feeling about that Berringer guy all along!" he shouted. "You didn't mention the money. Does it say anything there about the money?"

"Not a word."

"Berringer must have it," Davis mused.

Doc looked nervously over at the briefcase on the bed. "Must have," Doc mumbled.

Davis cursed. "Try to locate Berringer before the police do. He must be after the specimen." A coughing spasm interrupted his tirade. "First he picks up her dead body, then he personally attends the autopsy, and now this!" He spit into a cup beside his easy chair. "You don't suppose he already has it, do you? Maybe he stole it from Donovan."

Doc shook his head. Donovan hadn't turned it over to Berringer as of last night, he knew that for sure. "I don't think so, Mr. Davis. Donovan was pretty adamant when he talked to us. He wouldn't have given it up."

"Not without a fight at least," their employer responded slowly. "Maybe we've misjudged this Berringer." He pondered the facts. "I want you to find him. Don't just watch him this time." He raised his voice. "Locate him, and grab that specimen!"

◆ ◆ ◆

Ursula smiled as she smoothed her lab coat with her hand. She was on the phone with Kevin Schwab and obviously enjoyed his coming to her to ask a favor. "Having a little fit of conscience, are we? I would think you'd be a bit more objective by now." She spun around in her desk chair. "Why should you care about this Berringer's trouble anyway?"

Kevin sighed. "I feel responsible, that's why. They were my cells."

"Your cells?" She laughed. "Kevin, they were never your cells. Besides, you have no control over this lab, and you're not responsible for what we've done."

"That's not how the public will see it." He fidgeted with his baseball cap. "That's not how the Vatican will—"

"Oh, so now you're worried about God too?" she sneered. "I've never known you to care about—"

"Ursula, please," he interrupted.

She sighed heavily. "OK, OK, now tell me why I should meet this guy and give him information about Lisa Dale. What kind of trouble is he in that I can help him out of?"

Kevin launched his chair toward the middle of the floor as he began to fill in his former associate on the story of Lisa Dale, Seth Berringer, and Eric Donovan.

Ursula's smile disappeared. "Wait a minute—he says she died how?"

"Exsanguination after a uterine perforation. Obviously someone was after that baby."

Ursula's eyes went wide, and she shook her head. "I was told she died in a pedestrian accident." She paused as she tried to digest the new information. "When you called before and said you had a tissue sample from a murder case, I thought you were confused. Are you sure of all this?"

"What Donovan told me matches the description Berringer gave me exactly. It sounded like some sort of back-alley job."

"That's disgusting. Our scientists wouldn't—"

"Ursula, think!" Kevin interrupted. "Who else knew what you were doing? It had to be someone who knew who that baby was."

"No one knew. No one."

"Not even Lisa? You didn't even tell her, did you?"

Ursula let the accusation drop. After a pause she refocused. "So what do you want me to tell Berringer? I can't divulge anything about the project."

"Just give him enough information to prove Lisa was pregnant. You don't have to tell him more than that. Maybe just the surrogate implantation record—but nothing that would disclose the nature of the baby."

Her sarcasm returned. "We wouldn't want anyone figuring out where we got those cells, would we?" Pondering the implications, she decided to take a harder tack. "I won't talk to Berringer. No information goes out on this project. You can understand our position on that."

"I understand," he responded slowly. "How about Davis? Maybe he'd speak with Berringer."

"I doubt it." She shrugged. "But I'll ask. After all, it's his project. I was just about to go up to see him anyway. I'll call you right back."

She hung up the phone and walked to the window, troubled by the news Schwab had delivered. Lisa Dale had died from an abortion attempt? That surely wasn't the work of their harvest team. Davis would have told her about that. She shook her head. Lisa must have figured out what they'd done and gone to some back-alley clinic. But why would an intelligent, young girl do that?

As she walked up the hall toward Wilson Davis's office, the doubts continued. He never had told her whom he sent to do the harvest.

◆ ◆ ◆

Davis's office looked like a library of the rich and famous. Walnut cabinets and shelves lined the walls from the floor to the ten-foot ceiling. Wilson Davis stood on a mobile ladder, attached to a groove along the highest shelf. Holding a large book in his hand, he looked up just as Ursula Baumgarten entered.

"Ah, Ursula. I have good news and bad news, I'm afraid." He stepped off the ladder with slow, deliberate movements.

"What's the good news?"

"I'm almost positive the clone is still available."

"And the bad?"

"Donovan has been killed. I just got off the phone with a member of the retrieval team."

She nodded. "That's sad. What will we do now?"

"There's still hope of getting our specimen back. It may have been stolen by Donovan's killer." He sat in a leather chair. "If so, I would expect him to contact us—to work out a deal." He stared at her. Was she the one who'd leaked information to Berringer? How else would he know about the project? Why would he cover for them except to obtain the upper hand in negotiations?

Meanwhile, she was studying him. Did she really know this man? How important was this project to him—important enough to justify taking a life?

"Now, why have you come here? Surely not to see a pitiful, old man climbing a ladder."

She forced a smile. "Dr. Schwab called. He wants me to set up a meeting for you." She shrugged with apparent disinterest. "With someone named Berringer—a physician, I believe. He has some questions about the project."

"Berringer." Davis repeated the name slowly. "Of course." He turned away as a spasm of coughing assaulted his gaunt frame.

Ursula frowned at hearing the rattle in his chest. "You know of him?"

"Of course." He was sure Berringer was no stranger to her either. The old scientist cleared his throat. "Set up the meeting. The sooner the better."

Ursula nodded. "Will do." She began to leave but turned back.

Davis probed, "Is there something else on your mind, Ursula? You're acting like a nervous cat."

She looked up and offered a timid question. "How did Lisa Dale die?"

He stared at her, wishing he could discern her thoughts. "She fled to her hometown." He shook his head. "It was my fault, Ursula. I shouldn't have insisted on so much secrecy; it just seemed to increase her fears. I never anticipated her being able to figure things out. We can tell the next volunteer more about what is going on, like you believed we should do in the first place."

Ursula pressed, "But how did she die?"

He coughed, barely able to get out his handkerchief before a spasm hit him again. He looked up. "Sorry. I was getting to that." He paused. "She died of a freak pedestrian accident—a hit-and-run actually."

Ursula's eyes hit the floor. "That's what I heard." Why was he lying to her? She turned to go. "I'll set up the meeting with Dr. Berringer."

Davis followed her with his eyes until she was out of sight. He smiled. Berringer had been turning up again and again, showing an interest in the project. So now he wanted a meeting with Davis. The institute leader shook his head. Just how much would Berringer want for the clone? He must know its incredible value to the project. Why else would he be willing to kill for it?

CHAPTER
32

SETH looked at the alarm clock again. It had been over an hour. Schwab should have called by now.

Seth paced around the small room, stretching out on first one double bed, then the other. Then he'd rise, sigh, and stare at the phone.

He sat up and held his head in his hands. He was on the run again, trying desperately to redeem himself—to salvage his reputation—and he was running out of options. *Just look where trusting in yourself has taken you!* He shuddered. *Taking inventory is no fun if you're jobless, wanted by the police, and embarrassed by your own behavior.*

He thought about the events of the last few days. Everything had changed. He'd gone from being a respected physician to hiding in a motel room.

If Schwab didn't come through, then what? He couldn't go back to Deer Falls. No one would believe his story without proof. How had he gotten himself into such a mess?

What was it Kerri had told him? "You're no different than anyone else, Seth. We all need God. We all need to be restored, to solve the problem of our evil nature. You're not unique, Seth. We all need a Savior to make a way back to God."

Was that what he needed? Could he ever believe it? His eyes moved to a red book on the nightstand. He read the words on the cover: "Placed by the Gideons." They were after him too. He sighed. Everywhere he turned, someone was talking about God. The chaplain at the funeral home. Kerri.

Ms. Templeton. Ms. Anderson. Everyone seemed to know what he needed except him.

He opened the Bible and turned the first few pages. There, in twenty-seven different languages, he found John 3:16. Seth read the words slowly in his mind: "For God so loved the world, that he gave his only begotten Son, that whosoever believeth in him should not perish, but have everlasting life."

Believe me, Seth, I love you. I gave my only Son for you.

"Whoa," Seth whispered, closing his eyes. "I'm starting to think I'm—"

Ring! The sound startled him, and he jumped up, sending the Bible to the floor with a thud. Seth grabbed the phone.

"Hello!" he yelled more loudly than he'd intended. He repeated it more quietly. "Hello."

"Dr. Berringer?"

"Yes."

"It's Kevin Schwab. I've arranged a meeting for you."

◆ ◆ ◆

Sheriff Boatwright sat across his desk from Dave Trainum. "We're nearing the twenty-four-hour mark, Dave."

The detective nodded.

"And forty-eight will follow soon after that." He sighed. "We both know the trail gets cold real fast then." He nodded agreement with his own statement. "We've got to keep pushing."

"We still haven't found Ms. Barber." He shrugged. "I checked with the nursing coordinator at the hospital. She's not on duty again until next week."

"She's not at her apartment?"

He shook his head.

"Ten to one she's with Berringer." The sheriff hit his hand on the desk. "Blast it!"

"What else do we have?"

"There are other possibilities."

"I'm listening."

"I haven't completely ruled out Ms. Donovan. She could've been striking out against her husband because of the affair."

Dave shook his head. "My gut says no. Besides, she was seen by the grocer at 2, a gas attendant at 2:30, and was with her friends for a least three hours before we came by."

"What about Ms. Gaskins? It's not entirely implausible to think everything she told me was a fabrication and that she killed him because he wouldn't leave his wife."

"I don't buy that theory either. I spoke to the physician who'd prescribed her antidepressants. Completely off the record, he told me she's never been that stable but always seemed more suicidal than homicidal."

The sheriff wasn't sure about that. "Then again, the new information she spilled this morning about Berringer makes sense. If I can get just a little more confirmation, I'll bring serious charges against him."

Dave raised his eyebrows but declined to comment.

Boatwright drummed his fingers on the desk. "And then we have the mysterious Mr. Yamatsu, whom both Tammy Lynn Gaskins and Ms. Donovan implicate."

"Did either give a description?"

He nodded. "Gaskins saw him. Described him as muscular, short, Asian, dark mustache." He continued drumming his fingers. "You know what's interestin'? I saw a man of that description up at Lou Ellen's place the night Lisa Dale was killed. In fact, I think he was visiting her room." He leaned back in his chair and folded his hands behind his head. "I answered a noise disturbance call. Made the report myself." He shrugged. "Lou Ellen won't call anyone else. I had to leave Lanny's just to check it out."

"And?"

"I can't say for sure, but after hearing what Ms. Gaskins said this morning, Berringer and this Yamatsu guy might both be involved. This whole mess, starting with Lisa Dale and ending with our dead pathologist and his secretary, might all be tied together somehow." He looked the detective in the eye. "To tell you the truth, I didn't want to think any criminal types would be using the Inn like that. But the more I think about all the loose ends in this case, I think we'd better send an evidence tech over there to see if he can find any prints—maybe match 'em against those we found at the medical examiner's lab."

"There are probably a lot of other prints in that room by now."

Boatwright shook his head and chuckled. "My sister's paranoia may have helped me in this case. She thinks the room was cursed, so she hasn't rented it since."

Trainum nodded. "It sure would be interesting if we found a Berringer print in Dale's room."

"That would sure confirm the wild story Tammy Gaskins told."

They were silent for a moment before Trainum added, "There is one more unofficial suspect."

"Oh?"

"Donovan himself. Until we have the autopsy, I'd say we don't have secure proof that a homicide occurred at all."

"Technically you're right. But I don't believe that for a second."

"Me neither."

Boatwright started to scowl. "Just the same, put some pressure on the chief medical examiner involved in his case. I want that autopsy done, and I want it done now!"

◆ ◆ ◆

Hearing the news about Tammy Lynn Gaskins's death only heightened Kerri's fear level. She wanted to talk to Seth. She wanted to know he was safe. She wanted, above all, just to hear his voice again.

She had jumped up to answer the phone half a dozen times, and each time she'd frowned as she handed the phone to Angie or her mother.

As darkness approached, she found herself expecting each call to be bad news. The sheriff—a hospital—anyone but Seth himself.

She looked at Angie. "Do they still give you one phone call if they put you in jail? Certainly, if the sheriff had him, he'd call me, don't you think?"

Angie huffed. "You've seen too many movies." She studied her friend for a moment. "You're not serious, are you?"

Kerri made a face. "Maybe."

The phone rang, and for the first time Kerri didn't make an Olympic effort to answer it.

Angie looked at her. "Well?"

"You get it. I can't."

Angie rolled her eyes and picked up the portable phone. "Hello."

"Angie?"

"Yes."

"This is Seth Berringer. Is Kerri there?"

"Oh, I think I can find her somewhere." She held the phone out to Kerri. "Guess who?"

Kerri snatched the phone and walked off toward the front sitting room. "Seth, are you OK?" The anxiety in her voice was unmistakable.

"I'm fine." He paused. "Sorry I didn't call earlier. It's been a long day."

Kerri's relief kept her from finding fault. She bit her lip. "Did you meet with Dr. Schwab?"

"Yes. He had the specimen, Kerri. I was right about that."

"Did he let you have it?"

"No. He *had* the specimen but destroyed all traces of it."

"But why—"

"Something very weird is going on, Kerri. This may be darker than we ever dreamed. First, he tells me he knows about the specimen and that Donovan sent it to him, but then he tells me it will never prove Lisa was pregnant."

"But you said DNA studies would show—"

"The baby wasn't hers, Kerri. She was just housing it. She was a surrogate."

"A surrogate?"

"Don't ask me how he knew. He just said he recognized the fetus as something that would have been impossible for her to conceive herself."

Kerri shook her head. "And besides that, he claims it's not available?"

"Right."

She hesitated for a moment. "Oh, Seth, I'm sorry. I know how much it—"

Seth interrupted again. "The story doesn't end there. He knows one of the researchers who was involved in the project Lisa was enrolled in. He called her for me." He shrugged. "Evidently she refused to give me any information but took my request to her boss, and he said he'll meet with me."

"What will that accomplish?"

"Don't you see? He can give me the data I need to show that Lisa was involved in the research project and that she was indeed pregnant at the time of her death."

"Why didn't Schwab tell you all this before?"

"I asked him the same thing." He waited a moment as he remembered Schwab's words. "He got this weird look on his face, then said, 'There's something very special about the child Lisa was carrying—something very special and very hideous.'" Seth spoke the words in a slow, hushed tone to imitate the scientist.

"Seth," Kerri responded with a chill, "you're scaring me."

"Sorry, but that's what he said." He paused. "And you know what else is weird? The man heading up the project is none other than Wilson Davis."

"Am I supposed to know that name?"

"I thought you might. He's a well-known philanthropist. When Schwab gave me the name, I asked him about it, but he just blew it off. The question seemed to make him nervous, so it sparked my curiosity. I had a vague memory I'd seen his name somewhere. So when I got off the phone with Schwab, I ran back to the main hospital at the N.I.H. to check it out. Sure enough, there was a plaque with Davis's name on it in the lobby. He donated five million dollars toward human genome research."

Kerri stayed silent.

"Don't you see the connection? That's Schwab's area. That money would have gone straight to Schwab."

"But what does that have to do with the research they were using Lisa for?"

"I'm not sure, but it's just another clue that this thing may be more twisted than we ever imagined."

"Seth, things haven't exactly been quiet around here today either."

"Did Boatwright—"

This time Kerri interrupted. "Tammy Lynn Gaskins, Dr. Donovan's secretary, was found dead."

"Dead! What . . . How . . . ?"

"No one's saying anything. The news reported she was under the eye of the sheriff's department when the death occurred."

"They were watching her?"

"Trying to protect her, I think."

"Protect her?"

"Maybe from whoever killed Donovan?"

"Oh."

"Seth . . ." Her voice had a slight tremor. "This whole thing is starting to scare me. If Donovan conspired to change his autopsy report to cover up the real reason Lisa died, who else would know about it?"

Seth nodded his head. "His secretary?"

"Maybe. But the point I'm making is that now they're both dead. The only person left alive who witnessed the autopsy is you. Maybe someone isn't so thrilled about the truth getting out."

He began to protest, "Kerri—"

"Seth, if we're right, and the researchers who were after Lisa's baby were responsible for her death, and now suddenly everyone who knows anything about the real cause of her death is turning up dead, do you really think you should go out and meet with them?"

He sighed as he ran his hand through his hair. "Kerri, I have to go. It's my only chance to—"

"To clear your reputation, is that it?" She raised her voice in frustration. "What's that worth, Seth? Your life?" She broke down and began to sob.

Seth felt sad and frustrated as he listened. "Kerri, I—"

"Oh, Seth, I—I'm s-sorry." She wiped her tears on her sleeve.

"I'll be OK." He sighed heavily.

Her reply was timid. "But what about me? I haven't been so quiet about my feelings either. I've spouted off to Donovan and to the sheriff about the autopsy findings. If someone wants to hide the truth . . . well, maybe they'll want to silence me too."

"Is there someone you can visit? Maybe your family? Maybe just lay low at Angie's place for a while?"

"I can't just stay here hiding from Boatwright and from whoever else might be looking for me. I almost drove Angie crazy waiting for you to call." Her thoughts went to the two men who'd visited Sue Bergy looking for Lisa. She shivered. "I want to come with you."

"Kerri, I'm not sure that's a good idea."

"Why not? That way I won't be tempted to worry about you, and I wouldn't be easy to find. Besides," she added, "Lisa was my friend. The least I can do is try to get to the bottom of this."

He wanted her to be with him, but . . . "Kerri, I'm not sure what to say. I think you'd be safer if you found some other place to chill out for a while."

"I don't want to chill out for a while. I want to go with you."

"Is there any way I can talk you out of this?"

"No."

Seth smiled and formulated a plan.

"Seth?"

"OK."

"OK, what?"

"You can go, OK?"

Her voice was childlike. "OK."

Seth looked at his clothes and ran his hand over his chin. "A flight leaves Chesapeake Airport at 6:15 every morning for Pittsburgh. They always have room for a few extra passengers. We should be able to catch a flight to Denver once we get to Pittsburgh."

"I understand."

"Do you think you can do me a favor? It might be a little risky—I imagine the sheriff is watching my place. But I need some clothes." He stretched his shoulders. "And my razor. But don't take any unnecessary chances."

Seth and Kerri carefully worked out a plan to acquire Seth's supplies and avoid detection by the sheriff.

"We should probably get to the airport by 5:45," Seth suggested.

"Ugh." Kerri looked at her watch. "You'll need to leave by 2. Are you sure about this? You'll fall asleep!"

"Thinking about seeing you will keep me alert."

"Seth!"

"I'm serious."

She smiled. "I'll see you in the morning. And I'll be praying."

"Kerri?"

"Yes?"

"I'll be praying too."

Kerri felt a tear coming. Seth Berringer—what a man!

◆ ◆ ◆

Tracy sauntered up to the counter and eyed Lou Ellen, who quickly put a makeup mirror in her purse.

"What's up, Lou Ellen?"

"Nothing. Everything's fine."

Tracy frowned. "I'm no psychiatrist, honey, but I can tell that everything's not OK in River City. You practically have steam coming out your ears. Besides," she added, "you always put on lipstick when you're nervous."

"I'm not nervous." She glared at her friend. "And why do you always say . . ." She waved her hand in the air. ". . . that this is River City? This ain't River City!"

"Calm down, Lou Ellen. I heard it on TV, OK? I thought it sounded neat." She sat down behind the counter. They were alone. "Now, what's wrong?"

Lou shifted uncomfortably.

Tracy probed again. "I see you're opening 12 back up. That man fixin' the heater or something?"

"That man is an evidence tech from the sheriff's department. He's looking for blood—and fingerprints—and I'm not opening up 12!"

"Fingerprints?" She squinted and leaned forward. "Why?"

"That's what I'd like to know!" exploded Lou Ellen. She looked up sheepishly. "I'm sorry, honey. It's just that Wayne won't tell me anything this time. All I know is that suddenly he started to listen to me about that room. I told him all along something wasn't right in there—that those two men were up to no good. But he wouldn't believe me, oh no." She fidgeted with her purse. "He also didn't believe that girl who tiraded in here the other day claimin' that Lisa girl was murdered."

"Lou Ellen, he—"

"And he didn't believe Momma either—until now."

"What do you mean?"

Lou Ellen sighed. "Oh, he gets like this about once a year—when someone gets killed in his county. He goes on some sort of private rampage. He walks around mumbling about the clock—the first forty-eight hours of the hot evidence trail or some such rot. It's like he takes every such crime as a personal assault on his character." She raised her nose in the air. "And he won't share any of it with me. It's all top secret."

"You think this has something to do with that doctor and his secretary?"

"How should I know?" She shook her head. "But something is going on, I know that much. And if Wayne has finally decided to listen to me, so much the better."

The bell on the front door sounded as a short, balding man entered. "I'm finished for now, Ms. Boatwright."

"Thanks, Peter." She stood. "You didn't use that yellow tape to rope it off or nothin,' did you? That stuff ain't good for business, you know."

The man smiled. "No, I didn't use the yellow tape." He turned and added, "It would be a good idea to leave the room locked and unoccupied until we get back to you."

"Don't worry about that," she said intently. "I've known something was wrong in there for days." She looked at Tracy. "Do you think a room can be cursed?"

Tracy was preoccupied with trimming a cuticle. "Are you harpin' on that idea again?"

Lou Ellen rolled her eyes and waved to the technician. "Tell Wayne I want to know what's goin' on."

He nodded politely. "Sure thing, Lou."

She took a parting shot as he opened the door. "And tell Wayne that Momma wants to see him."

CHAPTER
33

SETH rose early, yawned, showered, dressed, yawned some more, and climbed in his van. He looked at his watch. Two A.M.

He stopped at a mini-mart for gas, a carton of powdered donuts, and a large cup of black coffee. He glanced at the local and national headlines on the newsstand. At least he wasn't making the news here—yet. He smiled and paid the attendant.

"Have a nice day," the young man offered.

Seth yawned. It wasn't day yet—not for another five hours. "Thanks."

He pointed his van toward the interstate, his lonely headlights mingling only with those of a rare trucker or an unusually committed D.C. commuter. Soon he lost himself in thought, playing the memory tapes from the last two weeks of his life.

What was it the chaplain had prayed? Seth squinted to refresh his thoughts. "I pray especially for the driver of the automobile that struck Lisa. I pray that you would hold that person in your arms and comfort him. Give him the courage to acknowledge his wrongdoing. Bring him forgiveness and healing. Show him your love and tender direction. In Jesus' name, and by the authority of his blood sacrificed for us, Amen." *He was praying for me, and he didn't even know it.*

Seth stared at the lonely road and sipped his coffee.

Kerri had been hesitant to approach him that first time at the funeral home. He smiled at the memory. "Dr. Berringer? Could I talk to you for a minute?" That was the last time she'd ever asked permission to involve herself in his life. He reflected on some of the statements she'd made to him after he told her what he'd done.

"I do believe God shows his love to all kinds of sickos. That's what's so amazing about him. He loves us in spite of everything we do to hurt each other and him. He just keeps on loving. It's his nature, Seth."

"I just know it's true—based on the Bible, based on faith, and based on my own experience. No one's perfect, Seth. Not me. Not you. None of us deserves God's love. But that doesn't change the fact that God goes on loving us just the same."

"You seem to be hurting, Seth. I think you're trying to be perfect or something."

"Being acceptable to God isn't about being our best or being good enough. No one is good enough, Seth. We're all made of the same stuff, all in need of someone who can take away our evil desires and make us clean and acceptable to God again."

Seth blinked back a tear. Why couldn't he believe that?

He sipped his coffee and ate a donut, dropping powdered sugar onto his shirt. He hoped Kerri would be able to get some of his clothes.

After another mile, his mind drifted again. It hadn't only been Kerri. Others had seen the need to talk to him about God too. His patient, Ms. Anderson, seemed to have such peace.

"I'm ready to die, Dr. Berringer. When I die, I'll see the Savior."

How could she be so sure?

She sure loved reading the Bible. He couldn't keep her from reading it to him. "He that covereth his sins shall not prosper: but whoso confesseth and forsaketh them shall have mercy." Believing that had put him in a lot of trouble!

And what about good old Ms. Templeton? She wouldn't let the President go by if he had a frown on his face, not without telling him how to solve his problems. "Dr. Berringer, you look like you're carryin' the worl' on your shoulders. You need to do what I do, I'll tell you right now. You need to carry them burdens right to God and lay 'em down. That's what I do, for sure. He takes care of me, he does."

What was it with all these people? He knew what Kerri would say. "God has been speaking to you, calling you, wooing you through all the people around you who have been talking to you about him. Conviction is his way of getting you to see that you need him, that you can't be good enough on your own."

He thought about the Gideon Bible back in the motel. "For God so loved the world, that he gave his only begotten Son, that whosoever believeth in him should not perish . . ."

Seth turned down the van's heater. Why did he feel so warm?

I promised Kerri I would pray. Did I say that just to please her, or do I really believe it would make a difference? I'm beginning to believe. I want to. But I'm not even sure I know how to pray.

He strained to remember a prayer from his childhood—something he'd heard in Sunday school long before his mother left him.

"Now I lay me down to sleep." That didn't seem appropriate.

"God is great, God is good." That was perhaps closer.

Slowly a remote memory gained color and clarity.

Haltingly, with his voice barely above a whisper, he began, "Father, who art in heaven, hallowed be thy name . . ."

◆ ◆ ◆

"OK," Kerri said with a forced smile, "I'll see you in a few minutes, right outside the doctors' entrance. Just beyond the visitors' lot."

Angie twisted her auburn hair. "Yes, I know where it is. We've only been over the details a dozen times!"

Kerri started her light blue Taurus. She revved the engine nervously, sending a white flume into the still, early-morning darkness. After a moment she pulled out, checking her rearview mirror several times to confirm that Angie was indeed following.

Once they entered the city limits of Deer Falls, Kerri turned right toward Seth's residence, and Angie traveled on toward Chesapeake General Hospital. Except for a teenager delivering morning papers, Kerri was alone, traveling slowly on a street paralleling Seth's. Once she spotted a two-story white house with green trim, she pulled to a stop, parking behind a Ford Bronco. If she'd done this right, Seth's backyard was directly behind the house.

She opened the car door and pulled out a black carry-on bag. Her breath fogged the night air, and when she shut the door, she winced at the thud. She moved quickly across the driveway and into the backyard. Seth's dark house was easily visible.

Once at the back of her friend's house, she turned and walked to the corner of a patio. She struggled momentarily with a loose tile, then lifted it to find a plastic bag containing a key. She breathed easier. She slowly crossed the patio to a wooden deck leading to the back entrance.

The back door creaked as she entered, and she froze momentarily to listen. She hoped she was just being paranoid. Once inside, she ascended the stairway and found Seth's bedroom. It was darker upstairs since the shades kept out the light from the street lamps. She allowed her eyes to adjust, then walked to the middle of the room, brushing the edge of the bed. She turned on a small penlight and glanced around the room. It felt strange being in Seth's bedroom, looking at his personal items. But she had to admit, she also felt a flutter of adolescent excitement.

She moved to the dresser and opened the top drawer. *Good. At least he joins his socks.* She opened another. *Good. He doesn't fold his underwear.* She went to his closet and took out a suit coat, a pair of pants, and two shirts, stuffing them into the carry-on bag. She could always get them ironed later.

She moved to the bathroom, where she found Seth's razor. She picked up his well-used toothbrush as well. She hoped he'd bought another one in Rockville. She threw it in the bag and reached for a bottle of aftershave. She held it close to her face and inhaled. She paused momentarily, again aware she was enjoying her visit a bit more than planned.

Moving downstairs, she stepped softly to the front window and pulled back a corner of the shade. There, in full view under a street lamp, was a county patrol car. She was glad she'd come in the back way. She let the shade fall back into place and turned toward the rear of the house.

At that moment a dark figure grabbed her from behind. Strong hands clamped over her mouth and shoved the barrel of a pistol into her neck.

She emitted only a muffled scream, then struggled to breathe again. Just when she thought she would faint from lack of oxygen, the assailant slipped his gloved hand down a fraction, leaving her nose partially free. She sucked air frantically through his fingers.

"Don't scream, Kerri. You don't want the officer to find you running off with the doctor's bag, now do you?" The voice was a forced whisper and revealed a distinct Asian accent.

Her eyes widened as a second man stepped out from the dark shadows. He wore a ski mask and motioned toward the stairs.

"Come on, let's take her to the doctor's bedroom!"

◆ ◆ ◆

Dr. Alden Rust sipped black coffee from a large styrofoam cup. He used Styrofoam in spite of his daughter's complaints that it would be around for the next millennium. In fact, he used it just because she said it would be around for the next millennium. He was cynical by nature, a quality evident in his professional conversations and on his Volvo's bumper stickers— "Save the Males" and "Visualize Whirled Peas."

This morning, a Saturday, normally his golf day, he found his cynicism reaching new peaks. Maybe it was because he was doing an autopsy at an unheard-of hour. Maybe it was because a pouting sheriff had pulled rank on him. And maybe, just maybe, it was because he was performing the autopsy on a long-time colleague and friend, Dr. Eric Donovan.

He held the cup at the bottom, careful only to touch the lower half. He wore rubber gloves and certainly didn't want to spoil his morning brew with an autopsy contaminant.

He looked at his watch. 5:45. He couldn't believe he'd let Boatwright talk him into working on a weekend, and at this hour!

He sighed. Maybe if he hurried, he could finish the gross inspection and get some samples to the histo techs in time to see Janey's volleyball game.

Before him lay the body of Eric Donovan, exposed and cold. As Dr. Rust examined, he dictated, carefully describing the head, face, neck, back, chest, abdomen, pelvis, perineum, and extremities. Other than a superficial scalp laceration measuring less than five centimeters and a few pigmented moles, the body was normal. There were no visible needle tracts or signs of an injection. Why had he died? Certainly not from external trauma. The sheriff had told him Donovan had been murdered, but there were no external signs of strangulation or suffocation.

He pried open the dead man's mouth and carefully examined the oral cavity. Nothing there except for some residual food particles. He must have vomited shortly before death. Nothing too unusual about that. Rust deeply insinuated his index finger into his upper airway. No signs of any foreign body or choking. No signs of a hidden stab wound or open-mouth gunshot wound. But he knew that traumatic injuries, even serious stab or gunshot wounds, were not always visible on the outside.

He slipped on an extra glove and completed the anorectal exam. Nothing there except for mild prostatic enlargement. Normal for the age of the deceased.

By the time he completed the gross inspection and dictation, Nelson O'Hare, his sleepy autopsy technician, arrived.

"Let's get to it, Nelson. Coffee's on the counter."

He nodded.

They donned gowns, gloves, and masks before proceeding. Unlike surgery, where sterile wear is used mainly to protect the patient from infection, autopsy personnel use the items to protect them from whatever killed the patient.

Rust started with a large Y-shaped incision over the chest, extending across the abdomen to the pubic bone. Before they quit, every organ would be removed, inspected, described, weighed, and prepared for microscopic analysis.

"Do we get to do a crainy?" Nelson asked, referring to opening the skull to inspect the brain.

"Absolutely. He was found dead with just a little scalp laceration. We need to make sure the brain was OK."

Nelson probed the forehead laceration with his gloved finger. "This is nothing. I'll bet he hit his head when he went down. It was probably his heart," he added.

Rust shrugged his shoulders. "That certainly is high on my list, but . . ." He paused. "The sheriff swears Donovan was murdered. Even has an arrest warrant out for a local physician."

"Hmmm. A physician, eh?" He tapped his foot. "How would a doctor kill someone without external signs of trauma? Maybe a lethal injection through a scalp vein hidden in the laceration?"

"You watch too much TV," the examiner complained. "I bet he died of an acute cardiac event. Remember, when you hear hoofbeats, think . . ."

"Horses. I know, I know," the technician added, completing the pathologist's oft-repeated statement. "Not zebras."

"I can't believe it. You've actually learned something from me!" Rust held his moist hands high in the air.

The assistant rolled his eyes and slurped his coffee noisily to let it cool between his teeth. "Let's see what's in his stomach. I'm bettin' beans. A lot of people eat beans before they die."

◆　◆　◆

Ian Brothers smiled. "May I help you?"

"I'd like to purchase two tickets to Pittsburgh."

Ian spent a moment tapping a computer console. "Name?"

"Seth Berringer." He watched the young man work. "And Kerri Barber."

"Are you checking any luggage today, Mr. Berringer?"

Seth looked around for Kerri. Where was she?

"Sir?"

"Uh, no, I guess not. My traveling associate hasn't shown up yet. She's bringing the bags." He frowned, then added, "They should be small enough for carry-on."

"How will you be paying for the tickets?"

Seth handed him his VISA card. He'd have to find a job before he used this thing too much.

Ian's fingers ran over the keyboard. "May I see a picture I.D.?"

Seth pulled out his driver's license.

The attendant nodded perfunctorily and initialed a boarding pass, then handed it to Seth. "Gate 4. Just up the escalator." He pointed to his right. "Ms. Barber needs to check in here to validate her I.D."

Seth looked around again and checked his watch.

"Boarding is in fifteen minutes."

"Right."

Seth walked away from the counter scratching his chin, which supported a two-day beard. He'd hoped she'd show early enough to give him time to shave. He looked at his watch. She sure was cutting this close!

He walked over to the front entrance area, bordered by a large glass wall facing the front parking lot. He watched each vehicle driving in. Where was she!

A nagging thought began to chew at his comfort zone. She wasn't coming. Maybe he'd frightened her away. Or perhaps she'd been delayed by the sheriff's department; perhaps they'd seen her going into his place.

He checked his watch again. Kerri!

◆ ◆ ◆

Jerry "Doc" Ling pressed his face into the nape of Kerri's neck. "You like doctors, don't you, pretty one?"

Kerri pulled away and screamed.

He slammed his hand over her mouth again, then lowered his face over hers and pushed her back onto the bed. "I know you like doctors. I'm a medical doctor too."

The taller man touched the younger on the shoulder. "Come on, man. We just want the doctor."

"That's what you want," he hissed.

Kerri could smell his breath. She strained her neck, forcing her head deeper into the mattress, away from her attacker's suffocating hand.

Doc moved back an inch. "Tell us where the doctor is—and don't scream! You were going to see him, weren't you?"

Kerri gasped as he removed his hand for the second time. "I don't know where he is," she said haltingly. "That's the truth."

"Take us to him."

"You were taking his clothes. You must know where he is," Bill interrupted.

Help me, Father.

Tears streamed down Kerri's checks, blurring her vision.

"You were going *somewhere*." Doc pressed his face against hers again. "You fixed yourself up, didn't you? You smell so nice." He laughed quietly. "You were going to him all right."

"You're hurting me!"

She watched as the second man pulled back the shade to look at the street. She could only make out his outline. She silently memorized it—as tall as the top of the window, medium to thin. She couldn't see his hair or face. His voice was mature; he was probably at least fifty.

As Doc buried his face against her neck and groaned, she envisioned the muscular man carrying the box of Lisa's possessions. It was him!

Rescue me, Father.

"Get off her." The voice was from the other man. "The police are outside."

Doc cursed. "Just kill her then. If she won't tell us where he is, kill her."

"The police would hear the shot," Kerri responded with more courage than she felt.

She searched her memory. What was that guy's name—the man in charge? What did Seth say?

Help me, God!

Doc slowly lifted himself from the bed. He glanced out at the street. "Just one deputy. If he hears a shot, we'll have a few minutes until his backup arrives. He'd never investigate on his own."

Wilson Davis! That was it!

"You work for Mr. Davis, don't you?"

The two men exchanged glances.

"You wouldn't want to mess up his plans, would you? I'm on my way to meet Dr. Berringer. We have a meeting with Wilson Davis in the morning."

"You know him?"

"A meeting has been arranged for Dr. Berringer."

"You're lying."

Kerri took a deep breath. "If you don't let me go, you're going to mess up Dr. Davis's plans. Call him—he'll tell you he's located Dr. Berringer. Certainly he told you?"

"It's too early to call. It's only 4 in the morning there."

"I'm telling you the truth," Kerri pleaded. "You have to let me go!"

Bill looked at Doc. "It's going to get light soon. Let's get out of here while we can."

Kerri sighed. "How would I have known his name? Dr. Davis will really be upset."

"We can always pick her up again."

Doc shook his head. "We know where you live."

"If you've lied, Mr. Berringer will pay," the other man warned.

Kerri slowly sat up.

Bill pointed a gun toward the door, barely visible in the dim light. "Get out of here."

They followed her down the steps.

Doc grabbed her arm again and shook a gun in her face. "If you walk toward the cop, I'll shoot. Go out the way you came in, across the backyard. We'll be right behind you."

Kerri picked up the bag she'd packed for Seth.

Slowly, she pulled open the back door.

"Straight across the backyard. No screaming. No barnstorming!"

Kerri ran across the frosty grass. She could see her car!

◆ ◆ ◆

Rick Zander heard the tires squealing and quickly set down his coffee. Someone was in a big hurry this morning. Through the trees, on an adjacent street, he could see a car accelerating dangerously. He started the car and flipped on his flashing lights. Judging from the distance to the corner behind him, it would be quicker to circle the block.

He sped along, taking the first right with only a light touch of the brakes. The paperboy looked up to see the headlights of the patrol car. With a calculated left swerve, Zander guided the patrol car onto the opposite sidewalk, nailing a metal trash can before lurching right and back into the street. Against the quiet morning, the noise seemed explosive.

With a blue Taurus two blocks ahead and the trash can bouncing down the sidewalk behind him, the deputy's adrenaline rush approached a malignant high. "Gooood mornin', Deeeeer Faaalls!"

Ahead, Kerri turned right, down a connector street, across an intersection, and onto Chesapeake Avenue.

Zander slowed to allow a milk truck and two cars to pass. Worried he might lose his quarry, his eyes followed the disappearing Taurus. He flipped on the siren and pulled onto the street, now four blocks behind.

Kerri turned into the hospital parking area and immediately turned left into the employee lot. She held her magnetic I.D. to a sensor mounted on a small pole, and the bar blocking her entry lifted. She pulled into the first available slot, grabbed the two carry-on bags, and ran for the E.R. entrance.

Zander pulled into the hospital lot. Where had that car gone?

Movement caught his eye, and he saw a lady running toward the well-lit entrance. It was the Barber woman!

He smiled. Late for work? Lives to save?

He parked his car in the E.R. lot. The sheriff had hoped she'd show up. Maybe she could tell them where her boyfriend was hiding.

◆ ◆ ◆

Waiting on the other side of the hospital, just outside the doctors' private entrance, Angie Blackstock looked at the car clock again. Where was Kerri? She wondered if she should go to Seth's to make sure Kerri was OK.

She turned on her lights and started the car. How had she ever let her friend talk her into this?

◆ ◆ ◆

Kerri dashed through the E.R., dodging a nurse wheeling an open suture tray and an intoxicated man on a stretcher. She ran into the back hall, past the X-ray department, the main elevator bank, and the medical library. When she saw the entrance to the doctors' lounge, she bounded left and down the stairs to the outside exit door. She hit it at a full run, depressing the lever with the carry-on in her right hand.

Ahead, she could see Angie pulling away in her Jeep Cherokee. "Angie!"

The brake lights lit up as the Cherokee slowed to approach the parking lot exit.

Just as Kerri yelled again, she saw the reverse lights flash on.

"Thank you, God!"

◆ ◆ ◆

The airport lobby was nearly deserted as Seth sighed, checked his watch a final time, and turned toward the escalator.

Ian Brothers called to him, "Your flight's boarding, Mr. Berringer."

He nodded resolutely. He had to face it—she wasn't coming.

Just then a Jeep Cherokee skidded to a stop in front of the terminal. Kerri jumped out, gathered her luggage, and hurried through the automatic doors. "Seth!"

He ran to her as she dropped the bags and fell into his arms. "What happened?"

She began to cry, no longer able to quench the emotion she'd held back since leaving his house.

Ian watched the couple with concern. "Uh, Mr. Berringer, Ms. Barber, you're going to miss your flight."

When they looked at him in a daze, he motioned them over. "Ms. Barber . . . ?" He paused, aghast at her appearance. "Do you have a picture I.D.?"

She nodded. With her mascara smudged and a small amount of dried blood at the corner of her mouth, she quickly retrieved her hospital badge.

"OK. Gate 4. Up the escalator. I'll call ahead and let them know you're coming."

He waved them on as Seth picked up the bags and hurried ahead. "What happened to you?"

Kerri bit her lip, unable to speak without a tremor in her voice. "I'll explain later. Let's get on this plane!"

CHAPTER
34

KERRI collapsed into the airplane seat beside Seth, closed her eyes, and prayed.

A stewardess placed a hand on Kerri's trembling shoulder. "Can I get you anything, ma'am?"

She kept her eyes pinched shut and shook her head.

The stewardess looked at Seth, who mouthed, *It's OK.*

In a few moments they were in the air, and the engines drowned the noise of Kerri's soft sobs.

"Oh, Seth, I ran from the police—I ran from those men—I was so afraid!" Her tears flowed freely as she buried her face in Seth's shoulder, finding comfort in his warm flannel shirt.

Seth, touched by her tenderness and fear, held her shaking body until a calm returned. He nestled his cheek into her hair and whispered, "It's OK now. You're safe." He consoled her softly until her sobs subsided and her gasps changed to settled breaths.

Kerri told the story, with more tears emphasizing the terror of her encounter with the two assailants.

"Why didn't you tell the police?"

"I don't know. I wanted so much to be here with you." She sniffed and raised her eyes until they met his.

His smile melted her again, and she replaced her head against his shoulder. "I took off so fast to get away from those men, and then I saw the police, and then I was afraid to stop, afraid they wouldn't believe—"

"It's OK, Kerri. Everything will work out."

"Angie said she'd go to the sheriff and explain. She'll tell them about those men."

"I hope they believe her. They're not going to like hearing that you and the two men were able to get into my place without their knowing it."

Kerri lifted her head again and smiled as she imagined the sheriff's consternation.

Their eyes met as they silently communicated their feelings.

Seth reached for her and gently brushed her lower lip with his fingers. "Your lip is swollen."

She nodded. He leaned forward and softly placed his lips against hers. He waited for a brief moment before slowly withdrawing until he could focus on her eyes again. He could see there the trust and love she offered him. He basked in a closeness he'd not allowed his heart to feel for a long time.

He could not remember ever knowing a love like this, an acceptance unrelated to his performance, position, or money. She had seen him at his worst, and yet . . . Why did she look at him that way? He couldn't be worthy of this!

A knot rose in his throat, and his eyes moistened with tears.

Kerri raised her hand and brushed away a tear, her touch lingering upon his face. "Just look at us," she whispered with a smile.

She lay her head against his shoulder for a long time without speaking. Then she sat up and reached under the seat for her carry-on. "I think I'll see if I can clean up a bit in the bathroom. I don't want to get off the plane looking like this."

He stood up and let her pass. He watched her move gracefully up the aisle in spite of the bulk of her overstuffed bag. When she disappeared into the lavatory, he closed his eyes.

In two minutes he was sleeping.

◆ ◆ ◆

Sheriff Boatwright wasn't any too happy to be at the office at 6:30 A.M., and even less to be hearing the tale that Angie Blackstock reported. He had known Angie since she was a little girl, when he worked with her father, a state patrolman, the same man who now opposed him in his reelection bid.

The sheriff put his hands on his hips. "How long has your father been in police work?" He didn't wait for her reply. "You know I can't get a warrant to arrest anyone unless the victim of the crime is willing to swear out a warrant against them."

"But it sounds like these are the same men who were looking for Lisa Dale! They may have even been involved in Dr. Donovan's death. And now they assault Kerri as they trespass in Dr. Berringer's house!"

"You'll have to ask Kerri to come down here herself and give us a sworn deposition. Then we'll see what we can do."

"Like I told you, she's out of town."

"With the doctor, right?"

Angie nodded.

"You're aware that we want this man for homicide."

Angie nodded again.

"Where did they go?"

"That is something I really don't know." She wouldn't have wanted Kerri to tell her, even if she'd been willing. "She didn't tell me." She knew Kerri was protecting Seth.

The sheriff sighed and looked over at Rick Zander, who'd been called in to verify the story Angie told. He'd confirmed the part that he could— the chase from Seth's residence until he lost Kerri at the hospital.

"This whole thing stinks. Every time I turn around, this Berringer guy is somehow involved in making this department look bad," Boatwright moaned.

"Sir," she responded, "Dr. Berringer had little to do with the fact that not one but three people entered his residence while under the watchful eye of your department."

Boatwright huffed. Score one for the cute redhead. He looked at his deputy. "Call the airport. There can't be that many flights out of there at this hour. Find out where Berringer's going. Hopefully, we can arrange someone to meet him on the other end."

Zander nodded. "Yes, sir."

"It can't hurt to look a little closer at Seth's place. Those men might return," Angie suggested.

"I refuse to ask for a search warrant for his residence." The sheriff sighed. "But I guess it wouldn't hurt to take a look around outside—see if there was any evidence of forced entry." He called after his deputy. "Zander! Tell Pheiffer to check out the Berringer place. Nothing on the inside—just check around outdoors to see if anyone's broken in."

Rick Zander nodded and sighed. "Yes, sir."

Angie softened. "Thanks, sheriff."

She turned to go.

Down the hall in a second office, Rick Zander found Todd Pheiffer filling out an accident report. "Man, Boatwright's in rare form this morning. He takes every little thing about this Berringer case personally." He shook his head. "I'm beginning to wonder if he's losing perspective."

"What is it this time?" Todd looked up as he sipped his coffee.

"A report that three people entered Berringer's house unnoticed." He cleared his throat. "Unnoticed while I watched the house."

"Oh, boy," Todd groaned. "Did the big guy lean on you?"

"Not very hard. He really couldn't say too much. Captain Blackstock's daughter was standing right there."

Todd smiled. "Angie? What's she doing here?"

"She brought the report. Her friend, Kerri Barber, was one of the three in Berringer's house."

"Who else was there?"

"Two unidentified men. One sounds Asian, one taller, older. Scared Kerri to death."

Todd stared out the window for a moment. "What time did you start watching the Berringer place?"

"I relieved Joe just after midnight. Why?"

"Those men may not have entered while you watched. They could have been waiting in there all night, for all you know."

Zander grunted. "Maybe so." He paused. "I'd like to think so anyway." He poured a cup of coffee, his fifth since midnight. "The sheriff wants you to go down this morning and do an external search of Berringer's place—see if there's any sign of forced entry. If so, we may want to pursue talking to the magistrate about a warrant to search the place. Maybe we'd pick up some prints on the guys, see if we can find a match."

Rick picked up the phone-book, shuffled the pages, then sank into a wheeled office chair. He dialed the main number for the Chesapeake Airport.

"Chesapeake Airport." The voice was masculine and precise.

"This is Deputy Zander from the Chesapeake County sheriff's department. I need some information about early flights this morning, say before 6:30."

"Only US Air Express has a flight that early, sir. Would you like me to transfer you to their desk?"

"Sure."

"US Air Express. How may I help you?" Ian Brothers answered.

"This is Deputy Zander with the Chesapeake County sheriff's department," he repeated. "I'm seeking information about a potential passenger on a flight early this morning."

"Arrival or departure?"

"Departure. Did any flights leave this morning?"

"Yes, sir. Flight 1077 with service to Pittsburgh departed at 6:20. Flight 1088 with service to Philadelphia departed at 6:45."

"Hmmm." Zander sipped his coffee. "Can you confirm whether a passenger, Seth Berringer, was on either of those two flights?"

"Sir, without talking to my supervisor I am only allowed to tell you if a passenger had a reservation for a particular flight. Safety regulations prohibit me passing on information regarding whether a person actually boarded a specific plane."

Bureaucratic red tape! "That's fine. Just tell me if Seth Berringer had a reservation for either flight then."

Ian tapped his computer keyboard for a moment to confirm what he already knew. "Mr. Berringer purchased a reservation for flight 1077 bound for Pittsburgh."

"Thanks." Rick hung up the phone and looked at his watch. 7:15. It couldn't be much more than an hour's flight to Pittsburgh. He knew he'd better get on the phone if he wanted to intercept Berringer on the other end.

Wouldn't the good doctor be surprised when an escort was waiting for him?

◆ ◆ ◆

Nelson O'Hare started his third cup of coffee after weighing the liver and the spleen. The stomach was next.

Alden Rust slit open the stomach with scissors, displaying the contents against the backdrop of a clean blue towel. "No beans here, my friend," he reported.

"What'd he have?" He tapped his foot. "I can't believe he didn't have beans. Seems like everyone lately has—Bernie Smith, Emma Duncan, that kid from up near Beaver Creek—"

Dr. Rust cut off his assistant's jabbering with a stern look. "No pill fragments either. He certainly didn't have a fatal ingestion."

He picked up the heart, weighed it, and turned it several times in his hands. "After looking at the lungs and not seeing any congestion, I'd say whatever got this guy came on pretty quick. Let's see how these coronaries look."

He started at the root of the aorta where the coronary vessels originate before they branch out and supply the heart muscle itself with oxygen-carrying blood. He carefully sliced through the left main coronary artery, doing cross sections every centimeter. "Uh-oh."

Nelson looked on. "Uh-oh what?"

"I told you so," Rust said, pointing to a fresh blood clot in the coronary artery. "A widow-maker, that's what we call these big ones."

"How long has the blockage been there?"

"Shortly before death. See the red color?"

Nelson nodded.

"That's fresh. These other clots . . ." he reported, looking at the other coronary vessels, ". . . are yellow-brown, indicating they've been around for a while."

"Boy, would you look at that! He's loaded with the stuff."

"He was lucky to make it this long. I'd be surprised if he wasn't havin' angina."

Nelson frowned. "Do we still get to do the crainy?"

"Yes. We still need to prove he didn't have any brain damage or a bleed associated with the laceration."

After finishing with the abdominal organs, Nelson put on his goggles and started the bone saw. This was his favorite part. He placed a series of cuts on the skull to allow the bone overlying the laceration to be popped free.

"Completely normal, grossly."

"I guess we have our answer."

"Most likely," Rust concurred. "Looks like our good doctor died of natural causes." He slapped his hand against the metal table. "That's the last time I let that sheriff from Chesapeake County push me into doing an urgent homicide case on a Saturday morning." He snorted angrily. "This wasn't murder at all. Somebody probably found his body and thought it'd be a real hoot to shove the stiff into the refrigerator."

Nelson shrugged. "There are some real weirdos in the world." He touched the brain's surface with his fingers with childlike fascination. "Want a donut or something? I'm starving."

"No, thanks. Not here." Rust took off his gown and gloves and walked to the phone-book.

"What are you doing?"

"That Sheriff Boatwright is running for reelection against an old college buddy of mine. I'm going to call him, just to make sure he knows Sheriff Boatwright is investigating murders that haven't even been committed."

"Don't you think you should tell Boatwright?"

"Oh, I'll tell him. You can bet on that." He smiled. This would be the last time he'd let Boatwright push him around.

◆ ◆ ◆

The flight attendant knocked gently on the lavatory door. "You'll need to get back in your seat now, ma'am. We're getting ready to land." She hadn't seen such a bad case of fear of flying for a long time. The woman must have hidden in there for fifteen minutes.

The stewardess waited a moment, then gently knocked again. Maybe the passenger was sick. "Ma'am, are you OK?"

Kerri opened the door and smiled sheepishly as she maneuvered past. "I'm fine. Thank you."

She arrived at her seat just as an announcement about landing preparation jarred Seth from his slumber. He yawned and looked up. Smiling, he pushed back in his seat to let Kerri pass. "You look nice."

"Thank you," she responded demurely. With a hint of a concealed smile, she added, "You need a shave."

Seth rubbed his chin and grunted.

She giggled.

Moments later they were on the ground again and slowly made their way up the aisle behind a row of passengers. In another moment the cold air hit them as they moved down the steps and onto the hard surface below.

Seth looked at Kerri. "The next time we won't have to go outside. That only happens on these Express flights."

They sprinted the last few steps into the warmth of the terminal, then walked along the E Terminal wing into the lobby housing the main US Air Express desk. They took a short subway ride over to the main terminal to look for connecting flights to Denver.

As they exited the train, three uniformed Pittsburgh police entered. "Clear the doorway, people! Official business!"

◆ ◆ ◆

Dr. Rust held the phone on his shoulder with his cheek. This was a call he would enjoy.

"Mr. Boatwright, Alden Rust here. Chief medical examiner."

"Yes?"

"I just called to check on some details about the Donovan case, just to make sure I had all the facts straight."

"Did you finish the autopsy?"

"Just the gross." He paused. "You said this was a murder case, correct?"

"Yes. We're hot on the trail of the main suspect."

"Homicide investigations require the body of a victim, correct?"

"Of course. What are you saying?"

"Well, we have a dead body here all right, but he wasn't murdered."

"What are you talking about? Berringer hit him in the head and stuffed him in a freezer."

"The head wound was superficial. It probably occurred when the deceased fell over due to his acute myocardial infarction."

"What? Use layman's terms, doctor. What are you saying?"

"I'm saying you don't have a murder case on your hands. Dr. Donovan died of a heart attack."

"Wha—" Boatwright took a breath. "Are you sure?"

"Very. I still have the blood chemistries and toxicology screen to look at, but I've never seen a coronary look this bad and not be the immediate cause of death."

Boatwright cursed.

"I think you'd better rethink this arrest warrant, sheriff. Then again, I'm just a pathologist. What do I know?" He smiled.

Boatwright slammed down the phone. "Debbie?" he yelled. "Get Zander in here. Now!"

CHAPTER
35

IAN Brothers gasped as he read the morning paper.

SUSPECT NAMED IN DONOVAN CASE

Seth Berringer, local family physician, has been named as a suspect in the recent homicide of medical examiner Eric Donovan. He has not been formally charged; however, an arrest warrant has been issued. He is still at large.

Berringer, the confessed driver in a recent hit-and-run case involving the death of local collegian Lisa Dale, was released from Evergreen State Hospital the day before Donovan's body was discovered. Physicians there had no comment.

Coast Care, Berringer's employer, responded quickly, stating that the physician was no longer employed by their corporation. A reason for his dismissal was not disclosed.

Police are speculating about a possible link with a second death, that of Tammy Lynn Gaskins, who worked as an administrative assistant to Dr. Donovan. Her body was found in her apartment yesterday. Suicide is suspected, but an autopsy has not yet been performed.

He set the paper aside as customers approached the counter, but he couldn't stop thinking about Berringer. He had seemed awfully stressed out. Hadn't shaved. Checked his watch every two minutes. Ian had let a murderer onto that plane!

"Good morning." He smiled at an elderly couple with two suitcases and two sets of golf clubs. "Where are you heading this morning?" Somewhere safer than Deer Falls, he hoped.

◆ ◆ ◆

Lou Ellen's feet landed on the cold wooden floor in her private bedroom at the Deer Falls Inn. Her fitful sleep had been troubled by dreams about Lisa Dale, with the intervening hours marred with anxiety about police investigations, Kerri Barber, and Lou Ellen's mother.

She winced at the light peeking out from behind the curtain. She pulled it back and assessed the weather. Another cold, overcast morning, the kind that made Lou long for the simpler days of her childhood—the days when her mother would guide her through whatever complex situation life offered.

Maybe she was making too much of all this. She scanned the side of the Inn, visible from her window. She stared at the door of room 12.

Was she worried about nothing? She shook her head. Momma hadn't spoken since her stroke. Maybe Lou Ellen had been under such pressure . . . Maybe it only happened in her mind. She needed to get away for a while.

She let the curtain fall back and flipped on the desk lamp before walking to the bathroom to lay her makeup foundation. What was it she'd seen on that talk show? Something about visualizing your way to inner tranquility?

She closed her eyes. She imagined a quiet place—palm trees, quiet blue sea—warm waters surrounding her . . . She opened her eyes. She could never wear her bathing suit in public! There had to be a better way to find some peace!

◆ ◆ ◆

Rick Zander began speaking as soon as Boatwright looked up. "They missed him, boss. Arrived five minutes after the plane was empty." He shook his head. "I called the US Air central desk, and they say it's impossible to tell what flight he took without going through every individual flight—that is, assuming he's getting on another plane. I gave a description of Berringer to the Pittsburgh City Police and the State Police. They promised to share it with airport security and—"

"Save it, Zander. It's no use." The sheriff sighed. "Besides, it looks like we may have to drop the charges."

"What?"

"The medical examiner called. He says Donovan died from a heart attack. There was no evidence he died from the head wound."

Rick sank into a wooden chair opposite the sheriff's desk. "Oh, man." He snapped his finger. "But what about his fingerprint match? I looked at that one myself. What was Berringer doing there?"

"And what about the motive?" Boatwright asked. "Dave Trainum even located a nurse up at Evergreen who swears she heard Berringer arguing with Donovan on the phone." He cursed. "But all of that is pointless if we have no victim."

"Maybe Berringer *was* there. Maybe he scared Donovan into having a heart attack. Maybe he pulled a gun on him, and the stress killed him or something." He paused. "I've read about things like that."

The sheriff grunted. "Maybe, but it can't be proven without a witness." He pushed back from his desk and held a box of donuts toward the deputy. Zander took one.

"Thanks."

Boatwright took the only two chocolate-covered donuts left.

"The thing I don't understand," Boatwright mused aloud, "is how Donovan ended up in that refrigerator."

"And who cleaned up the blood?"

"And why did he run?" His slapped his hand on the desk. "This doesn't add up. Berringer has done nothing but make this department look bad. Now I'm going to have to retract the arrest warrant and somehow save face with the public." He cringed, wiped his mouth with the back of his hand, and nodded solemnly. "Berringer's not getting off this easy. I know he's behind all of this somehow." He shook his head slowly. "If I could only put this all together. Lisa Dale's death—Donovan's death—Tammy Lynn Gaskins's sworn deposition and then her death. I need one more piece of evidence to show me who's telling the truth. Then I'll bring him in."

Zander wondered if Boatwright was perhaps taking this a bit too personally. He watched his sheriff closely, imagining steam blowing from his ears.

"I'll get him," the sheriff repeated. "He won't make this department look foolish again."

◆　◆　◆

By mid-afternoon Colorado time, Seth and Kerri were heading south on Interstate 25 toward Colorado Springs. They had purchased round-trip tickets, with plans to return to Pittsburgh on Sunday. The round trip was cheaper than one way, and the Saturday layover brought the too-expensive price into a range Seth could tolerate. He only hoped his meeting on Friday with Wilson Davis would be fruitful and that his mission would be accomplished before his time ran out.

If he had the evidence he needed by Sunday, he would return to Deer Falls. If not . . . He hadn't thought that far ahead, but he knew he couldn't run from Boatwright forever. Seth was an innocent man, but he wasn't confident that truth would win out with Boatwright in control.

Seth looked out the passenger window at the mountains. Kerri had told him it wasn't Boatwright who was in control but, ultimately, God. He shook his head. If God was in charge of this mess, that was one more reason to question his judgment.

Kerri broke into his thoughts. "You're supposed to be sleeping." She smiled.

"You're supposed to be watching the road."

"Can't help it if I wanted to enjoy the scenery."

Seth reached over and touched her cheek. "You look like you're feeling better."

"Nothing like thirty minutes in an airplane bathroom to refresh the soul."

He chuckled. "Forty-five."

"You wouldn't know. You were sleeping. Besides, the flight was only fifty-five minutes. I couldn't have been in there a minute over thirty."

Seth smiled. Kerri had a way of making him forget the seriousness of his quest.

"Try to get some sleep."

"I'm hungry." He tipped an imaginary cowboy hat. "Those peanuts aren't holdin' me, Kerri darlin'."

She rolled her eyes. "Now you're starting to sound like a Stephen Bly novel." She smiled at him again. "Get some sleep, cowboy. I'll stop if I see a good place to eat."

Seth turned down the car heater and closed his eyes.

In a few minutes, when Seth's breathing returned to normal, Kerri turned the heat back up. What was keeping him so warm? She was freezing!

◆ ◆ ◆

Dave Trainum closed his laptop computer and pushed a crumpled McDonald's hamburger wrapper toward the back of his desk to make room for his feet. Just as he was leaning his head against the wall and beginning to make up for lost sleep, an incoming fax announced its arrival. He took the transmission out of the machine and returned to his desk.

"Well, what do you know," he muttered. "Another quirk in an already complicated case. Won't Boatwright love this one."

He picked up the phone and punched the appropriate button for the sheriff's extension.

"Afternoon, sheriff. I got some news back from the national data bank. It seems we have a clear match on a print taken from the telephone in Donovan's office. The print belongs to a William Guessford. He has one felony arrest on a drug charge in Colorado."

"Are they sure?"

"Ninety-nine point nine percent. The print was very readable."

"What about Berringer? Did they confirm his print from the refrigerator door?"

"Yep. Experts confirmed our analysis. He was there too."

Boatwright scratched his chin. "What about the lab? Anything from forensics on the blood?"

"The blood on the paper towels in the trash is Donovan's. The blood on the corner of the desk was also his."

"The corner of the desk?"

"Right. The evidence tech saw it when he was combing for prints. It looked like someone cleaned most of it up, but there was enough in a small crack to give us a positive i.d." Trainum shrugged. "Apparently Donovan fell and struck his head on the corner after his heart attack."

"But why did someone put him in the refrigerator?"

"I don't know." He tapped a pencil on the desk. "If Berringer was there when he died, or found him dead, would there be a reason to stash the body away to make it harder to find?"

"I don't know." The sheriff shook his head. "What about this other guy? Guessford, you say? What does he have to do with all this?"

Trainum was silent for a moment, then responded, "Maybe this guy was posing as the Yamatsu character Ms. Donovan told us her husband was supposed to meet."

"Hmmm. From what she says, Donovan must've been involved in some sort of shady deal. Maybe the deal went sour, and the participants freaked out when Donovan croaked, so they cleaned up the lab and stuffed him in the refrigerator." He paused. "I don't know. It's theoretical at this point."

"Don't ask me."

"What about other prints? Anything from the doorknobs?"

"Only Berringer's. The curious thing is, the doorknob leading to Donovan's lab was completely clean except for prints by Berringer. Normally, those things are covered. We didn't even find a match for Donovan himself. It's as if someone had wiped it clean before Berringer arrived."

Boatwright looked at his watch. It was time to think about dinner. "Good work, Dave. Let me know if anything else comes in."

◆ ◆ ◆

"Look, honey, it'd be best if you kept this news quiet. I don't want it getting out that I had anything to do with spreading dirt around concerning Sheriff Boatwright." Phil Blackstock looked at his daughter until her eyes met his, and he knew he had made his point. "He'll have to take care of this one himself. He doesn't need me pointing out his mistakes."

Angie frowned. "At least let me tell Kerri—if she calls me, that is. She'll be so excited!"

The former state police captain shook his head. "I'm not sure what's going on at the sheriff's department. It's not like Boatwright to rush an investigation like this. Usually you have to practically push the guy into action." He huffed. "Not getting the medical examiner's confirmation first is a cardinal sin of homicide investigation. Now he's confused everyone, especially by leaking Berringer's name to the media."

"Do you think Dr. Rust told the sheriff?"

"I'm sure of it. He was peeved that Boatwright had pushed him so hard. I'm sure he enjoyed telling him the news. In a way, it's good that Berringer ran off. If he'd stayed around and the sheriff had arrested him, the department would've been liable for false arrest."

"What about defamation of character? Dr. Berringer can't show his face around here without someone wondering why he was in a mental hospital or what really happened to Donovan or Lisa Dale."

Her father sighed. "That case would be harder to make. I mean, Berringer will have to own partial responsibility for all this. Whatever he's

◆ ◆ ◆

Angie turned up the radio's volume to better hear the news.

"In late-breaking news regarding the death of medical examiner Eric Donovan, the sheriff's department has retracted the previous ruling of homicide. Autopsy reports reveal that Donovan suffered from severe coronary artery disease and died from a massive heart attack. The arrest warrant for Dr. Seth Berringer has been dropped. When asked about Berringer's mysterious disappearance or a possible link to the hit-and-run death of Lisa Dale, the sheriff's department simply said, 'No comment.' This new tight-lipped policy by the department follows a recent stream of confusing information about Dr. Berringer and his possible association with several recent deaths . . ."

Angie was alone, but she had to say something. "Finally Boatwright says, 'No comment.' Boy, does this town need the leadership of Phil Blackstock!"

◆ ◆ ◆

Ursula Baumgarten made her way down the steep, winding road leading from the research facility. The mountain view and sunset were picturesque, but she could not appreciate them due to her inner turmoil. Why was Davis lying to her about the girl? Was Schwab misleading Ursula so she'd be disenchanted with private research just as he'd predicted? Could he be wrong about the way Lisa Dale died? She kept the Jeep in low gear to avoid traveling too fast along the mountain road. And why did Davis insist on such secrecy?

She thought about Kevin Schwab and the years of work they'd accomplished side by side at the N.I.H. Schwab was possibly naive, but he wasn't dishonest. Either Berringer had pulled the wool over Kevin's eyes, or Kevin was telling the truth and Lisa really died during an attempt to harvest the clone. But why by the gross abortion technique? Could it be that someone had heard of their research and would do anything to stop them, even using outdated, back-alley techniques? That didn't seem probable, given the high level of secrecy at the institute.

She arrived at the highway and turned to the north. The other possibility bothered her the most. Could it be that Lisa's death was the result of their harvest team's using a technique designed to prevent anyone from

guilty of, he has admitted to misleading the sheri
public about Lisa Dale."

Angie nodded. "But at least he's not wanted for m
tell Kerri!"

Blackstock sensed his daughter's excitement
"Remember, no one hears about this from you or me exc
glanced at his watch. "At least until Boatwright issues a sta
dropping the murder charge warrant."

"Agreed," she responded slowly. She wished Kerri would ca

◆ ◆ ◆

Kerri and Seth stood at the counter of a Holiday Inn in Colorado Spri

Seth looked at Kerri, then back at the young man behind the count
who had just handed him a room key. "Uh, we'll be needing two rooms."

The man looked first at Kerri, then at Seth. Was this guy crazy? He
tapped on his computer keyboard. "Would you like adjoining rooms?"

Seth hesitated.

"Better not," Kerri interjected. It would be hard enough being out here
all alone with Seth.

"No," Seth agreed.

"Suit yourself." The man completed the registration.

The couple walked to the middle of the lobby, and Seth handed Kerri
her room key. "Would you join me for dinner?"

Her face lit up. "I'd love to."

Seth rubbed his chin. "I'll need some time."

"Let's make it a late dinner." She thought that would be romantic.

"How about 7:30? That way we can rest and get cleaned up."

"Good." She squeezed his hand. "Seth . . ."

He looked at her and waited.

"This will be our first date."

"We've been out before," he protested softly.

"They don't count. You didn't ask me in advance. This time I get to
prepare."

"You're already beautiful."

She looked away to hide her thin smile. She picked up her bag and
headed for her room.

He checked his watch and smiled.

◆ ◆ ◆

Angie turned up the radio's volume to better hear the news.

"In late-breaking news regarding the death of medical examiner Eric Donovan, the sheriff's department has retracted the previous ruling of homicide. Autopsy reports reveal that Donovan suffered from severe coronary artery disease and died from a massive heart attack. The arrest warrant for Dr. Seth Berringer has been dropped. When asked about Berringer's mysterious disappearance or a possible link to the hit-and-run death of Lisa Dale, the sheriff's department simply said, 'No comment.' This new tight-lipped policy by the department follows a recent stream of confusing information about Dr. Berringer and his possible association with several recent deaths . . ."

Angie was alone, but she had to say something. "Finally Boatwright says, 'No comment.' Boy, does this town need the leadership of Phil Blackstock!"

◆ ◆ ◆

Ursula Baumgarten made her way down the steep, winding road leading from the research facility. The mountain view and sunset were picturesque, but she could not appreciate them due to her inner turmoil. Why was Davis lying to her about the girl? Was Schwab misleading Ursula so she'd be disenchanted with private research just as he'd predicted? Could he be wrong about the way Lisa Dale died? She kept the Jeep in low gear to avoid traveling too fast along the mountain road. And why did Davis insist on such secrecy?

She thought about Kevin Schwab and the years of work they'd accomplished side by side at the N.I.H. Schwab was possibly naive, but he wasn't dishonest. Either Berringer had pulled the wool over Kevin's eyes, or Kevin was telling the truth and Lisa really died during an attempt to harvest the clone. But why by the gross abortion technique? Could it be that someone had heard of their research and would do anything to stop them, even using outdated, back-alley techniques? That didn't seem probable, given the high level of secrecy at the institute.

She arrived at the highway and turned to the north. The other possibility bothered her the most. Could it be that Lisa's death was the result of their harvest team's using a technique designed to prevent anyone from guilty of, he has admitted to misleading the sheriff's department and the public about Lisa Dale."

Angie nodded. "But at least he's not wanted for murder. I can't wait to tell Kerri!"

Blackstock sensed his daughter's excitement growing again. "Remember, no one hears about this from you or me except Kerri." He glanced at his watch. "At least until Boatwright issues a statement about dropping the murder charge warrant."

"Agreed," she responded slowly. She wished Kerri would call now!

◆ ◆ ◆

Kerri and Seth stood at the counter of a Holiday Inn in Colorado Springs.

Seth looked at Kerri, then back at the young man behind the counter, who had just handed him a room key. "Uh, we'll be needing two rooms."

The man looked first at Kerri, then at Seth. Was this guy crazy? He tapped on his computer keyboard. "Would you like adjoining rooms?"

Seth hesitated.

"Better not," Kerri interjected. It would be hard enough being out here all alone with Seth.

"No," Seth agreed.

"Suit yourself." The man completed the registration.

The couple walked to the middle of the lobby, and Seth handed Kerri her room key. "Would you join me for dinner?"

Her face lit up. "I'd love to."

Seth rubbed his chin. "I'll need some time."

"Let's make it a late dinner." She thought that would be romantic.

"How about 7:30? That way we can rest and get cleaned up."

"Good." She squeezed his hand. "Seth . . ."

He looked at her and waited.

"This will be our first date."

"We've been out before," he protested softly.

"They don't count. You didn't ask me in advance. This time I get to prepare."

"You're already beautiful."

She looked away to hide her thin smile. She picked up her bag and headed for her room.

He checked his watch and smiled.

detecting their research? If that was true, Davis was guilty of the worst type of deception, and his arrogance had taken an innocent life.

She sighed and turned on the radio. She longed for a distraction to push the anxieties about the project away.

It didn't work. Could it be that Davis's hatred of the Christian religion had blinded him to the point that he would stoop to this kind of violence?

CHAPTER
36

THE restaurant population had thinned, leaving only three couples besides Seth and Kerri at the quaint little inn in Manitou Springs.

Seth gazed across the table at Kerri. "It's hard to believe that come Saturday it's only been three weeks since Lisa died. It seems like a lifetime ago."

"So much has happened," Kerri added with a nod.

He stared at her a moment without speaking.

"What are you thinking?" she prompted.

"I don't know. I've never known someone so well, yet felt so . . . so like I . . . well, like you remain a mystery to me."

She wrinkled her forehead, unsure how to respond.

He continued, "I feel so open with you, like I can tell you anything. But at the same time, I don't understand the simple trust I see in you. Even when you're afraid, you seem to radiate a confidence that everything will be OK."

"A person would be lost without hope, Seth." She paused. "It all comes back to my Christian faith."

Seth shifted in his chair. "I knew you'd say that." He looked down. "I never thought much about God before . . . well, before I found Lisa that night."

She nodded and sipped her coffee.

"When I was driving down to meet you at the airport, I found myself wishing I could think like you do, that somehow I'd have the evidence in my hand to tell me that what you believe is the truth."

"Seth Berringer, you're always on a quest for evidence, aren't you?" Kerri spoke softly. "There are some things you can't prove. Some things you just have to take on faith."

"I even tried to pray again, but I didn't know how."

"Prayer doesn't have to be anything formal or fancy, Seth. It's like a child talking to his father. God doesn't require fancy forms or platitudes. He looks past that stuff. He hears the yearnings of our hearts."

"Maybe someday, when I get my act back together, I'll understand." He shook his head. "I have some straightening up to do before God could accept me." He looked at Kerri. "When I look at you . . . Well, I understand how God could love you, how he could be sympathetic to your prayers. But me? I've done too many crazy things lately—"

"Seth . . ." She kept her voice low. "That's the whole point of the Gospel. God sent his Son not because we were good enough, but because no one was worthy. God doesn't love me more than he loves you. Nothing you could do would make him love you more than he does right at this moment. All you need to do is to ask him to forgive you, to accept the death of his only Son as a substitute for the punishment you deserved. In simple language, you need to release control of your life and put God in the driver's seat." She tried to sense whether he was uncomfortable. "Do that, Seth, and I guarantee that I'll be less of a mystery."

"Give up control?"

She nodded.

"I don't know, Kerri. I'm not sure I'll ever believe the way you do. A God of love? Someone I can trust? How could I ever believe in something I can't see or touch?"

"Look around you, Seth. Do you think all this beauty came from nothing? I seem to remember you telling me once about the magnificent logic of the human body. You know God exists."

Seth nodded. "But a God who loves me personally? I don't see the evidence for that."

Kerri thought of a familiar Bible verse—"Faith is the evidence of things not seen"—but remained quiet. She had said enough.

After a few moments Seth spoke again. "Schwab told me we should be in the parking lot of a place called the Garden of the Gods by 10 in the morning. Someone from Wilson's lab will pick us up there."

"Why the weird rendezvous?"

Seth shrugged. "Maybe we'll understand tomorrow."

Seth paid the bill and drove them back to their motel.

Throughout the ride she remained quiet, lost in her own hopes and fears for Seth Berringer. *He's searching for you, Lord. He's so open with me— so vulnerable. He's so intelligent, caring, courteous—and so handsome. I melt when he touches me, Lord, but I know I shouldn't give my heart away as long as he doesn't love you the way I do. I just can't resist when he looks at me like he does. I know he loves me, Father. Can it be wrong to love him in return?*

She looked over at Seth and wiped a tear from the corner of her eye.

Seth parked and walked her to her room. He gently slid his arms around her neck. "I've never felt so close to someone," he whispered.

She resisted for a moment, then surrendered to the passion that he offered and that she desperately wanted to return. She pulled him close, her arms locked around his waist. Relaxing, she forced her caution to the side, concentrating only on the warmth of Seth's embrace.

After a moment she pulled away, hoping he wouldn't misunderstand the tears that filled her eyes. "You'd better go. We have a big day ahead of us."

He nodded and slowly released her, watching her disappear into her room, staring at the door until he heard the dead-bolt slide into place.

He was alone, suddenly struck with the fear that the woman he loved might not be free to love him in return. He shook off a chill.

He trudged mechanically toward his room. Why did he feel so alone?

◆ ◆ ◆

Because of the late hour, Kerri waited until the next morning to call Angie.

Angie picked up after two rings. "Hello. Blackstocks'."

"Hi, Angie."

"Kerri! Where are you? I've been waiting for you to call!"

Kerri smiled. Having a close friend was a great treasure.

Angie didn't wait for Kerri to say anything. "The charges against Seth have been dropped!"

"What? Did you talk to the sheriff about the two men at Seth's—"

"No, Kerri. Well, I mean, yes, I did talk to him about the two men, but that's not the reason. The autopsy showed that Donovan died from a heart attack—he wasn't murdered!"

Kerri let the words sink in. "B-but," she stuttered, "w-why did they f-find him in the refrigerator?"

"I don't know. Daddy's trying to discover what's going on down there. If I hear any more, I'll let you know. Now, where are you?"

"Colorado Springs. We're going to meet with Wilson Davis this morning. Hopefully, we can learn more about the research Lisa was involved in. Seth hopes he can obtain evidence that will clear up some of the mud that has tarnished his reputation in Deer Falls."

"Colorado Springs? Well, uh, in a motel . . . with Seth?"

"Yes, in a motel with Seth." She let her friend stew for a moment.

"W-well, I th-thought . . . Well, certainly—"

"In separate rooms, silly. You know me better than that!"

Angie paused. "I think I do, but sometimes I worry about you, girl."

"Angie . . ."

"Kerri, you are behaving yourself, aren't you?"

"I'm not a schoolgirl."

"And I'm not your mother. I just know that some things might be hard to . . ."

"Resist?"

"Yes."

"Listen, Seth is a perfect gentlemen. Don't worry. Pray, yes—but don't worry. I'll call you after we meet with Mr. Davis."

"Bye."

Kerri hung up the phone, grabbed her room key, and dashed for Seth's room without her coat.

"Seth! Seth!" She pounded on the door.

He opened the door, and she stumbled into his arms. She kissed him enthusiastically before breaking away and telling him the news. "You're off the hook! The sheriff doesn't want to arrest you! The autopsy showed that Donovan died from a heart attack!"

"Slow down!" He stepped away and sat on the bed. "Now, what are you talking about?"

"I talked to Angie this morning, and she told me the medical examiner revealed that Donovan died of natural causes. The murder investigation has been canceled."

Seth shook his head incredulously. "I wonder who put him in the refrigerator."

"Maybe the men who were in your house?"

"Maybe." He slapped the bed in excitement. "This means I can return to Deer Falls. At least I'm clear in that case. I just hope I can get to the bottom of the Lisa Dale situation. There's no telling what Boatwright might do to me for disturbing the evidence like I did."

"If he believes you. I think he's still convinced you had something to do with her death."

Seth nodded and stood up.

Kerri stepped toward him. "At least there's no warrant out for your arrest."

He moved closer. "That's a reason to celebrate." He reached for her hand and drew her to himself. Her hand slipped naturally behind the small of his back and urged him forward. Their lips met in raptured celebration.

Kerri lingered for a moment before stepping back and looking into Seth's eyes. She'd promised herself she'd stop doing this. She knew she couldn't have him. Not yet.

"What's wrong?" Seth sensed her indecision.

She hid a thin smile. "I—I need to finish getting ready." She turned to go.

Seth looked at his watch. "I'll come by your room in a few minutes."

"OK. I'll be ready."

In a moment she was gone, and Seth stood puzzling over this latest news and the diverse feelings he sensed in Kerri, the woman who had captured his heart. He needed to get his reputation cleared up, his job back, and his feelings sorted out about this woman! That was a tall order for anyone.

He sighed and returned to putting on his tie.

◆ ◆ ◆

Peter Layman seemed balder than he really was since, because of his short stature, everyone looked directly on his central bald spot. He handed the fingerprint comparison to Dave Trainum. "I've not run it by the state's expert, but it sure looks like a match to me."

"Where did you get this?"

"From the footboard in a room over at the Inn. The sheriff asked me to dust the whole place. Evidently the girl, Lisa Dale, spent her last night there, and there was a report of two male visitors." He shrugged. "This doesn't prove anything, and it doesn't prove this guy was there at the same time as Ms. Dale. But at least we know that this Mr. Guessford was present at the Inn and also used the phone at the medical examiner's office."

The detective studied the prints. "Sure looks like a match." He scratched his head. "Beats me how to put all this together though. Lisa Dale and Eric

Donovan—what did they both have to do with Guessford? And where does Seth Berringer fit into it all? He confesses to running Lisa over, or at least to making it look like she died in a hit-and-run. Then he visits the autopsy suite at the medical examiner's office and leaves a clear print very close to a dead man—the very man whose autopsy report contradicted the account Berringer gave us of the way Lisa died. And then Tammy Lynn Gaskins comes forward, recants her previous testimony, and swears that—"

A shrill ring from the phone interrupted the detective's tirade. "Trainum here."

He listened for a moment. "The new prints? Got 'em right here. Peter and I were just—"

He nodded. "Yes, sir. I'll bring 'em right down." He looked at his evidence technician and set the phone down. "The boss wants these. Let me know when the expert analysis comes in."

With that, he walked out. Peter followed, anxious to hear the rest of the detective's thoughts.

◆ ◆ ◆

Seth stood in the cold wind beside their Honda Accord rental car, unable to appreciate the incredible beauty of the surrounding mountains and the sheer rock formations in the area known as the Garden of the Gods.

"This is awesome, Seth. Just look at that one." Kerri pointed to another giant rock protruding from the earth like a natural skyscraper.

He nodded and checked his watch.

"I've heard about this place since I was a kid, but being here . . ." Her voice trailed off when she looked at Seth's worried expression.

"What if he doesn't come? What if I took the details down wrong? It's not like I can just call him. I have no idea how to contact this man."

"He's only a few minutes late." She squinted into the wind. "I'm freezing. Maybe we should sit in the car."

He nodded, and they climbed into the rental, which they had parked in the first parking slot next to the entrance to the popular tourist spot, per the specific, mysterious instructions passed on by Kevin Schwab.

After another minute, a stretch limousine pulled up and stopped in the next slot. The windows in the back were deeply tinted, preventing Seth from seeing whether the man was alone. A chauffeur rolled down his window and looked at Seth. Seth did the same.

"Dr. Berringer?"

Seth nodded.

"Mr. Davis asked me to meet you here. Please come with me."

Seth looked at Kerri, then back at the man. "That's what we're here for. Should I follow you?"

The man shook his head. "No. Leave your car. It will be safe here. You must ride with me."

The couple shrugged and got out. The chauffeur opened the back door, allowing Seth and Kerri to enter. The plush limousine had two bench-style seats facing each other on opposite sides of a small table. There was a corner bar, a television, a small sink, a phone, and a refrigerator.

"Help yourself to the bar," the chauffeur invited. "I'll be in front. Press 6 if you need anything." With that, he closed the door. An electronic lock snapped shut.

Seth instinctively reached for the latch. He looked at Kerri, whose eyes widened with a hint of alarm. "We're locked in."

They settled together on the velour seat facing the rear of the limousine. They were alone, with their faces lit by a single dome light on the ceiling.

"Seth?" A slight tremor in her voice betrayed her apprehension. "Did you notice anything funny about the windows?" Kerri gripped his arm.

"Yes," he sighed. "We can't see through them."

"We can't see where he's taking us!"

CHAPTER
37

THEY drove for thirty minutes before the noise beneath the tires changed as the crunch of gravel and ice replaced the steady, quiet hum of the pavement.

Seth pressed his face against the window again. He could only behold his own eyes. "It's no use. I can't see a thing."

The limousine slowed, and the terrain became irregular, as if the road was rocky or filled with potholes. Twice they could hear the wheels spin, as if the road had not been completely cleared of snow.

"We must be at high altitude. There wasn't any snow in Colorado Springs," Kerri whispered.

Seth nodded and sat back in his chair. His inability to be in control frustrated him. "I wish I could tell where we are."

In a few minutes the car stopped, and the door opened. The man offered his hand as they exited the limousine. "Welcome to the residence of Wilson Davis."

Seth looked around, straining to recognize any landmarks. He looked at their escort, a burly man of about thirty. "Is this his research center?"

"The research facility, his home—all in one." He pointed to a brick path that had been cleared of the snow that otherwise covered the ground. "This way please."

They followed him up to an expansive facility that looked more like a public building than a home. Glass and steel framed a central atrium in a structure in which brick otherwise predominated.

They opened the door and were greeted by a butler. The inside was warm, and the rich, colonial interior provided a stark contrast to the building's modern exterior. Painted wood paneling and eight-inch crown molding accented pastel colors and textured wallpaper. The floors were oak.

"Mr. Davis will be right with you. May I take your coats?"

They surrendered their outer garments and waited in the front vestibule.

"Did you see Pike's Peak out there?" Seth whispered.

Kerri shook her head. "Why?"

"I was just thinking—I'll bet you can see that mountain from everywhere around Colorado Springs. But not here. Maybe that means we're on Pike's Peak."

"It might be on the other side of the house. We didn't get a look that way," she whispered.

I think that direction is east," he responded, pointing back out toward the door. "Judging from the position of the sun."

They stopped talking when they heard footsteps—an elderly gentleman accompanied by a woman with long, black hair. Seth judged her age to be around forty. The man, who appeared very thin, had skin that was noticeably yellow in color.

"Dr. Berringer?" He held out his hand, and Seth shook it. "I didn't realize you were bringing a guest." He looked at Kerri. His mouth hinted at a smile.

"Yes, well . . . Pleased to meet you, Mr. Davis. This is my friend, Kerri Barber."

"This is Ursula Baumgarten." He nodded toward the woman at his side. "Dr. Baumgarten runs this research facility. Her accomplishments are manifold, I assure you. Without her, this project would have failed long ago."

Ursula held out her hand to Seth but did not offer a greeting to Kerri. Seth nodded.

"Welcome to our beautiful state," he continued. "Will you stay to take in some sights? Or are you only here on business?"

Seth looked at Kerri, then responded, "We're here until our flight back on Sunday." He shrugged. "Perhaps we'll enjoy the sights tomorrow."

Davis nodded toward his researcher. "I stole Ursula from the N.I.H. They were wasting her talents."

"Mr. Davis, you are too kind." She forced a nervous smile.

Mr. Davis cleared his throat. "Well, shall we get on with the discussion? Let me just say that I'm very pleased to meet you face to face, Dr. Berringer. We have been following your actions in Deer Falls with much interest."

Seth looked at Kerri.

"I have been anticipating this visit for some time." The research head paused, stricken by a wet cough. "Certainly you understand the importance and urgency of our business transaction, but I thought you'd enjoy seeing the facility up close before we talk." He raised his left hand to Ursula.

Before Seth could reply, Davis continued, "Ursula, show Dr. Berringer and Ms. Barber just how far we've come in our project. Let's make sure they appreciate the depth of our program and the benefit of our working together. I'll meet Dr. Berringer in my study upon the completion of your tour. Perhaps you can show Ms. Barber the library during my visit with Dr. Berringer. She may enjoy seeing the collection of Christian artifacts we have collected there."

"S-sir," she said, leaning in close to whisper in his ear, "the Turin Project?"

He waved her on. "Of course. That's why they're here."

Ursula shrugged. "Shall we?" Ursula led the couple down the hall. While she walked, she glanced back at Mr. Davis. What was he thinking? She'd only told him Schwab wanted her to set up a meeting with Dr. Berringer. Just what did he think this meeting was about? A "business transaction"? What did Davis think this guy wanted?

Seth obviously had the same questions. "Uh, Dr. Baumgarten," Seth began, "just what business transaction was Mr. Davis referring to?"

"I had hoped you would know," she quipped. "I guess you'll find out sooner or later. This has all been arranged by Mr. Davis." She was beginning to think she knew very little about Davis's real agenda.

At the end of the hall, they took an elevator to the second floor. There she entered a number on a keypad beside a metal door. With the door unlocked, they proceeded forward to a second set of doors. To open these, Ursula pulled her I.D. badge through a slot in a small rectangular box mounted on the wall. She stepped back and allowed the two doors to part automatically, then motioned with her hand. "After you."

They stepped into a central room with large glass windows on three sides that looked out onto a large scientific laboratory. It appeared much like any other hospital lab, the exception being that the few workers present were dressed in sterile scrubs with disposable hats, masks, gloves, and shoe-covers. Seth noted several instruments he couldn't identify. He thought some were perhaps automated fluid analyzers, such as might be seen in a hematology lab.

Ursula pointed to the scrub sinks. "Anyone who goes beyond this point must enter through the locker rooms. After the appropriate garments are put on and a full arm and hand scrub is accomplished, the workers enter the lab by walking across the dust-collectors." She pointed to a large blue mat in front of an inner door.

"The most important project in recent months involves Mr. Davis's fascination with human cloning."

Ursula watched Kerri's eyes widen, then continued, "To date, we haven't allowed a human clone to go through more than several cell divisions prior to disposal."

She pointed to the central lab. "That area houses our DNA sequencers, which unravel the basic core of the genetic code."

"Through those doors," she continued, pointing to the back of the lab, "is our animal facility." She sighed. "But cloning animals is old business. Mr. Wilson is on the very cutting edge."

Kerri couldn't hold her tongue. "Isn't the cloning of human embryos illegal?"

Ursula smirked and simply responded, "Not at all." Her eyes took on a glassy stare. "And even if the government did decide to regulate the industry again, it would be very difficult to control privately funded facilities like this one." She suppressed a laugh. "Our nation's leaders don't even know we exist."

Ursula continued to point to various instruments, answering Seth's questions about techniques and instrumentation for a few minutes before Kerri probed a little deeper. "What about the project Lisa Dale was involved in? What can you tell us about that?"

Ursula moved closer to Seth and away from Kerri. Kerri responded by slipping her hand around Seth's arm.

"I'm getting to that," she said. "Mr. Davis indicated you would be interested in that." She pointed to some chairs. "Would you like to sit down?"

They nodded.

Ursula continued, "Mr. Davis has been enthralled with new DNA retrieval and restoration processes I developed while at the N.I.H. With it, DNA can be taken and mapped from samples as small as one cell." She watched them closely, especially Seth, and seemed enraptured by his interest. "Going a step further, if our new cloning techniques are utilized, we can create a clone from DNA from any isolated cell, even if that cell is not an egg or a sperm."

Kerri looked at Seth. She wanted to ask about Lisa. He gave a barely perceptible head shake.

"Which brings us to the Turin Project." She let the name have its desired effect. "Mr. Davis has been fixated on historical relics of religion for a long time. He has financed huge archaeological expeditions seeking to prove—or more accurately, disprove—certain elements of religious history." She waved her hand in the air. "For whatever reason, when the N.I.H. research seemed to validate the shroud of Turin, Mr. Davis made it his final life's goal to examine the cells himself—here in his laboratory. Finally there would be proof of Christ's humanity—indisputable evidence that he was a man and no more."

She rolled her eyes and looked at Seth as he leaned across the table. "Mr. Davis knew a full examination of the historical Jesus would take more than educated guesses based on his genes, and he seemed incensed when new data from Jesus' DNA analysis only caused increased interest in the Christian religion. He became obsessed with showing modern men and women the man they never knew in the flesh—and proving once and for all how silly it would be to put one's faith in him."

Kerri gasped. She couldn't speak. This was hideous!

Seth was amazed. "So Lisa . . . was a surrogate in the—"

"Yes, yes," Ursula interrupted. "Lisa was the second successful surrogate mother carrying a clone of the historical Jesus."

"The second?" Seth was incredulous.

"Yes," she responded bluntly. "But the first miscarried at four weeks, and the embryo was lost when an incubator was set too high." She shook her head. "The DNA was denatured far too much for repair." Her brow furrowed in response to the memory. "Of course, Mr. Davis holds me responsible."

"So Lisa carried a clone of Jesus?"

"This is news to you?" She shook her head.

"Y-yes. I knew she was pregnant, and Schwab told me she was a surrogate, but I had no idea . . ." His voice trailed off.

Kerri finally found her voice. "So this is why those men were after Lisa's baby."

"It was not Lisa's baby! That tissue is very, very valuable, and she agreed to the conditions at the beginning of the experiment. That clone was ours!" she pouted. "It was never our intention to allow this clone to be born. We only wanted enough DNA so we would have a multitude of chances in the future to grow a clone to maturity. And now we've lost the only source of Jesus' DNA in the world."

"Certainly the N.I.H. has more," Seth offered.

"Dr. Schwab has been stricken with a sudden bit of conscience, I'm afraid. After their studies, he personally destroyed every cell he had." She shook her head. "The clone Lisa carried is the only material left that gives us any hope of completing the project."

"She wasn't even told she would be impregnated. She was told you were studying birth control pills!" Kerri charged angrily.

"Who gave you that information? Did Lisa tell—"

"She never had a chance! I talked to another one of your human guinea pigs."

"Who?"

"It doesn't matter." Kerri sat with her eyes fixed boldly on Ursula's.

Ursula showed her first hint of compassion. "I argued with Davis about this—the information we gave to the girls. He insisted on the utmost secrecy. He knew that certain fringe religious groups would be upset by our work and that our research could be revealed only under very controlled conditions." She shook her head with a hint of regret. "He didn't want to risk the surrogates going out and spreading information he couldn't control." She slapped the desktop. "Maybe next time we'll know better." She sighed. "Lisa's lack of knowledge caused us to lose the second clone. If the pregnancy hadn't been such a surprise to her, maybe she wouldn't have run."

Seth shook his head. "Why are you telling us the details of your work here?"

"I am puzzled by that very same question, Dr. Berringer. All I know is that Mr. Davis controls the flow of information about the project, and he specifically told me to share it with you." She shrugged. "I suspect he thinks you already knew or he wouldn't have brought you here."

They sat quietly for a moment, each trying to make sense of the situation. Finally, Ursula spoke. "Mr. Davis has connections, Dr. Berringer. He has been keeping close tabs on all the information surrounding Lisa Dale. Perhaps you have done something that makes him think you know more than you really do."

Seth nodded but kept silent. If Davis's team was responsible for Lisa's death, and Seth had covered for them by altering the death scene and going to the autopsy, Davis must think Seth knew about the clone. Had Davis also had something to do with Donovan's altering the report to hide the existence of the clone?

Seth looked up. "Look, all I really wanted was some proof that Lisa was pregnant—an outline of the research project or a report of the surrogate implantation—anything that will show the authorities back home I've been telling the truth all along."

Ursula nodded with understanding. "I see. Kevin gave me most of your story." She pointed to the exit doors. "All I can do is let you talk to Mr. Davis. As I said, he is personally in control over the flow of information about this project."

She stood. "Come. I'll let you talk to him."

◆ ◆ ◆

Connie Donovan endured a constant stream of visitors and family, a memorial service, and a closed-casket burial ceremony. Finally she found herself alone, but unwilling to rest and unwilling to process the tumultuous relationship that had begun in indiscretion and ended in sudden tragedy. She sat at her husband's desk with a trash can between her legs, discarding the clutter. Scrap paper, sticky-notes, and to-do lists that held meaning just a few days before were trashed along with countless copies of old autopsy reports and forensics magazines.

The loss numbed her, but in reality it only capped a slow process of emotional withdrawal from life, a process that had started when she first suspected Eric's unfaithfulness.

She completely emptied the bottom two drawers of his old rolltop desk before she was interrupted by yet another sympathy-laden phone call.

She hung up the phone, poured herself a glass of wine, and turned on the answering machine.

After a moment she relaxed a little and decided to change from the funeral dress into something less emotionally stifling. She went to the bedroom and selected a pair of sweats, but not before stripping off the black dress and heaving it into a wad in the corner. The small act of defiance somehow invigorated her, and she returned to Eric's old desk with an increased fervor to straighten the disarray that characterized it.

She slowly pulled open the top drawer, allowing its overstuffed contents to cascade onto the floor. Letters, addresses, and copies of old speeches, along with a host of flyers on medical conferences, predominated. Connie pitched each one into the trash with minimal notice.

She briefly considered a flyer highlighting a pathology review seminar in Jamaica. Eric had mentioned this. He thought it might be fun to get away. She looked at the picture of the white sandy beach and palm trees. It could have been a time of healing for them.

She sipped her wine as the phone started to ring. She decided to let the machine get it.

"Hello. You've reached the Donovans' . . ." The voice was Eric's. It was the first time she'd heard his voice since he'd been gone. She was unprepared for the tears that evoked.

". . . Connie and I aren't available right now . . ." She regretted now how she had pulled away from him.

". . . Please leave your name and number after the beep." Connie wiped away a tear and stared into her glass.

"Connie, this is Barb. I didn't get to talk with you at the funeral. Is there anything you need? I talked to Janet, and she said she's bringing dinner tonight, so I'll bring something tomorrow. Call me if you want to talk . . ." Barb's voice weakened, and she sniffed. She continued, her voice barely audible, "I'm so sorry. OK?"

The machine clicked off. Immediately the phone rang again.

"Hello. You've reached the Donovans'. Connie and I aren't available . . ." Connie covered her ears. She didn't want to hear his voice again.

When she finally pulled her hands away, she caught the end of a message.

". . . So if there's anything we can do, please call."

Connie looked at the trash. She hoped there was nothing here the police would want. If Eric really had been involved in something criminal, his correspondence might be important. She decided she'd bag the trash but not discard it. She grabbed some garbage bags from the kitchen and deposited the first one in a corner of the garage.

The phone rang yet again. Connie immediately stuck her fingers in her ear and began humming. Anything to keep from hearing Eric's voice again. The first thing that came to her was the title song from The Sound of Music, which she'd seen a hundred times.

She cautiously removed her fingers to hear the computerized message from a local catalog store. "Your order is in and may be picked up at our Deer Falls outlet."

She turned off the answering machine and impulsively unsnapped the connection to the wall. Now she wouldn't have to hear that message again.

She returned to the top drawer, now almost completely empty. At the very bottom she found a manila file. On the outside tab, a single name had been typed on a sticky label: "Lisa Dale."

Connie's heart quickened as she opened the folder. Gasping, she sorted through the contents. She began to shake.

Oh my! That Dr. Berringer was telling the truth!

◆ ◆ ◆

Ursula ushered Kerri into the library. "You may wait here. Mr. Davis requests a private audience with Dr. Berringer."

Kerri gripped Seth's arm. "Be careful," she whispered.

Ursula pointed at the display cases. "These artifacts from ancient Christianity may be of some interest."

With that, she turned, and held up her hand. "Dr. Berringer, I believe Mr. Davis is waiting."

They walked down another hallway, passing a large dining area, a kitchen, and several closed doors. At the end of the hallway was a massive study. Wilson Davis struggled to his feet and nodded at Ursula. "You may go. Perhaps you will keep the woman company until we are finished."

The scientist nodded and receded into the shadows, closing the door enough to obscure her vision, but not so tightly as to hinder the transmission of sound.

"Have a seat, Dr. Berringer. I trust you had a pleasant tour of my facility?"

Not yet knowing Davis's agenda, Seth wasn't sure how to respond. He mumbled a perfunctory, "Of course."

Davis folded his hands. "First of all, Dr. Berringer, I would like to congratulate you. You have been able to accomplish what my team has failed to do, even with their tremendous head start and full knowledge of the project."

"Sir, I haven't—"

"Don't be modest, doctor. I know you must have had some help," he interrupted. "But you must be congratulated on your ability to recognize and seize the rare opportunity afforded you."

He paused. Seth sat quietly confused.

"How did you come to this knowledge?" He looked at Seth. "I am not angry at *you*. You have acted like most capable men under the circumstances. So before you name your price, at least give me the honor of knowing my betrayer." He sat down in a padded, leather chair opposite Seth. "Who hired you, Dr. Berringer? Dr. Baumgarten perhaps? She would be one of the few capable of such an act."

Seth shifted nervously in his chair.

Ursula jerked her head and bit her tongue. He thought she had betrayed his secret plot! Her anger threatened to erupt.

Davis continued, assuming he had hit upon the truth. "Greed has contaminated her sense of professional pride. The reward of scientific discovery is apparently not enough for her anymore."

Ursula clenched her teeth. He had it all wrong!

"I'm not working for anyone, Mr. Davis."

Davis squinted.

"I am here seeking information to clear my own record. I'm afraid I've only stumbled upon your research in a twist of circumstances that have upset my whole life."

"Your whole life?" He coughed. "You didn't come to ask for money? You don't have the clone?"

Seth shook his head. "I didn't come to sell you anything. I seek only scientific proof of Lisa Dale's pregnancy. Some record perhaps that will help clarify the way in which Lisa really died."

Davis's countenance hardened. "Records of her involvement in my research?" He lifted his eyebrows in suspicion. "Records that would implicate some ethical indiscretion perhaps? Or perhaps reveal a critical lack of informed consent?" He shook his head. "The subjects were naive perhaps, blinded by their reimbursement maybe, but they were not uninformed. The risks were spelled out, Dr. Berringer, as were the true nature of what they were submitting to. Can I help it if they did not read the fine print?" He broke into a forced smile and met Seth's gaze. "If you're seeking a target to bring down with you, doctor, you must seek one you have a remote chance of hitting."

Seth remained undeterred from his original goal. "Please, Mr. Davis, I am not trying to bring scandal to your facility. I am only seeking to undo some of the damage that Dr. Donovan's report has caused my reputation."

"Dr. Donovan's report?" He pointed a jaundiced finger at Seth. "It was you who altered the evidence surrounding her death, not the medical examiner!"

Seth dropped his head and responded slowly, "That was a terrible error on my part—an action I've regretted every hour since."

"But if you did not know of our project, why did you seek to cover up our complication?"

"Complication? Is that what you call Lisa's death, her murder?"

Davis shook his head. "We certainly didn't mean for her to die, doctor, although it certainly isn't your place to demand an explanation from me. Murder? You were the one who altered the evidence. You are the one to answer that question."

"I recognized the girl. I thought I knew who killed her—a patient of mine who had confessed to me his intentions."

Davis erupted in a slow, coughing laugh. "You were worried about your reputation."

Seth nodded. After a moment he raised his eyes to meet the cold stare of Wilson Davis. "Why not come forward, Mr. Davis, if Ms. Dale consented legally to the risks of the procedure? Why not reveal the true cause of her death?"

Ursula pressed her ear to the door. Finally she would get to hear the truth.

"I had planned to do just that," Davis responded slowly, revealing a hint of humanity. "But when you quickly came forward with a solid alibi for me, we waited, wondering what you knew. We took advantage, as anyone would, of the attention being drawn away from the truth. Just as you did, Dr. Berringer. You are no different than I. We both allowed misconceptions to rule in order to protect ourselves."

Seth understood. "Did you force Donovan to change his autopsy record?"

"Force is a strong word." He looked away. "Donovan was a smart man—and very lucky. He alone, as it seems apparent to me now, was capable of discovering what our project was all about. He alone knew the value of the clone."

"Your actions made me look foolish. When I told the sheriff what the true cause of death was, and it clashed with Donovan's report, he—"

"He had you committed, didn't he?" The institute leader smiled. "I have been keeping up on the externals of your story, Dr. Berringer. But now I understand your motivation." He stood and leaned against the back of the tall chair. "You have caused your own downfall, boy." He raised his finger again. "What would make you change your story and confess the truth after such a clever cover-up? Don't you see? You covered for us, and we covered for you by making sure Donovan's report would be consistent with your little scheme. Why did you suddenly change your strategy?"

Seth cringed. Hearing it that way made him feel simple-minded. "I . . . well, I . . . I felt guilty. I needed to tell the truth."

Davis shook his head in wonder. "You are an intelligent man, doctor. And yet this . . . this worthless emotion . . . this guilt you acted upon has cost you dearly." He walked to a window and stared out at an aspen forest. "Evolution gave us the flight or fight response to protect us from natural enemies. Now we are so sophisticated we don't have to protect ourselves from being hunted—and we turn this protective fight response upon our-selves." He looked at Seth, whose eyes were on the floor in front of him. "Certainly you realize the uselessness of such a measure."

Seth sank lower in the leather chair before coming up with an angry defense. "Perhaps you could use a dose of it yourself after the murder of Lisa Dale!"

"You call me a murderer? Perhaps I should call the authorities. I'm sure your sheriff would be glad to have you extradited to stand trial for the mur-der of Dr. Eric Donovan!"

"S-sir, you have it wrong. I—"

"I've seen the newspaper reports. I only agreed to see you because I thought you would stop at nothing to get your own way."

"It's not true! His autopsy proved it. He died naturally. I just found him—"

They looked up as the large door creaked, and Ursula entered. "He's telling the truth, sir." She nodded at Seth. "Kevin Schwab called this morn-ing. It seems he has developed his own private fascination with Dr. Berringer's plight. The newest reports are saying the charges have been dropped, and Donovan's death is no longer being treated as a homicide."

Seth sighed.

Davis raised his hand. "But what about the money, Berringer? I had advanced Donovan a sizable sum just before he died. I assumed that you—"

"I promise, sir—I did not receive any money."

Davis heaved a long sigh. "Take him out. This talk has wearied me. Get the chauffeur to take them away immediately."

"But, sir, the information I have requested—"

"Give him what he needs, Ursula! Why should I care?" He waved his arms. "But only the records of the surrogate implantation—none of the work before that—and nothing about the clone—the clone for which I was willing to pay five million dollars," he muttered, walking slowly to the edge of his desk.

Seth stared at the man's emaciated frame as he picked up a check from the corner of his desk. Davis continued, "That was my final offer for the clone. That is what it is worth to me." He tore the check into pieces and threw them into the air in disgust.

"Now take him away. I can't tolerate any more disappointment today."

CHAPTER
38

SETH read the copies Ursula had made for him as he huddled with Kerri in the passenger compartment of the limousine. Somehow the victory of finally having the proof he'd sought seemed hollow compared to the darkness they'd encountered at the research facility.

Seth sat silently, pondering the guilt he felt after talking with Davis. Maybe the institute chief and Dr. Interman were right. Perhaps guilt was indeed a useless emotion or a useless by-product of evolution.

Kerri felt the darkness too, though she understood what it really was. The research at the institute was darker than she'd imagined. It was not only an attack on Lisa Dale, but on the very core of the Christian faith.

Seth finally spoke up. "I can't believe he was going to give me a check for five million dollars!"

Kerri shuddered. "He's an evil man who will stop at nothing to destroy Christianity."

Seth restrained himself from expressing admiration for the awesome lab facility they'd toured. He studied Kerri's expression. "He really got to you, didn't he?"

She nodded. "What he doesn't realize is that his goal is an impossible one."

Seth's questioning expression prodded her to continue.

"Don't you see? If anything, his research confirms the story of the Gospel—the claim that Jesus was fully God and fully man. Showing us the body of the historical Jesus could never prove he wasn't also God."

She paused, then went on, "If they were able to create my own personal clone, would that be me?" She shook her head. "No. No more than the fact that the real Kerri Barber is not this physical body," she added, pinching her arm. "If you take out my heart, my liver, my spleen—is that me? Can I be defined on a cellular level? Can my identity be found in the organization of my DNA? Do my molecules define Kerri Barber?" She shook her head again. "No. When I die, I'll leave my body, my heart, my cells, even my DNA behind. My spirit will live on in heaven with Christ. My DNA only helps determine what kind of physical tent I dwell in on earth, but it isn't me."

"Why are you so upset with the idea of cloning Jesus?"

"It's not just the cloning. It's everything about the way it was done— covertly, sacrificing a baby just to get more DNA, treating Lisa like a tool, then casting her aside." She sighed. "And, of course, if Davis was successful, there would be a number of people whose Christian faith would perhaps be shaken." She shrugged. "Just as people in Jesus' day stumbled over his humanity, thinking, 'He can't be the Messiah—he's just a carpenter's son.'"

Seth nodded as Kerri continued to think.

Finally she looked up and caught Seth's eye. "There is one thing I think we shouldn't miss."

"What's that?"

"All along you've sought Lisa's baby as proof that you were telling the truth, to clear your record. And all along I've contended that the only solution to the stain we all feel, our tarnished souls, is Christ. Only his blood can cleanse us."

Seth massaged his brow.

"Don't you see? All along you've been seeking Christ, and you didn't even know it." She looked deeply into his eyes, hoping for a glimmer of understanding.

Seth wasn't sure how to respond. In his hand he held evidence that would absolve his stained record. So why didn't he feel relieved?

He looked at Kerri. Was she right? Had he been searching for Jesus all along? "There's so much on my mind. So much has happened to me in three weeks." He shook his head. "Part of me thinks that what you say makes sense. I'd like to believe his blood is powerful enough to do everything you say . . ." His voice trailed off.

"What about the other part, Seth?"

"Part of me says the blood on the shroud is what caused all my misery in the first place. I had a good job, respect, money until someone found that stain."

Kerri winced inside. *Seth! That stain isn't the problem. It represents the only solution!*

Their conversation was interrupted as the limousine pulled to a stop in the Garden of the Gods parking lot.

They exited, thanked the driver, and watched him pull away.

Their eyes followed the receding limo. An aftertaste of the surreal lingered. Where had they been? Would anyone believe what they'd seen?

◆　◆　◆

That Saturday marked three full weeks since Lisa Dale's body had been discovered in Deer Falls. Three weeks Sheriff Boatwright would have rather forgotten.

That noon, being hungry and tired, he sought refuge and fuel at Lanny's. He nodded at the other customers, avoided his usual central table, and slid into a corner booth.

Lanny brought over a tall, iced Coke, Boatwright's drink of choice regardless of the temperature. "What can I get you, sheriff?"

"Give me a Caesar salad. A big one," he added.

Lanny squinted at his long-time customer. "Really?" Was the sheriff feeling OK? A salad for Wayne Boatwright?

Boatwright huffed. "Really. Now go on before I change my mind."

The sheriff quietly sipped his Coke, occasionally making notes on a small pad. There was none of the normal back-slapping or boisterous visiting with other diners that so characterized his usual lunchtime visits. Today the sheriff sat alone with his thoughts and his pen.

Soon Lanny delivered the salad and caught the sheriff's eye. He nodded toward the opposite seat. "Mind if I sit down for a moment, sheriff?"

Boatwright grunted. "Suit yourself."

"You OK? You seem a little down, quiet. This ain't like you."

The lawman shrugged it off. "It's been a tough few weeks on the department," he responded with a sigh.

"Has Dr. Berringer shown up yet?"

The sheriff studied him. Did anything happen in this town that Lanny didn't know about? "No."

"Why'd he run?"

"One of two reasons, Lanny. Either he's really guilty or he feels guilty."

Lanny shook his head. "He used to come in here a fair bit, but not anymore. Not since the hit-and-run."

"That was only what he wanted you to—" The sheriff stopped abruptly, then added, "You haven't seen him since?"

"No. And the last time I saw him was the very night of the girl's death. I remember it like yesterday. The doctor never drinks. I mean never. But that night he had a few, and when I started to ask him about it, he got real put off, told me to stop preachin,' you know?" He lowered his voice and leaned forward. "And you know what he said next? I remember it plain as day. 'I've done some things today I'd rather forget.'"

The sheriff's eyes widened. "He said that? He'd done something he'd rather forget?" That could mean anything, but still . . . "That was on the very night Lisa Dale died?"

"I'm sure of it."

Lanny looked over as two new customers walked in. "I've got to go."

The sheriff mulled it all over in his mind. What really did happen on the day Lisa Dale died? Berringer claimed he found her in a field, but they'd searched there and found nothing. He claimed he left her shoe by the road, but they found it lodged under his vehicle. The autopsy report contradicted Berringer's testimony, the medical examiner who saw Lisa was now dead, and Tammy Gaskins, who typed the report, told a different story altogether. And now Boatwright knew that Berringer confessed to doing things he'd rather forget on the same day Lisa died. Coincidence? The sheriff needed some concrete proof. If only they hadn't cremated her.

◆ ◆ ◆

Kerri spent Friday afternoon and Saturday seeing the sites in and around Colorado Springs with Seth. The hours passed quickly as they hiked around the Garden of the Gods and Seven Falls, visited the quaint tourist shops in Manitou Springs, and ate in local restaurants. Laughter punctuated their conversation, and hand-holding and an occasional stolen kiss both excited and frustrated Kerri. Her emotions seemed to be at the reins of an inexperienced driver who, not knowing whether to brake or accelerate, did both with unbridled enthusiasm.

They talked little about their experience at Davis's facility. The differences in their interpretation were obvious to Kerri. She approached it at a heart level, Seth with head knowledge.

Her enjoyment of being with Seth, their common love of helping people and medicine, and his open and friendly personality provided a strong attraction that Kerri found nearly irresistible. But the closer she came to opening her heart, the brighter the caution light flashed in her mind. She wanted desperately to love him but felt frustrated, knowing she could not give herself to a non-Christian.

She looked into her hotel room mirror. She was preparing for their last dinner together before returning home—a celebration over finding the information Seth had sought so intensely. Expecting to be happy, she felt bewilderment.

I love him. There, I've admitted it again, Lord.

Tears flowed down her cheeks.

She loved everything about him. She thought back to past dates she'd accepted with men of whom she knew her mother would approve. They were all perfectly nice, stable Christians with perfectly average looks, intelligence, and personality—all perfectly suited for a completely boring life!

Seth beat those other men hands down in every category. So could it be wrong to give her love to him? *He's coming closer to you, Lord. But I can't let my love get in the way of that.*

He'd come so far. But he couldn't lead her or walk beside her spiritually, she reminded herself. Not yet.

"You've gone too far, Kerri," she whispered to the reflection in the mirror. "You've already given him your heart. He's seen it in the way you look at him, and you've seen it in the way he looks at you—at me. He wants me. He loves me."

She finished getting ready just as she heard a gentle knock on the door.

She whispered a prayer. "Help me, Lord. I want to do what's right."

◆　◆　◆

Sonny Gaskins unloaded the packages he'd picked up at the post office, four of them, all addressed to Tammy Lynn, all arriving within a few days after her death.

He sighed as he looked at the return addresses. All from the home shopping channel. Tammy Lynn liked to spend money when she was depressed. He set the boxes aside. He'd have to mail them back. He hoped she hadn't ordered much more.

He sorted through her mail and set out two large boxes for her clothes. Tammy Lynn had been so confused, not knowing what she wanted.

Sonny packed her clothing and set the boxes aside. On the bed he had laid out her finest Sunday dress. The mortician had requested it for the viewing the following afternoon. He remembered when she wore that dress—when they visited a community church in Gleason.

He wiped a tear from the corner of his eye. He never thought she'd leave him. He knew she wasn't happy, but he didn't know how to help her. He thought letting her go would be the right thing. That's what her counselor had told her too. He shouldn't have let her leave.

Now he'd lost her forever.

◆ ◆ ◆

Over dinner, Seth talked excitedly about finally having evidence that would vindicate him and about formulating a plan to reenter the field of medicine. He was optimistic about the sheriff's response, but not overly so. Past experience dictated that he proceed with caution.

They talked about the people they knew at the hospital, about the stigma of doctor-nurse dating relationships, and about the fact that Seth hadn't been seen with any other nurses previously.

"I was waiting for you," he responded with a smile.

"You should hear the nurses in the E.R. You could have your pick."

He searched her eyes, wanting to see the meaning of her statement. He ventured forward. "I hope I have my pick." He studied her a moment. "I've never met anyone like you." He looked into her eyes, longing for affirmation that she felt the same.

Instead, he sensed only fear and saw only tears.

Had he gone too far? "Kerri, I love you."

She stared into his eyes. "Seth," was all she could say. She placed her hand against his receptive palm.

Later they took a slow walk in a small, deserted park. Seth leaned against a tall tree and put his arms around her. The night was clear and cold, and their frosty breath mingled between their faces. For a moment they did not speak. Seth explored the eyes that were locked with his. When he spoke, he didn't let his gaze waver. "I had a dream the other night," he started softly. "You and I together on a lovely beach. When you looked at me, your eyes were like they are now—soft, and deep, communicating how you feel without words."

Kerri bit her lip to keep it from quivering.

Seth continued, "In my dream I couldn't believe you could love me, and I was afraid to say, 'I love you.'"

He yearned to hear those three words that would bring rapture to his captive soul.

"I've never held someone like you," she responded softly as she encircled his waist with her arms. "I've never wanted to hold someone so badly. But . . ." Her voice trailed.

Seth's heart sank. "You can't say, 'I love you.'"

"Seth," she pleaded, "understand when I say I've never wanted to say it more, but—"

"What is it, Kerri?"

"It wouldn't be fair to you."

Seth shook his head. "Fair to me?" His eyes widened. "If you want to say it, then say it." His voice was soft but intense, with a slight tremor. "There's nothing I want to hear more."

"Oh, Seth . . ." She buried her face in his coat and began to cry.

He didn't understand but kept his arms around her, holding her, gently supporting her.

"You know I love you. You've said it yourself. You've seen it in my eyes," she sobbed, lifting her eyes to meet his again. "But I didn't plan to love you—not at first. I just wanted to support your search for the truth. I wanted to help you, not fall in love with you." She forced back a tear. "I can't expect you to understand, Seth, but I can't let my heart rule over me. I can't love you now. I . . . just . . . can't."

He watched her for a moment until her breathing was regular. "This is about your Christianity, isn't it?"

She looked at him, searching for a way to make him understand. She felt him retreat emotionally.

His expression became childlike. "If I—if I believed like you do, then would you give yourself to me?"

She shook her head. "I could never make my love a promise to entice you to believe in Jesus the way I do. I want you to come to him because you need him, not to make it possible for us to be together."

"Kerri, I would never make the kind of commitment you have just to please you." He shook his head. "Understand what I say. I do want you to accept me." He caught her eye again. "I've never wanted someone to want me so much. But I could never make myself believe the Christian faith just to please another person, not even you."

"I love you, Seth. That's why I need to set you free. You have to make an objective choice—without conditions." Seth kissed her softly as she began to cry again.

She offered him a salty kiss and placed her hand against his face.

They turned and walked to the car, maintaining a walking hug as they moved forward slowly in the crisp moonlight.

The silent walk, rich with communion, was broken only by their footfalls on the sidewalk. Seth's heart beat uncertainly with a growing ominous alarm. He sensed it might be the last time he would ever hold her.

◆ ◆ ◆

Wilson Davis knew full well what his giving the information to Seth would mean. Suspicion and guilt would be cast directly at his harvest team. The project was in severe jeopardy, but not yet lost. He still hoped to locate the clone. Donovan had reported that he had it shortly before he died. Davis wasn't about to give up.

He tapped his fingers on his desk. If Donovan died of natural causes, what had happened to the pay-off? He'd hoped Berringer would reveal the location of the missing specimen, but now Davis was no better off than before. In fact, the situation was worse because Berringer now knew the real reason Lisa Dale had died. Why had he let Berringer get away? He'd responded with his emotions, not his reason. Berringer had to be stopped!

He thought about Kerri too. They both had to be silenced. Davis could not allow the content of his research to go public before he presented the real Jesus people had been idealizing for so long.

Lisa's death was a mistake, but who would believe that if they knew the institute's true research objectives?

He picked up the phone and dialed Dr. Jerry Ling.

After two rings, Doc picked up his cellular receiver. "Hello."

"Doc, Wilson Davis here. I have bad news. Berringer knows the truth—he knows how Lisa died. He can get us in a lot of trouble."

"He knows about me and Bill?"

"Yes," Davis lied. "I'm afraid so."

"What about the clone? Did he have the clone?"

"No. He's a loose cannon. He only stumbled across the research. But he and his girlfriend know everything."

"Loose cannons can cause a lot of trouble."

"Definitely."

"What should we do?"

Davis wanted the message to be clear without spelling it out. "He's going to talk—I know he will." He paused. "I know you didn't mean for Lisa to die. But . . . well, it looks pretty bad for us, Doc."

"I know this project is important. I know what to do, Mr. Davis."

"They told me they were going back home tomorrow."

"We'll meet them at the airport—a regular welcoming committee."

Davis cringed. He didn't like doing this, but he had to protect the project. "Do what you have to do. I'll see you get generous compensation."

"Sure, Mr. Davis. You won't have to worry about Dr. Berringer or his girlfriend again."

CHAPTER
39

THAT night Connie Donovan's rest was fitful. Dreams of Eric while she slept and memories while she stared at the ceiling pushed the needed slumber away. She couldn't sleep in that bed—their bed.

She reached to the other side of the mattress. He was gone, and she couldn't get him out of her mind.

Finally she headed to the guest room, hoping to escape her husband's memories that haunted her.

Closing her eyes, she fought other recurring images that stole her sleep. A body lying on an autopsy table. A pelvis, badly misshapen and crushed. A dark street with a reflective purple jacket. An organ, purple-red like a grape, cut in half and lying open on a blue towel. Another image flashed in her mind. What was it? She'd seen it before. It was a fetus!

Connie let out a loud sigh. She looked at the clock. Four A.M. She tossed back the sheets. She might as well get up.

She walked to the kitchen and started a pot of coffee. She sat at the table with yesterday's unread paper and tried to concentrate enough to read. Her thoughts, however, were drawn to the manila file she'd found in Eric's desk.

Should she show it to the sheriff? That suggestion made her uncomfortable. Didn't she owe it to her husband to preserve his reputation?

Besides, who would benefit by seeing the document now? Dr. Berringer? No. The sheriff's case against him had been abandoned. Lisa? No. And she had no family. Connie decided she might as well let it rest. It was all history now.

She nodded her head and tried to read. But Lisa's file was never far from her mind.

◆ ◆ ◆

Later that morning, Kerri and Seth boarded a plane for Pittsburgh. Although their conversation was friendly and Kerri still held his hand, Seth could sense she was pulling away. Even the brief kiss she offered him at breakfast was different, void of the previous desire.

Armed with the papers Ursula had given him, clearly indicating Lisa Dale's involvement in the research, Seth felt neither relief or victory. Sure, he was about to win a battle, but had he really found what he'd been searching for?

He looked over at Kerri. Her eyes were closed, her face a picture of tranquillity. Seth heard her voice in his mind: "Seth Berringer, you're always on a quest for evidence, aren't you?"

That was the way he'd been taught! It was his whole approach to science, to medicine—to life. He pulled a magazine out of the seat-back in front of him, but his thoughts refused to be silenced. "There are some things you can't prove," Kerri had said. "Some things you have to take on faith."

Was that what he was missing? Was that what he'd been looking for?

"All along you've been seeking Christ, and you didn't even know it."

Seth stared out the window at the clouds below. He wanted to stop the turmoil in his mind.

He haphazardly thumbed through the magazine. Why so many photos of couples? Couples eating dinner. A man and woman walking hand in hand on a sandy beach. A man holding the woman he loved, enjoying her perfume. Another making his wife cry with an anniversary diamond.

He closed the magazine and stole a look at Kerri again before pushing his seat into a slight recline. He tried to relax but couldn't. He was beginning to understand that his heart didn't want to go on without Kerri.

He pinched his eyelids together to shut out the sunlight, but he couldn't stop hearing Kerri's words.

"All along you've been seeking Christ, and you didn't even know it."

Seth sighed. He didn't want to go on without her God either, and yet . . .

◆ ◆ ◆

Sunday morning wasn't a rest time for Sheriff Wayne Boatwright. It wasn't a morning for political church appearances either. The only way he'd salvage his image in Chesapeake County was to do his job to the best of his ability. He needed to put a cork on the Lisa Dale case, preferably before the voters had a chance to determine his fate.

He looked across the conference table at the few men he'd assembled. "Let's see if we can make any sense of the facts at hand."

"We know the doctor lied to us about the shoe," Zander reported.

"And we suspect, by his own testimony, that Lisa may have been dead before the hit-and-run occurred," the sheriff responded.

"A fact that is supported by Ms. Gaskins's most recent deposition," Detective Trainum added.

"Add to that the findings on Berringer's van," Zander responded. "The front of his van is surprisingly undamaged. It would have been a mess after a frontal pedestrian impact."

"And we have the report from the psychiatrist saying that Berringer is off the scale with hostility and guilt." Boatwright tapped the table with a pencil.

"It all points to a cover-up. The evidence has been altered to disguise the real way she died," Trainum concluded.

"We still have the problem of the conflicting data in Donovan's medical examiner's report, which still stands as a legal document. And with Donovan and his secretary dead, we have no one to refute it—except Berringer," the sheriff replied slowly. "What we need is some hard evidence to support the truth or falsity of the autopsy."

"If the hit-and-run is a cover-up, what would motivate Berringer to do such a thing?" the deputy questioned.

Trainum looked up. "Guilt?"

The sheriff nodded. "Exactly." He stood and began to pace. Methodically he recounted the story Lanny had told him about Berringer's comment on the day of Lisa's death.

Trainum fidgeted. "Sounds like a confession to me."

The sheriff nodded. "Berringer sure has been an albatross around this department's neck. I have him committed, and the psychiatrist lets him out. Then Donovan is found dead, and Berringer's fingerprints are found at the scene. He may not have killed Donovan, but he's surely guilty of *something*." He shook his head. "Then Ms. Gaskins is so afraid of him that we offer her protection and end up lookin' silly when she commits suicide right under our nose. Yeah, Berringer's guilty all right. Why else would he disappear right when things are heatin' up?" He clenched both fists. "He's a loose cannon—one I'm really going to enjoy nailin' to the wall."

Zander looked at the sheriff curiously. He again wondered why his boss was taking this so personally. He was the one who went after the arrest warrant before they had the autopsy results. He was the one who made the department look silly, not Berringer. It wasn't Berringer's fault that Tammy Gaskins's death made them look bad.

Zander decided to raise another issue. "What about this Guessford fellow? He has a criminal record, and his prints were found at the Inn—in the very room where Lisa Dale spent her last night—and at the medical examiner's lab, on his phone. That has to mean something!"

The sheriff pulled a picture from a file folder—a faxed photograph of William Guessford. "It's the same guy I saw at the Inn, all right." He accelerated his pacing. "I just wish the Barber girl would show up again. I'd like to know if she got a good enough look at the men at Berringer's residence to see if she could positively identify Guessford."

He walked back to the folder and retrieved a second image, this one a composite photograph drawn by a police artist, taken directly from the description the sheriff had provided. "This is the artist's rendition of the second fellow I saw at the Inn that night."

"Could this be that Yamatsu fellow Ms. Donovan and Ms. Gaskins told us about?"

The sheriff nodded. "Possibly. But that's probably an alias. And the link between Yamatsu, Guessford, and Berringer remains a mystery." The sheriff pointed at the drawing. "Keep an eye out for these two. Circulate their pictures to all the staff. Something's bound to turn up."

Trainum spoke up. "Regardless of the role of these two, I'd say the case is tightening against Berringer, especially with Lanny's testimony. It sure looks like he was covering for something."

"I want to do it right this time, boys. This time I want to wait until I'm sure. No more arrests 'til then."

"Todd located Berringer's van at the airport, just where Angie Blackstock said it would be," Zander pointed out.

"Why don't you spend some time out there today, Rick? If Berringer shows up, maybe you can talk to him, lean on him a little. Sooner or later he's going to crack. One of these days all of this is going to make sense."

Zander smiled. He liked airport duty. The people were interesting, and the new restaurant had decent food. "Won't the doctor like that? A welcoming committee."

◆ ◆ ◆

Once they were back in Pittsburgh, Seth and Kerri stood in a line to purchase a ticket to get back to Chesapeake County.

Kerri held back as the line moved forward. "Seth? I've been thinking. I don't want to go back to Deer Falls—not just yet."

"Where will you go?" He squinted. "What about your job?"

"I'm not worried about that. There's always someone looking for extra shifts." She avoided his gaze, not looking forward to being apart from him. "I—I think I'll visit my parents for a few days. Maybe even go to the coast. I need some time to think."

Seth nodded. He was right—she was pulling back. He'd lost her.

The line moved forward, and an impatient man behind Kerri cleared his throat. Seth edged ahead. "OK. I understand, I think." Kerri stood with him in line until he purchased his ticket.

The woman behind the counter pointed to her right. "Your flight leaves in twenty minutes."

They nodded and walked away.

"I'll stay with you until your flight leaves," Kerri offered softly. "Then I'll call my folks—make some plans."

He looked at her, memorizing her face, longing to caress her delicate and perfect smile. He wondered if he'd ever touch her or hold her again like he had this weekend.

She wondered what he was thinking. He looked distressed. "Seth," she offered, "I'll be OK."

They found a seat at Seth's gate and waited. The boarding announcement came ten minutes later.

They stood and gazed into each other's eyes. Kerri didn't want to cry but couldn't keep the tears from beginning again. "Bye, Seth." She encircled him with her arms.

He squeezed her hard, not wanting to be away from her, not wanting her to leave him alone again.

"You'd better go, Seth. Your flight . . ."

He nodded. He thought ahead to his meeting with the sheriff. "Pray for me."

"Always."

Seth hesitantly crossed the distance to the airplane through the cold air. On the steps to the plane, a dread seized him, and he turned to see Kerri one more time. He lifted himself on his toes and caught a glimpse of her timid smile, the one he'd seen the first time she approached him just a few weeks before.

He entered the plane and found his seat. He felt like he'd known her all his life.

◆ ◆ ◆

Jamie Edwards drove for the Blue Cab Company every Sunday. With his mother's hospital bills piling up, the extra money gave him a chance to help her financially.

He received a call to pick up an elderly resident at the Quiet Haven Home for Adults. It wasn't an unusual call, but it did involve a wheelchair transport, so it would mean some extra work, and hopefully a hefty tip.

He pulled up to the front of the home, a large southern-style house with a broad porch. The temperature was cold, so he left the car, and the meter, running. Why not? He was already putting in time as he went in to wheel Ms. Strickland out to the cab.

He looked at the front porch. He was glad to see they'd outfitted the place with ramps. That would make it easier to get her outside.

He opened the door and approached a desk in the foyer. A pleasant young lady in a pink smock looked up.

Jamie looked at the card in his hand. "I'm here to pick up Ms. Strickland."

"Hmmm," the woman responded, standing. "I think she's in her room." She shook her head. "That's peculiar—she always has me call for rides if she needs them."

"You didn't call?"

"Nope. Maybe old Frannie is asserting her independence again," she laughed. "I'll get her."

She disappeared down the hall. In less than a minute she was back, shaking her head. "Are you sure you have the right name? Frannie doesn't want a ride anywhere."

"Frannie? Frannie Strickland?"

"She's the only Strickland we have here." She threw up her hands. "Sorry."

Jamie rechecked the small card. "Well, don't that beat all." He smiled at the young woman. "Maybe she just forgot." He turned to go.

Once he was back out front, he looked down the wheelchair ramp to the empty street. Where was his cab?

◆ ◆ ◆

The blue taxi pulled into the shopping center parking lot beside a shiny BMW. Bill hopped out and smiled. "It was easy. He left it running, so I didn't even have to hot-wire it."

Doc popped the trunk of the BMW as Bill did the same to the blue cab. "Help me with this junk, would you?" Doc snapped before walking around to the driver's seat of the taxi.

Bill grunted. He grabbed a leather bag full of instruments and heaved them into the taxi. Only a plastic bag of discarded trash remained in the BMW. He chuckled, tossed it into the taxi, and slammed the trunk lid.

Bill slid into the passenger seat as Doc tapped a nervous tune on the steering wheel. "This was a stroke of genius." Doc winked at his associate. "Are you sure the van's taken care of?"

Bill nodded. "It'll never start."

"Good. What about my instruments?"

"Taken care of. Everything's in the trunk."

"Good. Let's get to the airport."

◆ ◆ ◆

Seth's flight was uneventful. In an hour he was in Chesapeake County again. It was time to make a new start, and Seth knew just how to begin— by visiting Sheriff Wayne Boatwright.

Rick Zander didn't notice Seth until he was out of the terminal and across the parking lot beside his van. The deputy pushed away the last of his cheese-steak sub and squinted toward the lot. Seth's maroon van was easily visible, sitting alone in the far corner. Berringer wasn't wasting any time getting on his way.

Seth hopped in the van and threw his bag on the floor. He put the key in the ignition and turned it. Nothing. He tried again. He banged the steering wheel impatiently. Perhaps the cold was too much for the old engine. He tried again.

Seth looked up and saw the deputy. He was definitely walking toward Seth since no one else was around. He shook his head and sighed. Great! He probably wanted to harass Berringer again.

Seth looked up just as a blue taxi approached. The window was down. "Need some help?"

Seth jumped at the opportunity and opened the back door. As he got in, he could hear the deputy shouting behind him, "Dr. Berringer!"

He hesitated, then pretended he didn't hear, and quickly slid in and shut the door. He looked up as Bill Guessford pointed a gun in his face. "Welcome aboard, doctor."

Doc punched the accelerator, and the tires squealed as the cab raced away.

"What're you doing?" Bill screamed. "Didn't you see that cop?"

Behind them, Zander sprinted for his car. Within seconds his lights were flashing as he took up the pursuit.

Seth pressed himself against the backseat and stared at the gun. He couldn't think, couldn't move.

Doc cursed and began braking. He turned on his blinker.

"What're you doing?"

"It's no use. I can't outrun him in this old wreck."

Guessford cocked the handgun. "Nothing funny from you, doctor. Stay quiet, you hear?" He held the gun in his left hand, with his arm draped over the back of the seat, so he could keep the gun low enough to be hidden from easy view but steadily aimed at Seth.

Seth turned his head in time to see Zander park his car on the shoulder behind the blue cab. He turned around as the deputy approached. As Doc began to roll down his window, Seth kept his eyes trained on Guessford and the gun.

When Guessford momentarily looked at the deputy, Seth grabbed Bill's wrist just above the handgun, forcing it toward the side of the vehicle. He screamed, "Zander!" just before the gun fired.

The noise inside the car was deafening. The bullet blasted through the left rear window and in and out of Rick Zander's right thigh.

Zander stumbled forward as Doc nailed the accelerator again, sending a stream of gravel from the soft shoulder

Instantly, the deputy drew his weapon, rolled into the street, and leveled his gun at the rapidly retreating vehicle. He fired once, then twice. The second bullet found its mark.

A trickle of blood appeared from behind Doc's left ear, and he slumped forward with his foot fully depressed against the accelerator. Seth held fast to Bill's wrist as he dropped the handgun in a desperate attempt to grab the steering wheel.

The car careened off the road and impacted the concrete base of a tall streetlight.

Bill Guessford's body ejected through the windshield into a free flight slowed only by the impact of his head against the pole.

Seth lunged forward against the backseat, crushing his right rib cage before coming to rest with his right leg draped over the seat at a sickening angle.

Doc's body rested motionless, pinned against the steering wheel.

Seth assessed the situation. He was conscious but finding it extremely difficult to get his breath. The terror of oxygen deprivation quickly gripped him.

All was silent around him. He opened his eyes and tried to focus but couldn't. Why was everything so dark?

He remembered his patient's words: "I'm ready to die, Dr. Berringer. When I die, I'll see the Savior."

He gasped for air, unable to call for help.

"I'm not ready to die! I need to know the Savior."

After that, Seth knew only darkness.

◆ ◆ ◆

In the next twenty minutes, in response to Zander's distress calls, the accident scene hosted a flurry of activity. Two additional Chesapeake County patrol cars, including the sheriff's, two ground rescue units, and the air evacuation university helicopter arrived with sufficient personnel to quell a small natural disaster.

As they loaded a comatose William Guessford into the helicopter, Steve Lambert and his paramedic staff gathered around Seth Berringer.

Boatwright cursed. "Hey! I've got a deputy down over here! You should treat my deputy before you help him!" He pointed at Berringer's still form.

Steve gave him a condescending glance. "It's triage, sir. This victim's life is in the balance."

"Victim?" Boatwright roared. "He shot my deputy!"

Zander lay quietly on a blanket provided by the second rescue unit. "It's OK, sheriff. It's only a flesh wound."

Steve Lambert continued his primary survey on Berringer. Seth was comatose, with shallow, ineffective respiration. While a second paramedic, Sue Gentry, established two large bore IV lines, Steve inserted an endotracheal tube to assist the ventilations.

"Pressure's way down. I can't hear it with my scope," Sue responded.

"Let's open up the fluids." Steve cut off Seth's shirt and felt along his right chest. He listened with his stethoscope. "No movement over here." He quickly retrieved a large needle from the supply case. He prepped a small area of Seth's chest with alcohol and inserted the needle inward, over the third rib. A rush of air followed.

Sue looked on. "Good job. Let's get him over to Chesapeake General so they can put a real tube in."

They quickly loaded him into the back of the rescue squad van and, much to the consternation of the sheriff, left in front of the unit that would transport Deputy Zander to the same facility.

In the E.R. after a chest tube had been secured, Seth's oxygen intake began marginal improvement. He drifted into consciousness, aware only of a surreal atmosphere surrounding him. Occasionally he recognized a voice or could hear partial comments, as if he were listening through a long tunnel. His vision was clouded because of blood in his eyes. The room was spinning, allowing Seth to discern only snatches of the action that constituted the fight to save his life.

He could hear a woman's voice, perhaps belonging to a nurse. "It's Dr. Berringer!"

Seth thought he recognized the voice of a paramedic as well. Steve? "They said he shot a policeman."

He faded back into a sea of confusion.

"There's too much blood in the chest tube drainage bag."

"He's bleeding from the lung."

"I can't get a blood pressure!"

Seth drifted in and out.

"More fluids. Wide open. Now!"

A doctor's voice. "He's starting to respond. Look at the EKG."

"Get rid of these clothes." A female voice. Cold scissors against his skin.

Seth was vaguely aware of his shirt and pants being cut from his body. *The papers—the evidence about the baby—in my shirt pocket!* Seth tried to raise his hand in protest, but the restraints held firm.

He started to fade again.

"Look at this leg! Let's get X-ray in here. Julie, have you sent the trauma labs?"

"His pressure's down!"

"Uncrossmatched blood."

Seth heard the words through the fog.

"Only blood can save him now. Only blood can save him."

He wanted to cry out. O *Jesus* . . . !

"Open up the crash cart. It looks like he's going to code!"

CHAPTER
40

K ERRI sighed and looked out of the plane's windows. Deb had agreed to take her E.R. shifts, and her parents were thrilled to have her coming home for a while. Staring at the clouds, she wondered why, since everything was working out, she felt so alone.

She dabbed the corner of her eye as her thoughts turned once again to Seth. *I did the right thing, Father. I told him it's over. I was obedient, wasn't I?* She choked back a sob. *So where's the joy of Christian obedience? Why do I feel so lonely?*

She opened a magazine, but every page reminded her of Seth. She saw his smile in a photo promoting a cellular phone giveaway. Her finger traced an advertisement of the Caribbean that brought back Seth's dream about the two of them walking on the beach. A men's clothing ad featured pants like the ones he often wore. She turned the page only to see an ad for a perfume she frequently wore that Seth had complimented.

Kerri shut the magazine in frustration. She opened her carry-on and slipped out her well-worn Bible. She didn't care where she read—just so it got her mind off Seth. She let the book fall open to the Old Testament. To Genesis. The beginning. A new start—that's what she needed.

She opened to the fifth chapter and began to read: "This is the written account of Adam's line. When God created man, he made him in the likeness of God."

That's how it had all started, before man messed everything up with sin. Adam, made in the image of God, had an open pathway of communication with his Father.

Kerri smiled. She read further and noticed that a different phrase marked the description of man after the fall in the garden. "When Adam had lived 130 years, he had a son in his own likeness, in his own image."

After sin entered the picture, she reflected, Adam's son was created in Adam's likeness. No longer perfectly in the image of God, man was now separated from the Creator, without the open path of communication Adam had earlier.

The next phrase came like a cannon shot: "And he named him Seth."

She blinked and stared at the page. She remembered reading about Cain and Abel, but . . . Seth?

Kerri looked at the verse again before shutting the Bible. She was seeing Seth everywhere! In the magazine—and now even in the Bible!

After she stared forward for a minute, another inspiration dawned. *Seth represents all of us—fallen man—separated from God—searching for the truth— the evidence that will wipe the slate and clear our records. But so often we search for you, Lord, without even realizing what we're searching for.*

She slipped her Bible back into her carry-on bag. She shook her head. Seth, son of Adam, created in his likeness. Why hadn't she ever seen that before?

◆ ◆ ◆

The next morning Angie Blackstock stood next to Seth's intensive care unit bed. Her father had heard the news about the shooting and accident and told Angie.

She was relieved to learn that Kerri was not with him in the car but was frustrated to no end at not knowing where her friend was or how to contact her.

She looked at Seth's chest, rising and falling rhythmically with the mechanical ventilator. A nurse adjusted an IV rate. She touched Angie's arm. "Is he family?"

Angie shook her head. "No. A friend." She paused. "Is he responding to treatment?"

"Not much. But we have him heavily sedated. Last night he wanted to fight the ventilator, and he wasn't getting enough oxygen, so Dr. Overby prescribed some medicine to keep his breathing under better control."

She looked at the myriad of tubing and wires connected to various monitors and collection chambers. She closed her eyes. "How's—how's his head—his brain?"

"It's hard to say, given the level of sedation we're using. He had a head CT last night before surgery, which was OK."

"Surgery?"

"The surgeons put a rod in his right femur." She lifted the sheet to reveal a bandage. "He had a pretty bad break."

"Oh."

She thought about Kerri and how much she cared about Seth. Kerri would want to be here.

Angie squeezed his hand.

No response.

She leaned forward and whispered in his ear. "Seth?"

She raised her voice a little, just in case somehow he could comprehend her. "Seth? I'm Angie Blackstock, a friend of Kerri's. You have to get better." She pulled back. She felt stupid. He couldn't hear her. Besides, what a thing to say to a person in a coma, as if he has any control over getting better! But what should she tell him?

"I'm praying for you." Angie looked at her watch. She wished she knew where Kerri was!

◆ ◆ ◆

Late Monday afternoon, more than a full day since the accident, activity at the sheriff's department continued at a feverish pace. The taxi, by this time identified as the one Jamie Edwards had reported missing, had been thoroughly combed for evidence.

Boatwright looked up just as Rick Zander entered, with Todd Pheiffer holding the door. Zander maneuvered his way across the room using a pair of crutches.

"I thought I told you to take a few days off."

"I am off. I'm just hanging around," he said with a smile. "You know I can't stay away from you guys." He looked at Boatwright and faked a cry. "I love you, man."

"Spare me, Zander."

Trainum walked in just then. "Hi, Rick. You OK?"

Rick propped his leg on the table. "Really, it's nothing. The E.R. doc just told me to keep my weight off it for a few days."

"Good. Well, you're just in time for the evidence news," Trainum began. "The gun, found in the backseat next to Berringer, has only one set of prints—belonging to none other than . . ."

"Doctor Seth—" the sheriff guessed.

"Don't interrupt. To William Guessford."

Boatwright snapped his fingers. Obviously he'd been hoping to nail Berringer.

"And get this," Trainum added, "they searched the bag of trash in the back of the trunk and found two pairs of bloody surgical gloves. The guys from the lab gave me a preliminary on the blood match. They are 99 percent sure the blood is Eric Donovan's."

Boatwright's jaw dropped.

"We had the evidence techs carefully invert the rubber gloves and lift a print from the inside, and bingo—William Guessford again."

"So now we have a Guessford print at the scene of Donovan's death and a glove Guessford wore that has Donovan's blood on it." The sheriff shook his head. "Very interesting. You said two pairs of gloves. Did both pairs have Guessford's prints?"

"No. The other pair is being examined. They have a good print but no immediate match. We'll check them against the driver."

"Any I.D. on him yet?" Zander questioned.

"His Colorado driver's license says Jerry Ling. It appears to be valid."

"Did you find anything else in the car?" Boatwright eyed the detective.

"Just a leather bag of surgical instruments. Fingerprint analysis isn't complete, but we ran them quickly against Guessford and came up negative. I'd guess we'd better check those against the dead guy too."

"Good work, Trainum." Boatwright stiffened. "Now all we need to figure out is what Berringer had to do with these two guys and why he'd hop in a taxi and run from the law the way he did."

Trainum thought back to his conversation with the sheriff just after he'd interviewed Tammy Lynn Gaskins. "Do you suppose this guy Ling could be using a false name? Maybe he's Yamatsu. Perhaps Tammy Gaskins was right, and Berringer and Yamatsu were working together to cover up the murder of Lisa Dale."

The sheriff nodded slowly. "There's a good chance of that, Dave. And now only Berringer is alive to reveal the truth."

Zander looked up. "Only Berringer?"

Boatwright nodded again. "Guessford died this morning."

Trainum responded solemnly, "Only Berringer, huh? After all the trouble he's caused around here, let's hope he survives to get his due."

"If he lives," Boatwright joined in, "I'll make sure he receives what's comin' to him."

◆　◆　◆

Whenever Kerri came home, she'd spend some time at her father's general store, helping out wherever needed, just like when she lived at home before college. She would walk the aisles, straightening, sorting, commenting on new products, or just asking her father about the business. In warmer seasons, she'd sit on the front porch and talk to the customers or play checkers on an old wooden barrel-top. For Kerri, this was a good escape. She came here to renew, to mend. Whenever she felt wounded by the world, this is where she came.

This visit was no different, and her father, Grant Barber, knew she would tell him the reason for her unexpected visit when she was ready.

Finally, during an afternoon lull, with the store empty, Grant looked over at his daughter as she stared out the front windows. "You look just like your mother when you do that. You know, when you raise the corner of your mouth like that. Your mother does the same thing when she's thinkin' real hard."

Kerri touched her mouth. "I didn't realize I was doing anything." She looked back at him. "Daddy?" She stopped.

"What is it, Kerri?"

She sighed. "Momma's so lucky to have you."

He smiled and sat down on a tall stool behind the counter. "When are you going to tell me why you're here? Is it a man? Your faith? Your mother is dyin' of suspense, honey."

"Oh, Daddy, it's both!"

"Both?"

"A man *and* my faith." She suddenly felt self-conscious. She lifted her fingers to her mouth. "Am I doing it again?"

Her father nodded.

She smiled this time. "I met a man, Daddy—a doctor. He's so loving and gentle, so giving to others, so intelligent, so handsome."

"Does he love you?"

She nodded.

"And do you love him?"

She nodded again. "But, Daddy, he's not a Christian. Not yet anyway."
Grant folded his hands. "I see."

"I didn't mean to fall for him. I just wanted to help him along. I talk to
him about the Lord all the time." Her eyes fell to the floor. "He's so open
with me—so vulnerable. It's like there are no masks with Seth." She
paused. "Seth. That's his name."

"And this Seth—does he know how you feel?"

"I think so," she replied with a nod. "Unless I've completely confused
him by telling him we can't be together."

"You wanted to help him, you reached out to him, and now you find
that your heart is involved."

"Yes."

Her father sighed. "You say he's vulnerable." He weighed what to say.
"Kerri, all your life you've been reaching out to people in trouble. Their
troubles become yours, their hurts your hurts. It's a trait that makes your
mother and me plenty proud. You are very special, Kerri." He caught her
eye. "Are you sure you aren't just tryin' to rescue him? Is he another lost
puppy you want to give a home?"

"I don't think so, Daddy. I thought about it for a long time. I knew I
had to tell him it was over." Her eyes teared, and her voice quivered as she
added, "It was the hardest thing I've ever done."

Grant stood and gathered his daughter into his arms. When she'd cried
for a minute, he let her go, but not before kissing her forehead. "You did the
right thing, honey. But the right thing isn't always easy."

She bit her lip and nodded.

"Your mother and I will pray for Seth. Perhaps the things you've shared
will bear fruit."

She wiped her cheeks. "Thanks, Daddy."

"Now, do me a favor and talk to your mother. She'll want all the details
about your special friend."

◆ ◆ ◆

John Overby, M.D, stood next to Seth's bed and assessed the bedside
chart. "If we have to go any higher on the PEEP, I'm going to have to float
a swan." He used the medical lingo common to the I.C.U. to indicate the
need to monitor the pressures around the heart in case higher base pressures
were necessary to properly ventilate the patient.

The nurse nodded.

"How's his H and H?"

"Hemoglobin 10, hematocrit 30."

"Good," he grunted. "Has his urine picked up?"

"Sixty in the last two hours."

Overby nodded. "Any more from the chest tube?"

"Minimal." She pointed to the collecting chamber. "Only what you see above the mark I made." She handed him the chest X-ray report.

"Good." He leaned forward and talked to Seth, even though he was unmoving because of the sedation. "You're in the I.C.U., Seth. This is John Overby. You were in an accident. Everything is stable right now. You're on the ventilator because of a pulmonary contusion. We were having trouble with your oxygenation. Tomorrow morning I'll have the anesthesiologist put in an epidural catheter to give you better pain relief. That way we can try going without the ventilator."

He looked up at the nurse and smiled. "It's not often that I can talk like this to a patient without stopping to explain."

CHAPTER
41

ON TUESDAY the sheriff paid an early-morning visit to Connie Donovan, out of legitimate concern for her welfare but also with the desire to see how she would answer more of his questions.

It was before 8 A.M., but Connie was up and expecting the sheriff, who had called ahead.

When Connie opened the door, she was dressed. But with her hair in disarray and dark circles beneath her eyes, she appeared as if she hadn't slept in days.

"Ms. Donovan?" The sheriff was tentative. "Should I come back? Would there be a better time?"

"No, no," she sighed. "Come in. I've prepared coffee."

She led him into the kitchen and motioned for him to sit. She poured steaming coffee into two large mugs. "Cream or sugar?"

"None for me." The sheriff studied her for a moment before asking, "Is there anything I can do?" He wasn't making a legitimate offer. He just thought it was the thing to say.

She shook her head. "You're here to talk about my husband. Let's get to it."

The sheriff nodded and glanced around the room. On the kitchen counter were two empty wine bottles.

He cleared his throat. "Ms. Donovan, we have reason to believe that your husband may have been part of an intentional cover-up to mislead the public about a death."

"Lisa Dale," she muttered.

"You know of her?"

"Only what I told Detective . . . Trainer, I believe."

"Trainum," he corrected. He leaned forward after sipping his coffee. "Is it possible your husband could have altered the autopsy report to disguise the way Lisa Dale died?"

"I believe that's what that girl, Ms. Barber, accused him of the day she came ranting and raving into my husband's office."

"What I'm looking for is proof. Anything that might help us sort through the discrepancies."

"What do you want from me?" She pushed back from the chair. "I stayed out of my husband's business. I helped him with typing occasionally, nothing more."

"Did he ever mention the case to you or indicate in any way that he may have been involved in a cover-up?"

"I don't know of any cover-up," Connie lied. She looked at the sheriff. "Besides, Lisa Dale is dead, my husband is dead, his secretary is dead, and now two other men have been killed. What possible difference can any of this make now?"

"Dr. Berringer isn't dead. It's his word against your husband's report. Finding evidence of the truth could directly influence any charges the state brings against Dr. Berringer."

"Hmmm." Would it be right to betray her dead husband? "It would affect Dr. Berringer?"

"Very likely."

"No," she said after much consideration, "my husband never mentioned a cover-up to me."

She stood, signaling an end to the conversation.

◆ ◆ ◆

Dr. Arthur Pollack positioned Seth on his side and prepped his back with an iodine solution. He numbed a small spot in his mid-thoracic area and inserted a needle, aiming for the space between two vertebrae. He advanced the needle until he reached the epidural space, then passed a narrow, flexible catheter through the needle. He withdrew the needle but left the catheter tubing in place.

He secured the catheter with tape, rolled Seth over on his back, and looked at the nurse who was assisting him. "How long has he been off his morphine drip?"

"Two hours."

"Seth?" He put his face right above the patient's and spoke again. "Seth?"

Seth blinked and opened his eyes.

"I'm Dr. Pollack with anesthesia. I've finished with your epidural catheter. I'm going to give you a test dose. Squeeze my hand if you're in pain." He slipped his hand into Seth's.

"Ouch!" the anesthesiologist responded. "OK, OK, I'll get you some pain relief. Then you'll be able to breathe easier."

He looked at the nurse. "It's time for a test dose. Did pharmacy send up the drugs?"

She nodded and handed him a syringe with two labels—Marcaine and Dilaudid.

He fitted the syringe into the end of the epidural catheter. After injecting a small dose, he monitored Seth's blood pressure and respiratory rate. After ten minutes without a change in blood pressure, he hooked the catheter up to an electronic pump and set the infusion for eight cc's per hour.

He looked at Seth. "Feel better?"

Seth slowly raised his right hand and stuck his thumb into the air.

The anesthesiologist excused himself and went to find Seth's chart.

Once the morphine drip had been removed, Seth had slowly emerged from his drug-induced coma. He felt like he'd awakened from a long sleep, as if he'd finally reached the other side of a massive fog-bank. Now fully awake, he was only too aware of the noises around him. He knew he was on a ventilator in the I.C.U.

He strained to think. He remembered the taxi—the gun—the accident—and then darkness.

He also remembered well the last fear that had gripped him, and now it returned. *I'm not ready to die. I know I need Jesus in my life. I need to start over. I need to pray, but I can't. I can't even talk with this tube in my throat. God, I hope you can hear my thoughts. I'm not sure how to pray.*

What had Kerri said? "Prayer doesn't have to be anything formal or fancy, Seth. It's like a child talking to his father. God doesn't require fancy forms or platitudes. He looks past that stuff. He hears the yearnings of our hearts."

OK, God, you'll have to look at my heart, 'cause I can't talk to you just yet. But, God, how could you love me?

The Holy Spirit nudged his memory again.

"Nothing you could do would make him love you more than he does right at this moment. All you need to do is to ask him to forgive you, to accept the death of his only Son as a substitute for the punishment you deserved. In simple language, you need to release control of your life and put God in the driver's seat."

OK, God, here goes. No fancy forms or platitudes. I'm just talking to you from my heart. I know I need you in my life. I've known it for a while, but I've been running. I know I don't deserve your love, but Kerri said you love me, and right now I'm starting to believe it. Finally, huh?

Tears began flowing down Seth's cheeks, slowly at first, then so much that his chin was getting wet.

I've messed up so much, there's no way I could ever pay the debt I owe. I guess that's why you sent your Son to die in my place. At least that's what I read in that Gideon Bible. Forgive me, Father. I accept the sacrifice of your Son—your innocent Son who shed his blood for me!

A nurse looked in on him and noticed the tears streaming from his eyes. "Gloria, come here. Have you ever seen anything like this? I'm going to page Dr. Pollack. I think he's having an allergic reaction to the Dilaudid or something."

No! I'm OK. I'm really OK. For the first time in my life, I'm OK!

The blood. The precious blood.

Seth's mouth formed an awkward smile around his endotracheal tube. *I tried to blame my problems on that bloodstain, Father, not realizing it was the only way to bring me to you. From now on I'm giving control to you. You're in the driver's seat of my life now!*

Seth looked at the monitor. His heart was beating so fast, he was afraid it would jump out of his chest. *God loves me! I know he loves me!*

The nurse looked at the monitor. "What's going on? Look at his heart rate!"

Seth continued to smile and to cry. *I'm not afraid to die! My sin is gone! My stain is gone!*

"Dr. Berringer, settle down! I've called for Dr. Pollack."

Seth had never known such exhilaration, such freedom. The earlier fear that he had lost everything—his health, his reputation, his job, even Kerri—paled in comparison with the brightness of this new life.

The anesthesiologist arrived and looked at the cardiac monitor. One hundred thirty.

"What's his blood pressure?"

"One fifty over eighty."

He drew back the sheet and studied Seth's chest and abdomen. "No skin rash here. Urine output still OK?"

"Over fifty in the last hour."

"Fever?"

"No."

He looked at Seth. "Any pain, Seth?"

Seth continued his silly grin around the tube and shook his head.

The nurse dabbed his tears with a cloth.

"There's no sign of allergic reaction. And with his blood pressure stable and his urine output up, and with the absence of fever, I'd say he's just excited."

Seth shook his head slightly.

Pollack shrugged. "Any reason we can't remove the endotracheal tube? Maybe that will make him less agitated."

"His last set of respiratory mechanics were good. I don't see why not."

Pollack untaped the tube, deflated the balloon cuff sealing it in place, and instructed Seth to cough.

Seth obeyed, and the doctor pulled out the endotracheal tube.

Seth coughed once more and lay his head back slowly on his pillow. His nurse fitted an oxygen mask around his face and turned to go.

He grabbed her arm and motioned for her to lean closer. She shook her head. "Dr. Berringer, you shouldn't try to talk. We just took you off your ventilator."

Seth insisted and motioned more rapidly.

She leaned down to hear his weak voice proclaim, "God loves me!"

It was a new thought for Seth, but somehow he knew without a doubt that it was true.

◆ ◆ ◆

At supper that evening, Kerri told story after story about her recent experiences with Seth—from Deer Falls to the mysterious research facility hidden in the Rocky Mountains. Her mother gasped when Kerri told about her visit to Donovan and gripped her apron so tightly that her knuckles blanched when Kerri told about the two men in Seth's house and her reckless run from the patrol car.

"Kerri, you didn't!"

Kerri nodded meekly and let a smile escape. "It all seems so strange and faraway now, almost like a dream."

After dinner they sipped coffee, and her mother reached out and touched her hand. "Don't you think you should call Seth, to ask him how things went with the sheriff?"

Kerri gritted her teeth. "I don't know, Mom. I've been thinking that a few days without hearing from me might make it easier on us both."

Her mother nodded. "You know best." She stripped off her apron and hung it on a hook in the pantry. "Maybe you should at least call Angie. She's probably worried, too."

Kerri shook her head. "Angie won't worry about me. She knows I'll call when I want to talk about Seth. Besides, I won't be here much longer."

Her father smiled. "I think she likes the idea of being over here in Buck County where no one knows where she is. She's hidin' out with us, Mom. If she goes back, that deputy might still be waitin' for her in the hospital parking lot." He chuckled at his own joke.

"I, for one," her father continued, "am worn out."

He stood to leave. Kerri kissed him on the cheek. "Night, Daddy."

"Good night, honey." He turned to go up the stairs. "How long will you be with us, Kerri?"

"Could Mom drive me home tomorrow?"

He nodded and smiled. "I'm glad you came, Kerri. I'll see you in the morning."

The phone sounded. Since Grant was standing, he waved his arm. "I'll get it. It's probably Ray calling about the store." He picked it up. "Hello." He smiled. "Yes, she's right here." He held the phone out to his daughter. "Looks like one of your friends figured out your hideout."

"Hello."

"Kerri?"

"Hi, Angie."

"Kerri . . ." Angie said the name again, but this time her voice betrayed a hint of anxiety.

"Is something wrong?"

"It's Seth. There's been an accident. He's in the I.C.U."

Kerri gasped with fear.

"Kerri? Kerri?"

There was silence as Kerri's face paled.

"I've seen him, Kerri. You'd better come."

CHAPTER
42

KERRI'S response to the phone call about Seth was to go to him *yesterday*! Unfortunately, she didn't have her own car, and her parents didn't want to drive her there at such a late hour. She finally settled on a phone call. If he was dying, they'd go tonight after all; if he was stable, they'd make an early start in the morning.

"I.C.U. This is Madge."

"Hi, Madge. This is Kerri Barber. How is Seth Berringer?"

Madge had heard those two were an item and had been wondering when Kerri would call. He'd been here for two days! "I'll have to get Elsie. She's taking care of him."

In a short while, his nurse picked up. "Kerri? We thought you might come by."

"I'm at my parents' place. I just heard about the accident. Is Seth OK?"

"He's doing better. Dr. Pollack put in an epidural, and that seems to be working. At least we were able to extubate him."

"Extubate? He was on the ventilator?"

"Yes—since the accident. But he's off now and seems to be holding his own."

"What all was injured? My friend who called me wasn't sure." She hesitated. "How's his mind?"

Elsie thought about Seth's first words. "I think he's OK. He's talking a little. He seems to know where he is, but he lost a few days. He thought it was Sunday today." She paused. "He has a right chest tube because of the rib fractures and an injury to his lung. He had a pretty nasty right femur fracture, but Dr. Chappell took him to surgery and fixed that. Otherwise, I think he's stabilized."

"W-would you tell him I called? I should be back in Deer Falls tomorrow."

"Sure, Kerri. I'll pass it on. He did ask about you."

"He did?" She wiped a tear from her eye. "Thanks, Elsie. Take good care of him."

"I will. Bye."

Kerri slowly hung up the phone and looked at her mom. "It sounds like he's stabilized." She turned to the stairs. "I think I'll get my bag ready. Can we leave early in the morning?"

Her mother nodded. "Sure, Kerri. I'll be up—and I'll be praying."

◆ ◆ ◆

The following morning, Connie Donovan dragged herself out of bed at 5. She couldn't get those images out of her mind.

She felt so bad for Dr. Berringer. He seemed to be telling the truth. But why had Eric hidden the evidence?

She wanted to be loyal to her husband, but she couldn't shake what the sheriff had said—the evidence could have serious implications for Seth Berringer.

Connie looked at the file folder still lying on the desk. *Forgive me, Eric. I have to do what's right.*

◆ ◆ ◆

Wayne Boatwright sat at his desk. He needed a breakthrough in this case. Berringer was obviously hiding something. Murder? But if he'd killed Lisa Dale with an abortion attempt and then covered it up, why would he claim the autopsy report had been falsified? Maybe he felt so guilty for lying that he had to come forward but couldn't bring himself to make a full confession.

Was Tammy Gaskins correct? Were "Yamatsu" and Berringer linked in a conspiracy to deceive them all?

Seth Berringer was such a complicated man—full of guilt and hostility. The sheriff didn't need the psychiatrist to tell him that. Berringer was deceitful, too. He'd lied about the shoe. He was covering up the truth, and he had confessed to intentionally running over Lisa's body.

The sheriff nodded his head. No one would do something so gruesome unless they were trying to hide an even worse crime.

Something else struck him. Dr. Berringer was at the autopsy. He probably wanted to see if his whitewash would work, and when he saw that Donovan was clearly able to see through it, he feared he'd be found out. So he concocted his convoluted story to try to explain it away.

When he made his confession to Sheriff Boatwright, he was surprised Donovan hadn't listed the true cause of death. He had no idea that "Yamatsu" had taken care of the report for him. That little slip-up in communication just might cost Dr. Seth Berringer his freedom.

The sheriff was more sure than ever that Berringer had covered up Lisa's death because he was guilty of botching her abortion. Berringer was guilty of murder!

But how could he confirm Gaskins's testimony that "Yamatsu" forced her to change the report? Unless he could disprove the medical examiner's report, this case seemed to be going nowhere.

He needed evidence to nail Berringer to the wall. And then the fine doctor would no longer be an embarrassment to the sheriff and his department.

◆ ◆ ◆

After morning rounds Seth was transferred to the orthopedic floor. There, for the first time, he was given something to drink. He looked at the tray in front of him and frowned. Cranberry juice, black coffee, green Jell-O, and clear beef bouillon were not Seth's idea of an appetizing breakfast.

It felt weird to be on this side of the stethoscope.

The evening before, Seth had remembered the papers Ursula had given him—his proof that he was telling the truth. Now they were gone, discarded with his bloody clothing.

Two days earlier Seth would have been completely disheartened by the loss of such evidence—testimony he'd hoped would restore his reputation and clear his record. But not now.

He'd started a new life. His sins were gone, and it didn't matter what Sheriff Boatwright or the newspaper or anyone else thought of him. His Heavenly Father loved him. That was all that mattered now.

Maybe Kerri had been right. He hadn't known what he was really looking for. He'd almost lost everything in his quest to justify himself.

A soft knock at the door interrupted his thoughts. He looked up to see

a well-dressed female in a navy suit. She was holding a manila folder. "Dr.
Berringer?"

He nodded.

She held out her hand. "I don't believe we've met face to face. I'm
Connie Donovan—Dr. Eric Donovan's wife."

Wondering what she was doing there, Seth shook her hand gently. "I'm
sorry about your husband, Ms. Donovan."

She nodded. "Eric hadn't been taking care of himself. I'd been after him
to see a physician about his 'indigestion' for a long time."

Seth looked at her. Certainly she hadn't come to tell him about her
husband.

"I—I know you had a disagreement with Eric over Lisa Dale's autopsy
record."

He squinted. She didn't think their dispute hastened his death, did she?

"I . . . well, I thought these pictures might help clarify the facts—maybe
help the sheriff believe you." She handed him the folder.

Seth opened the file to see pictures of Lisa's autopsy. Of course! Medical
examiners document everything with photographs! Donovan may have
changed the report, but he didn't destroy the film!

Seth looked at the glossy images, clearly labeled with Lisa's name and
her case number. Each photo was initialed "E.D." There were pictures of
each injured organ—pictures of the uterus, with the wooden cervical dilator penetrating the back wall—several pictures of the small fetus the
deceased was carrying.

Seth looked up. "What . . . Why did you bring these to me? Where did
you find them?"

She sighed. "I found them in the bottom of a drawer in Eric's desk—at
home. He must have intended to throw them away later—or to use them
to blackmail the person who . . ." She paused. ". . . who did that to her," she
added, pointing to the pictures and twisting her expression.

"But why me? Why now?"

"I just found them the other day, when I was cleaning out his things."
She shrugged. "I didn't want to show it to the sheriff's department unless it
would make a difference. Eric's gone, and . . . I know he wasn't the best husband, but . . . well, I loved him and I didn't want to see his name disgraced."
She thought it over. "With Eric dead and Lisa dead, I wasn't sure if any of
this mattered. But the sheriff said information about the autopsy might still
make a difference to you."

Seth nodded. He handed the folder back to Ms. Donovan. "I think the sheriff ought to see these—but from you, not from me."

She nodded, stood still for a moment, then softened as she looked around the room. "Is there anything I can do for you? Anything at all? My husband has caused you a lot of trouble, hasn't he?" She prattled on nervously. "Are you feeling OK?"

He nodded. "Your husband's actions . . . Well, don't worry, Ms. Donovan. It's pretty strange, but . . . I believe everything in this strange chain of circumstances had a purpose. In a way your husband helped me. Through this whole situation, as troublesome and misguided as it may have been, I've found a new life."

Connie looked at him curiously. She didn't know how to respond. "I'd better go. You need your rest." She walked to the door. "I'll give these to the sheriff."

With that she was gone, and Seth lay back, pushed away the green Jell-O on his eating table, and closed his eyes.

◆ ◆ ◆

Later that morning Boatwright again assembled his staff and presented his new theory. Seth was involved in a complicated plot to cover up the murder of Lisa Dale. He was linked to Jerry Ling, alias "Yamatsu," and to William Guessford, both of whom were witnessed as present in Lisa's room on the day of her death. Berringer had disguised the murder scene in a deliberate attempt to mislead the law. "Yamatsu" forced the pathologist and his secretary to alter the autopsy report. Berringer, unaware of their work and afraid Donovan's report would reveal how Lisa Dale had really died, concocted a wild story of stumbling over an already dead body.

"We know also that though Donovan died of natural causes, both Guessford and Berringer were present at or around the time of his death." He looked at his staff. "While I suspect they had something to do with the examiner's passing, we won't be able to prove it in a court of law."

He continued, "What we do know is that we can link Berringer firmly to 'Yamatsu' and Guessford. Their fingerprints were both at the scene of Donovan's death, and they were all fleeing from the law together after Guessford and 'Yamatsu' picked up Berringer at the airport."

"So," he added, lifting the file of pictures Connie Donovan had brought him, "what we needed was concrete proof of Berringer's little cover-up—

proof that Lisa Dale died from a botched abortion—something Berringer would have had the training and expertise to provide." He scattered the pictures in front of them, watching them wince as they looked at her body on the autopsy table. "These photographs are from Donovan's private file. Although he had changed his autopsy report, he saved these pictures in his desk at home."

The sheriff went on, "The psychiatrist said Berringer was off the scale with guilt and hostility. Well, now we know why. Lisa Dale was dead when she was run over. These pictures prove it." He walked around the table. "Berringer was afraid we would find out the truth from the autopsy. He was so nervous, he attended the event himself. But he lied to us about finding her in the field. We found no evidence that she'd been there. We found no evidence of the shoe he said he left behind. Instead, it was under his van. We caught him in that lie—another part of his camouflage of Lisa Dale's death."

He pointed to the photographs. "There's only one reason someone would run down a dead body."

Dave Trainum shook his head. "The guy is sick. He obviously saw no other way to hide what he'd done."

"When will Berringer get out of the hospital?" the sheriff asked Zander.

"Not for a few days," the deputy answered. "I checked this morning. He still has that tube sticking out of his side."

"Good. Talk to the magistrate. Lean on him hard about this one. Berringer's run before, and he'll run again if we let him. I want a warrant for his arrest for the murder of Lisa Dale!"

◆ ◆ ◆

Kerri opened the door quietly. Seth was breathing regularly, with his eyes closed.

She stood over him for a moment, staring at the IV, the oxygen mask, the epidural pump, and the collection chambers for his chest tube and urinary catheter. She began to cry. Though she knew about Seth's injuries beforehand, she was unprepared for the emotional impact of seeing him in this condition.

As her quiet sobs mingled with earnest prayer, tears cascaded off her cheeks and onto Seth's right hand.

He opened his eyes and smiled. "It's OK, Kerri. It's OK."

She met his gaze. Trembling, she touched his cheek. "Oh, Seth, I didn't know or I would have come sooner."

He nodded. "I know."

She stood hesitantly.

"Sit down," he said. "I have something to tell you."

"Are you in pain?"

"Not much. This thing works wonders." He pointed to the epidural pump.

She sat by his bed, holding his hand, listening as he related what had happened since they parted—his flight, his van not starting, the taxi ride, the gun, the accident, his clouded memory of the E.R., losing the papers Ursula had given him—and waking up relieved to be alive and to have a second chance. He told her about the visit from Connie Donovan, then paused. "There's one more thing I need to tell you."

Seth began to cry as he told her about his experience in the I.C.U.—his prayer of faith and the release he'd found in knowing the forgiveness of God.

"You should have seen them, Kerri. My heart was racing—I was crying so hard that the tears ran across my face—and they thought I was having a medication reaction!" He smiled. "Kerri, I've been running so long. You were right—I didn't know what I was searching for. But now I know God loves me and that his Son died for my sins." His voice broke. "I know it's true." He gripped her hand.

Kerri was crying too.

Their eyes met. "I did it for me, Kerri. I couldn't have done it for you."

Unable to speak, she nodded rapidly, biting her lip, unable to stop her quivering chin.

◆ ◆ ◆

That evening two young women approached the nursing station of the orthopedic floor at Chesapeake General Hospital.

"We're here to see Dr. Berringer."

The nurse eyed them suspiciously. "Are you family?"

The two shook their heads. One raised her voice, with a note of hesitation. "We're reporters. We hoped Dr. Berringer would give us a statement."

The nurse frowned. "I'll check with him."

She disappeared down the hall and relayed the question to Seth.

He shrugged. "My name's been dragged around too much lately. Maybe this will give me a chance to tell my side of the story."

In a moment the nurse returned with the two reporters. She eyed them again. "Thirty minutes max. The doctor needs to rest. Dr. Berringer, press your call button if you need me."

"Dr. Berringer, I'm Karen Scott, from *The Daily Record*. This is Mary Turner, from *The Coast Chronicle*. We know you've been through a lot. Would it be OK if we talked to you at the same time, to make this a little easier for you?"

He nodded and pointed to Kerri. "This is Kerri Barber. She can help fill in the details."

Karen began the interview. "We've all seen your name in the papers in association with your confession in the hit-and-run case, then with Dr. Donovan's death. People are also talking about your dramatic accident and your possible role in the wounding of a Chesapeake County deputy."

Mary nodded. "We want to hear your side of the story."

Seth relaxed, looked Kerri in the eye, and shrugged. "It's a long story."

Karen looked at Mary. "We have thirty minutes. We're all ears."

Seth took a deep breath and launched into the tale, starting with his frustration with Coast Care and ending with the trip to the hidden research facility in the Rocky Mountains and his accident when he returned home. He included a detailed story of finding Lisa's body, his evaluation at Evergreen State, the loss of his job, finding Donovan's body, and the Jesus clone research.

By the time they were interrupted by the nurse, the two journalists were shaking their heads in wonder.

By the time the morning editions were out and digested, everyone in Deer Falls would have a similar reaction.

CHAPTER
43

Wayne Boatwright was livid. "Who does Berringer think he can fool with this stuff?"

"It is pretty interesting," Trainum conceded.

"Interesting? They should be shot for printing such speculation. Listen to this!" He picked up *The Coast Chronicle*. "'A fortunate blunder, without which we never would have seen the deeper lurking evil.'"

"Is that what they call what Berringer did? A fortunate blunder?"

"How about this one?" Trainum lifted a copy of *The Daily Record*. "'An intentional criminal cover-up, a despicable shadowing of a plot that can only be called the most heinous attack on Christ since Judas Iscariot'." The detective howled. "This stuff is great, sheriff."

"Great? It's a smoke screen, that's what it is—more of Berringer's desperate antics to sway public opinion in his favor." He walked to the door. "Did the magistrate give us a warrant?"

The detective nodded. "But that was before—"

"I want you to arrest him— for murder!"

"But, chief, what if some of this is true? He's not going anywhere—"

"Go to the hospital and make the arrest. Is that clear?"

Trainum nodded again and turned to leave.

"And, Dave," the sheriff called out, "put a twenty-four-hour-a-day guard at his door. I don't want him disappearing again."

"Yes, sir."

"One more thing—I want you to let these reporters, whoever they are, know about the arrest. Make sure they're aware there's a side to this that Berringer's not telling!"

◆ ◆ ◆

Seth's reaction to the formal charges was something of a letdown to Detective Trainum. Half the fun is getting a good rise out of the accused. Seth merely took it in stride, viewing it simply as another challenge to deal with, this time with the confidence that God was somehow in control.

Kerri was impressed by his lack of outrage. In fact, she was more upset than he was and encouraged him to fight. "You heard him, Seth. You have the right to hire your own attorney."

"I don't know any. At least, not any that I'd want."

"Let me call Rodney Busch. He goes to my church."

"Hmmm."

"He'll believe your story, Seth. He's done this before. He defends criminals all the time—" Kerri caught herself and put her hand to her mouth. "Oops. I didn't mean it that way."

Seth waved his hand. "Call him. But tell him it might be a charity case." He smiled.

Kerri went out, casting a glance at the guard as she passed. This was crazy. Seth wasn't going anywhere. Kerri found a phone-book, called Rodney Busch, and poured out the complex story.

An hour later Seth's phone rang. It was the attorney. They made a preliminary verbal agreement. Busch would come by later that evening to formalize their contract and make initial defense plans.

At supper that night, Seth received his first "real food" since his accident. Even the hospital menu didn't seem so bad, at least when he compared it to slimy, green Jell-O. He was just finishing when Busch entered.

"Dr. Berringer?" He held out his hand. "I'm Rodney Busch." He greeted Kerri, whom he recognized from church.

Rodney dressed the part. A gray suit, white button-down shirt, a print tie, and wire-rimmed glasses complemented his leather briefcase.

"Hope you don't mind my court clothes. I'd be more comfortable in sweats."

He went over the basics of the attorney-client relationship, including the issue of confidentiality. He lifted the newspapers off the bed, which Kerri and Seth had been reading before supper arrived. "First of all, no more newspaper interviews. If they get in your face, all you say is, 'No comment.'" He caught Seth's eye.

Seth nodded.

"Hey, I've read the papers," Rodney conceded. "You have a great story to tell, but from now on, considering the serious charges against you, we'll have to fight back a little more carefully."

He looked at Seth and Kerri, who indicated their understanding and agreement.

"OK. How much do you know about the case against you?"

Seth shook his head. "Not that much really. I thought once Boatwright saw the pictures of the autopsy, he'd believe me." He shrugged. "I've gone to an awful lot of trouble to find proof I was telling the truth. Now when it finally shows up, I'm accused of murder."

"I kind of figured as much, from what Kerri explained to me over the phone. So before I came over, I had a little chat with Sheriff Wayne Boatwright."

Kerri looked at Seth. "I told you he was good."

Rodney seemed embarrassed by her praise. "I told him I'd been retained by you and that you had a right to a full understanding of the evidence he has against you. He's so proud of finally figuring out this case, he was eager to tell me what he has—almost like if he revealed his strong hand, I'd fold."

"Well?"

Rodney only offered a hint of a smile as he continued, "It seems Boatwright's thinking about Lisa's death took a turn when Tammy Lynn Gaskins was interviewed about Donovan's decease. Until then he was convinced you were guilty of something but thought the evidence pointed in the direction of involuntary manslaughter or even intentional vehicular homicide caused by your vehicle during the hit-and-run." He paused. "After hearing Tammy confess that she'd altered the autopsy report, he changed his mind."

"She admitted to it?"

"Yes. She said she was forced to do it by a man named Yamatsu. She claimed that you were working with him and that you probably killed Lisa Dale during a botched abortion."

"What?"

"That's what she claimed."

"And Boatwright believes her?"

"Not entirely. She also thought you'd killed Donovan, and she demanded that they protect her from you."

Seth shook his head. "Incredible!"

"Anyway, Boatwright has added that information to his belief that you're lying to him. As proof of your deceitfulness, he mentions Lisa's shoe being found under your van. . . Did you know about that?"

Seth nodded yes. "But I have no idea how it got there. I left it beside the road."

"Anyway, he also relies on the apparent association between you and the two gentlemen with you in the taxi—and with your psychiatric evaluation indicating excessive hostility and guilt."

Seth sighed. "So what will we do?"

"We'll attack every point of his logic. Kerri told me earlier that she feels certain the two men who picked you up were the ones waiting in your house and that they work for Wilson Davis. Any chance you could get information about that?"

Seth frowned. "Extremely doubtful. We have no idea where the facility is."

Kerri winced. "We don't even know the name of the company. Sue Bergy, another gal who participated in the research project, said it was Genetic Concepts or Genetic Concert or Gene Conquest or something like that, but even she wasn't sure."

Rodney shrugged. "We have to try." He was thinking rapidly. "What about your van? Kerri told me it wouldn't start. That's why you got in the taxi with the two men, right?"

"Yes. So?"

"Maybe we should have a mechanic check out your vehicle. There's a chance it was disabled. Maybe that's how the men knew you'd be looking for a cab."

Seth nodded.

"One more thing—would you mind if we called in our own expert psychiatrist to examine you? Maybe we could find some information to counter the Evergreen Hospital psych who said you're so full of anger and guilt."

Seth smiled. "Sure. I think they'll discover that my anger and guilt have been taken care of."

Kerri squeezed his hand in encouragement.

"So what are we looking at here? There's a chance I'll be discharged in a few days, if I get this chest tube out. What happens after that?"

"The deputy out there," Rodney began, pointing toward the door, "will take you before the magistrate to set bail. It's customary in cases like yours to say that the offense is so serious, it's unbailable. From there you'll be taken to jail, with the promise of a bail hearing before a judge on the next business day. The judge will briefly review the charges against you, make sure you understand them, and review the bail."

"Then what?"

The attorney shrugged. "The judge will agree with the magistrate, you'll go to jail, and you'll sit there until trial."

"Jail?" Seth swallowed hard.

"Unless the state drops its case against you."

"Fat chance that'll happen."

Rodney shrugged again. "Hey, these are only my first ideas. I'll be in touch."

CHAPTER
44

Ursula Baumgarten's anxiety had steady increased since Seth and Kerri's visit. She was all for objective scientific study, but the revelations about Davis's deceitful tactics and his apparent flippant attitude toward the death of one of their surrogates appalled her.

Further, the idea that he'd suspect her of betrayal, even asking Berringer about it, made her blood boil.

She had to leave this place. With the information she'd given Berringer, this place was going to have a meltdown. And she knew Davis would make sure someone else took the fall for Lisa's death. She was determined to make sure it wasn't her.

But where could she go? Back to the N.I.H.? That would be ideal, but she doubted Kevin Schwab would allow it.

She sighed. Wilson Davis had promised to make her the most celebrated DNA researcher in history—the scientist who resurrected the historical Jesus.

Now all she could see was scandal.

She had to make plans—and soon if she was going to salvage any reputation at all.

◆ ◆ ◆

Kevin Schwab looked at Friday's paper and shook his head. The Lisa Dale scandal, complete with a futuristic claim about the child she was carrying, had hit the Associated Press wire. And now there was a new development: "LOCAL PHYSICIAN ARRESTED FOR MURDER."

He read and reread the story. Good—no mention of the N.I.H. Only a mysterious hidden research facility in the Rocky Mountains was cited.

Berringer's story was so far out, they'd probably never believe him anyway. Murder?

Kevin twisted his baseball cap. They couldn't make that charge stick, could they? He looked again at the article. "Although no details have been given, the sheriff displayed confidence in a successful conviction and hinted at new autopsy evidence that confirms the real cause of death."

He stared at the page for a few moments longer, the words blurring in front of his eyes. If he hadn't sold the cells, Berringer wouldn't be in this trouble. Indirectly, he was responsible to bring the truth to light. Schwab winced at the stabbings of his conscience.

What was it Berringer had said? "You're a scientist. Truth has to mean something to you."

He looked at the article again and scanned for the name of Berringer's attorney. "When asked about his client's defense, Rodney Busch replied, 'No comment.'" *Counselor Busch, maybe there's a way I can help you.*

◆ ◆ ◆

The surgeon, Alvin Daniels, gave Seth specific instructions. "Take a deep breath, hold it, and bear down."

Seth looked at him and wrinkled his forehead. "Is this going to hurt?"

"Not with the epidural in." He smiled. "That's comin' out next." He paused and placed one hand on the chest tube and one hand on Seth's chest, just above the exit site of the tube. "Take a deep breath and hold it."

Seth obeyed.

The surgeon swiftly removed the tube and sealed the hole in the chest wall with his hand. "You can breathe now." He finished applying tape to the dressing. "There."

"When's the epidural coming out?"

"As soon as I can get anesthesia up here to do it."

"And the foley?" Seth pointed to the drainage bag. "I hate this thing."

"As soon as the epidural is out."

"When do I get out of here?" Seth wasn't really in any rush. The idea of going to prison didn't appeal to him.

"I'll check with Dr. Chappell about your leg." He turned to go. "Now that the chest tube is out, I'll call the physical therapist to get you walking with some crutches."

Seth nodded. "Great."

It's nice to be getting better, Lord. But with jail on the horizon, wouldn't it be good for me to stay here a little longer?

◆ ◆ ◆

Ursula twisted her long, black hair and shrugged. Maybe the plan would work. She'd help Kevin, and he could reinstate her at the N.I.H.

Kevin Schwab was insistent. "Come on, Ursula, what do you say? You said yourself the project is likely to go bust if the authorities find any evidence that Berringer's story is true."

She had let him stew long enough. She pressed her lips closer to the phone. "I'll do it."

"But, Ursula, nothing about the grant from Davis and nothing about the N.I.H., agreed?"

"I'm not a complete idiot, Kevin. I may have shown poor judgment by linking myself with the project, but I recognize the need to jump from a sinking ship. I'll see what I can get."

She hung up the phone and set her alarm for 2 A.M. It wouldn't do to have Davis see her collecting the data, would it?

◆ ◆ ◆

The next morning Seth, flanked by Kerri on one side and a physical therapist, Heidi Kristophel, on the other, took his first steps in the hall. Behind him, a Chesapeake County deputy trailed along at a leisurely pace.

"Put your weight on your hands," Heidi instructed, pointing to his crutch.

"I can really feel it in my ribs," he complained.

"It's always tough the first few times. It'll get better."

They went for a few feet, then stopped to rest. His first trip up to the nursing station and back to his room took ten minutes.

He sat back on the bed, exhausted. "Man, I can't believe a short walk could feel like such a marathon."

Just then a visitor appeared carrying a large bouquet of cut flowers. It was Connie Donovan.

"Dr. Berringer, may I come in?"

Seth nodded. She cast a leery glance at the deputy at the door and entered.

"Don't mind him. He's my ride when I get to leave." Seth attempted a smile.

She set the flowers on a shelf. "I read your story in the paper—the one with your side of all this. Then I read about your arrest." She took a deep breath. "Dr. Berringer, I feel just awful. I thought the pictures I gave the sheriff would convince him you were telling the truth. I had no idea—"

She glanced back at the deputy again.

Seth leaned forward and touched her hand. "Why did you believe me?"

"I'm not sure. I just felt after talking with you the other day that you were interested in the truth. If you thought the pictures would get you in trouble, you'd never have urged me to take them to the sheriff."

He nodded.

"I'm really sorry about the way this turned out." She looked around the room. "Is there anything I can do?"

Seth shook his head. "Kerri's been looking after most things. She comes in before and after work." He shrugged.

"When will they let you go?"

"It looks like I'll be discharged tomorrow." He looked down. "After that, it looks like the Chesapeake County Jail will be my home—at least for the time being."

She nodded uncomfortably.

Kerri looked at him. What would it be like visiting him in prison? O God, maybe he should stay here a few more days.

◆ ◆ ◆

Rodney Busch sat at his desk. Although it was Saturday afternoon, he'd hoped for a break, any kind of break, that would save his client the further humiliation of confinement in the county jail. He pored over the notes he'd made and the other information he'd received.

He looked at the mechanic's report on Seth's van: someone had cut the wires leading from the distributor. Now Busch just had to convince the sheriff's department to get fingerprints from the van in order to discern if the tampering had been accomplished by the two men in the cab.

The lawyer only had a few hours before Seth would go to jail. He needed some solid evidence that Seth's wild story was true. He'd looked up every possible genetics company west of the Mississippi. There was nothing around Colorado Springs that was remotely similar to what Seth had described. Another dead end.

His fax machine suddenly chirped to life.

Curious but preoccupied, he returned to the notes he'd made after talking to Seth and Kerri. There had to be a breakthrough here somewhere! *Father God, help me find the answer.*

Unnoticed by the anxious attorney, paper poured from the fax machine.

Rodney studied the autopsy on Eric Donovan. Nothing noteworthy here.

He studied Seth's account of the story again. He wished he had the papers his client had received at the institute. But the nurses in the E.R. said his clothes had been cut away and discarded.

The fax machine's loud, lengthy transmission cascaded onto the floor and looped into a large paper mountain.

Rodney looked up, finally drawn from his thoughts by the noise. He walked over to the machine, lifted the paper from the floor, and stared at the first page of a sixty-page transmission. What on earth!

He pulled the paper through his hands, scanning forward to the last page. A phone number was printed there, along with a number to call for validation of the message.

Rodney pulled the paper out of the machine and dialed the number.

"Mr. Busch? This is Kevin Schwab."

◆ ◆ ◆

Two hours later Rodney Busch tightened his court tie and walked into Sheriff Boatwright's office.

Dave Trainum sat in a chair opposite the sheriff, sitting proudly in his desk-chair.

"Mr. Boatwright, thanks for agreeing to meet me on such short notice." The confident attorney extended his hand.

"This had better be good, Busch. I don't need to remind you that it's Saturday evening." He pointed at the other lawman. "This is Detective Trainum."

Busch nodded. "Nice to meet you."

Boatwright sighed. "What's this all about?"

"I have new evidence in the Berringer case."

"Is that all? Why couldn't you tell me on the phone? Certainly this could wait until Monday—"

"Sir, with all due respect, by Monday my client will have laid in jail for two days—an insufferable humiliation for a man of his stature."

"Cut the lawyer stuff, Busch. This had better be good."

Busch slapped a copy of the fax on the desk.

"What's this?" The sheriff stiffened. "You want me to read a novel?"

"It's a research proposal detailing genetic research involving a volunteer subject, Ms. Lisa Dale. It reveals her involvement as a surrogate mother in said project and the plans for retrieval of the fetus she carried by a harvest team employed by the researchers. In addition, we have here the employee records of the research corporation, clearly identifying the members of the retrieval team—Jerry Ling and William Guessford."

Boatwright sat up straight. "What!"

"Furthermore, there is no mention of my client ever being employed by the research firm." He flipped several pages and pointed to a small chart with Lisa Dale's name clearly visible. A fine line was drawn through her name with a handwritten notation: "Deceased. Clone not retrieved."

"Where did you get this?"

"It doesn't matter. What matters is that I have it. I also have," he added, pulling a cassette tape from his pocket, "a sworn, taped deposition from a world authority describing the study and a page-by-page explanation of the document you are holding."

"This is gibberish." Boatwright slapped the paper onto the desk. "This is a scientific smoke screen." He looked at the attorney. "What do you want?"

"Drop the charges against my client. Unarrest him."

"Because of this?" The sheriff laughed. "What do you take me for? I've acted in the best interests of the people of this county on the knowledge I had in hand at the time the arrest was made."

"And now there's more information at hand, isn't there, sheriff?"

"I'll take it to the judge on Monday. I'll see what he thinks."

"I don't think so, sheriff. You know what you should do. Drop the charges."

"It will take a month for a layperson to work through this document and give an opinion. Until then the charges will stand and the public will be safe from Seth Berringer!" he huffed. "Just because he hires a lawyer, he thinks he'll get out of this—"

"Have you ever heard of false arrest, sheriff? Or defamation of character? If my client is taken to jail, he will likely suffer further humiliation in the eyes of the public. And hasn't he suffered enough? He's lost his job, he's had his mental competence questioned in the papers—and all because of news releases from your staff!"

"This is an abomination. Get out of here!"

Busch held his ground. He picked up the stack of paper. "I'll file my false arrest suit in court on Monday. Let's see," he began to count on his fingers, "compensatory damages to my client, which will be sizable—a career of lost earnings at his previous salary—not to mention punitive damages against a department bent on ruining my client's reputation with a series of blunders. Wasn't it enough of an embarrassment when you nearly had my client arrested for the murder of a man who died from a heart attack, after identifying him to the media as your chief suspect?"

"C-come on, I—"

"When the media asks me about your incompetence, I'll have more to say than, 'No comment.'" He glared at the lawman. "Put my client in jail and I'll see you in court!"

Busch pivoted and strode out of the office, exhilarated by the showdown.

He looked at his watch. Time was running out for Seth Berringer. He hoped the sheriff would do the right thing for once.

CHAPTER
45

THE next morning Kerri came by with a small box wrapped in colorful paper.

"It's not my birthday."

She smiled. "I know. Open it." She smiled and added, "It's to celebrate your other birthday."

He opened it to find a new Bible. He held it like a precious treasure, stroking the cover lightly, as if it might break.

"Open it up, silly."

He opened it to the first page. There she had written his name and a date. Seth counted back the days on his hand. Last Tuesday.

"Your first day as a believer. It's your new birthday."

Beneath the date she'd written the inscription, "Seth, the son of Adam, became the son of God."

He wrinkled his forehead. "The son of Adam?"

She turned the pages to Genesis 5 and shared with him the understanding she'd gained on the plane. "I was praying, trying hard to forget you." She smiled. "And God showed me this." She pointed. "See, first Adam was made in the image of God. That was before the Fall, before sin, when Adam had open communion with his Creator." She lowered her finger and pointed again. "Then, after sin separated us from God, Adam had a son, made in the image of man, and he named him Seth." She smiled again. "I know maybe it's just semantics, but it meant something special to me."

Seth took her hand. "And to me. Thanks."

They were quiet for a moment. Then Seth asked, "Aren't you supposed to be in church or something?"

"I know it's Sunday, but . . . Well, I just had to be with you today, Seth. If you're discharged . . ." Her eyes fell. "I didn't know how much I'd get to see you for a while."

He understood. "I'm glad you came."

"Seth, don't you think you should tell your mother about this? Don't you think she'd want to know about you?"

"What should I tell her?" He changed his voice and held an imaginary phone to his ear. "Mom? Seth here—you know, your son? I've got good news and bad news. The good news is, I'm getting out of the hospital today. The bad news is, I'm going to jail!"

"Seth!"

He lowered his eyes. "Sorry." He paused. "Truthfully, I have been thinking about her. How can you go through something like this and not think about your own mother?" He blinked back a tear. "Look, I hardly know her. She left when I was small. We don't even visit." He shook his head and shrugged. "A card at Christmas is as deep as it gets."

"I was thinking—maybe you should talk to her. Maybe she's waiting for you to take the first step. Perhaps she thinks you hate her. Maybe she needs to know you've changed."

"I'll phone her when I'm a free man. And if all this goes to trial, I'll definitely call her."

"Seth, your arrest and Lisa Dale's story made the AP news service. She might have already seen it."

His eyes met hers. "I'll pray about this. I know I have some things to work on, but I'm making a new start and . . . I'll work on it."

She knew Seth would honor his word. His faith was too fresh for complacency. Kerri nodded. "OK."

A few minutes later Dr. Overby appeared. "I've looked over your chart. Looks like today is the big day."

Seth nodded. "I guess so."

"I'd plan on getting out of here late this afternoon. I want you to work with the physical therapists a bit more before discharge."

"OK."

"Dr. Chappell is going to follow up on your femur. I'll see you again for a follow-up chest X-ray in a few weeks."

With that, he disappeared.

Just as the doctor left, a breathless Rodney Busch arrived, this time without the suit but still looking dapper in a tweed coat and tie. "Did the sheriff come by?"

"Did you really think he would?"

"I'd hoped so." Rodney shook his head. He had explained the information he'd received from Schwab to Seth the evening before. They both knew that if Boatwright didn't make a move in a very short time, Seth would spend some time in jail. Just how long was still to be determined.

"You did your best, Rodney. I really appreciate that."

"I gave him both barrels, that's for sure." Rodney chuckled.

"I'd have given anything to have heard that—and to see Boatwright's face." Seth found himself snickering, too.

"What's going on in here?"

The trio looked up to see Rick Zander, standing tall, back on the job. "Well?" He moved cautiously into the room, disguising a slight limp.

"This isn't a time for fun and games, is it?" Zander persisted.

Seth looked at Kerri. What was going on?

A hint of a smile passed the deputy's lips.

Rodney began, "Deputy, if you don't mind, we'd—"

Seth held up his hand. "I think I owe you an explanation. I didn't mean for that gun to go off. I was only trying to—"

"Forget the gun, Dr. Berringer. I read the statement you gave to the detective after he arrested you. And the only prints on that gun belong to Bill Guessford."

"You probably saved my life," Seth responded earnestly. "Those guys had nothing in mind except my immediate termination. I had stumbled across a bit too much information about them, I'm afraid. I owe you."

"I know." He smiled. "But that's not why I'm here." He paused for effect. "I think you'll want to hear this. The sheriff sent me."

They stared at him for a moment, not speaking. Finally Seth couldn't bear any further silence. "Well?"

"He's issuing a statement in a few minutes." Zander cleared his throat. "Something to the effect that due to your present state of poor health because of the recent accident, and due to some new evidence that has just come to the department's attention, the department doesn't think Seth Berringer causes an immediate threat to the public. Consequently, the charges of murder will be dropped, though a full investigation of Seth Berringer will be completed in a timely manner."

Seth looked at Rodney. "What's all that mean?"

"You're a free man. He just says all that other junk to save face."

Rodney grabbed Seth's bedside phone.

"Who are you calling?"

"Remember that reporter, Karen Scott? I want to let her in on this. She did such a nice job telling your story before."

"I thought you didn't want us to talk to the media."

"Not when a trial case is pending. But now . . . If you haven't noticed, we have some major work to do to bolster the public opinion of the fine, young, misunderstood, abused Dr. Berringer." He smiled. "Besides, Karen is also a newswriter for WKSV on Sunday mornings. I think I'll issue a short statement of our own, complete with words like 'fully exonerated of all charges,' 'expecting a full return to a life of community service,' that kind of thing. Nothing fancy you understand. Just a little image repair."

Seth wrinkled his nose. "I don't know, Rodney. I don't really care what people—"

"Let him call," Kerri said as she grabbed the phone. "But he can use the pay phone in the hall." She turned to the deputy and Rodney. "Now, if you'll excuse the fine, young, misunderstood doctor, I think he needs some rest!"

After the two retreated, Seth wrinkled his forehead. "What was that all ab—"

She cut off his sentence with a celebration of her own, kissing him gently once, then a second time as Seth responded with matching desire. She pulled away enough to communicate with her eyes what she now felt free to give. Now it was right to love him.

She held him for a few minutes before speaking the words that would melt his heart. "I love you, Seth."

"I love you too."

◆ ◆ ◆

The traffic in Seth's room swelled as the news spread via radio and the hospital grapevine. Kerri fended off several reporters, in addition to well-wishers and those who were merely curious to hear Seth's side of the story. The physical therapists were just leaving as yet another visitor arrived.

This time Connie Donovan didn't bring flowers but rather an offer of a quiet refuge for the recovering physician. It seemed to Seth that she was a bit too fixated on making up for her husband's misdeeds. Perhaps she was feeling a little guilty herself—an emotion Seth had known well.

"I heard the good news on the radio," she began. "I imagine you've had more visitors than you'd like. Perhaps you'd like some escape." She held out several keys. "You're welcome to stay at my vacation home on Red Lake. It's deserted, it's spacious, and there are no stairs for you to navigate on your crutches. Better yet, no one will think to look for you there."

That did sound nice, but . . . Seth shook his head. "Ms. Donovan, I couldn't—"

She persisted, "Listen, every time I've come in here, I've been looking for a way to help. This is something I can do." She locked eyes with the young doctor. "I'm trying to make a new start too, you know."

Kerri appreciated her sincerity. "Seth," she said softly, touching his arm, "your place does have stairs leading to your bedroom."

He looked up. "I could pay you."

"That's crazy." Connie thought for a moment. "Besides, you'd be helping me. I'm putting the whole place up for sale soon. It'll be nice to have someone stirring up the dust." She smiled. "There's a stone fireplace, a great view of the lake, a dock, a boat, even fishing equipment. Feel free to use it whenever you're able."

Kerri imagined building a romantic fire. She looked at Seth. "What do you think?"

He shrugged. "It sounds great. I'll do it."

"Wonderful." Connie pulled over a table. "You're getting out today?"
Seth nodded.

"I'll draw you a map. I'm heading down there myself after I leave. I'll make sure the heat is turned on for you."

◆ ◆ ◆

By Wednesday Seth had fallen into a comfortable routine. He spent most of his days reading the ton of books Kerri had brought him—all of her favorite Christian thinkers, from Lewis and Schaeffer to Lucado, Swindoll, and Graham. By far, his favorite reading material was the Bible she'd given him in honor of his spiritual birthday.

He was sitting in a recliner in front of the fireplace with a book open in his lap and his right leg propped up on two pillows when Kerri knocked.

"Door's open."

"Dinner's here." She took two grocery bags to the kitchen before walking back to see Seth. She sat on the arm of the chair and tousled his hair. "Rough day at the office?"

"The worst." He heaved an exaggerated sigh.

She smiled and leaned close to his face. They kissed. Her cheeks were rosy and cold. "Warm me up," she begged.

He smiled again. "You're taking unfair advantage of the lame."

"I know," she giggled as she nuzzled her nose against his neck.

He squirmed.

"I think my car heater gave out." She pulled away again. "I love you."

"You're just using me to warm your nose."

"You arrogant, pitiful thing!" She struck him playfully with a newspaper she'd brought.

He winced. "Whatever happened to young, misunderstood, and abused?" he responded.

She laughed and turned away. "Here," she replied, handing him the newspaper. "You're still making the papers."

"Great." He scanned the first two pages without success. "Where?" he called after Kerri who had walked into the kitchen again.

"Check the editorial page."

Seth slowly read over the editor's opinion column.

Well, the word is out on the street, and if we're to believe the confession of our own town physician, Seth Berringer, his problems started in earnest when he decided to take matters into his own hands and protect his job, something most of us would do, even if it means bending the appearance of the truth a little. If, on the other hand, you believe certain local staff reporters, Berringer's guilt lies more with the suspicion that the whole event was conjured up by a criminal mind capable of not only covering up a murder, but committing it in the first place.

Since there are two opposing views in the community, and the media can't seem to help, I'll add my opinion here. After all, I'm the editor, and I can print what I want. Besides, it is apparent that this act, regardless of how you've judged it, isn't bound for the courts. It is likely that Dr. Berringer will only be tried in the court of public opinion, and so on that score, I'll give my two cents.

We should at least listen to the doctor himself. What did he have to gain by bringing the facts to light? If he is guilty of more than he's confessing, why bring the whole thing up in the first place? Certainly, he knew people were bound to suspect that he was only protecting a deeper wrong.

I, for one, would like to side with Berringer. He's naive, if anything. Certainly we should explore the facts that have led to the events as we know them. If our doctor is telling the truth, a portion of the blame needs to rest with the mega-health-care-provider Coast Care, for creating the impersonal environment that made the doctor fear for his job.

And what of the nearly unbelievable story of human DNA cloning and the assessment of Christ's divinity? What would motivate Berringer to twist such a tall tale in the first place? Most of us find this all a bit unbelievable and wonder if this won't be a larger stain on Berringer's image. If he's not a murderer, then he certainly has an imagination bent on the implausible.

How will history judge our local family physician? A hero who uncovered a diabolical plot? A murderer who confessed to a lesser sin just to hide his own guilt? An imbecile who sought national attention by his outlandish imagination? A compassionate physician who cradled the people of his own community as if they were his own family?

A hero? A murderer? An imbecile? A compassionate physician? I want more information.

And when it comes, I want to weigh my judgment in the light of Berringer's history in this town. Don't we at least owe him that? Wasn't he the only one to stay when other physicians had given up on Deer Falls? How many of us have bothered him in the middle of the night with calls about our sick children? Who else provided care for the uninsured in our town when the silo plant closed? Who organized the fund-drive to help pay for little Holly's bone marrow transplant?

Let's look at history, folks. Sure, all of this seems a bit outrageous right now. But he hasn't been found guilty in any court of law, so let's refrain from assuming he's guilty before all the facts are in.

Well, that's how I see it.

Tim Snyder, Editor
Deer Falls Gazette

"I think I like this guy. At least it's a bit more balanced than some of the other stuff out there."

Kerri walked back in.

"So what do you think?" he probed, pointing to the editorial. "Hero? Murderer? Imbecile? Compassionate physician?"

She echoed the sentiments of the editor. "I want more information." She smiled. "Where's the wood for this thing?" she asked, eyeing the fireplace.

"Back deck." Seth looked down at the paper.

Kerri busied herself with preparation of a fire and dinner as Seth editorialized over the day's news.

She positioned a card table next to his chair, then covered it with a tablecloth. She brought out place settings and a single candle.

Seth's eyes brightened as she served the food, turned off the lights, and lit the candle. The fireplace and candlelight created a romantic setting.

"I have something I want to say," Seth began gently, watching the candlelight reflected in her eyes. "My life is so different because of you." He felt his throat tighten. "You believed in me. You loved me when I was at my worst." His chin began to quiver. "You reached me, touched me, when I was searching, trying desperately to find my own way." He paused as if trying to remember. "I have never known someone like you. You know I love you . . ." His voice broke.

Kerri couldn't prevent the tears. "I know, I know," she whispered.

He reached beside him, retrieving a thin box hidden in the cushion of his chair. "I knew you were planning a special evening for me. I wanted it to be special for you, too." He placed the gift in her hand. "For all you are to me."

"Oh—" Her words caught in her throat. She opened the box and lifted out a gold necklace holding a single diamond.

Her eyes widened. "Seth!" She shook her head. "How did you—"

He smiled and pointed to a desk in the corner of the room. "I used Donovan's computer. With the Internet and my Visa, everything's possible."

"Seth, you shouldn't do this! You don't even have a job!"

"Kerri . . ." His voice was gentle but firm. "I have moderate savings. And I'll be returning to work soon. This town hasn't completely abandoned me. You'll see. Besides, God is in control now. He'll take care of us."

Kerri smiled. She liked the way he said that. Us. It sounded right. Like an old pair of slippers—a perfect fit.

CHAPTER
46

By THE end of two weeks Seth was developing a minor case of cabin fever. He stepped out on the porch, now able to manipulate his crutches without difficulty.

The temperature was unusually warm, and the view of Red Lake enticed him. He wondered if he could catch a fish if he sat on the dock.

Connie Donovan had told him to make himself at home. He inhaled deeply. He hadn't done something like this for a long time.

He went back inside, then into the garage, where he found the appropriate supplies. He walked to his bedroom to get ready for the outing when he realized he hadn't worn a pair of shoes since before his accident. He didn't even have any there. Slippers wouldn't be enough; he'd fall. Besides, it was still too cold for such scanty footwear.

He looked in the closet and located a pair of Donovan's old boots. He put them on and found the fit adequate after donning an extra pair of socks. He put on his winter coat and grabbed his crutches. Where had Connie said he'd find bait? The freezer in the garage. He walked there and started rummaging through the contents. He set aside frozen meat and vegetables and spotted a small plastic bag labeled "Bait." He was just about to close the freezer when a vaguely familiar container with a blue lid caught his eye. Where had he seen receptacles like that before?

As he lifted the receptacle from the bottom of the freezer, recognition dawned. It was a pathology container. He couldn't believe Donovan would use this—

His thought jerked to a stop when he read the label: "Lisa Dale."

Lisa Dale! His hand began to tremble as he turned the specimen over in his hand. Inside, Seth could barely identify a small, pink bit of tissue. The Jesus clone!

He shut the freezer lid as his mind began to race. The very thing he'd been searching for and nearly lost everything in attempting to find. Donovan must have hidden it there, knowing that even if anyone searched his house, they'd probably overlook his vacation home.

He crutch-walked back into the house, placing the specimen on the counter. Who should he tell? Kerri? The sheriff? The newspaper?

What should he do? He'd found the clone—the five-million-dollar clone!

With his fishing plans completely forgotten, he stared at the specimen and paced back and forth, striking his crutches on the floor in a rhythmic motion that helped him construct a plan.

He gathered what he needed—his cell-phone, a winter cap, and of course the specimen. He retrieved the keys to Donovan's boat from a hook beside the door. Slowly and deliberately, he made his way to the dock. Getting in the boat wasn't easy, but after pulling it over with his crutch, he was able to make the transfer without falling.

He started the engine and cast off the ropes. He carefully edged the throttle forward and headed for the center of Red Lake.

At the widest point, Seth shut off the engine. He was adrift in the middle of the lake, with his mind racing and a dark temptation assaulting it. Here he could be alone to think. Here he felt not only physical seclusion, but a cold emotional isolation as well. No one could see him, no one knew his mind, and no one could hear him talk.

The clone was worth at least five million dollars to Wilson Davis. If he contacted him, using the information Schwab had faxed to Rodney Busch, he could execute a secret deal and secure his financial future. He shook his head. Who would know? If his project succeeded, the public would only think Davis had some other DNA available, right? No one would ever suspect Seth.

Five million dollars. He fingered the cell-phone. A simple call to Busch's secretary would give him Davis's number.

Five million dollars. A guy without a secure financial future could—

Seth lifted the small specimen container from his jacket pocket. This wasn't the true Jesus anyway.

He turned the container in his hand. It had all started with a bloodstain.

A precious drop of his Savior's cleansing, redeeming blood. A treasure worth far beyond any earthly riches.

Seth slowly collapsed onto the padded boat seat. *You died in my place, spilling your blood for me. How could I ever betray the one whose blood washed the stain of sin out of my heart?*

He felt sick, ashamed that he had even considered . . .

"Forgive me, Father. Forgive me."

Seth sat quietly for a moment, appreciating the still water and gentle breeze and the wonder of his loving Father.

He stood and moved to the edge of the boat. He strained his eyes at the shore. Red Lake was a mile wide at this point.

He opened the container and held it over the side of the boat. He paused as he worked through the decision one more time. In a sense what he was about to do seemed sacrilegious. But it had to be done in such a way that no one could ever retrieve the clone. He had to do this. He frowned, then shook the contents into the lake. The specimen disappeared instantly, lost forever beneath the surface of Red Lake.

Seth flinched for a moment, thinking that perhaps a formal burial would have been more appropriate. No, he reasoned, it had to be like this so no one would ever find the clone.

He looked at the water, captivated by a sudden thought. Red Lake. Red like blood—his blood.

He lifted his eyes to the shore again, then turned and started the engine. *I did the right thing, Father. I know I did the right thing.*

Seth, the son of Adam, had become a son of God.

Epilogue

A MONTH later, Sheriff-elect Phil Blackstock noted a small story at the bottom of the second page of *The Coast Chronicle*. It was from the AP wire service.

WILSON DAVIS, PHILANTHROPIST, DEAD

Wilson Davis, the millionaire philanthropist, died yesterday at his residence outside Colorado Springs. The multimillionaire, best known for a large grant given to the N.I.H.'s National Center for Human Genome Research, had fought a valiant fight against pancreatic cancer.

He set the paper aside, making a mental note to tell Angie so she could tell Dr. Berringer.

◆ ◆ ◆

The next day a solemn Kevin Schwab shifted uncomfortably in his seat in the business class section of a jetliner heading for Dulles. He had just attended a memorial service for the late Wilson Davis, a service he went to because it looked right for him to be there, not because he admired the man or his mission.

Next to him, Ursula Baumgarten sipped a mixed drink and paged restlessly through a flight magazine. Her own inner discomfort stemmed more from the way Kevin had been treating her than from any remorse over Davis's death.

She leaned toward Kevin, the man she now related to as Dr. Schwab, her division chief. "You're awfully quiet."

Schwab grunted.

Ursula flipped a few more pages. "As a matter of fact, since my arrival back in Maryland, you've barely talked to me at all, other than about our current research projects." She closed the magazine. "We used to be friends. What gives?"

Kevin looked out the window. He wasn't sure how to articulate his feelings. Finally he shook his head and lowered his voice. "I just hope this whole thing is behind us. Davis is dead—I hope his project is dead too."

Ursula gave him an angry look. "Of course the project is dead. No one, other than those of us who were in Davis's lab, even knows about it."

"What about the folks in Deer Falls? What if they believe Berringer's story?"

She rolled her eyes. "So what?"

He sighed. "Do you really want it to get out that you were manipulating the blood of Jesus?" He looked down. "A lot of people would find that pretty offensive. It's like holy ground or something. You know, too sacred to mess with."

"Since when did you ever worry about offending people outside the scientific community?" Her voice was strained and barely audible. "And since when did you care about sacred religious symbols?" She pointed her finger at Kevin's chin. "Remember, it was you who sent us the cells in the first place."

He met her gaze and tried to contain his frustration. "I only thought Davis wanted to do what I was doing—analyze Jesus' physical makeup."

"Do you think what you were doing with that blood was less offensive than what Davis proposed?"

"That goes without saying."

Ursula took another sip of her drink and rattled the ice against the edge of the plastic glass. "Why should you care anyway?"

He shook his head and sighed. "It's hard to explain, Ursula. I've never been a religious person, but examining those cells, mapping the DNA of Jesus . . . Well, I felt like I was finally doing something important. People were talking about conclusive proof of his existence." He paused for a moment. "I guess I started wondering if the story might really be true."

"Come on, Kevin, you're a scientist—"

"You should have heard the way the Vatican officials talked. When I first discovered the bloodstain on the shroud. . ." He stared out the window for a moment, recalling his conversations with Roman Catholic leaders. "They talked about the blood as if it were the most holy and precious thing in the universe. They insisted that I handle the cells with the utmost respect and care."

Ursula smiled. "And you sold the cells to us."

He nodded. After a moment he replied, "I can't help feeling like something's terribly wrong about all this. Whether we agree or not, many feel that the blood of Jesus is too precious to desecrate."

"Do you think that's what I've done?"

Kevin studied her for a minute, contemplating the objective, cold, scientific way she seemed to approach all of life. Nothing was sacred to Ursula. The only reality she knew was what she could prove and comprehend. "I'm sorry, but, yes, I do."

She turned away. He had no idea what she'd really done. And now he was letting conscience rather than reason rule him. "Don't be silly, Kev. It's only DNA."

"Maybe to you." He didn't know what else to say.

She sighed and finished her drink. "It's over now anyway. Davis is dead. You'll have your wish—the project is dead too."

"That brings us back to Berringer. What if someone believes his story?"

"Unlikely. His credibility is shot." She touched his hand.

Kevin stifled the urge to pull his hand away.

"Besides," she added, "the information we sent to his attorney about the research project didn't reveal the real nature of the clone. No one can prove what really went on."

Kevin sighed again.

Ursula leaned even closer. "Stop worrying, Kev. It's behind you. No one can find out." She studied his youthful complexion. She feared that if she told him the rest of the truth about the project, he'd think differently about her.

He looked out the window again, wishing his anxiety would flee, but finding Ursula's words less than reassuring. He pulled a magazine from the seat-back in front of him.

"Stop worrying, Kevin. You're not responsible for what we did with those cells." She looked at him and shook her head. "You find the whole project despicable, don't you?"

He remained silent.

"And what do you think of me?"

He met her gaze only a moment before looking down. "You're a scientist, Ursula. One of the best. That's why I agreed to take you back."

It was what he didn't say that bothered him the most.

And for Ursula, what he didn't say forced a small crack in her cool, objective worldview.

She turned away. What if he knew what had really happened?

◆ ◆ ◆

For the next two weeks, Schwab's communication with Ursula was confined to an occasional perfunctory greeting or a conversation directly related to the genome project at hand. Their old style of cheerful, nearly playful interaction was a thing of the past.

During that time, Schwab mulled over their conversation on the airplane. He gave careful thought to what Davis and his team had done. Was nothing, even the blood of Jesus, sacred?

During those weeks, Ursula wondered about the advisability of sharing a secret that only she knew. Would he think less of her if he knew she'd lied about the research? Why did he suddenly seem stricken with the idea that this religious symbol might lie beyond allowable scientific manipulation? Why did the Turin Project seem like such a scientific monstrosity to him now?

Finally Ursula opted to rid herself of her turmoil and be honest with Kevin, even if it meant risking his disdain. That way, whether he liked what she'd done or not, at least he would be judging her on the basis of the truth.

On a Tuesday afternoon she walked into his office and closed the door behind her. In her hand she held a small computer disk.

He looked up from his desk. "Yes?" His face conveyed what he didn't say: *I don't remember inviting you in.*

"You need to see this."

Kevin squinted. "What is it?"

"The full details of the Turin Project." She paused. "The stuff nobody knows. The facts Davis had no comprehension of." She met his curious stare. "The data that only I know."

"What are you talking about?" He took the disk and turned it over in his hand. "I don't want to know anything about this. You should destroy it. The project's dead, remember?"

She shook her head and sighed. "I don't want to work like this anymore, Kevin. Every day I can't help sensing that you think I've done some horrible evil." She shrugged. "Maybe it shouldn't matter to me how you feel, but it does. Maybe this will help."

"What do you mean? What are you talking about?"

"Come on, Kev. Ever since we talked on the plane, I've known what you thought. Before that really, when you first learned of the Turin Project, when you first told me you knew what we were doing. I know you thought I had crossed the line, that somehow I had done something God had never intended." She shrugged again and pointed to the disk. "Do you really think some things are sacred? That some things are beyond some sort of moral boundary?"

He nodded and twisted the rim of his baseball cap. "Sit down." He pointed to a chair with his head. "I've been trying to sort out how I feel." He nodded his head slowly. "And, yes, I'm beginning to think there are some things that should remain sacred." He lowered his voice, even though they were alone. "Jesus' blood, for instance. If it really has the power the Christian community believes it does . . . Well, then anything we do to it should be carefully monitored by those who hold it in such high esteem." He looked at her eyes. "We both realize that I now think cloning Jesus' DNA crosses a line we should never be even close to."

Ursula sighed. "I know. And whether I agree with you or not, I thought you ought to know the truth about the project."

"OK." He held up the disk. "What will I learn from this?"

"It was a fake, Kevin. A Jesus clone, in the purest sense, never existed."

He rubbed his forehead. "What?" He sat up straight. "But I examined it. I looked at—"

"You never looked at the whole genetic map, Kevin. It would have taken weeks."

"But it was an exact match. Not one nucleotide out of place—"

"In what you examined, yes." She shook her head. "But you never looked at the appropriate sections to determine the exact nature of the fetus."

"What are you saying?"

"What I'm saying," she responded, then halted and looked at his expression of surprise, "and I trust this will remain only between us, is that I couldn't deliver what I promised to Davis. He hired me because of my expertise. He hired me specifically to create a clone of Jesus for him. But every time I tried, I failed." She shook her head. "I don't understand it myself. I used the very techniques that had brought me success before, and yet every time I tried it with the DNA from the shroud stain, it didn't replicate."

"Then how . . . ?" He hesitated to finish the question. "What was the fetus that Lisa Dale carried?"

"It refused to replicate until I spliced in other human DNA. That's the only way I could get it to work." Her eyes were on the floor in front of her. "At first I intended to tell Davis, but he became so fixated on a perfect DNA match . . . I knew he would never approve the small changes I'd made. I realized that anything short of perfection would be viewed as a failure by Davis." She looked up. "But he's dead now. There's no reason to keep the secret any longer."

"You were using the same restorative techniques that brought us success before?"

"Exactly." She nodded at the disk. "It's all documented."

"And it didn't work?"

"I don't know why." She shrugged again.

"It just wouldn't work." Kevin cracked a smile.

"You don't find my conducting the experiment differently than Davis had conceived it even more outrageous?"

Schwab shook his head in contemplation. "I still don't approve of what you were trying to do," he responded slowly. "But you made the genetic substitutions in an attempt to get the project accomplished, right?" He shrugged. "I suppose if a person approached this from a purely scientific standpoint, void of any considerations of conscience, I might not expect anything else."

Kevin stood and began to pace around his office. "This is very interesting, actually." He looked back at Ursula, whose expression mirrored his own confusion just moments before. "You say it just didn't work." He paused. "And yet you used the exact techniques you developed and had proved hundreds of times before."

Ursula nodded.

"Maybe there's a reason it wouldn't work."

"Everything has a reason, Kev. I just haven't discovered it yet." She pointed at the disk. "Examine the technique. Maybe you can figure it out."

"And maybe it was just not meant to be done."

Her forehead wrinkled.

"Maybe the project's not working proves it was never meant to be attempted in the first place."

"Come on, Kev. Be objective."

"Maybe, just maybe, this is one more bit of evidence that there are some things too sacred to change."

"Are you saying God kept the project from working?"

He raised his eyebrows. Was it possible that the Vatican officials were right—that the blood of Christ carries a power beyond human comprehension? Is it so precious that a holy God would never allow it to be desecrated?

Ursula looked at him and repeated her question. "Well?"

"When you look at what happened," he responded, twisting the bill of his cap around again, "I think there's only one answer."

Acknowledgments

No one stands alone.
Special thanks to . . .

Steve Schwab, whose idea during a church cell-group discussion, started my wheels turning.

Tim Kinney, who provided computer literary searches with enthusiasm.

Kelly Zander, my friend, and a county deputy who endured my many "What would you do if . . . ?" questions.

Sheriff Don Farley, for his advice on management of a suspect when the evidence just doesn't add up.

Dr. John Rust and Dr. Alden Hostetter, who gave valuable information on forensics and surgical pathology.

Dr. Jack Wright, our medical examiner, who provided insight into the workings of traumatic death investigations.

Author Randy Alcorn who provided a tough critique to my rough draft,which resulted in an extensive "tightening" of the final manuscript.

Author Angie Hunt for her support.

My parents and my sister, Donna Parrish, who made valuable suggestions to the first draft.

Cindy Kiple for the cover design.

Ted Griffin, whose meticulous editing can be compared to a fine surgical dissection . . . painful but necessary.

Len Goss, former Editorial Director at Crossway, for believing in me and the value of our projects together.

Lane Dennis, whose insight and suggestions helped provide appropriate balance.

My wife, Kris, for her faithful support and her thoughts about the significance of Seth's name.

This list is incomplete without thanking God. I was stained, and you rescued me.